DATE DUE

~~FE 6 00~~			
~~AP 24 00~~			
JY 18 02			
AG 8 02			
~~MAY~~			
~~AP 10 03~~			
NO 29 11			

Encyclopedia of Heaven

ALSO BY MIRIAM VAN SCOTT

Encyclopedia of Hell

P

Encyclopedia
of Heaven

Miriam Van Scott

Thomas Dunne Books
St. Martin's Press
New York

Thomas Dunne Books

An imprint of St. Martin's Press.

Pages (7, 20, 23, 24, 29, 30, 46, 48, 52, 58, 61, 65, 69, 71, 80, 82, 99, 111,
118, 144, 149, 151, 155, 157, 160, 162, 165, 181, 198, 203, 209,
219, 226, 237, 243, 246, 272). *Art Today* images courtesy of
Michael A. Gariepy, CEO Zedcor, Inc.
www.arttoday.com

Page (76). Photograph of *Lady Death* is a trademark
owned by Chaos! Comics.

Page (75). Photograph of Bradford Exchange Angel Plate
by artist Edgar Jerins. Copyright ©
The Bradford Exchange.

PRODUCTION EDITOR: DAVID STANFORD BURR
BOOK DESIGN BY JENNIFER ANN DADDIO

Library of Congress Cataloging-in-Publication Data

Van Scott, Miriam.
    Encyclopedia of heaven/Miriam Van Scott:—1st ed.
        p.   cm.
    Includes bibliographical references (pp. 275–77).
    ISBN 0-312-19870-1
    1. Heaven—Encyclopedias.   I. Title.
    BL540.V36   1999   98-43619
    291.2'3—dc2198-43619   CIP

First Edition: April 1999

10   9   8   7   6   5   4   3   2   1

This book is dedicated to my parents,
who first taught me about heaven

and to my husband and children,
who have given me a glimpse of how
wonderful it must be.

Introduction

Notions of a "glorious afterlife" have been part of the human experience for millennia. Such supernatural speculations have shaped our language, our literature, and even history itself. Ancient mythologies, organized religions, and secular works of art and literature through the ages offer elaborate descriptions of the sensual delights and spiritual pleasures that await souls in the world to come. Images of this blessed realm have inspired everything from epic poems to satirical songs about the hereafter and encompassing everything in between. And the fascination with eternity continues.

From the earliest civilizations, images of a pleasant afterlife have influenced the way people live, interact, worship, inter the dead, and remember deceased kin. In some cases, the promised paradise is reserved for specific individuals, such as heroes, royalty, and priests. Others connect eternal bliss to a person's manner of death, granting admittance only to those who are slain in battle or die through acts of selflessness such as childbirth. Most, however, link afterlife reward with lifetime behavior, creating a powerful incentive to obey societal standards and contribute to the welfare of the community. The awesome beauty of this eternal kingdom—elusive in the land of the living—is reflected in thousands of interpretations of paradise designed to motivate the faithful. And the possibility of joining this mystic society is extolled as humanity's ultimate goal.

Throughout history, this focus on the life beyond death has been taken up by scholars, philosophers, artists, writers, priests, and poets. There have been critics, too, decrying the "obsession with heaven" and its often dark consequences as divisive, insincere, and manipulative. Yet the vast majority see heaven as true human perfection: a grand world of complete fulfillment stripped of all ugliness and imperfection. Souls in paradise are often themselves considered deified, sharing in the radiance of some higher power. This belief helps unite the generations and transcends the boundaries of time.

Of course, not all theories agree on heaven's specifics. Over the centuries, cultures have embraced a wide variety of "blessed eternity" concepts, describing it as everything from a spiritual social club for the wealthy to a realm of justice where the downtrodden are finally compensated for years of neglect and abuse. Various mythologies have put a vast variety of gods at the center of this divine dimension while religious scholars have developed elaborate criteria necessary for salvation. Writers have attempted to pen poems, prose, and plays illuminating the unseen world. Artists have composed great works alluding to afterlife grandeur. In more recent years, scriptwriters have translated the hereafter into fodder for irreverent parodies about faith, religion, and even God himself. Representations of the "glorious beyond" have also found their way into the modern consumer culture, appearing on everything from T-shirts to coffee mugs. And still the quest for heaven continues.

This book chronicles the diverse interpretations of paradise and offers insight about their origins and implications. Various viewpoints are compared and contrasted, showing recurring themes as well as unique heavenly concepts. *The Encyclopedia of Heaven* illustrates the enduring enchantment humans have with notions of splendid eternity, a fascination that persists even in our "enlightened" age.

ABA Aba is the creator of earth and the lord of heaven according to the tradition of the Choctaw, Native Americans of the bayous of Louisiana. When members of the tribe die, they are said to go to Aba, where they will dwell in bliss and tranquillity. Aba is a loving god who will give his human children eternal happiness.

The Choctaw share the idea of a pleasant land of the dead with other tribes, such as the Ojibwa. Both view the abode of the departed as a land of plentiful hunting and perpetual good clime located in some distant place, perhaps in another country just beyond the horizon. Neither tribe considers this to be a reward for a good life, but rather a realm free of conflict where all spirits will dwell in harmony.

ADIRI Melanesian mythology includes belief in Adiri, the land of the dead. Adiri is said to be either a mountain or an island located in the west, beyond the sunset. The dead exist in Adiri in a quiet realm devoid of pain, hunger, and the travails of human life.

According to the myth, the soul survives bodily death and must make a perilous supernatural journey, past geographic obstacles and mystic gatekeepers who try to thwart the spirit's progress. Its fate is determined not by moral factors but by the status it enjoyed in life and the rituals performed in its memory. If a soul fails certain tests or if the proper rites are not conducted, then it will cease to exist. Souls can also fade from Adiri if the living fail to respect and remember them properly.

ADORATION OF THE TRINITY
Artist Albrecht Dürer offers his vision of CHRISTIAN PARADISE in the early sixteenth-century composition *Adoration of the Trinity*. His work shows a regimented heaven where every saved soul has a specific place and level appropriate to the spirit's piety. It reflects the celestial village suggested by SAINT AUGUSTINE's CITY OF GOD, in which heaven and earth are separated by only the thinnest of veils.

Dürer places God the Father in the center, holding up JESUS Christ on the cross while a white dove representing the Holy Spirit hovers above them. The Father wears the crown and robes of an emperor. Beside him to his left, the VIRGIN MARY, mother of Jesus, is adorned in dazzling blue. Behind the smiling Queen of Heaven is a plethora of female SAINTS waving palms in worship of the Trinity. John the Baptist sits on his right, kneeling before an army of patriarchs and MARTYRS, including Moses, Solomon, and Daniel. Below this realm is a layer of saved souls ranging from kings and nobles to peasants (recognizable by their garments) all praising the Godhead.

Adoration of the Trinity is a breathtaking splash of bright colors and crisp strokes. Dürer uses brilliant reds, blues, yellows, and greens to show the majesty of heaven. His paradise is a delight for the eyes as well as the spirit, where everything is lush and beautiful. The work is a compelling depiction of the joys promised to virtuous souls in the world to come.

ADVERTISING   Astute business people have been using heavenly images to peddle their wares for decades. Early examples include using ANGELS in print advertisements to suggest that their products are mystical and wondrous. Cherubs have been used to sell everything from soap powder to guitar strings. (This continues to this day, especially in advertisements for baby products. Promotional directors use angelic beings to imply that their wares are as innocent and miraculous as the children themselves, "fresh from heaven.")

Another favorite trick of the trade is adding a sales pitch to a familiar icon of paradise. An 1887 advertisement for Williams Shaving Products features a representation of MICHELANGELO's artwork from the Sistine Chapel showing God giving life to the first man. Underneath the illustration is the assertion that "Adam was created without a beard," implying that the ideal male face is clean-shaven. Those wishing to emulate the divine Father's creation should therefore stock up on razors and shaving cream.

The biblical image of paradise as a celestial city was similarly incorporated into Post Health Product's 1925 ad for its cereals. In the printed promotional piece, a family is shown embarking on a holy pilgrimage to good nutrition with the "shining spires" and glimmering walls of the heavenly "Wellville" blazing before them. Readers are invited to "lift up your eyes" and see the splendor of this promised land. It is the reward for healthful eating, the salvation of those who make the appropriate sweet and salty sacrifices.

Other advertising themes incorporate religious interpretations of the afterlife according to specific faiths. Concepts of CHRISTIAN PARADISE have provided a host of images for salespeople, often focusing on one particular aspect of the celestial realm. In 1885 Jordan Marsh (a prominent Boston department store) used an illustration on its catalog that transformed the storefront into a veritable cathedral of commerce. Adapting fixtures from CHURCH ART AND ARCHITECTURE, the picture shows a semicircular window reminiscent of the STAINED-GLASS WINDOWS that Christian churches

An ad for Story & Clark Organs
invokes images of paradise.

use to portray paradise as a realm of brilliant light. Through this mercantile portal flows not a cascade of light but a deluge of envelopes stuffed with mail orders. These letters are carefully collected by cherubic couriers who assure customers that their requests will be handled with the utmost grace and care. The angels subtly promise that both the products and services offered are truly divine.

Wanamaker's Department Store in Philadelphia went a step further, actually transforming its main showroom into a church during the 1928 Christmas shopping season. The lavish display included linen banners adorned with regal crests, stained-glass windows, and Gothic arches. At the center of the sales floor, a painting of the nativity showing all of heaven rejoicing at the birth of the Christ child was prominently displayed. The store's owner, John Wanamaker, was a great believer in the marriage of religion and capitalism and devised this presentation as an example of how gloriously (and profitably) the two could be combined.

Wanamaker promotions borrowed SYMBOLS from other religions as well. The store's 1913 fashion show had as its theme the Garden of ALLAH, the exotic paradise of the Muslim faith. Images of DJANNA, Islamic heaven, adorned the store's luxurious hall. Few residents of turn-of-the-century Pennsylvania had ever even *heard* of the enchanted garden with its rivers of wine and honey, flowering trees, and splendid orchards, and visiting the paradise vicariously was a unique thrill. Attendees were as dazzled by the opulence of the mystic decor

as they were by the new clothes being modeled. The effect worked perfectly: Elated buyers were left with the feeling that they had indeed undergone a supernatural experience, and they bought plenty of souvenirs to remember the journey.

Edison Electric reached even further back in time for its heavenly advertisements. During the early 1900s, the utility company—striving to depict electricity as something mythical, even godly—lit upon the symbol "Edison Mazda," patterned after the Persian deity AHURA MAZDA, the Zoroastrian god of light. The Mazda figure appeared on print ads and in promotional calendars as a vibrant, luminous beauty lounging amid the clouds. Implicit was the message that electric power is a mysterious, auspicious gift from above, and those availing themselves of this new technology shared in the bounty of heaven.

As technology progressed, television advertising brought new depth to the depiction of the celestial orb. Televised commercials routinely showed heaven as a place where those who have lived good lives are rewarded with eternal access to superior consumer products. This includes being attended by angels, chatting with the SAINTS and even interacting with the Almighty himself. In the ultimate embodiment of conspicuous consumption, paradise is even presented as a realm that can be custom-tailored to each individual's tastes.

An example of this is the 1996 Reebok basketball gear ad campaign. In one commercial, a black teen is shown "going up for the jam" in slow motion.

As he pauses at the rim, the hoop resembles a HALO glimmering in the muted light. The narrator then whispers, "This is my Heaven." A recent Roy Roger's fast-food ad offers this perspective as well, showing a newly deceased young man who is reluctant to leave his steady diet of roast beef sandwiches, fried chicken, and french fries. The celestial welcome wagon joyfully reassures him that in paradise he will be able to continue enjoying the restaurant's tasty treats.

Another common usage of the supernatural in electronic promotions paints the afterlife as a realm where humans who have made the right consumer choices will receive eternal reward. In an Orville Reddenbacher commercial for low-fat popcorn, the departed tells the guardian of the gate that she has restrained her passions while on earth, opting for the healthful snack over more caloric indulgences. She is immediately admitted into heaven. A 1996 Chesapeake Bagel Bakery radio ad echoes the sentiment that selecting a proper diet translates into eternity in paradise. The narrator sings about a dream in which "I died and went to Heaven—and I was wearing a bagel for a halo," sung in the style of old-time religious HYMNS.

Other ads visit the opposite end of the spectrum, depicting the HEREAFTER as an endless festival of carnal delights. In 1997, Miller Brewing Company pitched a "Party in Heaven" complete with dance music, beautiful women, and, of course, malted barely beverage. When one reveler discovers that the refrigerator is empty, accommodating "angels" cause a tree to fall back on earth, smashing a few cases of Miller Lite bottles on a passing delivery truck. As the bottles break, their "spirits" ascend to the hereafter, where they refill the heavenly refrigerator allowing the party to resume in earnest.

Many afterlife promotions hint that although advertisers have a sense of humor, the powers that be might not. A pitch for Snickers candy bars depicts a waiting line of newly deceased souls stretching from the PEARLY GATES to the distant cloudy horizon. When one of them shouts, "Does this line ever move?" a hole in the sky opens and the impatient soul plummets into hell. The heavenly gatekeeper wryly ask, "It's moving now, isn't it?" As the rest of the arrivals wait in shocked silence, the narrator coos, "Not going anywhere for an eternity?" and suggests that a chocolate bar might make the wait a bit more tolerable.

A number of modern commercials stick to traditional images of heaven as an enlightened bureaucracy. Alphagraphics recently aired an advertisement for a speedy copier service that shows a middle-aged angel as heaven's receptionist. She dutifully forwards calls from those desperate for miracles, but when a frantic caller declares, "I need five thousand copies of this report by Monday," the celestial office worker replies that such a feat is beyond even divine intervention. The narrator reminds viewers that paradise might fall short, but Alphagraphics can deliver.

Contemporary advertisers also like to use "heavenly" terms in product names or promotions, hinting at the "out of this world superiority" of their products.

This is especially common among sellers of FOOD NOVELTIES.

AENEID The Roman poet Virgil wrote his epic *Aeneid* in the first century B.C. It tells the story of the warrior hero Aeneas, founder of the city of Rome. Virgil left instructions in his will that the unfinished poem be destroyed after his death; however, emperor Caesar Augustus refused to carry out Virgil's request. In fact, he demanded that the work be hailed as a triumph of Roman literary accomplishment. The *Aeneid* has since become a pivotal work of Western literature.

The *Aeneid* opens as, Aeneas, his troops decimated in the Trojan War, searches for a new home for his fellow soldiers and the survivors of Troy. The gods send a messenger who tells him to found a new city and promises that Aeneas's empire will be a great civilization that will change the face of the earth. At first, the fallen hero sets out to perform this task as instructed. But during his travels, Aeneas falls in love with the beautiful Queen Dido of Carthage and decides to abandon his quest. He marries Dido and plans to remain in her kingdom, where they will rule together.

The gods, angered by this refusal to obey their orders, dispatch Mercury (HERMES) to remind Aeneas of his duty. With a great deal of sorrow, Aeneas realizes that he cannot stay in Carthage but must fulfill his divine destiny. He makes plans to set sail immediately. His wife, who has already lost one husband, is heartbroken to learn that her beloved Aeneas is about to cast off for Italy. She begs him to remain with her, but Aeneas replies that the decision is not his to make. He leaves Carthage the following morning, unaware that Dido has committed suicide in response to this "abandonment."

Unsure of how he should proceed in his quest, Aeneas travels to the underworld to ask the advice of his father, Anchises. With the help of a sibyl (an enchanted priestess of Apollo) and the magic of an enchanted golden bough, Aeneas enters the land of the dead. Here he views both the splendors of paradise and the horrors of the damned.

In the underworld, the road forks, with one branch leading to Dis, the city of the damned, the other going to ELYSIUM, the "place of delight." In the sweet paradise, souls "who in their lives were holy and chaste" are greatly rewarded, invited to "take ease among the Blessed groves" and enjoy games, music, and dancing. They move about freely, enjoying the companionship of their peers. As Aeneas travels through this mystic land, he recognizes that the REUNION of loved ones formerly separated by death is the truest pleasure of the afterlife.

When Aeneas first sees his father in Elysium, the two men begin weeping with joy. Aeneas tries three times to embrace Anchises, but his father's spirit slips through his arms, since they are of different worlds. Undaunted, Aeneas asks Anchises to explain to him the mysteries of the "otherworld," especially why some souls "leave upper heaven" to reincarnate on earth. The elder replies that not all spirits can "clearly see heaven's air" and must live again to purge themselves of "stain." Others have "turned Time's wheel a thousand years" and are sent back to reexperience the pains and pleasures of the temporal plane. Aeneas declares that he longs to remain in this "lush meadow" with his father, but Anchises tells his son that this is not an option.

For a grand destiny awaits Aeneas below, Anchises explains. He tells his son that Aeneas's unconceived child "will be king and father of kings," and his line will one day produce "Caesar Augustus, son of the deified." As Anchises speaks, tears of pride well up in his eyes. Hearing this fantastic prophecy and witnessing his father's joy, Aeneas excitedly vows to return to Italy and plant the seeds of the Roman Empire. He bids his father farewell and departs through the "Ivory Gate" (through which dreams ascend to the living as they sleep) and rejoins his men in the upperworld.

The story of Aeneas has been adapted into a number of operas and stage plays, including *Dido and Aeneas* and *Didonne Abandotta*.

AFRA, SAINT (ca. 280–304) St. Afra, a MARTYR of the early Christian church, saw a vision of CHRISTIAN PARADISE at the time of her death. As she was being executed for refusing to renounce her religion, the heavens "opened up to receive her sweet soul." Then the young girl was carried to her exalted reward on the wings of ANGELS.

St. Afra was the child of St. Hilaria. (One account claims that Afra began her adult life a prostitute; however, this is historically inaccurate. Afra's life story has often been confused with that of Venerea, another martyr of the early days of Christianity.) Records show that Afra died a virgin and was executed under the Christian persecution of Diocletian. Her only crime was refusing to deny her faith and swear allegiance to pagan gods.

Accounts of Afra's death declare that she was sentenced to be burned to death. While soldiers carried out this execution, witnesses claim that the girl's soul left its wilted body and soared toward the sky, escorted by luminous angels. The clouds parted, and the "hosts of heaven" welcomed the martyr into paradise. The feast of St. Afra is celebrated on August 5.

AFRICAN PARADISE Many African religions teach that souls of the dead live on and even continue to participate in community life. In most cases, the spirit inhabits a familiar place, such as a favorite chair or resting spot. Family members routinely ask these souls for advice, guidance, and protection and might make offerings of food or gifts to curry favor. Some believe that deceased kin are eventually reincarnated as grandchildren or other descendants. Ancestor worship is important, as many believe that death reunites loved ones from across the generations.

The Dinka attribute liberated spirits, called tiep, with the power to influence the affairs of the living. Members of the LoDagaa of Ghana teach that the dead travel to the Land of Ancestors that lies across the River of Destiny. A similar journey over supernatural waters

African ritual honoring the dead. ART TODAY

is a component of the teachings of the Mende of Sierre Leone. They believe that departed souls navigate a mystical river that leads to a dazzling village much like those on earth, only far more beautiful and serene. Similarly, SWAHILI PARADISE is an enchanted land of abundant food, temperate weather, and eternal joy where souls mingle with their ancestors.

Because fate in the afterlife is so closely tied to prosperity of the living, funerary rites are meticulously adhered to and respected. These complex ceremonies are meant not to bid farewell and offer closure to survivors but to prepare the departed for the journey ahead. In most societies, only the most virtuous and heroic souls will be elevated to "ancestor" status, and the rites offer a last push in that direction.

The Yoruba of Nigeria are one of the few African peoples who equate virtue in life with fate in the world to come. They

envision an afterlife in which good deeds are rewarded and evil actions punished. Yoruba paradise is ruled by OBATALA, a benevolent deity and guardian of souls who welcomes virtuous spirits to his eternal kingdom.

Other African cultures provide tales of heroes who have firsthand knowledge of the afterlife. The legendary Ashanti folk hero Kwasi Benefo journeys to the paradise of ASAMANDO in search of his departed wives. After meeting them in the next world, he is able to return to life on earth. In Congolese Upoto tales, LIBANZA, the "first man," routinely travels between heaven and earth and eventually becomes lord of paradise after his death. Now Libanza is the escort who carries human souls to heaven in his enchanted boat.

AFTERLIFE DIET, THE   Author Daniel Pinkwater, famous for his humorous children's books and lively National Public Radio commentaries, has long made a joke of his "circumferentially challenged" figure. In his 1995 novel *The Afterlife Diet*, Pinkwater elevates obsession with portliness to new heights. The supernatural satire depicts a heaven where not the soul but the body is judged. Far from being a place of ethereal beings freed from the bonds of the flesh, Pinkwater gives readers a paradise that is especially designed for the obese.

In *The Afterlife Diet*, the saved are strictly segregated according to their body fat quotient. Svelte souls ascend to stellar ecstasy; chubby spirits are relegated to a lesser realm that is "exactly like a Catskills resort." Since heavy humans are decried as a "blot on the landscape," the powers that be feel that their presence would detract from the beauty of heaven. Besides, the nubile dead do not want to see fat, unattractive people in the afterlife, so portly souls must be sent elsewhere to dwell among their own kind.

Eternal paradise is decidedly unpleasant for the plump. Rather than experience a REUNION of loved ones after death, new souls are greeted at the PEARLY GATES by an "enormous woman" who croons a warm welcome but provokes quiet fear. Arriving spirits are shattered by the realization that it is not morality but body size that determines their supernatural fate, and the true pleasures of eternity are out of their stubby grasp. Virtually everyone they meet is obese (except for the ANGELS, who serve in such "staff positions" as waiters, porters, hosts, and cooks). Even the supreme being himself is a bit on the hefty side.

In this second-rate dimension of bliss, rotund SAINTS enjoy picturesque mountain views, casino games, nightclub shows, and, of course, lavish banquets. But their joy is tempered by the fact that they must share living quarters with disagreeable strangers, endure unending "fat JOKES" from God, and refrain from drinking alcohol (which is strictly prohibited in heavy heaven). Even the former joys of life are no longer so joyous: Sex is tiresome, movies are stale and monotonous, the food is delicious but tainted by the taste of guilt. The bored, somber residents of this realm flock to encounter groups for the "vitality-challenged" in search of elusive comfort, only to find further disappointment.

But overweight souls are not completely without hope of redemption. Portly spirits are routinely invited to play "Bardo" (an allusion to the Tibetan BARDO THODOL, a manual for negotiating the never-ending life cycle), which is simply bingo with a metaphysical payoff. Winners are awarded such prizes as "oblivion," a state of nonexistence preferable to their current status, or better room assignments without the obnoxious roommates. The ultimate prize is reincarnation; however, each winner must be careful when choosing new parents. (Unfortunate souls can unwittingly be reborn as animals, and overweight animals at that.) Those lucky enough to win another chance at life strive to remain thin on earth so that they can ascend to true paradise after death, rather than be consigned once again to the otherworld of the obese.

But, alas, the cycle is never truly broken. Reincarnated souls are doomed to assume the same body shape time after time, despite the constant criticism from family, friends, and society and thus must endure the same divine judgment. Their inability to shed those excess pounds even follows them beyond the grave. For when one unhappy soul tries to start a weight-loss program, he is jeered by his fellow spirits and even incurs the wrath of the Almighty.

Pinkwater's satirical picture of paradise—while a very funny book—serves as a sad commentary on the current American attitude toward the overweight. For even in death, those who fail to meet the ascetic ideal are judged not by what they are but by how they look. A quick look at artistic depictons of the afterlife suggests a similar conclusion: Paintings, sculptures, works of CHURCH ART AND ARCHITECTURE, and other compositions of paradise historically feature only lean, svelte saints and angels.

AGAINST HERESIES   IRENAEUS, bishop of Lyons around the year A.D. 200, penned an extensive treatise regarding the nature of CHRISTIAN PARADISE titled *Against Heresies*. In this work, Irenaeus promises the faithful that all suffering will be vindicated in the world to come. Since followers of the Messiah JESUS were heavily persecuted during his era, the belief in an eternal reward (and corresponding punishment of persecutors) helped strengthen Christians' resolve and reassure believers that their sacrifices would not be in vain. Irenaeus describes paradise as a bountiful earthly existence rich with human delights that can never be taken away from Christ's beloved.

Unlike contemporary religious concepts of heaven, his was not a place of elevated spirituality but a material realm of human pleasures. Irenaeus's tome reminds believers that God not only created all matter but himself took on a physical body, and therefore material is intrinsically good. The final reward, then, focuses on unending fulfillment in a world of tangible joys.

The afterlife envisioned in *Against Heresies* was greatly influenced by the conditions of Irenaeus's day. The bishop saw hundreds of his fellow Christians tortured and killed by pagan rulers and became obsessed with reconciling his religious ideas to this atrocity. His response to the persecutions was to preach that every Christian's lost happiness—and lost life—would be restored and amplified in a glorious utopia. And those who sacrificed the most would receive the greatest reparations.

Against Heresies also unites the God of the Old Testament with the more complex Christian deity. The work asserts that Jesus, the Redeemer of Christian belief, does not contradict the teachings of the Hebrew prophets but in fact affirms and fulfills their prophecies. Irenaeus's book ties these ideas to the MILLENNIUM, the upcoming thousand-year epoch of peace when Christ will reign in a "new Earth," the Garden of Eden restored. *Against Heresies* urges weary Christians to be patient and steadfast, confident that their agony will ultimately be turned to joy.

AHURA MAZDA   Ahura Mazda (Ormazd, Ohrmuzd) is the chief deity and lord of ZOROASTRIAN HEAVEN, the pre-Islamic paradise prevalent in ancient Persia and the surrounding regions. He is the overseer of both the material and spiritual world and desires tranquillity for his subjects. A wise god, Persian artists depict Ahura Mazda as a bearded scholar wearing a robe decorated with stars. The deity dwells in the highest heaven with a legion of ANGELS continually praising him in his celestial court. He is often associated with the Christian Messiah JESUS, since Ahura Mazda is called by followers the "savior of human souls."

Ahura Mazda is the god of truth, light, purity, and order. According to the teachings of the prophet Zoroaster, Ahura Mazda is the benevolent force in the dualistic faith, locked in an apocalyptic struggle with his evil counterpart, Ahriman. The two are forever trying to influence the human actions and affect the soul's final disposition. Zorastrianism doctrine foretells that in the end, good will triumph and Ahura Mazda will emerge the inherent victor. In the meantime, however, wickedness can still corrupt the spirits of weak people. This conflict is described in GATHAS, an ancient book of the AVESTA about the battle between Ahriman and Ahura Mazda and the ongoing war for human souls.

According to the text, Ahura Mazda is aided in his work by the AMESHA SPENTAS, seven holy angels who help oversee the material world. Chief among them is VOHU MANAH, "firstborn of Ahura Mazda," who helps record and judge the lives of human beings. Ahura Mazda is also attended by YAZATA, an innumerable legion of celestial spirits who intercede between mortals and the Almighty. The foremost yazata is Mithra, "spirit of light," who will help heaven's armies wage war against Ahriman at the end of the world (a role similar to the Christian angel MICHAEL who defeats Satan and forces him into hell).

In the aftermath of Ahura Mazda's conquest of Ahriman, the soul of every human being who has ever lived will be called forth to give an account of its life. Following this LAST JUDGMENT, spirits of the blessed will be rewarded with eternal life on a renewed earth. They will have GLORIFIED BODIES purged of all human frailties and physical imperfections. Damned souls will be eradicated from existence after suffering unspeakable torments. Ahura Mazda's faithful will be left to populate the universe and spend eternity in peace and harmony.

AIOMUN KONDI Aiomun Kondi is the Guianan Indian lord of heaven and creator of all things. He dwells in the skies, where he watches over the affairs of his mortal children.

Myths regarding this great spirit find parallels in the Old Testament stories of the destruction of the cities of Sodom and Gomorrah and the flood of Noah. Like YAHWEH, Aiomun Kondi becomes enraged at the insolence and disobedience of humans and sends natural disasters to destroy the world. The first time, Aiomun Kondi purges the land with wrathful fire. When the new race of humans still refuses to heed his will, the deity sends a deluge to cleanse the earth. And as in the case of the patriarch Noah, Aiomun Kondi spares the family of one consecrated man and allows him to regenerate the human species.

AJYSET Ajyset is the goddess of birth according to Siberian mythology. She dwells in heaven (where all life originates) and oversees the consecration of new souls. When a woman gives birth, Ajyset delivers a soul to the new child, giving the baby life. Those expecting a child pray to Ajyset, begging her to bestow on their child a strong and kind spirit. If Ajyset does not favor a child with a hardy soul it will be stillborn or will die in infancy.

ALFADIR   Alfadir (All-Father), also known as ODIN, is the creator god of Norse mythology and the master of heaven. The epic PROSE EDDA, a lengthy collection of Nordic legends, says that he was not himself created but has existed from before time. Alfadir then produced everything else, including the earth and all its creatures to reflect his greatness. Humanity was Alfadir's ultimate work, for he bestowed on each person an immortal soul capable of attaining eternal bliss after the death of the body.

Those who live moral lives in accordance with his divine plan will enjoy eternity in the presence of Alfadir in his magnificent paradise of GIMLI. But the souls of evil people will be damned to never-ending pain in the palace of Hel. In other accounts, only the souls of warriors killed in battle will ascend to VALHALLA, the "Hall of the Slain." The *Prose Edda* states that Alfadir is also Valfadir, the "Choosing Father," who takes as his sons "all those who fall in combat." To reward their valor, Alfadir "has prepared Valhalla," an eternal abode of great joys.

ALLAH   Allah is the supreme deity of the religion of Islam, similar to the Judeo-Christian God. He is an all-powerful lord who created the world and oversees every aspect of his creation. Followers believe that Allah is aware of every falling leaf; he knows the position of every grain of sand in the ocean. Allah sends ANGELS to watch over the living world and guard his creatures. These celestial guardians also keep records of the thoughts and deeds of every person to use at the time of judgment in the afterlife.

The word *Islam* means "surrender to Allah and find peace," and a Muslim (a believer in Islam) is "one who surrenders." It is the will of Allah that all enjoy eternity with him in the garden paradise of DJANNA, but he will not force anyone to accept him. The path to salvation must be freely chosen by each individual. Some followers will be called on to make the ultimate sacrifice, surrendering their lives on behalf of Allah by dying in the JIHAD (holy war). MARTYRS who go to their deaths in defense of the Almighty will ascend immediately to paradise, where they will dwell in Allah's glory and be eternally revered as great heroes.

Followers of Islam must walk in the "light of Allah's truth" throughout their lives. When a person dies, Allah sends an angel to guide the soul to the afterlife. These messengers from "the source of light" escort the departed spirit through the barriers that separate Allah from humankind, purifying the soul in the process. In order to enjoy salvation, a person must embrace "the truth" and renounce "the lie" and must correctly respond to questions asked by the messenger angels. Those who do will enjoy "bracelets of gold" and "robes of embroidered silk" in the court of Allah. Any who refuse Allah, give incorrect answers to the angels' queries, or fail to overcome the many obstacles on the road to Djanna, will plummet into hell.

MUHAMMAD, the founder of the Islamic religion, renounced all other gods except Allah and demanded that his followers do the same. He promised that those who embrace Allah's word will experience never-ending joy and indulgence in the world to come. In Djanna, the righteous will find lush meadows, rivers of wine and honey, and beautiful virgins called HOURI. The pious will be clothed in robes of glory. But the ultimate reward will be in basking in the magnificent presence of Allah, a grand BEATIFIC VISION.

Although Allah is the omnipotent creator of the universe, his defining characteristic is his infinite mercy. The teachings of Islam decree that all Muslims will eventually be saved, even though many must wait until the LAST JUDGMENT to be "awakened" from death's sleep and purged of their sins. No infidel (nonbeliever), however, could ever enjoy the presence of Allah, since the infidel has indulged in the darkest blasphemy. When such a soul enters the divine realm, its inherent evil will cause it to burn and writhe in agony. This "nightmarish existence" is a result of its rejection of Allah's wisdom and compassion rather than a punishment imposed by the Almighty.

ALL DOGS GO TO HEAVEN The 1989 feature-length ANIMATED CARTOON *All Dogs Go to Heaven* offers an imaginative answer to the question of whether there are ANIMALS in the HEREAFTER. According to the film, there is in fact a special paradise for man's best friend, since canines are "naturally good and loyal." Its accommodations, however, are not necessarily to every dog's liking.

All Dogs Go to Heaven features the voice of Burt Reynolds as Charlie B. Barkin, a tough mutt who is murdered by the gangster dog Carface in the dismal docks of New Orleans. Charlie's spirit then floats skyward on a pink cloud, past jewel-encrusted gates to the Hall of Judgment, where an angelic guide dog welcomes him to eternity. It is a serene realm of peace and tranquillity where Charlie will never again have to face difficulties of any kind. He is given a HALO and a set of wings, which he promptly rejects. Charlie does not want salvation and demands to be returned to earth. The guide gently shows him a stopped watch that represents his life and encourages the perplexed canine to accept his fate. But Charlie wants no part of this monotonous world devoid of challenge, risk, and especially "surprise." He misses the thrills of life on the edge.

After distracting the guide, Charlie manages to steal the watch, rewind it, and return to his life on earth. As he descends, the frantic gatekeeper of canine paradise warns him that once he leaves heaven, he can never come back. Dismissing this grave assertion, Charlie happily resumes his antics, proclaiming, "I tried a life of virtue but prefer a life of sin!" But he soon begins having horrifying nightmares of doggy hell, where the demonic Evil Dog tortures him in a lake of fire. Suddenly, pooch paradise does not seem so bad.

Charlie's fears about his damnation, however, are abated when he does in fact die a second time while trying to save the life of a little orphan girl. Since he has made the ultimate sacrifice for this child, the powers that be allow Charlie to return to heaven. In the end, he is able win one small consession. The feisty canine is allowed to replace the dull "heavenly choir" with his own favorite music: New Orleans jazz. This is all the paradise Charlie needs.

In 1996, moviegoers learned that all dogs also come back from heaven. The sequel *All Dogs Go to Heaven 2* sends Charlie (now voiced by Charlie Sheen) and his muttly crew back to earth to retrieve the stolen horn of GABRIEL, the angel who will signal the end of the world. The enchanted instrument has fallen into the hands of the canine's old nemesis, who plans to use it in his nefarious schemes. Thankful for the respite from "boring" dog paradise, Charlie proves his worth not only by recovering the horn but also by helping out another lost child along the way.

Both films were heavily peddled to children and generated a tremendous array of MOVIE MERCHANDISING, ranging from T-SHIRTS to "sing-a-long" videos. The success of the *All Dogs Go to Heaven* movies also spawned a weekly ANIMATED CARTOON series in which Charlie and company spend their days doing good deeds for a variety of species.

AMA-NO-HASHIDATE   The Ama-no-hashidate is the mystic passage that links heaven and earth according to the legends of Japanese Shintoism. In some depictions the Ama-no-hashidate is a STAIRCASE, one of the most common SYMBOLS of paradise found in mythologies from all over the globe. In other versions it is a bridge spanning the chasm between the human world and the realm of the gods. Legend claims that the creator gods used the Ama-no-hashidate while sculpting the earth and its creatures, but it has since been destroyed.

AMESHA SPENTAS   The Amesha Spentas (Amshaspands) are the six supreme ANGELS of Zoroastrian mythology created by the supreme god AHURA MAZDA. These "immortal benefactors" reflect the Elohim (qualities of divine nature) and reside in heaven with the chief deity. Each of the Amesha Spentas has a specific defining characteristic: Ameretat is immortality, Haurvatat is salvation, Armaiti is faithfulness, Kshathra Vairya is omnipotence, Asha is truth, and VOHU MANAH is glorious achievement. Together they comprise the "ideals of Truth and Righteousness" taught by the prophet Zoroaster.

Vohu Manah is the first of Ahura Mazda's angels and helps in determining the fate of human souls in the afterlife. He sits at Ahura Mazda's right hand in ZOROASTRIAN HEAVEN and records the actions and thoughts of all people. This record is read back at the person's time of death and is used in final judgment to determine whether the soul will ascend to paradise or be damned to everlasting agony.

Some scholars of ancient religion believe that the Amesha Spentas are not separate beings but simply the seven aspects of Ahura Mazda himself. Others equate the Amesha Spentas with Judeo-Christian angels, celestial messengers and assistants of the divine. When Islam replaced Zoroastrianism as the main religion of Persia and the surrounding areas, belief in angels of ALLAH (the creator god of Islam) became an article of faith necessary for salvation. This emphasis on cherishing celestial beings is considered a holdover from the ancient reverence for the Amesha Spentas.

ANASTASIS FRESCO The *Anastasis (Resurrection) Fresco* in the Church of Christ in Cora, Istanbul, celebrates JESUS' harrowing of hell and ASCENSION into heaven. The early fourteenth-century work is located in the church's funerary chapel, where it offers hope and comfort to mourners that their deceased loved ones are in the arms of a compassionate savior. And although it shows hell as well as heaven, the *Anastasis Fresco* is a powerful affirmation of the glories of the CHRISTIAN PARADISE.

The fresco features the image of a Christ, robed in dazzling white and crowned with a HALO of shimmering gold, storming the gates of the underworld. Hell is dark and murky, a stark contrast to the Lord's gleaming presence and to the beauty of paradise. Above this is a celestial kingdom of bright blue dotted with radiant stars. This use of color symbolizes the triumph of light over dark, good over evil, truth over lies. Christ is shown pulling Adam and Eve out of hell, while John the Baptist, King David, and other virtuous patriarchs

rush forward to join them. The conquered Satan is bound with ropes under the smashed gates of the abyss at Christ's feet. A scattering of locks and hasps around the devil symbolize that the fiend will be imprisoned in hell until the LAST JUDGMENT.

The unknown artist achieved the brilliant color effects by using an unconventional fresco method known as *secco su fresco*. Using a mix of coloring agents, bindery material (most probably oil, egg, and wax), and wet plaster, the artist created a work that dries into a shell-like, uniform piece. The rich hues are thus not simply painted onto a surface but are in fact part of the architecture. This preserves their breathtaking brilliance and amplifies the overall impact. As a result, the *Anastasis Fresco* serves as a permanent testament to the Christian view of the next life according to the beliefs of the Byzantine era. It remains one of the most important examples of CHURCH ART AND ARCHITECTURE of the time.

ANGELICO, FRA (1387–1455) Giovanni da Fiesole, known in the art world as Fra Angelico, dedicated his career to depicting religious themes. His works include a number of illustrations of CHRISTIAN PARADISE as well as unique interpretations of church teachings. As pious as he was talented, the artist-monk painted his subjects with reverence and realism, breaking new ground in artistic compositions. During his career he portrayed a number of supernatural events, including CORONATION *of the Virgin* and *The Annunciation*, in

which the angel GABRIEL tells the VIR-
GIN MARY she has been chosen to bear
the Christian Messiah JESUS.

His *LAST JUDGMENT* differed from previous illustrations of the theme by depicting a paradisical garden in which SAINTS
and ANGELS jovially interact while Jesus
pronounces sentence on the human
masses. Earlier works placed sole emphasis on God, portraying no social contact
whatsoever between his creatures. Fra
Angelico's painting also shows a ring of
holy souls gathered in rapt attention
about the BEATIFIC VISION; however, he
supplements this with an array of human
pleasures transported to the supernatural
realm. In the garden splendor, monks
dance with angels, virgins embrace heroes, and kindred spirits forge on to the
distant NEW JERUSALEM with its PEARLY
GATES and streets of gold. Fra Angelico's
Last Judgment also features the traditional
EMPYREAN, where both angels and saints
gather around the Godhead. Biblical heroes in his holy circle include the Virgin
Mary, the angels MICHAEL and Gabriel,
and an array of Christian MARTYRS.

In the early 1400s, Fra Angelico was
commissioned by the board of Orvieto
Cathedral to decorate its Chapel of the
Annunciation. He began by creating a
magnificent depiction of paradise entitled *Christ in Glory* on the vaulted ceiling
directly above the altar. The work shows
a stunning and powerful Jesus reigning in
a kingdom of light and beauty. This
painting is supplemented by a gallery of
sixteen biblical prophets who adorn the
compartment to the chapel right. Before
completing the illustrations, however,
Fra Angelico abandoned the project,

never to return and complete his assignment. Eventually, the board nullified his
contract and hired Renaissance master
LUCA SIGNORELLI to finish decorating the
cathedral chapel.

ANGELS From the Greek *angelos* and
Hebrew *malakh*, meaning "messenger,"
angels are immortal, spiritual beings who
participate in supernatural matters but
can also influence the affairs of humanity. They are found in the Jewish, Christian, and Islamic religions as well as in a
score of mythologies. Angels can be either benevolent (as in guardians sent
from heaven) or evil (as in demons con-
spiring to corrupt human souls). In current usage, the term *angel* refers almost
exclusively to kind spirits in the service
of the divine. Their roles include protecting people from harm, aiding in
human salvation, and worshiping at the
throne of the supreme deity.

Angels have been part of belief systems for millennia. Zoroastrianism, a
Persian faith that predates Islam, includes tales of the AMESHA SPENTAS, six
powerful angels of the good lord AHURA
MAZDA, and of YAZATA, the immortal
"adorable ones." Each spirit has specific
duties, including guarding animals, bearing witness to the truth, and recording
the deeds of human souls to help determine salvation or damnation. They are
all reflections of characteristics of Ahura
Mazda or personifications of such abstracts as honesty, purity, peace.

In Jewish tradition, angels are usually
messengers sent from YAHWEH to reveal
God's word to the prophets and patriarchs. Abraham was visited by three an-

gels in the form of men who promised that they would visit him again in a year, and at that time he would have a son by his aging wife, Sarah. Two angels came to Sodom to warn Lot that he must move his family from the town, for the Lord was soon to destroy both Sodom and Gomorrah. When Daniel was thrown to the lions, God "sent his angel, and hath shut the lions' mouths," saving him from certain death. And in the time of Moses, Yahweh dispatches the Angel of Death into Egypt to take the life of every first-born son not protected by the sacred pact.

Christian tradition also views angels as divine messengers. The VIRGIN MARY was approached by the angel GABRIEL with the news that she had been chosen to give birth to JESUS, the savior. Immediately after his birth, a "heavenly host" of angels appeared in the skies to nearby shepherds, joyfully announcing the Christ child's arrival. The apostles Peter and John and friend Mary Magdalene were greeted at Jesus' empty tomb on Easter morning by a pair of celestial beings. Years later, when the Virgin Mary's earthly life was through, her body was borne up to paradise by a legion of angels. This supernatural event is called the ASSUMPTION.

God's angels have proven their allegiance to the Christian deity by going to war to defend the Almighty. St. John's Book of REVELATION gives an account of this war in heaven, in which the archangel MICHAEL leads the divine forces against Satan and his rebels. According to the tale, God's betrayers are cast into hell, where they will remain

Angels are often depicted as guardians.
EDGAR JERINS

for all eternity. Revelation further states that angels will play a major role in the destruction of the earth and will assist in the LAST JUDGMENT, when all human souls will be called on to explain their every action.

After years of speculation by scholars about the nature of angels, medieval Christian theologians divided the angelic ranks into nine distinctions. They are (from highest to lowest): seraphim, cherubim, thrones, dominations, virtues, powers, principalities, archangels, and angels. Each group has its own defining characteristics and corresponding duties in the celestial orb. Church doctrine states that every human has a particular spirit that is his or her special guardian, believed to be of the last order of angels. Children are taught to communicate with their supernatural shepherds, learning this popular prayer:

Angel of God, my guardian dear,
To whom God's love commits me
    here
Ever this day be at my side
To light and guard, to rule and
    guide.

This sentimental image has made statues of angels a common sight in cemeteries, especially to mark the graves of children.

Angels are likewise quite prominent in Islamic belief. Passages about their existence can be found in the KORAN, the Muslim holy book. They are referred to as servants of ALLAH and overseers of humanity. One of the key doctrines of Islamic faith—that must be accepted in order to attain salvation—is the belief that angels are divine creations who must be revered. These celestial messengers issue from the "source of light," bringing the word of Allah to humanity, and encourage their mortal brethren to remain faithful to "the truth." Angels are also sent to guide departing spirits up supernatural "STAIRCASES of light" that lead to the paradise DJANNA, Islamic heaven. In Djanna, one "angel day" is equivalent to fifty thousand human years.

Islam mentions several angels by name, many of whom have Judeo-Christian counterparts: The angel JIHAL is the Islamic equivalent of the Christian Michael, defender of heaven. Jibril is similar to the messenger Gabriel who delivers divine messages to the living world. Jibril is also identified as the "sacred one of Allah" who dictates the holy scriptures to the prophet MUHAMMAD.

The seventeenth-century philosopher EMANUEL SWEDENBORG spent decades studying the nature of angels. He eventually postulated the theory that angels are, in fact, the purified souls of human beings. He taught that when human spirits are purged of all the residue of their lower nature, they become elevated to the status of angels. This supposition has served as the basis for continuing religious debate and has formed the premise for countless stories, television programs, and theatrical releases. Foremost among these are the beloved classic film IT'S A WONDERFUL LIFE, in which an angel is dispatched to save a suicidal man so he can "earn his wings," and HIGHWAY TO HEAVEN, the television series about a celestial good Samaritan who returns from paradise to perform good deeds.

In recent years, angels have made major inroads into secular society. One of the biggest fads of the past decade is the proliferation of GIFT NOVELTIES bearing images of celestial guardians. These heavenly beings appear on GREETING CARDS, COLLECTOR PLATES, key chains, wall plaques, notepads, coffee mugs, magnets, and a variety of other trinkets. Perhaps the most commercially successful emissaries of paradise are the two pensive cherubs from Raphael's SISTINE MADONNA. This sprightly pair has adorned every type of ANGELWARE from T-SHIRTS to postage stamps, even making an appearance in charicature on the cover of a Black Sabbath record album.

Angels also remain a perennial favorite inspiration among Christian artists. Their images have been used throughout the world in CHURCH ART

AND ARCHITECTURE. They have also served as the inspiration for SHORT STORIES, CHILDREN'S LITERATURE, POETRY, and other creative endeavors. Guideposts Publications even publishes a bimonthly magazine called *Angels on Earth*, dedicated entirely to recounting supernatural encounters between humans and their celestial kin. Every issue is filled with art, anecdotes, and scriptural references about these angelic creatures.

ANGELWARE One of the best-selling merchandising phenomena to mushroom during the past decade is angelware, items adorned with images of angels. These heavenly products include COLLECTOR PLATES, T-SHIRTS, stickers, nightlights, salt and pepper shakers, and other GIFT NOVELTIES that depict the citizens of paradise. These items are popular with religious people as well as secular buyers who consider themselves "spiritual" but do not belong to any specific church.

Angelware runs the gamut from generic spirits to familiar angels adapted from classic works of CHURCH ART AND ARCHITECTURE. The cherubs of the *SISTINE MADONNA* decorate a myriad of items, such as key chains, note cards, and bookmarks. Original angels are especially popular on items of jewelry. Pins, necklaces, and charms of "guardian angels" offer wearers a constant reminder that they are being cared for by a higher power.

Other manufacturers have designed their own signature angelic products. Artist Kristin Haynes has created an entire line of childlike spirits called Dreamsicles, which can be purchased in the form of statuettes, stickers, plates, and

An assortment of angel-adorned items

other memorabilia. Dreamsicles even offers a set of twelve chubby cherub Christmas ornaments each with its own distinct character, recalling the "heavenly hosts" praising JESUS at the manger. Roman, Inc. has a series of more traditional celestial figurines titled the Seraphim Classics Collection. These angelic images are crafted in rich detail and vibrant colors representing the splendor of their stellar dwelling place.

Ancient tradition meets high technology with "virtual pet" angels, electronic toys that require owners routinely to press the right buttons in order to keep them "alive." Tamagotchi offers pet angels in a choice of pink, yellow, or white that must be cared for according to a strict schedule. If the owner feeds, exercises, and entertains it as instructed, the celestial being "will fly home to be rewarded with its wings" in paradise. These virtual pet angels playfully remind children that heaven awaits those who act responsibly and live up to their divine commitments.

The angelware fad also envisions a paradise where ANIMALS are welcome. Store shelves are laden with bears, dogs, cats, cows, pigs, and other friendly beasts complete with wings and HALOES. Plaques designed to ease the sorrow of losing a pet promise that the beloved creature is now "playing in paradise" where the "sun always shines." Licensed animal characters such as Garfield, Bugs Bunny, Mickey Mouse, and Winnie the Pooh have likewise appeared in angelic guise.

Our celestial overseers are also featured on GREETING CARDS celebrating Christmas, birthdays, baby arrivals, and other occasions.

Products displaying angels help bring thoughts of heaven to the temporal plane. They reassure humans that there is a paradise where beautiful creatures dwell in bliss and suggest that we might one day join them in eternity.

ANIMALS The question of whether animals exist in heaven has been debated for centuries. Some ancient mythologies feature beasts as protectors of the dead or escorts to the afterlife; other belief systems decry such assertions as sacrilege. Contemporary religious doctrines also differ greatly on the subject, ranging from complete rejection of the notion of animals in the eternal realm to unconditional acceptance of their place in paradise.

One of the first beasts to appear in the next world is the ancient Egyptian ANUBIS. This dog-headed deity is described in the BOOK OF THE DEAD as a benevolent guide who brings departed spirits safely through the treacherous maze of the afterlife. He also helps OSIRIS, the lord of the dead, determine whether the soul will find happiness in the supernatural realm. Belief in Anubis inspired legends about dogs having the ability to sense evil and to help people avoid its snares. Many people believe this to the present day, as indicated by modern SHORT STORIES and even an episode of the classic television series TWILIGHT ZONE featuring canines who lead their masters to everlasting bliss.

As the centuries progressed and alternate belief systems emerged, the concept of eternal animals became less important. YAHWEH, the Hebrew God of the Old Testament, condemned worship of bestial deities (such as the proverbial golden calf) and focused attention on human salvation. He directed humanity's attention toward its own behavior and emphasized the role each individual soul has in determining its fate. Once the object of pagan worship, animals such as birds, lambs, and rams now were used in sacrifices to the creator rather than revered as fixtures in the supernatural realm.

The Christian Messiah JESUS extends this practice, often using animals in his supernatural analogies (even referring the himself as "the Lamb"); however, he never definitively affirmed or denied that animals would be present in heaven. And although the Bible includes no explicit mention of them in CHRISTIAN PARADISE, many artists have added gentle creatures to the divine realm. Countless paintings, sculptures,

Animal heaven, from *Penguin Island*
ART TODAY

and other artworks portray the Holy Spirit as a dove soaring through the heavens. Others show paradise as a lush garden dotted with butterflies and songbirds, where humans and animals dwell together in harmony. Modern author C. S. Lewis, who wrote extensively of heaven in his nonfiction works and in the novel THE GREAT DIVORCE, suspected that pets who were beloved on earth would accompany their owners to paradise.

The Islamic heaven DJANNA not only includes animals but specifically names several who dwell within its borders. Muslim belief states that the whale that swallowed the patriarch Jonah, the ram Abraham sacrificed to seal a pact with God, and the dove that brought Noah a branch to signify the end of the flood are all enjoying eternity in paradise. Foremost among the divine creatures is the BORAK, the mule-beast that carried MUHAMMAD to Djanna for a tour of ALLAH's garden. And though he is not mentioned by name in the KORAN, Islam's holy book, many believe the faithful dog KATMIR also lives in eternal splendor.

Even in secular society, many people tend to believe in an afterlife for our fellow creatures. Young children who have lost a beloved cat or dog are routinely told that their pet has gone to heaven. Gift shops sell wall plaques explaining that the lost puppy or kitten is now enjoying paradise. Some even show the animal frolicking with ANGELS or with the child Jesus. (This approach, however, has recently lost favor with many parents, since it seems to imply that Christ killed the animal deliberately for his own purposes. Such a petty, insensitive Lord greatly detracts from traditional notions about Jesus and his heavenly home.)

Speculation about the eternal destiny of animals has been illustrated in recent years in ANIMATED CARTOONS. All manner of furry and feathered creatures are shown enjoying paradise tailored specifically to the beasts' desires. Examples include an episode of the popular *Simpsons* series in which a father tells his son that in canine heaven, "A dog can't turn around without sniffing another dog's butt." A less idyllic (although very opulent) version of this afterlife is described in the full-length feature film ALL DOGS GO TO HEAVEN. And the live-action films YOU NEVER CAN TELL and THE THREE LIVES OF THOMASINA portray the paradisical "happy fields" where all variety of species dwell in eternal harmony.

GIFT NOVELTIES also depict animals in heaven. Cats enjoy a magnificent afterlife according to COLLECTOR PLATES showing feline paradise. Winged pigs, dogs, cows, and other beasts make up an entire category of ANGELWARE, suggesting that earth's lower creatures will one day ascend to divine bliss. Products adapted from CHILDREN'S LITERATURE likewise show animals in heaven, sharing their owner's blessed fate.

It is improbable that religious leaders will ever reach a consensus about animals in the next life, so most leave the matter to individual belief. Many people find happiness in imagining heaven as a place of myriad creatures joining in the celebration of God's glory. Others consider including pets, cattle, fish, and fowl around the divine throne to be the ultimate blasphemy.

ANIMATED CARTOONS Illustrators have been using heaven as a background for cartoons since the medium was first developed a century ago. Animators have drawn on supernatural themes to convey everything from horror to humor, in comic scenes and cautionary tales. Donald Duck, Bugs Bunny, Tom and Jerry, Homer Simpson, as well as a host of other animated creations have visited the next world during their celluloid adventures. And the paradises they encounter are as diverse as the imaginations of their creators.

The most striking (and successful) example of cartoon afterlife is depicted in *Casper, the Friendly Ghost*. This chubby specter has been floating through the HEREAFTER since his debut in 1945. Early tales of the little spirit explain that Casper (a deceased eight-year-old boy) faced the "Spookreme Court" after his discorpulation and was sentenced to spend eternity "with humans." This truly *is* paradise for him, since his sole joy is making new friends and playing with an endless progression of children, ANIMALS, and other benevolent spirits.

In his afterlife existence, Casper is endowed with a number of supernatural powers. He is able to make himself invisible, to pass through solid objects, and, of course, to fly. Casper puts these skills to work in numerous humanitarian endeavors. Episodes show the young ghost saving children from fires and delivering Christmas toys to the underprivileged. In *Ghost of the Town*, Casper even appears as a guest on *The Ed Sullivan Show*, famous for his notoriety and heroism. These exciting escapades are a sharp contrast to the serenity of the rest of "ghost society," which is a bureaucratic monotony of dull days and dour doings. But Casper has earned his own unique eternal reward for his effervescent "friendliness."

Over the past half century, *Casper, the Friendly Ghost* has become an enduring cultural icon. He has appeared on all types of GIFT NOVELTIES, and COMIC BOOKS of his saga remain popular. The boyish spook even traveled to the moon in effigy, his image painted on the side of *Apollo 16*. Recently, Casper has been the subject of a live-action feature film of the same title, generating a new round of MOVIE MERCHANDISING. His embodiment of eternal bliss in a never-ending playground has truly captured the American imagination.

Not all cartoons are as extensive in their depiction of paradise. Many characters simply visit the higher realm between earthly adventures. In 1938, Disney's Donald Duck faced both good and evil, as an angelic and a demonic version of the famous fowl battle for control of the duck's soul. Bugs Bunny and his friends from Warner Bros. have likewise traipsed through heaven in their sprawling escapades. In most of these episodes, the celestial plane is a billowy world of clouds where everyone wears wings and a HALO and plays the harp. After a few wisecracks and sight gags, the animated antics return to the land of the living.

Cartoon cats are routinely depicted going to heaven one life at a time. Their proverbial nine lives depart as winged spirits, one following the next into the clouds, usually with harps in hand. They ascend to the skies to assume existence as feline ANGELS.

Illustrations of the afterlife have also been prevalent in more recent animated series, often with sarcastic overtones. *The Simpsons*, the most popular cartoon of the past decade, has offered several perspectives on paradise. In one episode, Homer tells his son Bart that their dying mutt is destined for "doggy heaven," a place where "A dog can't turn around without sniffing another dog's butt." Another installment shows Ben Franklin and Jimmy Hendrix playing air hockey in the skies above. Long-suffering daughter Lisa Simpson has a vision of her departed hero "Bleeding Gums," a saxophone player, belting out a divine version of "Jazz Man" from his heavenly home. And numerous episodes have featured benevolent angels sent to help the Simpson family out of its wacky predicaments.

Visualization of paradise has likewise been the subject of such animated theatrical releases as ALL DOGS GO TO HEAVEN (which also spawned a television series) and the Disney short *Peter and the Wolf*. In the 1946 classic, the lovable duck Sonia is believed to be devoured by the vicious wolf. Young Peter imagines the fowl arriving at the golden gates of paradise, which have distinctly Russian spires reminiscent of St. Basil's Cathedral.

ANUBIS Anubis is the Egyptian protector of the dead, similar to the Greek HERMES. According to the ancient legend, this jackal-headed deity guides departed souls to the Hall of OSIRIS, where spirits face judgment in the afterlife. He also aids Osiris (Anubis's father in some versions) in reading the record of each person's life in order to determine the soul's ultimate fate. Osiris asks the spirit for a complete account of both its good and bad acts, and Anubis helps review the records. Osiris then weighs the deceased's heart against the "feather of truth" to validate the its account. The scales tip toward good or evil, at which time Osiris renders final judgment. THOTH, the eternal bookkeeper, then records the decision in the annals of eternity.

Anubis figures prominently in the BOOK OF THE DEAD, a massive text describing funerary rites, religious rituals, and secrets of the supernatural. He is often depicted holding an ankh, the hieroglyph for "life force." The Latin poet

Anubis aids Osiris in the realm of the dead.
ART TODAY

Apuleius refers to Anubis as the "messenger between heaven and hell" since he shepherds both virtuous and evil spirits to the next world. In other legends, Anubis is the messenger sent by the gods to warn the pharaoh of his imminent death, appearing before the ruler carrying a viper (symbolizing mortality). When the pharaoh sees Anubis before him, he knows that his time on earth is short and he must prepare his successor to ascend the throne.

AO Ao, meaning "eternal light," is the paradise of Tahitian belief. In Ao, spirits will dwell in peace forever, basking in the sunshine of truth and goodness.

APOSTLES' CREED The Apostles' Creed, called "a faithful summary of the apostles' faith," remains one of the most enduring prayers of the Christian faith. The words of this office affirm numerous tenets of the faith proscribed by JESUS, the Messiah. Within the Apostles' Creed, the faithful express their belief in such mysteries as the Holy Trinity, the indestructibility of the human soul, and the interconnection between all who have ever lived. The prayer also includes insights into the nature of CHRISTIAN PAR-

ADISE, stating that Jesus: " . . . ascended into heaven and is seated at the right hand of the Father. He will come again to judge the living and the dead."

Thus, paradise is the abode of God where saved souls will enjoy the BEATIFIC VISION. The Apostles' Creed also describes the coming LAST JUDGMENT, when all people who have ever lived will be called before the divine throne to explain the actions of their lives. After this "resurrection of the body," the saved will inhabit GLORIFIED BODIES free of all imperfections. In this elevated condition, redeemed humans will enjoy "life everlasting" with Christ.

Another belief espoused in the Apostles' Creed is the COMMUNION OF SAINTS, a concept stating that all souls, whether living or dead, are linked through the divine plan. SAINT THOMAS AQUINAS explains that "since all the faithful form one body, the good of each is communicated to the others." Christ is the mystical head of this body. Members are therefore encouraged to pray for one another and can look forward to a grand REUNION in eternity.

The Apostles' Creed has been declared the official creed of the Roman Catholic church and is prayed by millions across the globe.

APSE MOSAIC OF OLD ST. PETER'S CATHEDRAL The mosaic in the Old Cathedral of St. Peter in Rome shows one of the earliest artistic interpretations of CHRISTIAN PARADISE. Based on a centuries-old original by an unknown artist from Constantinople, this sixteenth-century copy is rich with images and symbols of heaven from the first days of Christ's church. Later additions to the composition also give us some indication of the evolution of religious ideas regarding the afterlife.

The apse mosaic shows heaven as an ethereal dome above the earth. This representation of God's abode as a protective cover sheltering humanity is typical of early Christian art. JESUS, the Messiah, stands in the center flanked by SAINT PETER on one side and Saint Paul on the other. Christ is depicted extending his hands, blessing the world below. From the divine skies flow the four "rivers of paradise," symbolically giving life to the faithful. Stags (representing human souls) drink from the sapphire waters.

Below this supernatural realm is the earth, with the cities of Bethlehem (place of Christ's birth) and Jerusalem (the site of his crucifixion) at either side of the mosaic. Between them are twelve sheep (the apostles) adoring a lamb (Christ) seated on a gilded throne. The entire piece features brilliant colors that seem somehow illuminated from behind.

The original mosaic was altered during the thirteenth century, when Pope Innocent III had himself added to the work. He also had the artist insert a small chapel to symbolize the Roman Catholic church as part of Christ's history. The depiction of heaven, however, was left unchanged.

AQUINAS, SAINT THOMAS
(1224–1274) Italian-born theologian and doctor of the church Thomas

Aquinas wrote extensively on the nature of CHRISTIAN PARADISE. The Dominican friar dedicated his life to contemplation rather than works, spending decades pondering the mysteries of the divine. He had a special interest in ESCHATOLOGY, the "last thing," and devoted much of his attention to speculating on heaven. His theories were heavily influenced by SAINT AUGUSTINE, whom Aquinas considered a genius of after-life interpretation, and by the philosophies of the Greek scholar ARISTOTLE.

Aquinas believed in the concept of heaven as the EMPYREAN, a realm of pure spiritual light centering around God. He further theorized that there will be no plants, ANIMALS, or physical creations in paradise. These material works will ultimately separate into their elements of composure: air, water, earth, and fire. In eternity, all "movement," such as growth,

Doctor of the Church Thomas Aquinas
ART TODAY

planetary orbit, etc., will forever cease, and all creations will become fixed in their optimum.

Human souls in paradise will have GLORIFIED BODIES that shine "brighter than the sun." These luminous bodies will resemble the holy ANGELS who reflect the brilliant glory of heaven. And since humans were "created in the image of God," in their perfected form they must by logic resemble his dazzling presence. All of Aquinas's heaven is permeated with light, whereas hell is complete darkness. Activity in paradise will focus on adoring God's divine light, rendering all other joys insignificant.

Aquinas complied these ideas in his masterwork, SUMMA THEOLOGICA, called by religious scholars the "consummate work on Christian doctrine." According to the text, the philosopher also believed in LIMBO, a pleasurable realm for unbaptized souls, and in PURGATORY, a dimension for purging the residue of sin before ascending to paradise. He further expounded on the prophesied LAST JUDGMENT, when every soul ever created will appear be-fore the throne of God for divine adjudication.

The saint's teachings were sanctioned by Christendom and have influenced generations of religious scholars. (Not all of his students, however, accepted his conclusions about heaven's joys. His pupil GILES OF ROME came to very different opinions about the pleasures of the HEREAFTER and enumerated on them in his own writings.) Roman Catholic officials, as well as leaders of other Christian denominations, continue to teach Aquinas's theories.

ARISTOTLE (384–322 B.C.) The ancient Greek philosopher Aristotle was a pioneer in speculating on the great questions of humankind. His works pondered the nature of humans and their role in the universe, the meaning of life, and the possibility of life after death. Aristotle's students included the ancient warrior Alexander the Great, and his theories on science, logic, physics, and metaphysics shaped Western thought.

Aristotle taught his students that in the afterlife, pure souls will enjoy an enhanced version of earthly life. In this next existence, a spirit's greatest joy is the companionship of friends and the intellectual stimulation of divine discourse. Aristotle looked forward to an eternal forum where great thinkers could exchange ideas without fear of reprisal from civic authorities. He also anticipated the REUNION of loved ones as a key component of eternal happiness.

The ancient thinker's philosophies have had an enormous impact on history. His works greatly influenced later Christian scholars SAINT AUGUSTINE and THOMAS AQUINAS. His theories formed a starting point for their speculations about the divine. Aristotle was also revered by the medieval writer Dante Alighieri, author of THE DIVINE COMEDY: THE PARADISO, who drew inspiration from Aristotle's ancient concepts.

ASAMANDO Asamando is the land of the dead of Ashanti belief. It is a rich example of AFRICAN PARADISE where souls of the departed enjoy an earthlike existence in villages much like those of the living. In Asamando, the dead tend fields, enjoy feasts, and dance and sing in eternal community.

A famous Ashanti legend describes a poignant REUNION of loved ones in Asmando. The tale describes the sad life of Kwasi Benefo, an Ashanti farmer whose one wish is to marry and have a family. In time he falls in love with a beautiful woman, but she dies soon after the wedding, leaving Kwasi grief stricken. His kin eventually convince the man to try to forget her and find another wife, which Kwasi does. But she too becomes ill and dies, and Kwasi is more heartbroken then ever. When his third wife is killed in a freak accident, Kwasi leaves his homeland and vows to live a solitary life in the wilderness.

Alone in the wild, Kwasi begins taming the land and starting a new farm. Over time, his land becomes quite prosperous, and Kwasi longs to share his bounty. The notion of having a family returns to him, and once again he finds a young woman to become his wife. But before they have a single child, this fourth wife likewise becomes ill and dies. Kwasi then abandons his farm and returns "to die in my own village and be buried near the graves of my ancestors." He goes back to his family's village, tortured by the realization that when his own death comes, there will be no one to mourn him.

One night as Kwasi lies awake bemoaning his accursed existence, he decides to travel to Asamando to be with the spirits of his deceased wives. He walks to the edge of the forest where the women are buried, then ventures into the dense woods. Kwasi continues walking through the night, the forest becoming so dark he can see nothing in front of him. After forging on for what seems like days, Kwasi emerges on the other side of the trees, to the banks of a raging river.

Kwasi makes several attempts to cross, but the water is too deep and the current too strong. He is forced back every time. Dejected, Kwasi sulks that his journey must end, yet he has no reason to return home. Just then he sees an old woman at the other side of the river, sitting next to a large brass basket filled with beads and women's clothes. Kwasi recognizes her as Amokye, the benevolent spirit who welcomes the dead to Asamando. Upon arriving at the border of the land of the dead, newcomers must give Amokye an article of clothing for her basket. Kwasi sees in her basket items belonging to his lost wives, and a shadow comes over his heart.

Amokye calls out to Kwasi and asks why he, a living man, has come to this place. He responds that he has "no more desire to live" and wants to be with his wives. The kind woman tells him he cannot cross, since he is still alive. Hearing this, Kwasi sits down and vows to stay until his body dies so he can proceed. Moved by pity for the dejected man, Amokye agrees to let him enter Asamando but only for a brief visit. She stills the waters and lets Kwasi cross the river, then directs him to the place where he will find his brides. Since they are spirits, she informs him, he will not be able to see them, but he will know they are near. Kwasi thanks her and continues his quest.

At last Kwasi arrives in Asamando, which appears to be a deserted village. And though the houses seem to be empty, his ears ring with the sounds of laughter and activity. He enters one home and hears the voices of his wives, singing a song about how kind and loving a husband Kwasi had been. Inside the house he finds a washcloth to cleanse himself, a basket of food, and a sleeping mat. As he bathes and then eats, the lyrics of the song recall his many virtues, then invite Kwasi to lie down and sleep. As he does so, the song changes, and the women begin singing of the new life that awaits Kwasi back in his village, a life that will be rich with prosperity, children, and a bride who will spend many years at Kwasi's side. He falls asleep with these images dancing through his head.

When Kwasi awakens, he finds himself back in the dark forest. Cheered by the prediction of a future family, he rises and returns to his village and takes up farming once again. In time, he meets a beautiful maiden, and the two fall deeply in love. They marry and have many beautiful children. Kwasi and his wife enjoy many happy years together, living to see their children's children, before departing this world and making the final journey to Asamando together.

ASCENSION The ascension is one of the key beliefs of the Christian faith. According to the teachings of Christianity, the Messiah JESUS ascended to paradise after being crucified, dying, harrowing hell, opening heaven, and returning to earth for forty days of preaching. (This explains why no relics of Christ's body remain in existence.) The Gospel of St. Luke records the miraculous event: "Jesus led them out as far as to Bethany, and he lifted up his hands and he blessed them. And it came to pass, while he blessed them, he was parted from them and carried up to Heaven" (Luke 24:50–51).

Unlike other biblical figures (such as the prophet ELIJAH and Jesus' mother, the VIRGIN MARY) who were transported bodily to heaven, Christ ascended to paradise under his own power. While Elijah made his celestial trip on a fiery chariot and Mary was escorted to the skies by a legion of ANGELS, Jesus brought about his own elevation to the realm of God. There, he dwells in physical as well as spiritual form "at the right hand of the Father."

Christians believe that all saved souls will one day have GLORIFIED BODIES like that of the risen Christ. This means that everyone in heaven will assume perfect corporeal form, free of any blemishes, frailties, or imperfections. The only exception in Christ's case is the endurance of his stigmata, the wounds on his hands, feet, and side administered at the time of his crucifixion. This scar remains to commemorate his sacrifice on behalf of humankind.

ASCENT INTO THE EMPYRIUM
Fifteenth-century master Hieronymous Bosch painted his *Ascent into the Empyrium* five hundred years before modern descriptions of a supernatural "tunnel of light" became popular. The work shows disoriented human spirits, naked and listless, being guided by

richly robed ANGELS toward a luminous portal. At the far end of the tunnel, at the edge of the viewer's vision, is the silhouette of some welcoming figure, encouraging souls to make the passage.

This image of a dark portal that leads to a brilliant, luminous realm has since become a key component of many NEAR-DEATH EXPERIENCES.

ASGARD Asgard is the Norse dwelling place of the gods. It is a complex city of rich palaces, jeweled walls, and great banquet halls. One of its mansions, Valaskjalf, is the home of the supreme deity, ODIN. Within this castle is VALHALLA (Hall of the Slain), which is reserved for warriors who die in battle. In Valhalla the souls of dead heroes enjoy an endless feast, great games and competitions, and the camaraderie of fine companions.

Asgard lies beyond the BIFROST BRIDGE, which is guarded by a fierce giant. Only those anointed by the gods could safely pass. Norse legend says that after the destruction of the earth, Asgard will be adorned in even greater luxury and splendor.

ASSUMPTION OF MARY Roman Catholics (as well as members of some other Christians sects) believe that the VIRGIN MARY, mother of JESUS, was taken directly to heaven by a legion of ANGELS when her life was through. Because Mary was sinless, she was not made to suffer death and decay, which are punishments for sinning against God. Instead she was transported bodily to the EMPRYEAN, the divine realm of pure light. This supernatural event, called the Assumption, was made official doctrine by Pope Pius XII on November 1, 1950.

Unlike the ASCENSION of Jesus, who ascended into heaven under his own power, Mary had to be elevated through the will and force of the Almighty. She is not herself a god but is simply the recipient of this miraculous service rather than its instigator. The Virgin now dwells in paradise in physical as well as spiritual form. Mary (and her son Jesus) have GLORIFIED BODIES in heaven, free of all human imperfection.

The explanation of Mary's departure from the world of the living is not included in the Bible; however, oral tradition dating back millennia describes her mystic Assumption. According to the accounts of early church leaders, Mary was delivered body and soul to the afterlife. Religious scholars believe that Jesus could not bear to see his mother die and sent his celestial guardians to bring her to his side before death could claim her.

The feast of the Assumption is celebrated on August 15. It is one of the most holy days of the year throughout Christendom. In many Catholic countries, the Assumption is marked with pageantry and festivals similar to those held on Christmas and Easter.

Artists have long been inspired by the Assumption. This supernatural event has been a favorite subject depicted in Christian CHURCH ART AND ARCHITECTURE throughout the world.

One of the most striking illustrations of this event is Correggio's As-

sumption of the Virgin in Parma Cathedral. Painted in the early 1500s, the composition gives viewers the sensation that they are actually looking into paradise. The work, painted on the interior of the church's dome, creates the illusion of a hole in the roof through which heaven is visible. In the cloudy skies worshipers can see the Virgin Mary, dressed in rose garments tied with a sash of blue, being transported into a brilliant white light. The beautiful lady is carried on the wings of angels, past rows of SAINTS, patriarchs, and saved souls. Her face beams with joy and anticipation, envisioning a joyful RE-UNION with her beloved son.

Renaissance master Titian took up this topic in his own *Assumption of the Virgin*, painted from 1516 to 1518. In his vision, the crimson-robed mother of Jesus is borne to paradise by a contingent of ethereal angels. God, depicted as an elderly man with a white beard and face lined with age, awaits, flanked by the apostles who joyfully watch this miraculous event. The work, at the high altar of the church of St. Mary in Venice, glows with warm, vibrant colors, characteristic of Titian. His use of striking reds, blues, and blazes of gold suggests a resplendent realm of unspeakable joys.

Artist Paolo di Giovanni Fei takes the celebration a step further with his *Assumption of the Virgin*, showing Jesus awaiting his mother's arrival with open arms. Around the savior, a contingent of angels sing and dance with joy. Awestruck saints stare at Mary's open coffin, filled only with flowers, as her body resides in paradise. Fei's work conveys images of a paradise of human pleasures, where parent and child will celebrate the loving God who is the very author of love.

Other works portraying the Assumption include a vast array of witnesses to the miracle. Virtually all include angels as escorts to Christ's mother. And most feature prophets, patriarchs, biblical heroes, or other blessed souls rejoicing at the arrival of the Virgin in paradise.

AUCASSIN ET NICOLETTE Heaven is a monotonous realm of boring souls according to the twelfth-century drama *Aucassin et Nicolette*. The plot follows the star-crossed love affair of rich nobleman Aucassin and his amour, the lovely young Nicolette, a sweet maiden with "eyes gray and laughing, and a slender face . . . and lips redder than the cherry or the rose in summertime." Both fami-

Titian's *Assumption of the Virgin*. ART TODAY

lies are against the union, determined that the two should wed other suitors. Learning this, Aucassin considers taking Nicolette as his mistress and keeping their affair a secret. An elderly sage warns the youth that although this might bring him immediate pleasure, in the long run it will cost Aucassin his very soul. Aucassin considers this argument, then decides he would not want to go to the paradise preached by the clerics, for it is a dreary realm of pathetic wretches: "What would I be doing in Paradise? . . . For to Paradise go only . . . the old priests, the old cripples and maimed ones who, all night and all day, drag themselves before the altars and in the old crypts, and those who wear old worn-out clothes and are dressed in tattered rags . . . dying of hunger and thirst and of cold and of misery. These go to Paradise. . . . But to Hell I wish indeed to go; for to Hell go the handsome clerics, the fine knights who have died in the tourneys and great wars, and the good soldiers and brave men; with them do I wish to go. There also go the fair and courteous ladies who have two or three lovers beside their husbands. And there go the gold and silver and miniver and gray furs. . . . With them, I wish to go."

Aucassin would gladly forego this tedious paradise in order to have his fair Nicolette. In a last attempt to separate the pair, Nicolette's father sends her to "a distant land," hoping she will forget the cavalier Aucassin. But their love is strong and will not be denied. Eventually, the two reunite and marry, "then they lived for many days, and much

pleasure did they have." At the play's end, Aucassin "now has his joy," although he still faces the dim prospect of salvation to the insufferable heaven of his estimation.

AUGUSTINE, SAINT (354–430) St. Augustine of Hippo, a Christian bishop, and doctor of the Church, was a brilliant writer of many texts defending Christianity and its doctrines about the fate of the soul. The son of a pagan father and Christian mother, Augustine began his life as a polytheist and held no deep religious convictions. At times he embraced the beliefs of such ancient philosophers as Plato, PYTHAGORAS, and CICERO but never truly accepted any faith until he found Christianity.

Among his works is the classic CITY OF GOD, a massive twenty-two-book tome written from 413 to 422. The work was

St. Augustine. ART TODAY

immediately lauded by religious scholars as a triumph of Christian aesthetics and has had an enormous influence on both early and modern Christianity. In the *City of God*, Augustine describes heaven as an ideal spiritual community, a place of ultimate fulfillment with God at its center. Human souls find true peace in this blessed paradise, since, as the bishop states, "Our hearts are restless until they rest in Christ." The theories Augustine presents in this text crafted concepts of CHRISTIAN PARADISE and continue to shape modern notions about the HEREAFTER.

Augustine drew from his own diverse experiences when formulating ideas on human nature, God, salvation, and damnation. He began his life as an Agnostic, and Augustine spent much of his youth involved in debauchery, drunkenness, and selfish pursuits. He considered, then abandoned, a variety of philosophies, as none could logically answer his questions about theological matters and humanity's purpose in the grand scheme. His decadent lifestyle left him equally unsatisfied.

Augustine was eventually converted through the efforts of St. Ambrose, bishop of Milan, and the prayers of Augustine's mother, SAINT MONICA. (Both mother and son experienced powerful visions of heaven and speculated on the nature of the divine. After one especially moving experience, St. Monica told her son that she longed to leave this world and enjoy true paradise. She died less than two weeks later.) After being baptized into the faith of JESUS, Augustine spent the next several years studying and debating Christian doctrines. He flatly rejected the popular notion that all matter is evil, declaring that all God's creations are inherently good since they reflect their divine creator. He did, however, equate celibacy and denial of sensual pleasures with the "life of the ANGELS." Physical delights are "minor joys," while the eternal bliss of the afterlife gratifies humans' "higher nature," the spiritual self.

The focal point of Augustine's heaven is the BEATIFIC VISION, and the ultimate joy is being in the presence of God. Augustine called the heavenly Father "the end of our desires" and declared that the saved would enjoy forever his magnificence. He described this theory at length in a number of theological texts illuminating a THEOCENTRIC HEAVEN. Augustine's theories spread rapidly throughout Christendom and shaped the church's formative doctrines.

The saint's later works elaborated on the concept of eternal paradise, adding the elements of REUNION of loved ones to the afterlife. Augustine believed that human souls will not truly enjoy heaven until after the LAST JUDGMENT, at which time all are given GLORIFIED BODIES so that eternal pleasure is both physical and spiritual. He was convinced that human spirits are created to spend eternity celebrating the goodness of God in paradise and that this entails reflecting the physical nature of Christ as well as the supernatural nature of the Father. Until the time of final adjudication, the souls of the saved will exist in an interim state of bliss and natural joy. This model of the afterlife was incorporated into the teachings of Martin Luther, John Calvin, and scores of other religious leaders.

The writings of St. Augustine have had a far-reaching impact. In addition to defining paradise according to Lutheran and Calvinist sects, the bishop's works influenced generations of Roman Catholic scholars. Almost a thousand years after Augustine wrote his *City of God*, philosopher THOMAS AQUINAS relied on its conclusions for his own works of ESCHATOLOGY. And his postulations continue to be studied and discussed to this day.

St. Augustine remains a prominent saint of the Christian church. He is especially revered by writers who ask his intercession on behalf of their efforts. Augustine's feast day is celebrated by the Roman Catholic church on August 28.

AUPIEL   Aupiel is the "tallest of heaven's ANGELS," according to ancient Jewish tradition. He is believed to be the celestial escort who delivered the patriarch ENOCH body and soul to the throne of God. According to tradition, he towers over the rest of the heavenly hosts and is several "parasangs" larger than the next biggest angel.

AVALON   Avalon, also called the Fortunate Isle, is the paradise of ancient Celtic myth. It is a place of complete, timeless happiness where the dead enjoy endless feats, enchanted music, dancing, and celebration. In the realm of Avalon, there is no sickness, aging, or suffering of any kind.

The VOYAGE OF BRAN, one of the religion's oldest legends, describes an epic journey to Avalon. Bran and his army set out to find this promised land, encountering all sorts of fantastic places along the way. The sailors visit the Delightful Plain, the Land of Merriment, and the Island of Women on their supernatural trek through the magical otherworld. But when Bran and his men head for home, they are warned not to set foot on land lest tragedy befall them.

One foolish sailor disregards this advice and leaves the ship, only to turn to ashes the instant he reaches the shore. Bran and his bewildered followers then learn the truth: They have been traveling for centuries, protected from aging by the gods. Unable to live again in the mortal world, they cast off once more for Avalon, never to be heard from again.

Avalon is also incorporated into the Arthurian legend cycle. King Arthur is said to have been carried by faerie queens to Avalon (relocated to Glastonbury) after his final battle. There, he convalesced from his wounds on a bed of gold while enjoying the splendor of the royal palace, where he lives to this day. The legend claims that King Arthur will one day return from this paradise to resume his throne, earning him the title "the once and future king." In the meantime, Arthur patrols the shores of Avalon and keeps a lookout for souls of the righteous dead. Under his care, the shores of the Isle of Avalon remain open to all virtuous spirits.

King Avallach, a Celtic mythological hero, rules the Isle of Avalon. His daughter (Arthur's half sister, according to some accounts) Morgan le Fay, dwells there with him. She is a kind, gentle spirit skilled in the healing arts. Morgan was instrumental in saving King Arthur when he arrived at the gates of Avalon, bloody and broken from the war. She spends eternity ministering to fallen heroes and comforting the souls in her father's care.

Other legends place the Danish hero OGIER in the enchanted Avalon. According to the story, Prince Ogier is a mighty warrior who receives counsel from heavenly ANGELS. After traveling the seas in a series of adventures, Ogier comes to Avalon, where Morgan le Fay falls in love with him. She gives him a ring and a crown with magic powers that allow him to remain forever young. Ogier remains in Avalon still, like Arthur, waiting to return to his kingdom on some distant day.

AVESTA The *Avesta* is the ancient sacred text of Zoroastrianism, a faith that predates Christianity and Islam. It is divided into four parts: (1) the *Yasna*, liturgical texts written in old Persian dialect; (2) the *Visperad*, rites and invocations used for religious festivals; (3) the *Yashts*, HYMNS of praise to the divine; and (4) *Vendidat*, a collection of spells for exorcism of demons, protection against evil spirits, and purification of corrupted souls. Only about one fourth of the original *Avesta* remains in existence.

The first section of the *Avesta*, the *Yasna*, contains the GATHAS (songs) of the ancient prophet Zoroaster (Zarathustra).

In addition to providing older myths regarding the work of the gods, the book describes ZOROASTRIAN HEAVEN. Its text details the mystic voyage human souls must make after death to reach the realm of AHURA MAZDA, the "lord of light." Followers of the faith are encouraged to know this story so they will be ready when their time to depart this world arrives. The *Avesta* calls paradise "the happy realm of the future."

Within the *Avesta* are passages regarding the AMESHA SPENTAS, the six supreme ANGELS who assist Ahura Mazda in his divine work. These "beneficent immortals" have specific duties in overseeing the harmony between this world and the next. According to the *Avesta*, VOHU MANAH (Good Thought) is charged with keeping records on every living human being. These accounts will be used to determine each spirit's fate in the afterlife. Other members of this supernatural troupe help the living overcome evil, ward off disease, produce abundant harvests, and faithfully worship Ahura Mazda.

The first text of the *Avesta* was lost during the Persian conquest by Alexander the Great, around the year 333 B.C. The Greek forces burned Persia's capital and destroyed most of the records of Zoroaster and his teachings. Alexander then insisted on instituting Greek religion and culture throughout the world, forbidding worship of any other gods. For the next five centuries, scholars and magi (Zoroastrian priests) transcribed their recollections of the original works, adding commentary and interpretation as they completed their manuscripts. The result is a compendium of religious ideas and ancient tradition blended into a complex, exotic faith.

B

"BALDER DEAD" British author and Oxford professor Matthew Arnold wrote his narrative poem "Balder Dead" in the mid 1800s. However it was inspired by the tales penned centuries earlier in the "Viking handbook" PROSE EDDA. Both works feature tales of Norse god Balder (Baldur, Balldr) son of ODIN, the "All-Father" and lord of warrior paradise VAL-HALLA, and of Balder's tragic demise. Arnold's epic laments that the benevolent god falls victim to an evil plot that claims Balder's soul as well as his body.

According to the legend, Balder is "beloved of the gods," and every plant, animal, and element vows never to harm him. Only the mistletoe, a leafy shrub that grows in the eastern fields of Valhalla, is not asked to make the promise since it is considered too small to pose any threat to the mighty Balder. Loki, a trickster god who is jealous of the "fair-haired" Balder, learns of this and devises a scheme to kill Balder with a mistletoe twig. The wicked deity convinces a blind god to throw the seemingly harmless branch at Balder, but when he does so, Balder falls dead. Balder's mother is devastated by this catastrophe and begs Hela, goddess of death, to restore her son to life. However, Loki also manages to thwart this attempt at reviving Balder, and so he must remain in the land of the dead.

Since Balder did not die in battle, he is unable to ascend to his father's heavenly palace in Valhalla, which is reserved for spirits of warriors heroes. Instead he must take his place in Niflheim, the gloomy realm of departed souls. In "Balder Dead," Arnold also describes how Nanna, Balder's wife, dies of grief after her husband's death. The inconsolable widow is burned beside her lover on a great funeral pyre. Together they descend to Niflheim to give each other comfort and solace in the cold eternal kingdom.

In addition to recalling the legend of Balder and Nanna, "Balder Dead" details the delights of Valhalla, which include dining at the banquet table of Odin, engaging in great challenges and feats of strength, and preparing for an apocalyptic battle that will occur at the end of the world. Arnold's massive poem has been adapted for the stage and is the basis for several plays and operas focusing on age-old Nordic mythic heroes.

BARDO THODOL The Bardo Thodol, or Tibetan BOOK OF THE DEAD, is an ancient text that describes the human cycle of life, death, and rebirth according to Buddhist tradition. The book dates back centuries before Christ and details the underlying philosophy of many Eastern religions. Unlike the Egyptian Book of the Dead, the Bardo Thodol is not a collection of funerary rites but rather a manual that teaches "the art of dying," which, according to teachings of Buddha, is as vital to the spirit as the art of living. By practicing its principles, humankind can gain "enlightenment" and "freedom from self" in this world, assuring a pleasant eternity.

The word *bardo* means "gap," referring to the chasm between life and death. It also refers to the human gap between body and soul. The Bardo Thodol is a guidebook for negotiating the many gaps that every spirit will encounter while passing through the never-ending cycle of life. Buddhist tradition teaches that during each lifetime, a soul is constantly in flux between "excessive pain and excessive pleasure." This continues into the afterlife, at which time the spirit is assigned to one of six realms: deva Ioka, realm of gods; asura Ioka, realm of Titans; manaka Ioka, realm of humans; tiya Ioka, realm of subhumans; preta Ioka, realm of hungry ghosts; and nara Ioka, realm of damned spirits.

Each realm is characterized by its own "light, color, and essence." A departing soul naturally gravitates to the dimension it finds most appealing and continues its life cycle in that realm. In each incarnation, the spirit strives to purge itself of iniquity and move toward union with eternity, called NIRVANA in Buddhist tradition. This ultimate goal is not "heaven" but enlightenment in the "perfect Buddha state," and to achieve this a spirit must face and overcome conflict. Therefore a soul cannot proceed from a paradise to enlightenment; the only path to true bliss is through earthly existence.

According to the Bardo Thodol, there is no supreme being who judges souls in the afterlife; the spirits of humans who have lived exemplary lives will rise through their inherent radiance. Wicked, selfish souls will sink under their own weight into the dark realms of pain and suffering.

Likewise, there are no saviors who redeem human souls as in Hebrew, Christian, and Muslim tradition. An arbitrator named Yama will force every departed spirit to look into a mirror of its life, but he is only an objective observer. The soul's good and evil will be reflected, and then each soul must acknowledge its deeds, resulting in inner peace for the just, or great horror for the wicked. Spirits seeking higher levels of spiritual development will thus be elevated to better existences, while selfish souls will be drawn to unpleasant reincarnations.

Since each spirit chooses its own next life, prayers for reincarnation in a "good womb" are a vital part of the Bardo Thodol. Believers are encouraged to meditate on these ideals, thereby influencing their afterlife fate: "I will be born as an emissary for good . . . in a family rooted in faithfulness. . . . I will bloom as a lotus flower . . . in the Realm of Bliss. . . . Help me to cross the bardo's treacherous pathways and lead me to the perfect buddha state."

Another prayer stresses the desire to become one with the universe and "die to the self." This incantation for the "deliverance from the dangers of the pathway of the Bardo" asks:

May I know all sounds as my own
sound,

*May I know all light as my own
    light,
May I know all rays as my own
    ray,
May I spontaneously know the
    bardo of the three kayas
    (the personified metaphysical
    bodies of Truth, Enjoyment
    and Creation).*

The Bardo Thodol also mentions the paradise of MOUNT MERU, the "king of mountains" located at the center of the universe. Those who attain spiritual perfection can find comfort and repose at this holy site, once the place of meditation for the great sages of the past. In some legends, it is a place of temporary respite where virtuous souls are rewarded for their great progress before being returned to the life cycle. Other stories claim that the mystic mountain is a metaphor for eternal bliss.

Parts of the Bardo Thodol have been incorporated into later Eastern religions; however, the current emphasis on eternal reincarnation has greatly diluted the impact of its speculation on the afterlife. In many modern versions, the goal of enlightenment, where "recognition and liberation are simultaneous," has been replaced by a belief that human souls will return to earth forever, experiencing the sorrows and delights of humanity throughout the ages. With so many opportunities for a spectacular life, many find the notion of an impersonal Buddha state dull by comparison and have little interest in pursuing such a goal.

BASIL, SAINT (328–379) Basil was bishop of Caesarea during the rule of Emperor Valens, an avowed Aryan who despised Roman Catholics. Valens began a religious persecution of Catholics and made several attempts on Basil's life before the courageous bishop was able to convince Valens to relent. Using biblical quotes, logic, and eloquence, Basil eventually persuaded Valens to reject his heresy and embrace the faith of JESUS. Basil's oratorical skills were so acclaimed that he is credited with talking Satan into surrendering a soul promised to the fiend.

Another legend claims that St. Basil saw a vision of the VIRGIN MARY reigning as queen of heaven. According to the account, Basil was awakened in the middle of the night by a glorious explosion of light. When he looked up, he saw the mother of Christ seated on a jeweled throne surrounded by vast legions of ANGELS singing her praise. She then instructed the angels to rouse another of the fallen SAINTS to send him into battle against those who attack the Christian faithful.

The saint also took up the subject of ranking angels and studying their relationships to God and to humanity. He concluded that the archangel MICHAEL is the "prince of angels," since this supernatural guardian is named the defender of heaven in the Bible's Book of REVELATION. According to Basil, Michael is likewise protector of the people of God and custodian of human spirits who will assist in the LAST JUDGMENT at the end of time.

Basil has been declared a Doctor of the Greek Orthodox church, and his feast day is celebrated on June 14.

BEATIFIC VISION According to many faiths, the beatific vision—seeing God face to face—is the ultimate joy of paradise. This mystic communion with the divine is an aspect JEWISH HEAVEN, CHRISTIAN PARADISE, and Islamic DJANNA. Followers of many Asian religions likewise believe that virtuous souls will bask in the presence of the gods in the spiritual realm as a reward for their efforts.

In some cases, contact with the supreme being did not have to wait until the afterlife; pious spirits could be achieved this "foretaste of paradise." Buddhists who devote themselves to deep meditation and contemplation of the truth reach a "beatific state" during trancelike prayer. In this spiritual plane, they meet with the great Buddha and dwell with the divine lord. By concentrating their thoughts on "universal truth" and the "collective soul," these highly developed souls are able to leave their bodies for a period of time and soar to the heavens. According to tenets of the Buddhist faith, this communion with the higher powers anticipates the soul's ultimate goal, the state of "oneness with all that is" called NIRVANA.

In Judeo-Christian belief, true union with God does not occur until after death. In the Old Testament's Book of Hebrews, heaven is referred to as the "city of the living God, the heavenly Jerusalem." Righteous souls are promised citizenship in this holy village, where they will spend eternity with the Almighty. Later Christian texts echo this sentiment. St. Paul calls paradise "the abode of God," and in REVELATION, St. John writes: "And I heard a great voice out of heaven saying, 'Behold, the tabernacle of God is with them [the saved], and they shall be his people, and God himself shall be with them, and be their God.' . . . And the city had no need of the sun, neither of the moon, to shine in it: for the glory of God did lighten it, and the Lamb [Jesus] is the light thereof" (Rev. 21:3, 23).

Christian scholars have been studying the nature of the beatific vision for almost two thousand years. Doctors of the church SAINT AUGUSTINE and THOMAS AQUINAS dedicated volumes of text to expounding on this mystery, both men ultimately concluding that it is "unknowable" until the LAST JUDGMENT, when all secrets will be "laid bare." St. Ambrose wrote in the late fourth century that redeemed souls will "be allowed to see God, to be honored with sharing the joy of salvation and eternal light with Christ the Lord" in the ageless "Kingdom of Heaven." Fifteen centuries later, American archbishop FULTON SHEEN enumerated this, saying, "Heaven is not a place where we find the fullness of all fine things. . . . Heaven is the communion with perfect Life, perfect Truth and perfect Love."

The concept of the beatific vision has also been the subject of several official church proclamations. Pope Benedict XII declared in 1336 that "souls behold the divine essence" in heaven, dwelling "face to face" with the Almighty. During the Renaissance, humanist philosophers began postulating that paradise is a place of human joys where fulfillment of physical desires and REUNION with loved ones overshadow delight in the beatific vision. In response to this depiction, the Catholic Council of Trent decreed in 1566 that heaven is the "vision of God and enjoyment of His beauty," with the divine Father firmly at the center of eternal joy. Everything else, if it exists, is supplemental and secondary.

For many, the concept of spending eternity adoring the Godhead seems tedious and artificial. Detractors have lampooned the notion of the beatific vision in POETRY, drama, and prose, offering monotonous paradises of weary SAINTS mouthing meaningless praise. But theologians and philosophers counter that this is anything but boring. They describe the beatific vision as dynamic, not static, continually unfolding to reveal new truths, beauty, and mysteries. It is like an eternal kaleidoscope, forever changing to display new and glorious visions.

BEDE (673–735) Saint Bede (Baede, Beda, Bebe), called the Venerable Bede, was an Anglo-Saxon theologian, writer, and historian who broke new ground in VISION LITERATURE with his *Ecclesiastical History of the English Nation* in 731. The text includes several apparitions of the afterlife adapted from a variety of sources. Bede collected these stories from old records or acquaintances, embell-

ished them as he saw fit, then compiled them in his *History*. The book quickly became one of the most popular tomes of its time, inciting debate and conjecture among clerics interested in ESCHATOLOGY and providing a valuable reference for world historians.

The first vision of paradise described in *History* is that of an Irish monk named Furseus. The cleric claimed to have had many supernatural apparitions, ranging from visits with ANGELS to horrible trips to the burning underworld. In one particularly frightening vision (which occurred around 630), Furseus is warned that if he does not change his wicked behavior, he will spend eternity among the damned. After sampling the luminous glory of "high heaven," this prospect is unbearable, and he changes his sinful ways.

Another vision of the afterlife recounted in Bede's work regards a Northumbrian landowner named DRITHELM who "died" and was delivered to a fiery abyss. He also saw the tortures of hell as well as the anxious spirits in PURGATORY. While touring the netherworld, the farmer saw a valley of suffering souls and a dark ocean where damned spirits rolled in and out on black waves, screeching in hysterics. Demons would have seized him too if his angelic guide had not protected him. After reviving from his comalike state, Drithelm gave away his considerable fortune and dedicated the rest of his life to prayer and penance.

Bede's *History* greatly contributed to both the popularity and credibility of vision literature. The writer had a gift for stylish, compelling prose, which made his text especially appealing to a vast audience. Since he claims to have based his accounts on actual testimonies, readers were willing to accept the tales as authentic. Clerics quickly adapted these eyewitness accounts of heaven and hell into their sermons, offering them as compelling reasons to live a virtuous life. Bede's work also earned him a reputation as a prominent historian, as he is credited with devising the system for dating events from the birth of Christ. Scholars have called his *History* "the beginning of English literature."

Bede is mentioned in Dante's DIVINE COMEDY: THE PARADISO as a resident of the "Heaven of the Sun." Another Christian legend claims that the saint was given the title "Venerable" by an angel after his death. According to the account, a celestial messenger descended from heaven and inscribed the word on the dead man's MEMORIAL. St. Bede's feast is celebrated on May 27.

BERTHA Bertha is the Norse goddess who watches over the souls of infants, especially those who die before being properly consecrated. She is often portrayed as a white lady who slips through villages at night to observe the lives of her faithful. Because of her compassionate nature and dedication to innocent children, she is sometimes associated with the VIRGIN MARY, the Christian mother of JESUS, and Queen of Heaven.

BEST EXISTENCE The ancient prophet Zoroaster refers to the blessed afterlife as the best existence. This ZOROASTRIAN HEAVEN is a reward for virtuous souls who accept the truth of AHURA MAZDA and refuse to be taken in by Ahriman, the evil lord of "the lie." The faith teaches that all people have free will and must ally themselves with Ahura Mazda or his wicked counterpart, and that each person therefore accepts the corresponding consequences. Those who choose wisely and live according to Ahura Mazda's plan will depart to the best existence, where they will spend eternity basking in comfort and joy. Evildoers will sink to a murky hell of regret and retribution.

The voyage to the best existence is beset with dangers, but Ahura Mazda promises his faithful that he will see them through safely. When a person dies, the soul must cross CHINVATO PERETAV (Bridge of the Separator), a razor-thin passage to paradise that spans the pit of hell. In the GATHAS, the religious tome of this ancient faith, Zoroaster reassures followers that he will personally shepherd the just across this perilous bridge and deliver them to heaven. Other legends claim that Ahura Mazda will send ANGELS to escort the saved into paradise. Once across, worthy spirits will live forever in a realm of perfect bliss.

Zoroaster also teaches a LAST JUDGMENT, at which time the eternal fate of all will be reaffirmed. At this time a record of every soul's actions will be read. Righteous souls will enjoy the best existence for eternity, while spirits of the iniquitous will be purged from existence.

BEULAH LAND Beulah Land became popular around the 1600s to refer to

CHRISTIAN HEAVEN. It derives from a passage in the Old Testament about the marital "inheritance" of a woman named Beulah, in whom "the Lord delighted." The prophet Isaiah uses her situation to draw an analogy to heaven, invoking the image of the WEDDING FEAST: "As the bridegroom rejoices over the bride, so shall thy God rejoice over thee" (Isa. 62:5).

Based on this declaration, Beulah Land became synonymous with the paradise promised to righteous souls. Like land conveyed to women through marriage, heaven is the rightful inheritance of all who embrace the word of JESUS. In this way, Christ assures his followers that even though they have no formal "claim" to paradise, through union with the Messiah, all will receive a share in the eternal kingdom.

The metaphor began surfacing in works of Western literature and in sermons about the reward Christ has in store for his faithful. Its popularity soared after author John Bunyan included the name in his PILGRIM'S PROGRESS. The story describes a lovely hamlet called Beulah Land where the pilgrims rest during their grueling quest. It lies, mystically, somewhere between life and death. In this blessed place, the "sun shineth day and night" and the "air was very sweet and pleasant." The pilgrims stop for a brief respite in Beulah Land, which is "within sight of" the Celestial City. Since it lies "upon the border of heaven," the realm is frequently visited by the "Shining Ones" (ANGELS) who delight in walking its hallowed ground.

Beulah Land also appears in a number of Christian HYMNS as a synonym for paradise. Edgar Page envisions the distant heaven across a mighty ocean, which represents the journey each soul makes upon death. His lyrics describe a glimmering city of gold "where mansions are prepared for me," and he pines for this eternal "home." The song encourages others to lift their eyes to that dazzling sight and plot their own course to Beulah Land, reachable by living according to the teachings of Christianity.

In more recent times, Beulah Land has lost the popularity it had during the early part of the century. However, certain American fundamentalist sects continue to use the term when preaching about paradise.

BHAGAVADGITA   The *Bhagavadgita*, written around 200 B.C., is a sacred text of the Hindu religion, comparable to the Christian Bible and the Islamic KORAN. Literally translated, the title means "Song of the Blessed Lord," referring to the Hindu god Krishna, the "final resting place of the universe."

The *Bhagavadgita* is an excerpt of the MAHABHARATA, the longest epic poem ever discovered. Its text synthesizes traditional Indian myths, warrior codes, and contemporary religious ideas into a comprehensive philosophy. Later generations declared the ancient writ the inspired word of the gods. It has since become vital to the faith and practice of Hinduism.

The central theme of the *Bhagavadgita* is that humanity's ultimate joy is in liberation from self and from the "bonds" of material things. This liberation, called MOKSHA, can be obtained through education, meditation, and reflection. The book emphasizes the individual's role in society, which is harmonious with the will of the divine. By following the text, one can dissolve the "I" and become part of the "whole." The *Bhagavadgita* also focuses on reincarnation as an essential part of Krishna's plan for universal oneness.

The *Bhagavadgita* remains an important cultural as well as religious document. It was the favorite scripture of modern philosopher Mahatma Gandhi. With these sacred words as his foundation, Gandhi began a revolution of social reform that changed a nation and inspired the world. His tactics for effecting change through nonviolent means were later adapted by the American civil rights hero Martin Luther King Jr.

BIBLE ACCORDING TO MARK TWAIN, THE

Renowned satirist Mark Twain (Samuel Clemmens) offers his views of heaven, the Garden of Eden, and other religious concepts in a series of essays and SHORT STORIES collectively called *The Bible According to Mark Twain*. Written over a span of decades from 1871 to 1910, the author takes aim at contemporary depictions of CHRISTIAN PARADISE as well as traditional Christian doctrines. The result is a witty, often irreverent indictment of "preacher heaven" that Twain considers to be sheer hell.

One of his biggest targets is Elizabeth Stuart Phelps's *The Gates Ajar*, a best-selling novel about the afterlife that, according to Twain, describes "a little ten-cent Heaven much like Rhode Island." Its mundane trinket shops and "Sunday socials" are nothing less than "petty" and, in his opinion, insufferably boring. Twain, finding the whole image nauseating, ridicules the book in his own essays, although critics at the time accused the author of "borrowing" ideas from Phelps and using them in his own works.

In *The Bible According to Mark Twain*, the author paints his own unique picture of what happens to humans after death. His short story "Captain Stormfield's Visit to Heaven" was inspired by a dream recounted to him by real-life seafarer Captain Edgar Wakeman. Twain took elements of this dream, mingled them with his own ideas, and wove a fantastic tale of astral projection, space travel, and spiritual redemption. The story went through many forms (Twain crafted it as a drama, an essay, then a novel before finally settling on short story format), and Twain even considered expanding it into a lengthy volume detailing "all sorts of heavens." This never-completed embellished version would have offered differing paradises tailored to the tastes of the saved. And each paradise would have been set on a different planet.

In his final "Captain Stormfield," Twain sends the departed sailor on a tour of the vast unknown that takes him to the limits of the universe. After a long, perilous journey to heaven, the captain learns that paradise is the resting place of spirits from around the cosmos, not just of earthly beings. In this utopia, souls are given many options as to how and where they shall spend eternity. People can, for example, choose what age would best suit their desires. Stormfield heeds the advice to remain elderly, "bald and wrinkled on the outside" but "deep on the inside." The gruff captain also quits the heavenly choir and elects not to wear his wings on a daily basis, as he is having "considerable trouble" mastering their usage. He is informed, however, that for "official functions," everyone is expected to appear in full uniform, "wings, HALO and harp and palm branch and all that."

Like the rest of the blessed, Stormfield must choose which "district" he will inhabit in paradise. Twain uses this aspect of heaven to rebuke those who indulge in social and racial prejudices, revealing the ugliness of such tensions in eternity. In his story, bigoted souls decry the "Jersey" and "California" areas, as they are littered with "leather-headed mud-colored ANGELS." People tend to stay with "their own," congregating along racial, economic, and religious lines. Through this satirical (and distinctly distasteful) depiction of heaven, the author suggests that those who believe paradise means being insulated from all who are different would find such a segregated realm bland, tedious, and wholly unpleasant. Their prejudices would not beautify but pollute eternity.

Twain also offers some speculation on the nature of angels, as Stormfield discovers that they have distinct missions and duties. The captain learns that the celestial beings travel by the millions to appear "to dying children and good people," offering comfort in times of trouble. Each angel is also allowed to select its own color, filling the

heavens with a dazzling bouquet of "blazing red ones, and blue and green and gold." In sharp contrast to their human counterparts, these dear spirits delight in a grand mix of colors and create for themselves a much more beautiful world.

Also contained in *The Bible According to Mark Twain* is a short essay titled "Etiquette for the Afterlife: Advice to Paine." The text was written for an ailing friend as a way to take the sting out of death, but ironically it turned out to be Twain's last substantial piece. The author died in 1910, just weeks after penning the counsel.

"Etiquette for the Afterlife" is more dark and cynical than his earlier treatments of the subject, perhaps because of his own impending death. The essay is filled with jabs at Christians and traditional doctrines concerning heaven and hell. Twain comments that "religious" paradise is a dour realm where a saved soul might as well "leave his heart behind," since he would "have no use for it in THIS place." Sunday entertainment in heaven consists of smugly watching the damned roast in everlasting fire. Compassionate souls, he warns, should not consider trying to "smuggle water to those in Hell" or else they, too, might be damned for their kindness.

Twain's essay, though acerbic, offers numerous humorous touches. Among his bits of counsel to the saved: "Don't try to tip SAINT PETER," "leave your dog outside," and "do not look bored." And the author reassures his reader that "by and by, if you behave, they will give you a halo" and accept you into the lofty ranks. Beyond that, Twain has little advice for making his satirical paradise more heavenly.

BIFROST BRIDGE The Bifrost Bridge forges a passage between heaven and earth according to Norse mythology. It is a mystic rainbow that stretches to the ASGARD, the home of the gods. Bifrost Bridge is mentioned in the epic PROSE EDDA as a great work of art fashioned by the gods from before time. A fierce giant stands guard at the foot of the bridge, ready to warn the gods of approaching transgressors and to defend the borders of Asgard.

Within the city of Asgard is VAL-HALLA, the "Hall of the Slain," the final resting place reserved for warriors who die in battle. These fallen heroes enjoy an eternal feast given in their honor.

BILL & TED'S BOGUS JOURNEY The 1991 comedy *Bill & Ted's Bogus Journey* sends a pair of teenage "excellent dudes" on a Dantesque journey through heaven and hell. This pseudosequel features the dimwitted but likable duo from *Bill & Ted's Excellent Adventure* (played by Alex Winter and Keanu Reeves) in a rousing trek through the afterlife. In *Bogus Journey*, the boys must overcome such obstacles as evil robot duplicates, supernatural challenges, and even the devil himself in order to ascend to heaven to seek the assistance of the Supreme Being.

Winter and Reeves begin their otherworld travels after being murdered by mechanical look-alikes programmed by a sinister despot intent on destroying the boys. But when the pair attempts to make contact with the living through

an amateur psychic, the girl panics and believes she has unwittingly conjured demons. With the help of a "do-it-yourself" spiritualist guide, she performs a ritual of exorcism that plunges the two into hell.

In the murky underworld, the boys encounter their worst nightmares. Winter and Reeves also meet and befriend the Grim Reaper (played by William Sadler), who offers them the opportunity to challenge him to a test of skills, with the promise of release if they win. If they lose, however, the two must remain in hell for eternity. But when the duo defeats Death at the board game Battleship, he angrily demands they go "two out of three!" This contest is followed by a round of Clue, a Twister match, and finally a bout of mechanical football, all of which are won by the deceased teens. Sadler reluctantly agrees to take the pair to heaven to seek advice on how they might return to life on earth.

Winter and Reeves soon discover that getting into paradise is a somewhat difficult task. While approaching the PEARLY GATES, they learn that only the "serene and enlightened" may enter heaven, and they are having considerable trouble feigning serenity and enlightenment. The boys believe they have succeeded when a white-robed woman hands them a scroll and a map of the celestial grounds, cooing "welcome to heaven." But Sadler informs them that she is merely a receptionist; they still must get past "security." This will be much more challenging, since everyone else in heaven wears ivory robes or lavender garments, and Winter, Reeves, and Sadler stand out in their colorful clothing. Desperate, the boys mug three new arrivals, steal their linen garments, and present themselves to the gate-keeper.

Before allowing the trio into par-adise, the guardian of the gates asks that they explain "the meaning of life." Per-plexed, Reeves begins reciting the lyrics to Poison's song "Every Rose Has Its Thorn." Winters and Sadler pick up the lines, the Reaper disguising his voice so as not to be recognized in eternity. Sat-isfied with this response, the gatekeeper motions them forward, and the massive doors to paradise swing open. The de-ceased teens and their supernatural guide enter and search out the throne of God.

Everything in the city of heaven is dazzling white, almost too brilliant to behold. In paradise, the boys see such fa-mous faces as Thomas Jefferson, William Shakespeare, Albert Einstein, and CON-FUCIUS. They are among the crowd of SAINTS gathered to play charades. Other blessed souls sit above the scene in bal-conies overlooking the eternal court-yard. As could be expected, the genius Einstein is the first to guess the correct answer to the charade, happily shouting, "Smoky Is the Bandit!"

The Almighty dwells in the heights of paradise, enthroned at the top of a white STAIRCASE that rises beyond view. Reeves greets the deity (who is never shown onscreen) with a hearty, "Con-gratulations on earth, it's a most excel-lent planet!" The boys then ask the supreme being what they must do to re-turn to earth and stop the evil robots who killed them and now threaten their girlfriends. God responds by referring them to Station, the "most brilliant sci-entist in the entire universe." In thanks, the teens assure the lord, "You are a just and noble creator!" and take their leave of his divine presence.

Using the mystic map, Winter and Reeves find Station, who turns out to be an intergalactic scientist from some alien world. With his help, the boys are able to resume their existence among the living, destroy the villainous robots, and achieve their grandest dreams. But before exiting paradise, the two affirm their desire to return on some future day, leaving the Almighty with the en-thusiastic declaration, "catch you later, God!"

BLAKE, WILLIAM   (1757–1827) Artist, poet, and philosopher William Blake dedicated decades of creative ener-gies to interpreting his concept of the su-pernatural, including in his works many vivid illustrations of heaven. Blake claimed to be both a Christian and a polytheist, embracing JESUS as the son of God but also believing in a number of powerful deities, which he termed "Zoas." He was a follower of EMANUEL SWEDENBORG and mentions the philoso-pher's theories in many of his own works. Blake drew on his free-form ideas on reli-gion and philosophy and his mystic vi-sions of the supernatural as inspiration for a host of poems, paintings, and liter-ary works on ESCHATOLOGY.

Blake claimed to have had mystic apparitions throughout his lifetime, beginning with the vision of a "tree filled with ANGELS" at age eight. The author later wrote that such supernatural episodes continued for the rest of his life, giving him a unique perspective on the mysteries of the hidden world. He considered himself at home in both the physical and spiritual realms, having intimate dealings with both.

Blake detested "reason" and cherished "imagination." In his estimation, heaven is the dimension where all souls are creative and industrious, constantly producing great works of fantasy. This paradise coexists on the same plain with hell, which is an artistic vacuum. The damned do not suffer tortures and hellfire but are condemned to a fruitless existence of intellectual sterility. Seeing the prolific blessed spirits amplifies their agony.

With this model of the afterlife, Blake uses unconventional criteria in defining good and evil, each being related to artistic expression rather than to morality. Creativity is good, obstruction of the creative force is evil. Using this philosophy, Blake identifies the God worshiped in traditional religions as villainous, since this Almighty is too controlling and interferes with human passions. The deity of Judaism, Christianity, and Islam demands that his faithful follow a "narrow" road and adhere to a strict set of behavioral guidelines. Blake much prefers the proverbial devil, who encourages human souls to indulge themselves, test limits, and question authority. The controversial scholar once paid a great compliment to fellow writer Milton (author of PAR-

ADISE LOST), declaring that the man could better describe hell and demons than he could God and heaven because Milton "was a true Poet and of the Devil's party without knowing it."

Redefining supernatural terms to suit his own theories, Blake describes "Jesus the Imagination" and "Satan the selfhood," asserting that true salvation rests in eternal creativity, while damnation is ascetic frustration. Blessed souls will spend eternity reflecting the infinite creative power of the Almighty through exercising their own imagination both individually and collectively. By contrast, the damned are isolated in their own shallowness and superficiality. Blake further believed that in paradise the saved enjoy the REUNION of loved ones and the continuation of love that existed on earth.

Blake offers his most extensive interpretations of the Christian afterlife in his 1793 *The Marriage of Heaven and Hell.* The work offers a description of Jesus as impulsive and energetic, brimming with creativity. This, he asserts, is the true savior: a man of passion and fire, not the tedious "law giver" preached by contemporary reverends. Based in part on Swedenborg's models of heaven and hell, Blake's *Marriage* denies that people ultimately choose good and evil, stating instead that there are only good and evil "states." These states are permanent, and people pass through them on the journey of life but are themselves morally neutral. Therefore a soul can change its state at any time—even after death—if it simply "rejects error and embraces truth." (This assertion helped inspire C. S.

Lewis's THE GREAT DIVORCE, which soundly rejects this interchangeable concept of the afterlife.)

In addition to being a prolific writer, Blake created many intriguing paintings of religious, mythic, and literary themes. He began working as an artist while apprenticed to an engraver and specialized in etching Gothic tombstones, drawing on his visions for inspiration. Biblical concepts, too, inspired many of Blake's paintings. His *Death on a Pale Horse* is a haunting portrait of the description of the end of the world foretold in REVELATION. In his 1808 *Vision of the LAST JUDGMENT*, Blake depicts a landscape of couples embracing and kissing, mothers cuddling infants, and patriarchs greeting their descendants before the throne of Christ. A swirling legion of angels watches over this scene, smiling in approval. This incredibly complex illumination is the most recent depiction of this cataclysmic event to be painted by a major artist.

Blake has also transcended his era with the haunting painting *The Soul Hovering Above the Body*. The early nineteenth-century composition depicts a spirit escaping its physical shell and floating freely through space. Many believe that this is an interpretation of one of Blake's own supernatural adventures into the unknown. The work also bears striking similarities to descriptions of modern NEAR-DEATH EXPERIENCES, in which people claim to leave their bodies and become purely spiritual beings.

In addition to these creative endeavors, Blake penned POETRY focusing on the afterlife. His poems contain the same quixotic mix of traditional imagery and innovative symbolism. Contemporary musician Jim Morrison was greatly influenced by Blake's poetry, emulating his ethereal style in many of his song lyrics.

William Blake's *Jesus Offers to Redeem Mankind*
ART TODAY

BOOK OF HOURS During the Middle Ages, lay Christians began commissioning books of hours in order to organize their religious duties. The decorated schedules list specific rites that must be performed each day by the faithful. A typical book of hours contains a calendar of SAINTS' feast days, prayers and meditations, and portraits of religious themes. Many also listed the offices of the dead and other complex liturgical services. By the fifteenth-century, books of hours were common fixtures in finer homes throughout Europe.

The book was usually named for its patron. Since each edition had to be printed and illustrated entirely by hand, almost all early copies were commissioned by royalty or wealthy families. Artwork was provided by the finest painters and engravers of the era. The quality of the book's content and illustrations depended almost entirely on how much the patron was willing to spend on the project. More lavish examples were rich in gold-trimmed pages, exquisite drawings, and brilliant illustrations. However all books of hours featured common Christian themes, such as the sacrifice of JESUS, the CORONATION of Mary, and the LAST JUDGMENT.

The glories of heaven figured prominently in books of hours. In addition to text describing the various joys of paradise, many books had detailed portraits of the Messiah Jesus, the VIRGIN MARY, and God the Father enthroned in eternity. The *Rohan Hours*, a luxurious fifteenth-century masterpiece, includes an illustration of a "Dying Man Commending His Soul to God." The picture shows the heavenly father, a white-bearded patriarch, dispatching ANGELS to collect the departing spirit. Above the deathbed, a swirl of celestial spirits and glorified saints surrounds God in an explosion of heavenly beauty.

LES TRÈS RICHES HEURES DU DUC DE BERRY the most famous book of hours still in existence, features similar allusions to CHRISTIAN PARADISE. Readers are admonished to set their eyes skyward and avoid the horrors of hell (which is also graphically illustrated). Even the drawings of earthly life in *Très Riches Heures* are topped with a "dome of Heaven," represented by a royal blue sky dotted with golden stars. The purpose of this is to remind readers that the shadow of paradise is ever-present, even when worldly pursuits distract our attention.

Books of hours are among the examples of ILLUMINATED MANUSCRIPTS that graphically depict the afterlife and focus attention on the beauty of the world to come.

BOOK OF THE DEAD The Egyptian Book of the Dead, a collection of funerary rites, incantations, and directions for reaching paradise, dates back to approximately 1580 B.C., when Egyptians began placing scrolls of text beside entombed bodies. The book is said to be the work of THOTH, the powerful god of wisdom. In the text, Thoth offers his faithful hints designed to help departing souls enjoy a pleasant afterlife. The path to the otherworld is lined with treacherous obstacles, and the Book of the Dead provides methods for avoiding or overcoming these supernatural dangers.

The Book of the Dead contains explicit descriptions of the route a soul must take to the Hall of OSIRIS, the judge of the dead and lord of the underworld. If the proper procedure is followed, the spirit will find happiness and fulfillment in an eternal realm that closely resembles life on earth. This supernatural world offers the many pleasures of earthly existence but is without illness, hunger, sorrow, or other human pains. Failure to follow the book's guidelines would result in a horrific afterlife of torture and eventual annihilation.

Ancient Egyptians were the first to believe that souls are judged after death,

Artwork from an Egyptian sarcophagus shows a grant banquet in the afterlife. ART TODAY

and no culture was more obsessed with the question of immortality. Their complex mythology turns the afterlife into the ultimate private club, a place where the migrating spirit must know an intricate series of secret passwords and complicated rituals to negotiate the mystic maze. The great beyond is fraught with dangers, and souls who lose their way face numerous terrors. Over time, directions for escaping these horrors had become so involved that the data had to be transcribed in manuscript form. This "divinely inspired" text eventually became known as the Egyptian Book of the Dead.

According to the writ, when a person dies, the soul travels in the boat of RA (the sun god) along the "river of the sky" with many other newly deceased. If it makes the journey safely, the spirits will disembark in Duat, the "Valley in the Sky." Each soul must then pass through seven gates, calling every gatekeeper by name and giving the proper password. On this supernatural voyage, the spirit must also be able to discern

which paths are safe and which hold hidden dangers.

Once the departed makes it past the tangle of perilous roads, a dog-headed deity named ANUBIS meets the spirit and delivers it to the Hall of Justice. Anubis shepherds the soul to the court of King Osiris, judge of the dead. Osiris then asks the soul for a complete account of both its good and bad acts during life on earth. After the spirit gives its response, Osiris weighs the deceased's heart against the "feather of truth" to validate the soul's account. The scales tip toward good or evil, at which time Osiris renders final judgment.

During this hearing, a hideous monster named Ammut (eater of the dead) sits at Osiris's feet, ready to gobble up any unworthy spirits. To avoid becoming food for this ghoul, the spirit must also recite a specific series of invocations, prayers, and magic words to appease Osiris. If it fails in any of these tasks, or if Osiris renders an unfavorable verdict, then Ammut savagely devours the soul. (One illustration from a copy of the Book of the Dead dating to around 1310 B.C., titled *The Last Judgment Before Osiris*, shows Ammut drooling hungrily as Osiris places the dead man's heart on the mystical scales, ready to consume the unfortunate spirit.) Souls who survive this trial advance to the next life, where they enjoy banquets, contests, dancing, and other earthly joys.

The Egyptians also believed that spirits of the dead could take objects with them for use in the afterlife. Therefore, survivors often placed offerings of food, wine, tools, and other objects in tombs for the spirit's eternal enjoyment. In the case of the pharaohs and of the very wealthy, horses, pets, and even servants were also "dispatched" along with the master of the house to serve in the next world. Proper burial, adhering to a strict embalming procedure, was also essential to a happy afterlife.

Because of the massive amount of information needed by the dead, and its complexity, Egyptians began routinely placing scrolls of text in tombs around 1500 B.C. These ILLUMINATED MANUSCRIPTS, at first called *Chapters Coming Forth by Day*, were eventually compiled under the title *Book of the Dead*. In addition to such rites, the book features ideas on human nature and destiny, magic spells, and various incantations designed to curry favor with the gods. Originally, only priests and pharaohs were considered worthy of such information, so the poor were condemned to wander the afterlife without the benefit of instruction. After many decades, inexpensive copies were made available to the peasantry, but these no-frills editions contained only the bare essentials and had no maps or illustrations. The best a commoner could hope for in the next world was to serve as one of a pharaoh's slaves in his regal paradise.

BOORALA Boorala, an Australian mythical deity, is the rough equivalent of the Christian God the Father and the Hebrew YAHWEH. He is credited with creating the world and infusing it with inherent goodness and beauty. People who live lives of justice, morality, and kindness are welcomed into the House of Boorala after death, where they will enjoy a blissful eternity. The spirits of evil people, however, have no place in the afterlife and will be eradicated from existence.

BORAK The borak is the great beast of Islamic lore who carried MUHAMMAD to DJANNA, the paradise of Islam. The prophet's journey to the abode of ALLAH is chronicled in the KORAN, Islam's holy book; however, no details are given about the animal, not even its name. What is known of the beast has been supplied by later legends that became popular after Muhammad's death.

According to the description in *Ascension of Mohammed*, a stylized version of the holy man's travels, the borak is described as a powerful beast with a human head and the body of a donkey. One "stride" is equivalent to a hundred miles, covering a distance approximating "as far as the eye can see." His saddle was made of emeralds and lashed with ropes of pearl. Tradition also claims that the borak is one of the ANIMALS that will exist eternally in paradise.

BRAINSTORM   Ancient myth meets future technology in *Brainstorm,* a 1983 film about probing the mysteries of eternity. The movie is based on a story by Bruce Joel Rubin, whose treatments of the afterlife include GHOST, JACOB'S LADDER, and MY LIFE. In *Brainstorm,* high-tech scientists invent a machine that can record sensory experiences, emotions, and thoughts, which can then be played back by another user. During the development of the device, one of the project design-ers (played by Louise Fletcher) suffers a heart attack and uses the device to record her own death. Coworker Christopher Walken finds the tape and decides to relive his friend's experience, determined to "take a scientific look at the scariest thing a person ever has to face."

The journey to *Brainstorm's* afterlife begins as Fletcher's spirit discorpulates and floats above her body. Her freed soul then travels to a realm of silver bubbles, each of which holds a memory of Fletcher's life. She visits several of these, some happy, others sorrowful, enjoying one last glimpse of earthly existence before moving on to the next world. As Walken reviews this series of remembrances, he is touched to learn that his friendship with his deceased colleague was truly cherished and provided her with a measure of often-elusive joy.

The scene then abruptly shifts to a frightening montage of horrifying images of blood, mutilations, and faces contorted in agony. This part of the tape is so jarring that Walken has to stop before he, too, suffers cardiac arrest. When he resumes the review, the grisly phantoms are gone. Now Fletcher's soul is departing the earth and soaring through the cosmos toward a distant brilliant light. Magnificent bursts of color erupt all around the spirit in flight, and a sense of unknown peace overwhelms Walken as he approaches paradise vicariously through the strange machine.

At last, Fletcher's soul arrives in the realm of bliss. A myriad of ANGELS drift gently around that beautiful light. Their white robes and silken wings reflect the golden glow of God himself. Each movement of these celestial creatures is a miniature ballet, like milky butterflies fluttering through eternity. Walken is about to join them in their endless dance, but before he draws close enough, the voice of his wife (played by Natalie Wood) calls him back to earth. He departs the court of heaven, comforted by the notion that one day he too would take his place "among the stars."

The visualizations of the unknown for *Brainstorm* originated with director Douglas Trumbull, who distinguished himself as a special effects wizard with such films as *2001: A Space Odyssey, Blade Runner,* and *Close Encounters of the Third Kind.* The ascent to heaven bears striking similarity to the mind-spinning finale of *2001,* a swirling vertigo of flashing light and brilliant colors. *Brainstorm's* angelic legions are likewise reminiscent of the sci-fi classic's luminous alien images.

Ironically, this foray into life after

death marked Natalie Wood's last film. She drowned while on a boating excursion in 1981 before production was completed. *Brainstorm* had to be pieced together using existing footage and stand-ins.

BRALGU Bralgu is the Australian Aboriginal land of the dead. In Bralgu, deceased spirits enjoy a REUNION with their friends and ancestors. When a person dies, the soul is believed to be ferried to this paradise by an enchanted boat that sails upstream. In Bralgu, blessed spirits spend eternity in peace interacting with their departed comrades.

BRENDAN, SAINT (484–577) St. Brendan, also known as Brendan the Navigator, is the subject of many legends regarding the supernatural. The fearless sailor is said to have visited the ISLE OF THE BLEST during his seafaring adventures. According to the *Navigatio Brendani* (Travels of Brendan), written in the tenth century, Brendan was searching for the "Island of Earthly Paradise" and the "Land Promised to the SAINTS" on one of his many mystic quests. His voyage took him to the shores of paradise, where he met his destiny.

According to the legend, Brendan sails with a crew of devout monks in search of this holy place. He discovers many islands, including the mystic PARADISE OF BIRDS. Upon departing this isle, the sailors celebrate Easter Sunday on the "back of a friendly whale." After forty days (forty years in some versions), the navigator reaches heaven, a lush garden

laden with fruit-bearing trees, precious stones, and endless sunny skies. The realm is filled with ANGELS disguised in human form. They allow Brendan and his men to rest with them for a time, then send him back, since "no man may come to the other side while he yet lives." But the celestial messengers reassure Brendan that he will return one day, as all virtuous spirits shall one day be restored to paradise.

The *Navigatio Brendani* was widely read across Europe during the centuries following its publication. It contained extensive maps and illustrations of Brendan's travels and is believed to have influenced explorers such as Christopher Columbus. The supernatural travelogue is also believed to have inspired sections of Dante's DIVINE COMEDY.

BRIDGET OF SWEDEN, SAINT
(1302–1373) Bridget of Sweden, a wealthy noblewoman of the fourteenth century, received many mystic visions during her lifetime. She frequently saw images of heaven, hell, and the earth simultaneously, as a united universe in different layers. Her amazing mystical experiences are chronicled in a fascinating diary, and Bridget also wrote numerous scholarly works describing CHRISTIAN PARADISE. The saint's influential account of the life of JESUS, titled *Revelations,* is still studied in convents and monasteries.

Bridget married at age fourteen and bore eight children, including a second-generation saint, Catherine of Sweden. After her husband's death, Bridget spent her large inheritance on founding a

St. Bridget of Sweden woodcut
by Albrecht Dürer. ART TODAY

monastery and improving the plight of the poor. She was loved by the community and had a reputation for being compassionate and generous. A servant once said of Bridget that she was "kind and meek to every creature" and had "a laughing face." Both the wealthy and the destitute trusted the gentle woman, knowing that she was a wise and trustworthy friend.

Throughout her life, Bridget had visions of the supernatural and prophecies about the future. Word of her ability spread, and she eventually found herself being approached by kings, nobles, and political leaders for advice and counsel. She corresponded regularly with a number of powerful rulers, angering many with her suggestions that their habitual self-indulgence and abuse of power were impediments to salvation.

Among her more pleasant visions were soothing images of heaven. She described paradise as a realm of "infinite love" and joy where blessed souls enjoyed the BEATIFIC VISION. According to her accounts, the greatest delight of eternity is having endless time to reflect on the mercy and majesty of JESUS. No pleasure "imagined on earth" could approach this divine rapture.

Bridget died in 1372 and was quickly declared a saint of the Roman Catholic church. She is still dearly loved by the people of Sweden, who have adopted her as the country's patron saint. Her feast day is celebrated on July 23.

BUDDHIST PARADISE Buddhist beliefs in a pleasant afterlife include both spiritual and physical dimensions. Ancient tales describe the realm of KHUN-LUN, a blessed land where purified human souls ascend to dwell with the gods. Khun-lun is an earthly paradise, a resplendent garden of succulent produce and sweet waters in which birds of every color soar amid flowering trees. In Khun-lun grows a sacred PEACH tree with fruit that conveys immortality.

In other Buddhist lore, believers reject the notion that any "glorified earth" could offer the human spirit ultimate fulfillment. True eternal bliss is found through attaining NIRVANA, a state of enlightenment similar to the Hindu MOKSHA or Jain KEVALA. To reach this lofty height, a soul must purge itself of all evil, selfishness, and deception, which usu-

Silver and ruby Buddha ring designed by contemporary Hawaiian artist Margaret Wong

ally entails living through numerous incarnations. Before achieving Nirvana, a spirit must live, die, be reborn, and continue striving for perfection. Some souls might enjoy a brief respite in a paradisical realm or be detained in a temporary prison in one of many hells before the reincarnation cycle continues.

Once sufficient progress is made, spirits no longer have to return to the living world for improvement. Such souls have outgrown the "self." After reviewing the summation of their lifetimes' knowledge and learning the lessons of the temporal plane, enlightened spirits achieve Nirvana, a collective immortality in which they unite with the universe. In this contemplative state, spirits dwell eternally motionless, pondering the great mysteries of the cosmos.

BURIAL OF COUNT ORGAZ, THE
The Burial of Count Orgaz was painted in the late sixteenth century by famed master El Greco (born Domenikos Theotokopoulos), blending elements of mysticism, Byzantine imagery, and Venetian style. The composition depicts the interment of a man so holy that legend claims SAINT AUGUSTINE and St. Stephen descended from heaven to preside over the count's funeral. The two SAINTS are robed in rich red and gold vestments as they gently lay the deceased's body into the grave.

The top portion of the painting depicts paradise, where the VIRGIN MARY, JESUS, and a host of ANGELS look lovingly toward their new companion. A celestial guide adorned in glittering garments of gold satin escorts Orgaz's spirit to heaven, cradling it like a newborn child. Clouds part to allow passage, revealing countless angels and saints celebrating the latest arrival. The vibrant colors and dazzling tones provide a sharp contrast to the sea of black-robed mourners that line the bottom of the painting.

Like El Greco's reverent depiction of the ASSUMPTION, *The Burial of Count Orgaz* incorporates the artist's innovative use of color and elongated style to give his paintings spiritual depth and stir deep emotions. The work suggests a paradise more fantastic than any heaven conceived in the human imagination. The juxtaposition of the dreary mourners with the brilliant celestial court likewise implies that death is not an occasion for sorrow but a magnificent passage into CHRISTIAN PARADISE where souls will experience joy without end.

CAESARIUS OF HEISTERBACH (ca. 1180–1240) Caesarius of Heisterback was a Cistercian writer and monk, born in Germany and educated in Cologne, who advanced medieval notions of CHRISTIAN PARADISE that were quickly adopted throughout Christendom. His *Sermones* and *Expositiones* (Sermons and Exempla) are filled with vivid images of ANGELS, SAINTS, JESUS, and other heroes of paradise who eagerly await the arrival of virtuous souls. Caesarius emphasized devotion to the Holy Eucharist and frequent reception of the sacraments as essential to attaining salvation. His ideas were repeated at pulpits throughout Europe and greatly influenced ESCHATOLOGY of the thirteenth century.

Caesarius encouraged Christians to seek the intercession of the VIRGIN MARY, mother of the Messiah, for protection against damnation. He believed that Christ's mother had the power not only to save souls from being condemned but also to visit hell to retrieve sinners from the underworld. His writings include the example of a corrupt monk who had died and been damned but was restored to life through Mary's mediation. The man repented, led a devout life, and eventually became a saint. This legend was spread across the Christian world to serve as inspiration to the faithful. Caesarius's teachings also became instrumental in securing the Virgin's reputation as queen of PURGATORY and intercessor for people's souls.

CAROUSEL The famous songwriting team of Richard Rodgers and Oscar Hammerstein sets a rather unconditional afterlife to music in the 1945 musical *Carousel*. The drama (adapted from Ferenc Molnár's 1921 play LILIOM) features its hero in the next world trying to atone for the sins of his youth. It became one of the most successful stage shows of the decade, enjoying an original run on Broadway of 890 performances. The 1956 film adaptation was equally successful.

Carousel's plot centers around Billy, a handsome, cavalier carousel barker in late nineteenth-century New England. A flirtatious rogue, Billy loses his heart to a naive young girl, Julie, and the two elope, to the chagrin of the entire village. But when the restless (and now unemployed) scoundrel discovers that his young bride is expecting his child, Billy panics and tries to rob a wealthy tradesman. He is killed in the foiled burglary, and his tainted spirit proceeds to the next world.

In the afterlife, Billy demands to speak to "the highest judge of all" to beg for a chance to redeem himself. He pleads his case and convinces the Almighty to allow him one last chance to return to earth to help his child. The baby he never knew is now a rambunctious teenager about to graduate from high school. She is a troubled girl who has lived under the shadow of her father's dark reputation, enduring years of insults and jeers about being the daughter of a "criminal." Billy descends to earth to convince her that she can overcome this stigma and do anything she wishes with her life.

The film version depicts a rather drab afterlife where "lowlifes" such as Billy are given the task of polishing stars in an eternal workshop. Billy manages to steal one before departing heaven, which he gives to his daughter on earth. Instead of landing him in further trouble, this celestial theft convinces his heavenly "boss" that he truly loves his little girl and for once has placed someone else above himself. For this selfless act, Billy is allowed into paradise.

This classic of American theater has been imitated often over the years, with predictably tepid results. Films such as THE HEAVENLY KID and the failed Broadway play THE PINK JUNGLE could not duplicate Carousel's enchanting blend of supernatural themes, sentimental imagery, and notions of human redemption. Rodgers and Hammerstein's musical remains a perennial favorite.

CARRIE: THE MUSICAL Heaven is the setting for the finale of one of the most bizarre musical failures in theatrical history. The 1988 Carrie: The Musical is based on Stephen King's best-selling novel Carrie, the story of a gawky adolescent girl who is viciously tormented by her heartless peers. The beleaguered heroine must simultaneously deal with the onset of puberty, the cruelty of her contemporaries, and the wrath of her religious fanatic mother. Unable to cope with this onslaught of misery, Carrie resorts to use of her telekinetic powers in avenging herself. The book ends with the humiliated teen incinerating the entire senior class, leveling her hometown, and psychically stopping her mother's heart before dying herself from stab wounds. (In the film version, Mom is mutilated in a flurry of sharp projectiles hurled through Carrie's unique ability.) Needless to say, staging this story as a theatrical production requires significant changes.

Carrie: The Musical was launched with great anticipation and visions of grandeur. Collaborators included England's prestigious Royal Shakespeare Company, Cats producer Friedrich Kurz, Hollywood choreographer Debbie Allen, and the lyricists who made Fame and Footloose such blockbuster box office hits. Renowned actress Betty Buckley (who had played Carrie's benevolent teacher in the film adaptation) filled the role of Carrie's mother on stage. CBS even signed on as an investor, contributing to the project's $8 million budget.

But despite this remarkable send-off, Carrie: The Musical was doomed to failure from the start. The plot was revised so drastically in the name of staging that it became virtually incomprehensible. Characters and sequences vital to the story line were unceremoniously cut. The bloody carnage effects that made the movie so spectacular could not be replicated, so they too were dropped. And the finale, central to the impact of both the novel and the film, had to be completely rewritten. The results were nothing less than disastrous.

Carrie: The Musical ends not with ultimate destruction but with salvation.

Both Carrie and her repugnant mother are heaven-bound as the final curtain closes. This celestial effect is accomplished via a huge white STAIRCASE splashed with dazzling light that ascends into the divine realm. The two women, battered and bloody, make their way up as the play's musical score dissolves into an angelic chorus. This image of paradise, like the musical itself, is muddled and confusing, leaving audiences to speculate on what sort of God the producers envision presiding over this debacle.

CARTOONS Heaven has served as the inspiration for printed cartoons for decades. *The New Yorker* routinely offers humorous interpretations of the great beyond, lampooning everything from reincarnation theory to CHRISTIAN PARADISE. A typical example shows a nervous-looking man arriving at the PEARLY GATES wearing a T-SHIRT bearing an obscenity. He sheepishly tells a disapproving SAINT PETER, "I'd like to go home and change." Another depicts God reviewing the work of a departed cartoonist, noting, "Blasphemy, yes, but it *was* funny!"

Gahan Wilson, most famous for his macabre sketchings, pokes fun at paradise in his own unique style. An entry in his *Still Weird* collection portrays a shabby heaven of peeling plaster, littered grounds, and bent wire HALOS. A newly arrived soul dejectedly surveys the place, complaining that he imagined the abode of the blessed "would be a lot classier!" His equally disappointed peers nod their agreement.

In 1980, British humorist Robert Churchill published an entire book of divine comics titled *The Cartoonist's Bible*. In the text, Churchill presents major episodes from the Christian good book in cartoon form, including the creation of the earth, the birth of the Redeemer JESUS, and JACOB's dream of ANGELS descending a mystic LADDER. His drawings also depict God perched on a cloud while consorting with the blessed in paradise, overseeing the happenings on earth via a supernatural television set. *The Cartoonist's Bible* closes with "a glimpse of heaven," in which an angel sporting three halos tells his single-haloed counterpart, "I am holier than thou!"

Many HEREAFTER funnies result from newsworthy items or historical events. The death of Richard Nixon in 1994 inspired a flurry of cartoons about the statesman's demise. Artists were evenly split in their judgment: Some show the ex-president triumphantly entering heaven while others place him in the smoky pit of hell. In a more forgiving example, Nixon is pictured walking through the pearly gates giving a startled St. Peter his trademark "victory sign." A *Newsweek* cartoon depicts Nixon's good and evil aspects being weighed in the afterlife, in the tradition of the Egyptian OSIRIS. *Esquire* granted him admittance to paradise without question: Its caricature shows the young, vibrant ex-president being groomed by angels as he joins the celestial ranks. A similar cartoon commemorated the death of comic legend George Burns. He is shown in silhouette arriving in heaven announcing, "Gracie, I got the part!"

Cartoonist Wiley offers an ongoing interpretation of the afterlife as the staging ground for cosmic practical JOKES in his regular strip *Non Sequitor*. Wiley depicts the Almighty at the keyboard of his divine computer deciding what sort of "challenges" to put before his mortal creatures. In one instance, he sends bolts of lightning and rampaging bears after a soul in need of "more seasoning." Another has a recently deceased male being reincarnated as his worst nightmare: in the body of a woman.

On the more reverent side, artist Bil Keane has often used heaven as a backdrop for his long-running strip *Family Circus*. His warmhearted drawings depict a paradise where family members enjoy REUNION with loved ones, interact with angels, and savor the innocent joys of childhood. His characters make frequent reference to the world to come, asking questions and speculating on the pleasures that lie on the other side of the grave.

But by far, the most prolific heavenly comedian is Gary Larson, whose *Far Side* cartoons have parodied paradise for decades. One shows a truck made of "pressed ham" rolling through "Dog Heaven" so the canine "car chasers can decide for themselves whether or not to participate." Another classic has angels greeting the saved, cooing, "Welcome to heaven, here's your harp," while the bottom panel shows devils telling the damned, "Welcome to hell, here's your accordion!" A worried Colonel Sanders arrives at the "Pearly Gates" only to find angry chickens standing guard. Larson likewise parodies NEAR-DEATH EXPERI-ENCES, showing a doctor shining a flashlight in a patient's face, then laughing hysterically when she later enthusiastically recalls seeing "bright light at the end of the tunnel" on a TV talk show. During his career, the prolific artist has drawn hundreds of comics lampooning the blessed afterlife.

All of these examples illustrate the enduring interest humans have in unraveling the mysteries of the world to come. Whether reverent or raucous, such cartoons offer hope that there is another life that follows earthly existence, which it is hoped will be a place of eternal amusement.

CATHERINE OF SIENA, SAINT

(1347–1380) St. Catherine of Siena, a young Italian girl of great faith and piety, began having mystic experiences as early as age five. During her youth, she reported having glimpses of paradise and hearing "heavenly voices" that gave her advice and comfort. In one of her earliest visions, Catherine describes seeing JESUS enthroned in majesty surrounded by the SAINTS Paul, PETER, and John. These extraordinary episodes continued throughout her brief life.

When Catherine was eighteen, the infant Christ appeared before her and asked her to become his betrothed. As the astonished girl consented, the Christ child placed a regal ring on her finger and promised to remain with her forever. In this vision, Catherine also saw the VIRGIN MARY, mother of Jesus, a host of saints, and heroes of the Old Testament. The celestial contingent served as witnesses for the mystic ceremony, during which Jesus promised Catherine: "Thou shall celebrate with me in Heaven the eternal WEDDING FEAST."

As word of Catherine's supernatural experiences spread, she came under great scrutiny. Her story inspired deep faith among the common people but enraged family members who believed she was making up these fantastic stories to get attention. The bishops and nobles were equally angered, insulted by the notion that God would grant such dynamic visions to a young girl rather than visiting his divine favors upon them. Catherine did, however, receive support from clerics who shared her simple unquestioning faith. Ultimately, even the pope was convinced of her piety and accepted her advice on vital church matters.

Catherine died at age thirty-three, the same age Jesus was at the time of his crucifixion. After her death, the stigmata (the marks of Christ's wounds in his hands, feet, and side) became visible on her body. By this time she had been hailed as a great saint, and her claims to have seen Christ and heaven were accepted by church authorities. Catherine of Siena has been canonized in the Roman Catholic church and declared the patron of Italy. Her feast is celebrated on April 29.

CECILIA, SAINT (ca. 200–220.) Born of wealthy parents during the height of the Roman Empire, Cecilia was a deeply spiritual girl dedicated to chastity and contemplation of the Christian Gospels. She was also quite gifted musically, and some legends even credit her with inventing the organ. In other tales, Ce-

cilia was regularly visited by ANGELS who would come down from paradise to hear her sing HYMNS that she had composed. Their beauty, according to the celestial audience, did justice to the majesty of God enthroned in glory.

While still in her teens, Cecilia was given in marriage to a rich nobleman by the name of Valerian. The devout girl told him of her desire to remain a virgin, and Valerian was so touched by Cecilia's devotion that he agreed to respect her wishes. Within a short time he, too, converted to Christianity and dedicated his life to the service of JESUS, the Messiah.

Knowing his wife's piety, Valerian was not surprised to learn that Cecilia was routinely visited by angels. On one occasion he too was favored by the messengers of heaven. The angels crowned the couple with roses plucked "from the

St. Cecilia, patroness of music. ART TODAY

heavenly garden" and offered to grant them any request. Valerian asked that his brother, an arrogant rogue, renounce his ways and become a Christian. As Valerian said these words, his brother walked in and commented that he could smell—but not see—the most fragrant roses he had even encountered. Cecilia said a prayer over him, and the brother was converted. He could now see the roses of paradise.

From that day on, Cecilia and the two brothers spent their family fortunes tending to the poor and the sick. When word of their acts spread, the men were executed under Roman law as part of the Christian persecution. Cecilia retrieved their bodies and buried them in a religious funeral ceremony, which resulted in her arrest. She was tortured and finally killed, joining the brothers as MARTYRS of the early church.

Cecilia was officially adopted as the patroness of music in the Roman Catholic church in 1584. She is usually pictured with a musical instrument or with sheet music. Her feast is celebrated on November 22.

CEDAR TREE OF THE END African tradition includes teaching about the mythical Cedar Tree of the End. This is a magnificent plant with millions of leaves that grows in paradise. Each leaf of the cedar has inscribed on it the name of a living person. When the leaf falls, that person dies, and his or her soul either soars to heaven or plummets into hell.

The tale of the Cedar Tree of the End closely parallels the Islamic doctrine of the SIDRET-EL-MOUNTEHA in DJANNA. It is believed that Arab traders first introduced this concept to the Africans during the Middle Ages when there was a great deal of traffic between the two regions. Today, Islam is the dominant religion of northern Africa, and belief in this mystic tree persists.

CHAD, SAINT   (ca. 630–668) St. Chad, a seventh-century Northumbrian monk and abbot of the early Christian church, had a vision of heaven just before his death around 668. Chad was one of four brothers who became priests during the early 600s. He and his brother Cedd (also a saint) had worked together at a monastery before Chad was appointed bishop of Mercia. The brothers faced the separation with great sorrow but vowed to remain close despite the geographic distance between them.

Two years later, Chad was saying his evening prayers when he saw his brother Cedd coming toward him escorted by a legion of ANGELS. As they approached, they sang beautiful HYMNS that Chad had never heard before. The party then turned and began ascending a STAIRCASE to heaven and motioned Chad to join them. Chad responded that he still had work to do on earth but would look forward to a great REUNION with his beloved brother in the next life. Not long after the apparition, Chad died of the plague and was later declared a saint of the Roman Catholic church.

Because of this vision, St. Chad is especially revered by those who have lost close family and friends and anticipate being reunited in paradise. His biography is included in the writings of the Venerable BEDE, an early Christian historian. St. Chad's feast day is celebrated on March 2.

CHALMECACIVATL   Chalmecacivatl is the realm of paradise for infants and young children in Aztec belief. In many ways it resembles the Christian notion of LIMBO, a place of perfect earthly happiness for innocents who die without being baptized. (Cultural anthropologists believe that this supernatural dimension may have been adapted from teachings of early Catholic missionaries.) In Chalmecacivatl, pure spirits enjoy eternal existence free of pain, suffering, and all human frailty.

CHAMPS-ELYSÉES   The Champs-Elysées, famous Paris landmark, is named for ELYSIUM, the paradise of ancient Greek and Roman mythology. Its name means "street of paradise," and the regal boulevard claims to offer visitors a foretaste of heaven.

CHILDREN'S LITERATURE   Storytellers have been translating the intricate concepts of the afterlife into tales for children from time immemorial. Ancient legends from Africa describe the next world as a CITY IN THE SKY where an earthlike life continues forever. This simple explanation of what happens when we die is easily grasped by youngsters and helps reduce a child's fear and sorrow over the death of a loved one. Tales of the Nordic GIMLI, the Native American HAPPY HUNTING GROUNDS, and the Breton COCKYANE are likewise understandable by the very young.

Over the centuries, authors greatly embellished descriptions of the life to come and created endless variations of paradise. Hans Christian Andersen sends his Little Match Girl to heaven to escape the brutality of her cruel father. Forced to stand barefoot in the snow peddling her wares, the young child has visions of a grand feast, joyful dancing, and her beloved deceased grandmother. At last the girl perishes in the snow and is taken to paradise for a REUNION with her waiting grandmama.

Andersen was deeply moved by the plight of children during his time and penned stories to help ease their suffering in this world by anticipating great joy in the next. The tender author writes that: "When a child dies, an angel comes down from heaven and takes the child in its arms, and spreading its great white wings, visits all the places that had been dear to the heart of the child. From the favorite place, the child gathers a bouquet of flowers then flies up to Heaven with them, where they will bloom more beautifully than they had on earth. And the flower that is the most beautiful, most beloved, is given a voice, so it can join the chorus of heaven singing songs of bliss."

Andersen likewise concludes his *Little Mermaid* with a lesson about paradise. In the original version, the mermaid surrenders her voice—and ultimately her life—to an evil sea witch who tricks her into believing she can win the heart of a prince. When he marries another,

Mackerel sky, mackerel sky,
Never long wet, never long dry.

Rain before seven,
Clear before eleven.

Heaven is often depicted as a place of gentle magic in children's literature. ART TODAY

the mermaid must forfeit her life to the wicked spellbinder. According to the dark bargain, the mermaid is to be dissolved into "sea foam" and scattered on the waves. But the Almighty intervenes and transforms her into an ANGEL whose duty is to soothe children. In this new life, the mermaid spends eternity bringing good dreams to the world's babes.

Nineteenth-century playwright Oscar Wilde wrote many stories for his children featuring glimpses into heaven. His "The Happy Prince" features a jewel-encrusted statue that looks down over an impoverished village, heartsick at the suffering it sees. When a migrating swallow rests at the statue's base, the prince asks the bird to pluck off his gold and gems and distribute them to the needy. The swallow agrees, knowing that this delay will mean death. Over three nights the bird delivers the prince's riches to the poor, then freezes to death at the statue's feet. At this, the statue's "leaden heart snapped right in two."

The following day, the town elders notice the statue of the prince, now "shabby," looking no better "than a beggar." Declaring that since "he is no longer beautiful he is no longer useful," the major orders that the statue be torn down and melted for scrap. But the prince's lead heart will not melt, even in the fiery furnace, so it is thrown on a garbage heap where it lands beside the body of the dead swallow. Then God charges one of his angels with collecting "the two most precious things" in the village below. When the angel returns with the heart and the bird, the Almighty tells him: "You have rightly chosen . . . for in my garden of Paradise this little bird shall sing for evermore, and in my city of gold the Happy Prince shall praise me."

Charles Tazwell's contemporary classic *The Littlest Angel* tells the tale of a young boy who dies in an accident and ascends to paradise. Everyone in heaven is busy preparing for a great event: the birth of JESUS Christ in Bethlehem. The legions of angels devote themselves to creating the perfect gift to mark such an occasion, and a rather fierce sense of competition sets in. The Littlest Angel has nothing to offer, until he remembers his box of "treasure" left behind on earth. He descends to retrieve the collection of stones, feathers, bird eggs, and other little boy prizes, only to be teased on his return by the elder angels. They display silky gossamer wings, luxurious gold HALOS, and other celestial masterpieces. But are all amazed when the Christ child selects his favorite angelic gift: the array of earthly mementos presented by the Littlest Angel. The tender story was adapted for the small screen in the 1969 made-for-television musical.

Modern writers have likewise penned tales detailing the internal workings of paradise. Peter Mayle explores the afterlife from a child's perspective in his 1976 *Will I Go to Heaven?* The work discusses a variety of theories about what paradise is like, including the Happy Hunting Grounds, the Viking VALHALLA, and the traditional CHRISTIAN PARADISE. Using simple vocabulary and cartoony illustrations, Mayle explains such complicated concepts as, "Your body is what you look like. Your soul is who you are." *Will I Go to Heaven?* also offers numerous SYMBOLS of the afterlife, including the PEARLY GATES tended by the celestial gatekeeper SAINT PETER. Children are even encouraged to speculate that their beloved ANIMALS will join them in the next world.

Taking a more lighthearted stance, Margot Zemach paints a delightful portrait of paradise in *Jake and Honeybunch Go to Heaven*, published in 1982. Jake, a chronically unlucky man, is hit by a train when his stubborn mule Honeybunch tarries on the tracks. His soul then follows "Glory Road" to the "Pearly Gates" of paradise. But when Jake lets himself in and begins soaring all over heaven, he manages to anger the angels, Saint Peter, and even God himself with his reckless flying. Seeing the mess, the Almighty kicks Jake out of paradise.

As the dejected man sulks on the steps of "forevermore," the mule Honeybunch arrives, forces her way in, and immediately commences "rampaging all over Heaven." Only Jake can control her, so he is readmitted to paradise to subdue the beast. Impressed with his skills, God appoints Jake the "Moon Regulator," charging him with hanging the moon and stars each night and collecting them again every morn. In his spare time, Jake sails through the heavens on silken wings, "just like a flying fool."

More traditional notions of Christian paradise fill Merula Salaman's 1993 *The Kingdom of Heaven Is Like.* Her work, designed to convey images of paradise to very young readers, offers a series of beautiful illustrations based on the parables of Jesus regarding the world to come. These include the WEDDING FEAST, lush fields laden with fruit, and the "house with many mansions." By using Christ's two-thousand-year-old analogies as her sole inspiration, this modern author creates a vision of heaven that transcends time.

In the 1996 *Dybbuk: A Story Made in Heaven*, Francine Prose offers a whimsical look at JEWISH PARADISE. Her story is more a "before-life" than "afterlife" tale, describing how angels gather "forty days before a baby is born" to "decide whom the baby will marry" later in life. The dybbuk of the title is a mischievous spirit of Jewish folklore who intervenes when the lovely Leah, destined to marry Chonon, is forced by her parents into an engagement with "Mean Old Benya." Her celestial guardians, unwilling to see their decisions ignored, ultimately prevail.

Another contemporary tale, *Dog Heaven* by Cynthia Rylant, involves the paradise of man's best friend. In this utopia, canine spirits find comfortable cloud beds, delicious dog treats, and never-ending fetch games. Special angels oversee this mystic realm, where "dogs belong, near the God who made them." In addition to providing a flight of fancy, the book reassures children who have lost a pet that their beloved friend is enjoying its own brand of bliss.

These and other children's stories of the supernatural have inspired a proliferation of GIFT NOVELTIES, including calendars, snow globes, T-SHIRTS, dolls, and other items based on characters from heavenly tales.

CHING TU Ching Tu is the paradise of Chinese Buddhism. It is believed to lie in the west, beyond the sunset. Followers of the faith are destined to a constant cycle of life, death, and rebirth as they seek "enlightenment" and oneness with the cosmos. This can be accomplished by meditating on the Buddha (celestial truth) and allowing the self to die. An individual's metaphysical death allows that person's life force to shed its bonds and enter the PURE LAND of collective consciousness. In Ching Tu, there is total enlightenment and liberation from worldly limitations where souls dwell in eternal harmony.

CHINVATO PERETAV According to ancient Persian myths of ZOROASTRIAN HEAVEN, when a person dies its soul remains beside the body for three days. On the fourth it travels to Chinvato Peretav (the Bridge of the Separator, also called Al-sirat), accompanied by ANGELS of protection. The bridge is "finer than a hair and sharper than a sword" and spans a deep chasm teeming with monsters. On the other side of the bridge is the gateway to paradise.

Demons guard the foot of the bridge and argue with the angels over the soul's fate. The actions of the dead person, both good and bad, are reviewed, and the soul is either allowed to cross or denied access to the bridge. Spirits whose vice outweighs their virtue fall into the ghoul-infested pit to face eternal torment. But the souls of righteous people who have embraced the truth of the good god AHURA MAZDA cross safely into everlasting bliss.

The sixth-century religious leader Zoroaster had warned his followers of this obstacle to heaven but promised to lead his flock safely across. The ancient manuscript GATHAS (Songs of Zoroaster) explains that the Bridge of the Separator "becomes narrow for the wicked," whereas the holy can easily pass unharmed. (In *Gathas*, the fair god Rashnu is named as the judge who will help determine who is worthy of salvation and who must be damned. Other texts in the sacred *avesta* assign this role to Ahura Mazda.) All infidels (nonbelievers) will fall into hell, which the prophet says has been created especially for the "followers of the lie." The good will find their way to the BEST EXISTENCE, Zoroaster's paradise of "eternal light."

Chinvato Peretav is located somewhere in the far north. Souls who are unsuccessful in crossing Chinvato Peretav will suffer great torments until Ahriman, the evil god of Zoroastrian faith, is destroyed in an apocalyptic battle with Ahura Mazda. After this, the good lord will hold a LAST JUDGMENT to confirm the everlasting fate of every person who has ever lived. At this time, all virtuous spirits will be restored to the truth, since "the lie" will have been eradicated, and will enjoy unending paradise in the realm of truth and light.

CHRIST ENTHRONED BETWEEN SAINT PETER AND SAINT PAUL

Beginning around the sixth century, European nobles often commissioned illustrated diptychs (pairs of painted or carved panels hinged together) to give as gifts commemorating a special occasion or appointment to high office. Ivory diptychs were especially popular. These intricately crafted artworks were approximately twelve inches long and depicted significant events of Christian history. An example of this delicate treasure is the *Christ Enthroned Between Saint Peter and Saint Paul* diptych, which shows the Messiah JESUS in the glory of heaven.

The carving portrays Christ as an elderly man seated on a throne elaborately decorated with lions and beautiful flowers. This representation of the savior is a departure from typical representations of the Son of God, who is usually shown as either an infant or a young man in his prime. In the diptych, Christ sits at the center of heaven and serves as the judge of all creatures. (Perhaps the artist aged the Messiah to suggest the divine wisdom essential for this role). Jesus is flanked by SAINT PETER, legendary keeper of the keys to paradise, and St. Paul, biblical "apostle to the gentiles." The attention of the SAINTS is focused on the BEATIFIC VISION.

A companion piece to this diptych offers further illustration of CHRISTIAN PARADISE. The ivory miniature shows the VIRGIN MARY, mother of Jesus, arrayed in similar splendor. She is cradling the infant Christ in her arms. Around them, a gathering of ANGELS worships the Lord. Together the two carvings reflect common medieval images of the blessed HEREAFTER, where Christ is king and Mary queen of heaven.

CHRISTIAN PARADISE The Christian concept of paradise has many variations and in fact is still evolving. Fierce debate has raged over the centuries about the exact nature and description of heaven; however, there is little agreement on the specifics. Much of the controversy revolves around the origin of this eternal bliss: Will it be a rich social life, a REUNION of loved ones, a material bounty, an intellectual abundance, a spiritual enrichment, a communion with God and his ANGELS, or some combination of these? Perhaps the only real consensus is the universal belief that heaven is a realm of pure delight where souls will spend a joyful eternity, whatever that might mean.

Unlike many other religions of millennia past, most depictions of Christian heaven include dwelling in the presence of God. This sharing in the realm of the creator is known as the BEATIFIC VISION. Also breaking with faiths that predate Christianity, salvation did not depend on a person's status in life. From the early days of JESUS' church, followers viewed themselves as God's beloved children, and their actions were motivated by a desire to return home to him after death. Heaven occupied their

Heaven and the Throne of God woodcut by Albrecht Dürer. ART TODAY

thoughts constantly, and paintings, frescoes, sculptures, and other works of art were devoted to illustrating every detail of the HEREAFTER. Much celestial imagery developed as a result of this divine obsession.

During medieval times, concepts of a supernatural hierarchy emerged. All saved souls were not considered equal but would occupy varying "levels" of paradise depending on their sanctity. The holiest souls would exist on higher levels, closer to God, while less-deserving spirits would inhabit lower areas of heaven. SYMBOLS such as a LADDER or STAIRCASE were used to depict this ascendancy in art of the era.

Eventually, medieval paradise was portrayed as a somber celebration with a vast cosmic "seating chart" to determine who is placed where in order of worthi-

ness. In some versions of this scenario, angels and SAINTS occupied separate sections; in others, the citizens of heaven were ranked strictly according to merit. Thus John the Baptist might sit next to the archangel MICHAEL, followed by SAINT PETER and the apostles. In almost all cases, the VIRGIN MARY, mother of Christ, is closest to the Almighty.

By the mid-1100s, belief in a THEOCENTRIC HEAVEN was commonly accepted throughout Christendom. According to this theory, the saved ascend to a community where all action focuses on adoring God. Some artists combined this image with the symbolic hierarchy; others composed pictures showing circles of worshipers gathering around the Godhead. With eyes focused on the Almighty, souls offer praise according their own talents, comprehension of divinity, and degree of holiness. Jesus is seated "at the right hand of the Father," enshrined in splendor in accordance with the words of the Bible: "When the Son of man shall come in his glory, and all the holy angels with him, then shall he sit upon the throne of his glory" (Matt. 25:31).

St. John's prophecies extend this notion of God at the center of a fully integrated heaven. His REVELATION, the book of the Bible that describes the LAST JUDGMENT in great detail, calls heaven a place where people of every "race, tribe, nation and language" will gather around God's throne. This was a great departure from past belief systems, such as Greek and Egyptian mythologies. For Christian paradise extends an invitation to all humans—whether poor, sickly, "foreign," or otherwise downtrodden—to a place "at the eternal banquet."

During the Renaissance, new ideas completely supplanted hierarchy theory. Artists such as MICHELANGELO, Raphael, and others rejected images of saved souls sitting motionless in rows quietly adoring God. Influenced by contemporary humanist concepts of paradise, these innovative artists envisioned heaven as a dynamic realm of physical as well as spiritual delights.

Paintings began depicting paradise as a box or cube with God at the top and the saved, in a renewed "garden of pleasure," lining the bottom. Souls had no rank or set position and could move freely about. For the first time, the blessed are free to stroll through heaven, talk with one another, dance, sing, and indulge in all manner of human pleasures as the smiling Father watches from above. This new—and highly controversial—concept is reflected in CHURCH ART AND ARCHITECTURE of the era. Christian leaders tried to squash activity-oriented heaven and return focus to the divine. But the new paradise was immensely popular with the common folk, especially the idea that in the hereafter, decent souls would be reunited with parents, children, and other loved ones separated from them by death.

In the face of conflicting visions of paradise, the Council of Trent, a symposium of Catholic scholars, decreed in 1575 that our reward in the afterlife is the "vision of God and enjoyment of His beauty." Everything else is incidental. This allowed the faithful to embrace

such concepts as GLORIFIED BODIES and joyous reunions without detracting from the importance of the beatific vision. Works of the Doctors of the Church, including SAINT AUGUSTINE and THOMAS AQUINAS, reflect the notion of a multidimensional paradise that ultimately centers on the Almighty.

One notable exception to the common depiction of Christian paradise is MORMON HEAVEN, which is vastly different from the notions of both Catholic and Protestant sects. According to the beliefs of the Church of Jesus Christ of Latter-Day Saints (also known as Mormons), the great beyond is a hub of activity and learning that proceeds into eternity. In heaven, Mormons believe they will continue about the business of evangelizing nonbelievers, bear and raise "spirit children," and participate in communal activities. This temporary paradise will exist only until the "resurrection," at which time the saved will enter eternal joy on a lush, fertile "New Earth."

Most modern theologians and philosophers agree that there can be no complete description of Christian heaven, since the Bible itself declares that paradise is beyond human imagination. In a letter to the early believers, St. Paul explains: "Eye has not seen, nor has ear heard, nor heart of man conceived what God has prepared for those who love Him" (1 Cor. 2:9).

Believers are therefore encouraged to embrace Jesus, keep his commandments, and experience heaven firsthand.

CHRISTIAN TOPOGRAPHY *Christian Topography*, an odd treatise on ESCHA-

TOLOGY written by sixth-century Egyptian monk Cosmas Indicopleustes, offers theories of the logistic relationship between heaven, earth, and hell. The author envisions the created world as a flat plain upon which the mystery of humanity continually unfolds. Earth is shielded by the "dome of Heaven," a mystical arc that covers the world. When a "redeemed" person dies, the soul ascends to this realm to join the SAINTS and ANGELS enjoying the BEATIFIC VISION.

Indicopleustes speculates that this arrangement will continue until the cataclysmic events of REVELATION occur. When the prophecies of annihilation are fulfilled, all people who have ever lived will then be summoned from their graves to render an account of their lives. JESUS, the Messiah, will review each soul and pronounce final sentence. After this LAST JUDGMENT, virtuous spirits will be escorted into paradise to enjoy an eternal banquet hosted by God. This never-ending feast will feature an abundance of fruit, sweet waters, meats, and other harvests of "earth's bounty."

Sinners, however, will be forced to remain on the ravaged earth, now transformed into a withered, infertile desert. The protective dome will be dissolved, leaving the planet vulnerable to the ravages of the elements. With no vegetation or game, the damned will be forced to "eat dust" for all eternity while the saved savor the rewards of their virtue.

CHRISTINA, SAINT (1150–1224) St. Christina, orphaned as a girl, had a NEAR-DEATH EXPERIENCE at age twenty-two in which she visited the afterlife before returning to her body. After a violent epileptic seizure, Christina was declared dead and placed in a coffin for burial. During her funerary mass, however, she leaped up and flew to the ceiling where she perched, birdlike, on a beam. The priest ordered her to come down and explain herself. She refused, saying she could not stand the "stench of sin," which even the most virtuous humans carry. Eventually she returned to the altar, where she recounted her miraculous trip to hell, PURGATORY, and finally heaven.

According to her story, Christina left her body and plunged into hell, a foul-smelling bog of terror and confusion. She then traveled through purgatory, where she saw thousands of spirits purging themselves of the residue of sin before proceeding on to paradise. Finally, Christina ascended to heaven, where she enjoyed the BEATIFIC VISION, basking in the presence of the Trinity. God gave her the choice of staying with him in glory, or returning to earth to work for the salvation of other souls. Haunted by the suffering she had witnessed in hell and purgatory, Christina chose to resume her earthly existence. She dedicated the rest of her life to praying for souls in purgatory and warning contemporaries of the horrors of hell.

Christina became a nun and devoted herself exclusively to winning souls for heaven. Word of her remarkable experience spread, and she was constantly sought by nobles and clerics who valued her wise counsel. Her feast is celebrated on July 24.

CHRIST WITH THE SAINTS

MOSAIC The *Christ with the Saints Mosaic* was commissioned around 530 for the Church of Saints Cosmas and Damian, two MARTYRS of the early days of Christianity. It is similar to the APSE MOSAIC OF OLD ST. PETER'S CATHEDRAL, a depiction of eternal bliss from the same era. Both works of CHURCH ART AND ARCHITECTURE show JESUS in paradise with SAINT PETER and St. Paul at his side.

In the *Christ with the Saints Mosaic*, the two early Christian leaders are shown presenting the souls of Cosmas and Damian to God and welcoming the new SAINTS to heaven. The men are robed in shimmering garments to symbolize their purity. Christ, receiving the two spirits, is arrayed in regal gold. Behind the Messiah, paradise is represented as an explosion of orange, yellow, and crimson clouds set against a bright blue sky. The earth lies below, protected by "the celestial dome." In contrast to the richness of God's abode, the human world is depicted as a ribbon of soft green dotted with indistinct figures. The artists purposely shift emphasis away from the world and direct it toward heaven, suggesting that worshipers do likewise.

CHURCH ART AND

ARCHITECTURE Images of the afterlife have adorned places of worship for millennia. Ancient Egyptian MEMORIALS depict ANUBIS and OSIRIS in the next world, Japanese NISE-E show the pleasures of paradise, SARCOPHAGI of the ETRUSCANS include portraits of souls reclining in eternity. The earliest attributable illustrations of heaven date back

five centuries before Christ, to Greek artist POLYGNOTUS who decorated shrines to Apollo with scenes of ELYSIUM. And works of Renaissance master MICHELANGELO regarding the divine remain among the most celebrated artistic creations of human history.

In some instances, the entire structure is designed to reflect the "palace of eternity." The TAJ MAHAL, for example, is a grand monument to the deceased wife of seventeenth-century Indian emperor Shah Jahan. The structure is patterned in the architectural style of an Islamic mosque, and its walls are lined with inscriptions from the KORAN about DJANNA, Islamic paradise. Even the gardens of this chapel are patterned after the "flowers that grow in the garden of ALLAH."

Buddhist temples are decorated with images of the Indian philosopher Siddhartha, known as "the great Buddha," reclining in NIRVANA. The wise man and founder of the Buddhist religion is typically portrayed in the "perfect state" of detachment from the world, dwelling among the immortals. Some images include KHUN-LUN, the mythic paradise of "blessed spirits."

But the most graphic and detailed illustrations of heaven are found in churches consecrated to JESUS, the Christian Messiah. Artists have elevated the ascetic depictions of CHRISTIAN PARADISE to new heights, offering literally thousands of mosaics, frescoes, statues, columns, paintings, and other works showing the afterlife. Their compositions are designed to give worshipers a foretaste of paradise and remind the faithful that the riches of this life cannot compare to the beauty of the next.

From the early days of the Christian church, Jesus' followers have decorated their places of worship with countless images of ANGELS, SAINTS, the VIRGIN MARY, Jesus, the Holy Spirit, and God the Father dwelling in paradise. By surrounding themselves with depictions of those who reflect divinity, the faithful reinforce the notion that heaven is humanity's inheritance. After this life ends, the heavenly Father calls all his children home. The first portraits of paradise incorporated specific details from biblical descriptions of the afterlife, using gold, jewels, pearls, spires, and luminous beings to illustrate the realm of the blessed.

Use of precious metals and gemstones to suggest that the splendor of paradise became the standard for scores of Gothic cathedrals. Popular from the twelfth through fifteenth centuries in Western Europe, Gothic cathedrals are characterized by ribbed vaultings, pointed arches, and flying buttresses. Their luxurious jeweled interiors connote the incalculable value of salvation and hint that the joys of the afterlife must be even more opulent, invoking the scriptural passage about "storing up riches in heaven." Carvings of saints and angels abound, watching over the congregation. Huge edifices, the entire structure of the Gothic cathedral suggests the vastness and larger-than-life quality of paradise.

Supernatural grandeur is also suggested by extensive altar decorations. Duccio's 1308 *Virgin as Queen of Heaven*, a massive altarpiece, features a center panel showing Mary holding the infant Christ. The saints kneel before mother

Mosaic from St. Mark's Cathedral, Venice. ART TODAY

and child, while angels fill the background. A gallery of biblical patriarchs and Christian heroes stare in rapt attention at the holy pair. The work employs heavy use of gold, illuminating glittering HALOS and radiating throughout the circle of paradise.

The 1300s also saw the proliferation of STAINED-GLASS WINDOWS in Western churches. These formed another significant component of Christian art and architecture, appearing in cathedrals throughout Christendom. Their luminous, translucent beauty captured the magnificence of God's glory. With beams of colored light spilling through in a cascade of brilliance, stained-glass windows communicated divinity in a way no gray stone walls ever could. They also formed mystic portals through which worshipers could "see" heaven, and likewise the residents of paradise could watch over the living.

The Cathedral of Chartres in France has been called a "Gothic masterpiece" of Christian art and architecture. Offering a dizzying array of paintings, sculptures, and stained-glass windows representing the joys of paradise, the church has artworks depicting scores of religious doctrines. These include the ASCENSION of Jesus, and visions of paradise from St. John's *Book of* REVELATION.

The Renaissance ushered in an era of humanism, adding a physical dimension to the pleasures of paradise. No longer fixed around the BEATIFIC VISION, works of this time portray souls in heaven strolling through lush gardens complete with lovely orchards, majestic ANIMALS, and lavish celebrations. Cou-

ples kiss as they recline in splendor. Family and friends embrace, enjoying a REUNION in eternity. Even the angels are dynamic, playing instruments and tossing flowers into the air. Heaven became and all-encompassing festival of physical, spiritual, and emotional delights.

During this time, vaulted ceilings and domes were very popular, providing a new method for illustrating paradise. Artists decorated these interior surfaces with elaborate frescoes, giving churchgoers the sensation that they were "looking" into heaven. Johann Baptist Zimmerman's 1733 *Mary in the Glory of Heaven* adorns the ceiling of a German church. The composition shows the mother of Jesus amid a swirl of brilliant angels and adoring saints. Its circular pattern draws the viewer's gaze upward, to God at the pinnacle of paradise. The fresco achieves its heavenly effect via rich, lush colors, detailed robes with luxuriant textures, and finely detailed expressions.

The undisputed masterpiece of Christian ceiling frescoes is Michelangelo's Sistine Chapel. Taking more than four years to complete, the finished work tells the story of humanity from creation to the banishment from Eden to the promise of a Messiah who would one day open the gates of paradise. The most famous panel depicts God the Father extending his hand to the listless Adam, ready to give life to this new creature. This image has been adapted into GIFT NOVELTIES, ADVERTISEMENTS, CARTOONS, and countless parodies.

Modern Christian churches lack the opulence of older structures, due mostly to the economics involved. The Protestant revolt and its aftermath severed many ties between church and civic authorities, drying up the seemingly endless sources of funds for such elaborate projects. Many contemporary churches continue to feature stained-glass windows, statues of saints, and ornate carvings; however they cannot compare to the accomplishments of past eras. Age-old themes remain prominent, with the vast majority of heavenly art showing blessed souls in paradise.

CHURINGA According to Australian mythology, human souls leave their bodies at death and join the spirits of their departed kin. These divine spirits date back to the Dreamtime, the ancient past during which the gods walked the earth. People who have lived virtuous lives and who are respected and beloved achieve that status of "ancestors" and can be summoned by the living to provide advice, protection, and assistance. Churingas are sacred vessels that ancestor spirits inhabit. They are usually carved out of stone or wood and blessed through hallowed incantations. Within the churinga, a departed soul can enjoy continued existence with loved ones in his or her homeland.

CICERO (106–43 B.C.) Marcus Tullius Cicero was a Roman statesman, orator, and writer who speculated on ESCHATOLOGY in a number of literary works. Curious about the ultimate destiny of the human soul, Cicero concluded that happiness after death consists in enjoying a REUNION of loved ones in the next

Ancient philosopher Cicero. ART TODAY

world. His vision of paradise offers a realm where family and friends have eternity to talk and laugh with one another unencumbered by the constraints of time. This theme is prevalent is such works as his *De Republica* (which contains "SCIPIO'S DREAM") and *De Senectute* (On Old Age).

Due to his style as well as his subject matter, Cicero had a profound and enduring impact on Western literature. He was responsible for enriching the Latin language by adapting Greek words and concepts into the limited Roman vocabulary. He likewise introduced the Greek system of using the dialogue as a means of presenting theories. His works influenced generations of scholars, including SAINT AUGUSTINE, William Shakespeare, and Geoffrey Chaucer (who retells "Scipio's Dream" in *Parliament of Fools*).

CITY IN THE SKY Concepts of AFRICAN PARADISE vary greatly, but one common belief is that of a City in the Sky. This celestial village is the dwelling place of the dead. It is most often a mirror world where life continues much as it had on earth, only in reverse (inhabitants rise at night and sleep during the day, etc.). Social life resumes in this City in the Sky where it left off before death, with familial and friendly relationships intact. The worlds of the living and the dead are connected by rainbows.

One story from the Tonga people of Mozambique describes a visit made by a young girl to the City in the Sky. She travels to the upper village by means of a magic rope that leads to a paradise, populated by many of her deceased friends and relatives. They show her around the town and invite the girl to join them in a grand celebration.

When the girl has to leave, the deceased offer to let her take a baby home as a souvenir. She is presented with a white child and a red child and told to choose between the two. A helpful ant advises her to take the white baby. She heeds his advice and returns to her hometown with the enchanted child. Her sister becomes insanely jealous upon hearing her story and scrambles up to the City in the Sky to voice her anger. The dead offer her the red baby, but the wise ant admonishes her not to take it. She scoffs at the ant, even threatening to squash the small insect under her heel. But as soon as she takes hold of the red child, she is reduced to a skeleton and her bleached bones fall immediately to the earth.

CITY OF GOD SAINT AUGUSTINE of Hippo, a fifth-century Christian bishop and Doctor of the Church, offers his views on CHRISTIAN PARADISE his famous treatise *City of God*. The complex twenty-two-book text was written specifically to refute the popular notion that Christianity was responsible for the fall of Rome. Critics of the religion circulated the theory that Christians had incurred the wrath of the pagan gods in hopes of gaining support for a massive persecution of Christ's followers. But Augustine disputes this assertion, using logic, historical fact, and biblical quotes to prove that Christianity is a boon to humankind rather than a blight.

City of God evaluates the creation of the material world, the fall of Adam and Eve in the Garden of Eden, and the progression of human events since that time. His conclusion is that governments and civilizations come and go, but God never changes. People must therefore considers themselves first and foremost citizens of the City of God and members of their earthly society second. This latter membership is temporary and imperfect, whereas citizenship in the divine structure lasts throughout eternity.

Augustine further states that each individual must choose between salvation and damnation, since God respects human free will. People have been given the opportunity for redemption through grace earned by the sacrifice of Christ, but they are not forced to accept it. Behavior during one's lifetime will determine whether one is receptive to the grace necessary for salvation. Life on earth is therefore the prelude to eternal punishment or reward rather than an end in itself.

Augustine's *City of God* defines heavenly bliss as basking in the magnificence of God's presence, known technically as the BEATIFIC VISION. In paradise, humans will be forever united to the Almighty, whom Augustine describes as "the end of our desires." Thus in the glorious afterlife all souls will be radiant with love and truly fulfilled.

City of God also addresses the question of the LAST JUDGMENT, noting that at this time the body and soul will be reunited, resulting in both physical and spiritual pleasures for the saved. After this adjucation, humans will have GLORIFIED BODIES, free of any limitations or frailties. These restored bodies will be perfect and incorruptible, able to enjoy the delights of the flesh but not bound by them. Eating, for example, is a pleasure one can choose to indulge, rather than be limited by the "necessity of eating." The saved's heavenly forms will likewise delight in singing, dancing, and celebrating in eternity.

In later works, the bishop also asserts that in heaven saved souls will experience a great REUNION with loved ones, although this pleasure is supplemental to enjoyment of the beatific vision. Augustine's conclusions on the afterlife were officially sanctioned by Christian authorities at Council of Constantinople in 553. *City of God* has had an enormous impact on Christianity, influencing such diverse theorists as Martin Luther, John Calvin, and THOMAS AQUINAS.

CLOTILDE, SAINT (ca. 470–545) The Frankish queen Saint Clotilde (Clotilda) is credited with evangelizing France and with introducing the fleur-de-lis as the symbol of the French monarchy as the result of a supernatural vision. Born the daughter of Burgundian King Chilperic, Clotilde brought her beliefs about CHRISTIAN PARADISE when she wed the pagan Clovis and began advising him on regal affairs.

According to the story, King Clovis and the Franks were under attack by the Huns, a seemingly unstoppable force. Clovis had made offerings to a number of pagan gods, but his troops continued to lose ground to the attacking armies. Desperate, Clovis asked Clotilde to pray to her Christian God for a battlefield victory. She did so, telling her husband to place his "trust in Christ." After Clotilde's prayer for heavenly assistance, Clovis defeated the Huns and forced them into full retreat. Clovis returned home and announced that he would be baptized a Christian, since JESUS had succeeded in securing triumph for the Franks when all the pagan gods had failed.

Clovis was christened in a lavish ceremony presided over by St. Remi, a brilliant young bishop who later helped spread Christianity throughout the empire. During the baptism, the heavens opened, and one of the ANGELS of paradise descended with three lilies. He gave the flowers to St. Remi, who then presented them to St. Clotilde as a sign of the Holy Trinity, representing "heaven's favor." Clotilde decreed that her husband's coat of arms should bear this image sent from God himself, and had the fleur-de-lis declared the official emblem of France.

St. Clotilde remains revered throughout France. Her feast is celebrated on June 3.

COCKAYNE The mythical land of Cockayne (Cockaigne, Cochagne) is a fairytale realm of delicious treats, with streets made of gingerbread, houses of cake, and fields of candied flowers. In thirteenth-century England, stories of Cockayne were among the most popular and imaginative vernacular legends. Because of its emphasis on sweets and on "the fulfillment of wishes," Cockayne became a metaphor for heaven, especially among children. When a loved one died, consoling relatives would reassure the child that "he's off to Cockayne!" a place of sheer delight and tasty salvation.

The realm of Cockayne was revisited in the early twentieth century when Sir Edward Elgar, favorite composer of King Edward VII, composed his Cockaigne overture. The work is a musical tribute to the composer's beloved London, invoking images of the mythical paradise of sweets and treats.

COLLECTOR PLATES One of the most popular trends of the past few decades is the buying, selling, and trading of collector plates. These GIFT NOVELTIES are usually issued in a series with a unifying theme. Recently, ANGELS, traditional heaven, and interpretations of mythic paradises have been favorite sources of inspiration. Such supernaturally illustrated ceramic works are currently available from a variety of porcelain producers, including Lenox, the Bradford Exchange, The Franklin Mint, The Hamilton Collection, and others.

Many of these plates incorporate graphics of popular licensed figures in celestial settings. Precious Moments (a line that depicts biblical and Christian themes) offers a plate showing the Old Testament prophet JACOB dreaming of the divine STAIRCASE leading to heaven. The stairs are lined with childlike winged figures sporting delicate HALOS of gold. A similar plate called Hallelujah Square, from the Through the Gates of Heaven series, shows happy children laughing, talking, and playing in a courtyard outside a magnificent palace. A message board on the gateway reads, "No More Tears," and two beaming cherubs hold up a sign saying, "Welcome to your Heavenly Home."

Dreamsicles (a line of red-cheeked, chubby cherubs) shows a nervous angel perched on a cloud between two more experienced spirits. The pair, armed with a book titled *How to Fly*, is trying to help the new arrival get used to his gossamer wings in The Flying Lesson. In the background, a second set of baby-faced angels fly hand in hand through the sapphire sky. Its Heaven's Little Helper plate shows a celestial guardian descending from paradise to help a fallen baby bird back to its nest.

Lenox recently issued a line titled The Heaven Sent Plate Collection: Angels of the Masters. Each plate features a reproduction of the celestial creatures reprinted from Western masterpieces. Entries include angels from works of artists such as Raphael, Titian, and Guercino. On various plates, the classic cherubs play music, chat, and speculate on the divine against a billowy background of heavenly mists. Every dish is advertised as "a work of art," etched in ivory china and lined with twenty-four-karat gold.

Other collector plates are somewhat less highbrow. Holy Cats! from the Franklin Mint offers a more whimsical look at utopia. Award-winning artist Bill Bell presents a cathedral scene of feline faithful, complete with STAINED-GLASS WINDOWS depicting cats in paradise and a caricature of MICHELANGELO's God the Father giving Adam the touch of life (also portrayed as kitties). Even the CHURCH ART AND ARCHITECTURE boasts sculpted columns of angelic tabbies and sainted kittens.

The Bradford Exchange capitalized on the fiftieth anniversary of Frank Capra's heavenly classic IT'S A WONDER-FUL LIFE with a line of plates patterned after scenes from the film. The movie stars James Stewart as George Bailey, a hardworking businessman who has always placed others ahead of himself. When he falls on hard times one Christmas Eve, an angel is dispatched from heaven to help him resolve his problems. The first plate in the series, An Angel Gets His Wings, depicts the film's heart-warming finale, in which the divine messenger is rewarded for accomplishing his mission. (Greeting card company Hallmark commemorated the same scene with a 1996 Christmas tree ornament with a bell that really rings.)

Bradford Exchange also broke new

The latest innovation: an angel-shaped plate featuring art by Edgar Jerins. EDGAR JERINS

ground in collector plates with a series of plates actually shaped like angels. Award-winning artist Edgar Jerins, whose realist portraits of celestial guardians have adorned CD covers and been exhibited in the National Museum of Catholic Art and History, created a series of heavenly spirits for Bradford's Seasons of Joy line. Each issue shows a feminine angel, appropriately arrayed for the time of year, in flight. Jerins, who draws inspiration for his compositions from "FRA ANGELICO and other masters," calls angels "aspirations toward the right and beautiful" and reflects this reverence in his work.

Collector plates currently represent a popular component of ANGELWARE, offering consumers a small-scale glimpse of the blessed afterlife.

COMIC BOOKS Paradise is the setting for a number of comic book escapades, ranging from humorous forays into the HEREAFTER to frightening stories based on the apocalyptic Book of REVELATION. Supernatural adventure comics routinely feature afterlife exploits in the kingdoms of OSIRIS, VALHALLA, and ELYSIUM. And more reverent depictions of heaven likewise adorn the pages of religious pulps designed to bring the word of JESUS before new audiences. These comics often include ANGELS, SAINTS, and other Christian heroes.

Casper, the "friendly ghost" who has been haunting with humor for more than two generations, is an enduring favorite in afterlife comics. He made the leap from ANIMATED CARTOONS to comic books in the mid-1940s and remains on shelves. With the theatrical release of the live-action film in 1996, Casper made further inroads into Americana via a deluge of MOVIE MERCHANDISING and product tie-ins. A typical comic book adventure has the benevolent spirit helping locate lost puppies, playing with lonesome children, or trying to outwit his cantankerous fellow ghosts.

More sinister comic books such as *Lady Death* dispatch characters to paradise on mystic quests. The dark, occult series features numerous story lines about Hope, the immortal offspring of a sainted mother and demonic father. Hope struggles to discern her place in the dualistic universe, setting in motion events that will eventually result in an apocalyptic "war between Heaven and Hell." Episodes of *Lady Death* send the mistress of mayhem to the PEARLY GATES in search of her long lost "angelic"

Lady Death features adventures in heaven, purgatory, and hell. GREGG PISANI

mother. Artists Brian Pulido and Steven Hughes pen a paradise of white-winged ANGELS and castles of ivory, where good does not necessarily conquer evil. The cryptic series has overtones of the prophesied devastation from Revelation.

Religious comic books offer pious depictions of CHRISTIAN PARADISE. A large assortment of titles from Spire Christian Comics adapt the popular pulp format into effective tools for evangelizing teens. Examples include *Through the Gates of Splendor* and *The Gospel Blimp*. Some religious comics are annotated, illustrated versions of Christian best-selling books like *The Cross and the Switchblade* and *The Late Great Planet Earth*. Others, such as *Archie's Clean Slate*, use favorite secular characters in spiritual situations, promoting the notion that being religious does not mean being out of step with peers.

Spire also offers comic books based on biblical descriptions of the afterlife, most notably the 1973 *There's a New World Coming*. The pulp features three teens dressed in 1970s fashion witnessing the LAST JUDGMENT, the RAPTURE, and the apocalypse described in St. John's Revelation. Likening drug use and free love to the sins warned against in the sacred text, *New World* ends with a glimpse into paradise, depicted as the NEW JERUSALEM. It is a vibrant meadow dotted with flowers, where the "waters of life" flow from crystal waterfalls. In this heaven, souls will be rewarded "a hundredfold" for all the sacrifices they have made on earth.

COMMUNION OF SAINTS According to the beliefs of Christianity, all blessed souls—whether living or deceased—are members of the collective "body of JESUS Christ." As Doctor of the Church THOMAS AQUINAS states: "Since all the faithful form one body, the good of each is communicated to the others . . . The riches of Christ are communicated to all the members, through the sacraments."

This concept is known as the communion of SAINTS. The term describes the love, empathy, and kinship of all God's saved regardless of their era. This mystical body will be present in heaven, when members of Christ's faith family, formerly separated by time, will enjoy a great REUNION in eternity. An important aspect of CHRISTIAN PARADISE, belief in the communion of saints is affirmed in the APOSTLES' CREED as well as in many liturgical prayers.

Because of the familial ties among God's children, many Christians (and especially Roman Catholics) revere the saints and ask for their assistance in living the faith of Christ. Like a young child relying on the guidance of an older sibling, spirits on earth seek intercession from their saved elders. The mystic relationship between the souls in heaven and the people striving for salvation is described by St. Paul in a letter to the early Christians: "Wherefore seeing we also are compassed about with so great a cloud of witnesses, let us lay aside every weight, and the sin which doth so easily beset us, and let us run with patience the race that is set before us" (Heb. 12:1).

The "cloud of witnesses" refers to the saved enjoying eternal splendor with Jesus in paradise. They intercede for the living and offer powerful examples of fidelity and perseverance. These two groups, now in different realms, will be forever joined in the kingdom of heaven. Death, therefore, unites rather than separates those who do God's will. And in paradise, blessed spirits will pass the ages sharing their love of the Almighty and collectively reflecting his majesty.

COMPENDIUM OF REVELATIONS The *Compendium of Revelations,* an innovative treatise on ESCHATOLOGY, was written in the late 1400s by the Dominican friar Savonarola. It describes heaven as a brilliant realm of light encircled by a jeweled wall. Souls that ascend to paradise are at first overwhelmed by the unearthly splendor of the place and are blinded by its radiance. After becoming accustomed, however, they are able to discern the distinct realms of utopia.

The lowest level is a natural land of enchantment populated by "mild ANIMALS," "multicolored birds," and "delicious flowers" through which "crystal streams" endlessly flow. Savonarola refers to this as "paradise," a physical dimension of human pleasures. The author makes a distinction between this material utopia and true "heaven," which is the spiritual abode of God. In paradise, the saved inhabit GLORIFIED BODIES that can float effortlessly through eternity.

On mystical plane of heaven, the nine choirs of ANGELS form concentric, ascending circles in which the SAINTS dwell according to their degree of piety. At the summit is the throne of the VIRGIN MARY, mother of JESUS, just removed from the BEATIFIC VISION. Blessed souls can pass between the spiritual and physical realms via a mystic LADDER connecting the two.

Savonarola's tome is significant as it combines several dominant themes of CHRISTIAN PARADISE. The first level of paradise incorporates humanistic concepts of a perfected earthly place rich with lush plant life, gentle beasts, and sensual pleasures. This vision of bliss had been advanced previously in such works as the ELUCIDATION, written around the year 1100. But Compendium adds

the beatific vision, placing God at the center of heaven and describing the ultimate joy of salvation to be seeing the Almighty "face to face." Such a THEOCENTRIC HEAVEN had been espoused by SAINT AUGUSTINE from the third century A.D. These divergent views are linked—literally and figuratively—by Savonarola's ladder, one of the most prevalent images of the afterlife throughout the world. The result is a text that encompasses a variety of heavenly theories, designed to appease Christians of all convictions.

COMPUTER GAMES Computer games enthusiasts can enjoy an assortment of supernatural adventures in the form of electronic challenges. Titles such as *Afterlife: The Last Word in Sims*, *Adventures in Heaven*, *All Dogs Go to Heaven: The CD-ROM* offer players an opportunity to visit paradise vicariously while retrieving holy relics and thwarting nefarious demons. Others even allow users to view "divine" graphics and print "celestial images" of ANGELS, SAINTS, and mystic heroes.

Adventures in Heaven advertises itself as paradise for cyber junkies. Dubbed the "ultimate game collection," *Adventures* offers puzzles, mazes, "mind challenge," and apogee tailored to players with advanced skills. *Afterlife: The Last Word in Sims* takes users one step further, allowing them to build virtual celestial cities. Players open their own PEARLY GATES and add infrastructure, then the "dearly departed arrive in droves." Using such features as the "Brahmatic Bovine Bliss Ranch," "Cherubopolis," and "Good

Heavens Theme Park," *Afterlife* "lets you create the HEREAFTER in the here and now." This "ultimate adventure" game parodies everything from Buddhist NIRVANA to CHRISTIAN PARADISE.

Younger players can learn basic skills while discovering the paradise of ANIMALS with the computer game adaptation of the film ALL DOGS GO TO HEAVEN. The story of a feisty Fido who ascends to paradise has been digitized into an "animated storybook" that allows children to read the story, play games, and interact with the movie's characters. Sega Saturn likewise translates Casper "the friendly ghost" into computer game format with its *Casper Haunting 3-D Challenge*. These characters from films about the great beyond are popular examples of electronic MOVIE MERCHANDISING.

A more sublime interactive adventure is LIVE's *Angels: The Mysterious Messengers*, a CD-ROM providing simulated contact with the celestial beings. Users can click into tours of "angel history," partake in guided meditations, even view video clips of cinematic interpretations of heaven. Despite what critics call its lapses into "New Age drivel," *Angels* boasts gorgeous artwork and attention to detail. It is an ascetic foray into the divine realm, conveying a sense of actually touching eternity.

Other heavenly computer games are derived from afterlife films such as BILL & TED'S BOGUS JOURNEY and from COMIC BOOKS about the next world.

CONFUCIUS Confucius (K'ung Fu-tzu), the Chinese wise man whose quiet

insights evolved into a national religion, lived from 551 to 479 B.C. Born of a noble family that had lost most of its wealth, Confucius was a self-educated magistrate who devoted his life to dispensing justice in an often unfair bureaucratic system. He was a strong advocate of education, believing that each person had the right and obligation to develop the intellect to its full potential. The philosopher considered this the best (and sometimes the only) way to achieve peace and social justice in a turbulent world.

Confucius routinely spoke of the "Way of Heaven," declaring that the path to PARADISE consists of acceptance of personal responsibility, loyalty, and faithfulness. A prolific writer credited with scores of works, Conscious frequently invokes images of TIAN, a "great" and "august" paradise for virtuous souls. He demands that students revere heaven and the "supreme spiritual presence." Rejecting the ancient notion that only the rich

Jade carving of a Chinese magistrate

and powerful could expect a pleasant afterlife, Confucius was the first Eastern philosopher to change the criterion of salvation from anthromorphic to moral. He also taught an early version of the Golden Rule, admonishing that all people should "not do to others what you would not do to yourself."

Influenced by the constant wars and troubles that beset his homeland during his lifetime, Confucius supported the idea of a ruling class and hierarchy but sought to imbue the system with justice. His works were later used to justify the "Son of Heaven" doctrine, which states that the emperor of China has a supreme mandate from the gods and is himself divine. This "natural ascension" of moral authority continues into the Chinese afterlife. In the next world, souls will be judged by a complex bureaucracy using detailed records, scores of judges, and appropriate rewards and punishments for each soul.

CORONATION   Christian tradition holds that the VIRGIN MARY, mother of JESUS, was assumed bodily into paradise when her life was finished. There, she was crowned the Queen of Heaven by her divine son. This mystic event, called the coronation of the Virgin, has inspired hundreds of artistic compositions over the centuries. Interpretations of this sacred celebration have become prevalent in Catholic CHURCH ART AND ARCHITECTURE as well as in public and private artworks.

French artist Enguerrand Quarton provides a typical example of this theme. His 1453 *Coronation of the Virgin* was

Velazquez's *Coronation of the Virgin*, seventeenth Century. ART TODAY

commissioned to hang in a local hospital to provide patients a reminder of their ultimate destiny. The painting, which shows the three realms of heaven, earth, and the underworld, depicts a dazzling paradise splashed with blazing of red robes, golden HALOS, and blue sky. Mary is shown in the uppermost level of the work dressed in a sapphire tunic, humbly receiving her crown from the mirror image of God the Father and the Son. The Holy Spirit, depicted as a white dove, soars above them. This scene is attended by a legion of seraphim radiant with jubilation and by a contingent of SAINTS, Christian leaders, and biblical heroes.

Below on earth, ANGELS deliver pure souls up to paradise. The celestial escorts fill the skies. An image of Christ's crucifixion is at the center of the *Coronation*, between the cities of Jerusalem and Rome. Jerusalem marks the site of Christianity's origin, while Rome is the place where SAINT PETER founded the Catholic church. Because of their prominence in Christianity, these two cities are depicted as forever existing in the shadow of heaven.

The bottom layer of Quarton's *Coronation* illustrates hell. It is a black strip of chaos licked by flames. Amid the fires, horned demons strangle, rape, and mutilate the damned. The bloody souls writhe in agony, a frightening contrast to the splendor above. It is an ugly contrast the to the beauty of paradise and serves as a stern but subtle warning about incurring the wrath of the Almighty.

Tuscan artist Fra Filippo Lippi's *Coronation*, composed around the same time as Quarton's interpretation, offers a more informal and joyous celebration. His work shows a dome of heaven filled with excited saints and angels. God the Father places a crown on Mary's head as the citizens of paradise genuflect before her. The Virgin is robed in white linen, and a gallery of angels forms an arch behind and around her. In another variation, Agnolo Gaddi's *Coronation of the Virgin* has Jesus himself placing a jeweled crown on his mother while the saints and angels sing and celebrate.

The mystic event of Mary's coronation is among the most popular themes for Christian painters. Likewise, portraits of her meeting with the angel GABRIEL and her ASSUMPTION into paradise are common throughout Christendom.

CRISPIN, SAINT (ca. 300) Crispin and his brother Crispinian, both SAINTS

of the Roman Catholic church, found favor with the ANGELS but were constantly at odds with the civilian authorities during their brief lives. The two were shoemakers by trade, using leather and silk that were reportedly delivered to them by celestial messengers. The shoes were so beautiful that they drew a great price from the wealthy, enabling the brothers to give countless pairs away at no cost to the poor. Eventually, the two were beheaded during the Roman persecution of Christians and became MARTYRS of the early church.

The saints' feast day is celebrated on October 25, and one story claims that on the first feast St. Crispin spent in paradise, he asked God to allow his peers a vision of heaven. Eager to reward Crispin's piety, the Almighty lowers a LADDER to earth and invites all shoemakers to ascend. Those who do are stunned at the beauty of an angelic choir singing HYMNS to God. Many meet SAINT PETER and St. Paul and other blessed souls. In some versions, a rope supporting the mystic ladder is mistakenly cut, and many of the shoemakers fall back to earth, incurring permanent injuries.

St. Crispin has been immortalized by William Shakespeare in *Henry V*, in which Prince Harry rallies his men with promises of "glory" at the "battle of St. Crispin," which is to occur on the saint's feast. The soldiers are offered a glimpse of grandeur similar to that bestowed on the craftsmen allowed to see heaven.

CUTHBERT, SAINT (ca. 635–687) St. Cuthbert of Lindisfarne became a

St. Cuthbert. ART TODAY

monastery, eventually being named abbot. He wanted to live out his life as a hermit on a secluded island, spending his time in prayer and penance, but was called to serve as bishop of Lindisfarne. Cuthbert remained there until his death in 687.

Because of many miracles associated with Cuthbert both during his life and through his intercession after death, the bishop has been canonized a saint of the Roman Catholic church. His feast day is March 20.

monk after having supernatural visions instructing him to dedicate his life to God. His mystic experiences included witnessing other SAINTS being welcomed into heaven and talking with ANGELS about divine matters. The Venerable BEDE, an early Christian historian, compiled a biography called *The Life and Miracles of St. Cuthbert, Bishop of Lindisfarne* based on the legendary exploits of this holy man.

In one story, Cuthbert while still a child is instructed by a "heavenly emissary" to devote himself to the glory of the Lord. He presents himself at the Melrose monastery and becomes the pupil of St. Aidan. Cuthbert recognizes the monk's virtue, and the two become good friends. Later, Cuthbert is tending sheep in the fields when he sees the soul of his beloved St. Aidan being carried up to paradise by a celestial escort. Cuthbert then takes his place at the

DANIEL Daniel is the patriarch of the Old Testament who was given many supernatural powers. Beloved of YAHWEH, the God of Hebrew tradition, Daniel had visions of heaven, was visited by ANGELS, and was able to interpret cryptic dreams. In one incredible incident, enemies plot to have Daniel killed by throwing him to the hungry lions; however, the prophet is protected by the hand of the Almighty and left unharmed. Because of his piety and unflinching faith, Daniel is often included in artistic renderings of paradise.

The Book of Daniel, written about 165 B.C., describes the mystic experiences of the hero's life. In one passage, an angel visits Daniel and foretells the LAST JUDGMENT: "And many of them that sleep in the dust of the earth shall awaken, some to everlasting life, and some to shame and everlasting contempt" (Dan. 12:2).

Though Daniel transcribed these mystic apparitions, he often did not understand their meaning. In fact, many of these images left him confused and frightened. "The visions of my head troubled me," he wrote, and Daniel longed to understand the hidden truth of these revelations. In response, God sent the angel GABRIEL to explain certain events to Daniel to help ease his anxiety. The Book of Daniel concludes with soothing words from above, as the celestial interpreter tells the prophet not to worry over these things, for "thou shalt rest" until the foretold events are fulfilled.

DEAD HEAT Two policemen receive their "eternal reward" for laying down their lives in the line of duty in the 1988 dark comedy *Dead Heat*. The film stars Joe Piscopo and Treat Williams as a pair of cops investigating a recent rash of "zombie-related crimes." When they stumble on a fiendish plot orchestrated by mad scientist Vincent Price, the two are murdered and then miraculously resurrected via an ominous "life force" machine. Reanimated corpses, Piscopo and Williams set about tracking down their own killers.

Despite the fact that both heroes are dead, the movie manages to provide a happy ending by sending the two ghoulish officers to heaven. *Dead Heat* ends as Williams and Piscopo, friendship intact and joking about their fate, depart to a billowy realm of clouds and bright light. Audiences are left with the notion that in the HEREAFTER, the men will continue to enjoy a fulfilling existence without the pain, treachery, and avarice that plague the land of the living.

DEAD SEA SCROLLS One of the most significant archaeological finds of the twentieth century, the Dead Sea Scrolls were discovered in 1947 by a shepherd near the ruins of the desert city Qumran. Since that time, religious scholars have labored to decipher the ancient texts and determine their mysterious origin. And though authorities have not reached full consensus, most agree that these scrolls are actually the earliest texts of the Bible and describe critical events in Jewish and early Christian history.

Today, more than 80 percent of the eight hundred separate writs have been translated and published by the Oxford University Press in a series titled Discoveries in the Judean Desert. Their translators believe that the remaining texts will be available around the turn of the century. Included in the works, written between 200 B.C. and A.D. 50, are ancient Old Testament books, HYMNS to God, philosophical commentaries, and rules of religious etiquette. Some of the most startling scrolls also contain dire prophecies about the apocalypse and foretell horrific wars that will destroy the world.

The Dead Sea Scrolls describe a heaven where ANGELS sing around the throne of God, serenading the Almighty with "seven-word litanies" of praise and thanksgiving. One text goes so far as to name some of the celestial beings, including the archangel MICHAEL (defender of heaven), Raphael (guardian over sickness and injury), GABRIEL (messenger), and URIEL (hope and repentance). The very flapping of their magnificent wings creates a joyous music that fills paradise.

According to the Dead Sea Scrolls, a "final Day of Atonement" (or LAST JUDGMENT) is predicted to take place at some undesignated time in humanity's future. It will entail a huge battle between the "Sons of Light" and the "Sons of Darkness," and the armies of goodness shall ultimately prevail. Afterward, virtuous souls will be restored to their true status as "children of God." All sin and its residue will be eradicated, as will all vestiges of pain, suffering, and conflict. In the text, God promises, "I will give thee rest from all thine enemies," including the devil, forevermore.

A critical conclusion of religious scholars studying the Dead Sea Scrolls regards the origins of Christianity. Once dismissed as a blending of Hebrew notions of sin and justice with Greek afterlife myths and tales of relationships between humans and the gods, the Dead Sea Scrolls put the religion of JESUS on a more solid theological foundation. The texts describe belief in a "Son of God" who is both human and divine and other themes prevalent in early Christian worship being discussed in Judaism not long before the rise of Jesus Christ. Thus the key doctrine of Christ's new church—that the Messiah is himself Almighty and able to open the kingdom of heaven to all people— was not borrowed from pagan faiths but believed to be the fruition of Hebrew prophesies. This also puts a human face on paradise, making it a realm where the Son of God shares human nature with his creatures.

Because of this validation of Christianity's origins, the Dead Sea Scrolls help illustrate the evolution of theories regarding CHRISTIAN PARADISE.

DEFENDING YOUR LIFE   Albert Brooks presents his version of what awaits human souls in the next realm in his 1991 film *Defending Your Life*. The author/producer drew inspiration from pondering the possible fate of his own father, who died when Brooks was only eleven. The movie, advertised as "the first true story of what happens after you die," paints the supernatural dimension as a celestial courtroom where each soul must explain its actions and prove itself worthy of promotion to a higher plain. Those who fail to convince the court of their worthiness are sent back to earth for another try.

Brooks also stars in this comedy as Daniel Miller, a neurotic businessman who finds himself in "Judgment City" after perishing in a car accident. Rip Torn costars as Brooks's counsel, a modern ANUBIS whose job is to guide souls safely into the next world. *Defending Your Life* also features an updated version of OSIRIS, a stern judge who ultimately decides the fate of each spirit by weighing its actions.

As selected scenes from Brooks's life are replayed as "evidence," the court begins concluding that Brooks has been too worried about consequences to take any real risks and therefore has squandered much of his life. Fear is the "giant fog" that has blocked his happiness, joy, and development. He is sentenced to be reincarnated on earth for another attempt at greatness. But as he is departing, Brooks puts his soul in danger to reunite with Julia (played by Meryl Streep), a sweet spirit destined for better things. When Torn sees this, he decides that Brooks has learned his lesson, and the two are allowed to travel on together for a REUNION in some higher plane.

Brooks's vision of the supernatural is rich with comic delights. In his paradise, the departed can eat whatever they like without gaining any weight. For entertainment, new arrivals can visit the "Past Lives Pavilion" to see what incarnations they have lived before. (Streep has been a prince in the past; Brooks a meal for cannibals.) Judgment City does have its drawbacks, however. Its guests wear drab white robes, and the only mode of transportation is buses. But the film promises only "laugh after death," and Brooks's Judgment City is a place where humor goes a long way toward spiritual redemption.

DENG The Dinka of Africa's Sudan are said to be descendants of Deng, the creator god who dwells in the sky. Deng made humanity but became angry and disgusted with his creatures' greed and so decreed that all people must face death. He does not abandon the mortal beings altogether, though, bestowing the blessings of rain, plentiful harvests, and children on his creations.

After death, virtuous souls are restored to Deng for eternal rest. Those who are struck by lightning are thought to be especially blessed, since this means that Deng has hit the person with his club and personally taken its soul to paradise. People who die this way are not mourned but celebrated as the "favored of Deng," now reposing in unending joy.

DILUM Dilum (Dilmun) is the paradise and "place of sunrise" according to Sumerian mythology. Mentioned in *The Epic of Gilgamesh,* an ancient epic poem, Dilum is a lush garden of plentiful fruit and game where favored souls live forever. It is the oldest recorded paradise of human history, dating to around 2500 B.C.

According to the legends, Dilum at one time had no water, so the sun god Utu took water from the earth to create a great river. This linked the two worlds and created a conduit for human souls to travel to Dilum. In *Gilgamesh,* departed mortals are rewarded for their virtue with eternal life, sailing to this garden paradise to dwell among the gods.

Many later interpretations of heaven involve elements similar to those of Dilum. These include GAN EDEN, DJANNA, the HAPPY HUNTING GROUNDS, KHUN-LUN, and numerous other beliefs that equate paradise with a tropical garden. During the Renaissance, CHRISTIAN PARADISE was likewise depicted as a fertile meadow with fruit orchards and crystal streams, recalling the ancient images of Dilum.

DISPUTA The great Renaissance master Raphael painted his *Disputa* in 1509 for the Vatican, the home of the Roman Catholic pope. The fresco is done in two levels, the higher section showing heaven and the earthly plane depicted below. The *Disputa* is one of the most brilliant religious masterpieces of the era, including not only an interpretation of the divine but also illuminating a key theological debate.

The dispute illustrated is over the nature of the Holy Eucharist, the body of Christ consecrated at each Roman Catholic mass. Raphael's composition shows the Eucharist displayed on an altar while poets, popes, and philosophers discuss its meaning and significance. Among them are the Doctors of the Church (including SAINT AUGUSTINE) and Dante Alighieri author of the DIVINE COMEDY: THE PARADISO.

Above this debate scene is the plane of heaven, where all mysteries have been revealed. Raphael uses a burst of gold to signify the divine realm (marking the last example of a major Christian artist using gold to represent heaven and the majesty of the BEATIFIC VISION), God the Father sits at the top of the *Disputa*, with his son JESUS enthroned beneath him. The Holy Spirit, symbolized by a dove, proceeds from the two. ANGELS gather around the Godhead, completely filling the background. The apostles, SAINTS, and patriarchs worship nearby, their questions about the Eucharist mystically resolved. Four cherubs hold open the Gospels of Matthew, Mark, Luke, and John, indicating that the answers to all questions can be found herein.

Raphael offers another interpretation of paradise in his SISTINE MADONNA, also an important historical example of Christian CHURCH ART AND ARCHITECTURE.

DIVINE COMEDY: PARADISO, THE

The most extensive and imaginative fictional account of the afterlife in Western literature is *The Divine Comedy* by the Italian poet Dante Alighieri. Dante wrote this masterpiece during the early 1300s while living in exile from his hometown of Florence, Italy. The work incorporates his religious beliefs about sin, salvation, and justice with his political troubles, social background, and educational experiences. The result is a masterpiece of writing as well as an insightful and historic account of the times.

The Divine Comedy is divided into three separate books corresponding to the three possible destinations of the human soul: *The Paradiso* (heaven), *The Purgatario* (PURGATORY), and *The Inferno* (hell). Each offers a vivid description of the sights, sounds, scents, and feelings encountered in the afterlife. The *Comedy* is written in the first person and reads as an eyewitness account. This style, and the author's extensive details about the supernatural, led many readers to believe that Dante had, in fact, visited the afterlife and considered his account to be indisputable.

In the *Comedy*, Dante is joined on this metaphysical journey by historical figures who have had an impact on his life and work. The Latin poet Virgil, author of the epic AENEID, conducts Dante's tour of the underworld, since the ancient writer had so greatly influenced Dante's ideas about life after death. In *The Paradiso*, Dante has as his guide the lovely Beatrice, a woman whom Dante had loved dearly but who died in her youth.

The author transforms Beatrice into an idealized saint of breathtaking grace and beauty who shows him heaven and answers his questions about the divine.

The Paradiso begins at high noon on the day of the vernal equinox. Dante has just finished his journey through purgatory when he is absorbed by a brilliant white light. In this mystic place is the most beautiful music Dante has ever heard. He is so overwhelmed with ecstasy that he feels he has become part of this powerful radiance. Beatrice informs him that he has entered the Sphere of the Moon, the first level of heaven. In this sphere are souls who tried to do God's will but were compelled to violate their vows, such as those who wanted to remain virgins but were forced to marry. He meets several women who had been nuns but were made by their families to leave the convent in order to wed wealthy men. Beatrice explains that although these ladies did not willingly forsake their promises, they are guilty of failing to return to the convent when the opportunity arose.

Dante protests that this does not seem fair, but Beatrice reassures him that although these souls reside in the lowest heaven, they are perfectly happy. Each person, she explains, is given ultimate joy according to his or her capacity. She further informs Dante that in reality, all souls exist in the EMPYREAN (the shining presence of the Almighty), but they have assumed these positions for his education. This division is not a limit on their happiness but rather an order delineated so that he could understand the structure of paradise.

After leaving the Sphere of the Moon, the pair travels to the Sphere of Mercury, the second circle of heaven. Here are the virtuous souls who neglected God in their haste for fame and glory. They lived moral lives and did not abuse their power; however, their love for the Lord was secondary to their personal ambitions. In this plain Beatrice and Dante discuss why JESUS had to be crucified in order to redeem humanity. She tells him that this was necessary since as both God and man, only Christ could repay an infinite debt incurred by human beings. His death was simultaneously an act of human atonement and a feat of divine mercy.

The next level is the Sphere of Venus, a place for spirits who were more devoted to earthly love than to adoration of God. They, too, lived lives of virtue but did so predominantly out of devotion to other human beings. Dante speaks to several historical figures in the realm of Venus, some of whom the author had actually known in his lifetime. Beatrice tells Dante that this is the last circle of heaven that is in the "shadow of the earth" and that the remaining levels are for perfect souls who have shed all trappings of worldly life.

When they pass from the Sphere of Venus to the Sphere of the Sun, Dante is once again overcome by love, only this time it is for his creator. The author's vision is filled with beings of light who dance and sing their cantation of joy. This first level of perfect heaven is reserved for men of great wisdom and scholars of the Christian church. In this plane Dante meets

BEDE, an early Christian writer, as well as a number of SAINTS.

The next circle is Sphere of Mars, the paradise for soldiers who die in religious wars. Beatrice and Dante are joined here by Dante's great-grandfather, a valiant warrior who was killed in the Crusades. Dante is overjoyed to learn that the REUNION of loved ones is possible in the afterlife and lovingly embraces his forefather. The hero then leads the pair on a tour of the place for those who die defending the faith.

In the Sphere of Jupiter, a utopia for honorable rulers, Dante is introduced to a number of monarchs from the past. This circle is filled with political and social leaders who used their position to administer divine justice rather than to serve their own selfish desires.

This level is connected to the Sphere of Saturn by a golden LADDER laden with spirits traveling up and down its rungs. These are the saints who have spent their lives in quiet contemplation of the divine. Most have focused on one particular aspect of God or sought to refute some specific heresy. One such saint talks with Dante about the incorrect notion of predestination and réfutes the theory that God has chosen certain ELECT for heaven from before time.

The eighth realm of heaven is the Sphere of the Fixed Stars. Dante turns back after reaching this plane and sees the earth, tiny and insignificant, in the distance. In this moment he realizes how trivial is the pursuit of worldly things. Looking upward, he beholds the face of Christ, a sight almost too beauti-

ful to bear. In this realm the VIRGIN MARY, the angel GABRIEL, and the prophets of the Old Testament dwell in ecstasy. Dante pauses to speak with SAINT PETER, John the Baptist, and Adam before ascending to the next—and highest—stage of paradise.

Dante at last enters the Primum Mobile, the very presence of the Godhead. The nine choirs of angels are seated around their creator according to rank. Dante's eyes can hardly stand to view the Empyrean, which is pure light. The saved then form a fantastic white rose around God, every saint a petal in the mystic flower. Each blessed soul is robed in dazzling white and fitted with gold wings. Dante notices empty spaces in the rose, undoubtedly left for those saints who are yet to come. Above this is the Virgin Mary surrounded by a thousand angels praising the Lord.

Finally, Dante lifts his gaze to the BEATIFIC VISION, depicted as the light at the rose's center. Within this brilliance are three interlocking circles representing the Father, the Son, and the Holy Spirit. And through tear-filled eyes Dante sees that one of the circles—that of Christ—has a human face. Seeing this, Dante is suddenly overwhelmed by a sheer joy that no living soul can comprehend: the quiet unity of all creation and the final reconciliation of will and desire.

Dante ends his Comedy by informing his readers that this explanation of the supernatural is deeply flawed. The author apologizes for his inability to describe the divine but insists that the magnificence of what he has seen is beyond human vocabulary. He likens his effort to that of a baby trying to verbalize the most complex of mysteries; it is simply impossible. The only way anyone can hope to fathom the pleasures of heaven is to witness them firsthand in the world to come.

DIVINE ESSENCE Both the Hindu and Buddhist religions believe in karma (metaphysical residue of human actions) and reincarnation as essential components of paradise. Their belief is that those who have been evil or unjust in life build bad karma and must purge this blot by being born again and making amends in a new life-form. This is achieved through reincarnation in the body of either a human or an animal, depending on the nature of the sins to be purged. This cycle continues until all karma has been burned away. When this is accomplished, the soul attains its highest state: absorption into the divine essence.

The divine essence is a state of oneness with the celestial orb. It is known by many names: KEVALA, MOKSHA, NIRVANA. When a soul joins the divine essence it loses all individuality and becomes an indistinguishable part of the whole. The spirit is then "free" to spend the ages in "motionless" contemplation of the mysteries of the universe.

On the way to this perfect state, souls might also enjoy respite in a temporary paradise. Since few people go through life without accumulating any bad karma, almost all will have to be reincarnated in order to reach the divine essence. But those who have led good (but not perfect) lives are sent to one of several heavens for a time before returning to earth. In some legends, Yama, the judge of the dead, reviews each life through a series of meticulous records and then assigns the spirit to a particular heaven, to a hell (also temporary), or to an immediate reincarnation. Souls that are completely purified do not pass through the Hall of Yama for judgment but are instantly melded with the divine essence at the time of death.

DJANNA Djanna (al-Janna) is the paradise of the Islamic religion. In this "garden of ALLAH" (God), the faithful enjoy delicious food, fruit in abundance, and freedom from all pain and sorrow. In Djanna virtuous souls indulge in all the pleasures forbidden them during life. The saved wear robes of silk and recline on fine pillows while partaking of a great feast. According to Islamic belief, in Djanna flow rivers of milk, water, wine, and honey. These are most pure and delicious, far surpassing any delights of earth. In Djanna, Allah's children also receive the services of the HOURI, beautiful virgins with ebony eyes and creamy complexion who are dedicated to pleasuring their masters.

The celestial garden of Djanna is arranged in many levels, including the Garden of Eternity, Garden of Peace, Abode of Rest, Garden of Pleasure, and Garden of Paradise. Throughout the realm, fruit grows in abundance on fragrant hills lined with flowers blooming in a thousand colors. Handsome warriors and lovely maidens welcome new souls to Djanna and guide them through the various regions. On the planes of Djanna, the saved will be given "robes of embroidered silk" and "bracelets of gold" symbolizing the treasure of faith.

At the pinnace of this pyramid-shaped utopia is the SIDRET-EL-MOUN-TEHA, an enchanted "tree of life." This opulent plant has branches of pearl and emerald and leaves of shimmering gold. Every leaf bears the name of a living human. During the holy season of Ramadan, some of its leaves fall, indicating who will die during the upcoming year. African legends of the CEDAR TREE OF THE END are believed to have derived from the Sidret-el-Mounteha.

Islamic writings chronicle the travels of MUHAMMAD, founder of the religion, to this supernatural realm. The prophet is believed to have visited Djanna where he spoke with ANGELS and learned the sacred language of Allah. While visiting the heavenly dimension, Muhammad is enveloped in a luminous cloud of gold and brilliant light. Here, Allah gives the prophet the divine words of the KORAN the holy book of Islam, describing what is necessary for humans to attain salvation. The Koran explains that those who obey his word will "enjoy a banquet with Allah" featuring the finest foods and "goblets of wine."

According to the faith of Islam, in Djanna righteous souls will also enjoy the BEATIFIC VISION. Looking upon the radiant face of Allah and dwelling with him in paradise is the ultimate eternal joy. Other pleasures will seem insignificant, falling into the Almighty's shadow.

Islamic tradition states that ultimately all believers will be saved, even the most vile. At the end of the world, Allah will preside over the LAST JUDGMENT, after which time all Muslims will be purified by the mercy of the Lord and will enter Djanna. After this "Day of Decision," all family, political, and social relationships will pass away, and all humans will become "one brethren." But infidels (nonbelievers) can never enter paradise, no matter how virtuous they have been in life. Only those who profess faith in Allah will savor the splendor of Djanna. The rest will perish in the fire of their own "evil."

Unlike CHRISTIAN PARADISE, Djanna is the eternal home of ANIMALS as well as humans. Holy texts include a list of blessed beasts specifically named as belonging to the kingdom of Djanna. Among these are Noah's dove, Abraham's ram, and Jonah's whale. Foremost among the animals in paradise is the BORAK, the magnificent beast upon whose back Muhammad rode to heaven. And though KATMIR is not named specifically in the Koran, legend holds that this mystic guard dog is also a resident of Islam's paradise.

Djanna appears in numerous Arabic literary works, as well as contemporary western compositions. Singer-songwriter Don Henley alludes to the paradise in his 1995 "In the Garden of Allah." Djanna is also used as an exotic backdrop in ADVERTISING campaigns designed to transport consumers to a higher realm.

DONNE, JOHN (1572–1631) John Donne, one of the greatest English metaphysical poets, earned a reputation for his stirring Anglican sermons focusing on ESCHATOLOGY. His works are marked by a complex mix of startling metaphors, delicate argumentation, and a dazzling blend of wit and wisdom. Donne's published works include *Divine Poems*, *Elegies*, and *Satires*. Twentieth-century literary genius T. S. Eliot was a great admirer of the poet, calling Donne a master at "unification of sensibility" and extolling his interpretations of CHRISTIAN PARADISE.

During his career as an Anglican priest, Donne wrote more than 160 sermons, many featuring images of heaven. They offer imaginative explanations of complicated biblical themes and provide touching illustrations of God's love and mercy toward humanity. Among his more poignant works are a number of lectures regarding the nature of the afterlife. Donne piqued the curiosity of his congregation by assuring them that in heaven the saved shall be imbued with perfect knowledge. This means that everyone will understand the mysteries of the universe in a single instant and have all their probing questions answered.

Donne also had a talent for using satire to communicate complicated or distasteful subjects to his followers. He uses this tactic for talks about the LAST JUDGMENT as well, avoiding the grisly metaphors of fire, brimstone, and eternal suffering that were commonly preached to frighten the faithful into submission. Donne preferred a more optimistic approach, describing a loving God who dearly longed for all his mortal children to find their way to their eternal home. A poem from his *Holy Sonnets*

envisions the Last Judgment of St. John's REVELATION:

> At the round earth's imagined
>   corners, blow
> Your trumpets, ANGELS; and arise,
>   arise
> From death, you numberless
>   infinities
> Of souls, and to your scattered
>   bodies go.

The poem reassures Christians that an "abundance" of grace is available to cleanse human souls, and that JESUS himself has "sealed" a divine pardon with his own sacred blood. Thus the impending Last Judgment is a trial not to be feared but is the final checkpoint on the road to eternal bliss.

Donne also originated such common literary phrases as "no man is an island" and "ask not for whom the bell tolls; it tolls for thee." These images are from one of Donne's most famous sermons, given just before his death in 1631.

DORÉ, GUSTAVE (1832–1883) French artist Gustave Doré was the most prolific and popular book illustrator of his time. His woodcuts decorated the pages of almost one hundred texts, including collections of POETRY, ancient literary classics, and the Bible. But Doré's specialty was creating compelling images of supernatural themes. The artist was especially known for his grotesque style of portraiture.

Among Doré's works are illustrations of heaven for Dante's DIVINE COMEDY: THE PARADISO and Milton's PARADISE

LOST. His pictures feature beautiful AN-GELS, breathtaking landscapes, and mystic passages that the characters must negotiate on their metaphysical journeys. The artist strives to capture the supernatural aspects of heavenly creatures, giving them a radiance and beauty that are more than human. His subjects take on an ethereal quality that suggests loveliness in spirit as well as body.

Doré's unique compositions remain among the most hauntingly beautiful and compelling illustrations of literature. His magnificent pictures are still included in many reprints of these centuries-old stories.

DREAM MODEL   Over the centuries, scores of theories have been proposed suggesting that if death is eternal sleep, then salvation and damnation are unending dream states. Using this scenario, theorists conclude that in the afterlife human souls eternally revisit the memories of their lives. This is known as the dream model of the afterlife. As sleepers dream, so the dead likewise experience thoughts, feelings, and emotions in a purely spiritual realm. Virtuous souls who have lived well will therefore pass the millennia reliving their past joys; vile spirits will be forever trapped in the quagmire of their wickedness.

Variations of this philosophy have been embraced by such diverse scholars as CICERO and SAINT AUGUSTINE and continue to be advanced by modern eschatologists. The pagan philosopher Plato taught that the benevolence of civic-minded citizens would survive

death and comfort souls in the world to come. Oscar Wilde, a nineteenth-century Irish author, calls death "the brother of sleep" in one of his fairy tales involving paradise. Similar connections are drawn both in fiction works and scholarly treatises on ESCHATOLOGY.

The ancient BARDO THODOL (Tibetan Book of the Dead) expounds on this perspective regarding the fate of the human soul. The text asserts that there is no supreme being who judged souls in the afterlife. Each departed spirit must look into the "mirror of truth" and face the image that appears. For the righteous, the reflection will bring great peace and consolation. Enlightened by their good karma (the sum of a person's good and bad actions), these noble souls then gravitate toward beneficial reincarnations and bring themselves closer to the DIVINE ESSENCE (ultimate spiritual fulfillment). However, self-centered spirits, eyes turned inward, will damn themselves to destructive reincarnations that will bring further pain.

In the modern philosophy, Oxford professor H. H. Price teaches that the afterlife is an indestructible state of consciousness in which "life memories" are continually revisited. The soul, free of its physical shell, spends eternity reflecting on the deeds of its earthly existence. The nature of these acts determines whether eternity will be a pleasant recollection of joy and happiness or a bitter prison of despicable images and vile thoughts. Price believes that in the next realm, memories will be heightened to contain all the sights, sounds, smells, tastes, and feelings of the original experience. Heaven, therefore, consists of endless treks to past scenes of earthly happiness.

This theory has been explored in a number of contemporary fiction works as well. Modern SHORT STORIES about heaven depict paradise as a return to the glamour and vitality of some youthful experience. Playwright Thorton Wilder depicts a comparable afterlife in OUR TOWN, in which his main character, Emily, now deceased, revisits the simple joys of small-town life. Stories from tent TWILIGHT ZONE MAGAZINE further explore the dream model of eternity and the perpetual dream state, describing the unending bliss of savoring past events.

DRITHELM, SAINT (ca. 650–700) Drithelm (Drythelm), a Northumbrian landowner of the seventh century, was said to have died, lay dead for more than eight hours, and then been restored to life following an illness in 693. While "dead," his spirit visited heaven, hell, and PURGATORY under the guardianship of a luminous angel described as "a handsome man in a shining robe." His supernatural adventure is recounted in BEDE's historical works.

After "dying," Drithelm's spirit left his body and was transported to "a very broad and deep valley of infinite length." On one side, flames burned into the night sky, while a fierce blizzard raged on the other. Anguished souls flailed in agony on either side, jumping from one bank to the other in search of elusive relief. The angel told Drithelm that this was not hell but a purging place where

one's sins are burned away. Even in this wretched place there was the "seed" of joy, since these spirits would one day ascend to paradise.

The celestial guide then took Drithelm on a ghastly tour of hell. In the dark abyss, the terrified mortal witnessed souls being boiled, dismembered, and impaled by unearthly beasts. Drithelm recognized some of the spirits as those of friends and villagers who had recently died. Several of them lunged at him, but the angel repelled the attack. Sickened and seized with "unholy fear," Drithelm begged the somber angel to deliver him from this vile place.

Before returning Drithelm to his body, the angel explained to him that only the souls in the pit were irrevocably damned for their evil. As a result of the choices they had made in life, these bitter spirits placed themselves beyond hope of salvation. The ones burning and freezing along the chasm, however, would suffer only until the LAST JUDGMENT described in St. John's REVELATION. At this time, JESUS, the Christian Messiah, would deliver them to heaven, their sins finally expiated.

The angel gave Drithelm a quick glimpse of paradise, which resembled a beautiful city atop a verdant hill. The shining spires and lush fields were filled with SAINTS and ANGELS celebrating the magnificence of God. Drithelm longed to see more of CHRISTIAN PARADISE, but the angel delivered his spirit back to his body before he could draw closer.

Upon awakening, Drithelm sold all his property and declared that "hence forward, I must not live as I used to, and must adopt a very different way of life." He immediately entered the Melrose Monastery on the river Tweed and remained there for the rest of his life. Drithelm lived an exemplary life and "returned to heaven" after his death. Drithelm was declared a saint of the early Christian church. His feast day is celebrated on September 1.

DUMA Duma (Dumah, Douma) is the angel of silence according to Jewish legend to whom each departing soul must give an account of his or her life. Those who are able to convince Duma that they have lived virtuous lives are escorted to JEWISH HEAVEN. But spirits who are unable to justify their evil are cast into hell for everlasting torment.

Contemporary Jewish author Isaac Bashevis Singer includes Duma in his 1964 *Short Friday*, a collection of SHORT STORIES. In the tale, a husband and wife are just sitting down to Sabbath dinner when the great winged messenger arrives and informs them that the moment of judgment is upon them. The "thousand-eyed angel" swoops in, armed with a "fiery sword," and demands that the two answer for the actions of their lives. After listening to their stories, Duma declares them worthy of heaven and escorts them to paradise.

The supernatural creature also appears in some myths as the Babylonian guardian of the underworld. In other legends, Duma is an avenging angel and lord of hell, "charged with punishing sinners" in the afterlife.

E

EFÉ Efé is the first man according to Pygmy legends, similar to the Judeo-Christian Adam. At first Efé dwells on earth, but then God asks him to return to heaven to serve the Almighty as a hunter. God gives the man enchanted spears that soar "straight and true" and have remarkable precision. Efé spends many contented decades in heaven, but after some time he longs to return to earth and rejoin his family. God allows Efé to go back to his home and promises him that he and his children will one day return to their "home in the sky." When Efé reappears in his village he is hailed as a great sage and spends the rest of his life teaching others about God and the paradise he has seen firsthand.

EL El is the chief deity of the ancient Canannite pantheon. He is the chief creator god and lord of human destiny. He appears in the Old Testament as the deity of the patriarchs, later referred to as YAHWEH, which means "everlasting one." In Judeo-Christian tradition, El is the supreme being who first holds out to humanity some hope of departing to an eternal paradise.

ELECT The term *elect* has been used by many religions to signify those who have a special relationship with the gods. The elect are believed to be predestined to go to heaven or to dwell in everlasting paradise. Their status is not based on merit or morality; they have simply been chosen from before the creation of the earth to share in the immortal realm. This foregone assurance of salvation is a divine gift that requires nothing from the recipient.

In past epochs, certain humans (almost exclusively men) were said to be chosen by the gods to receive special favors and divine protection. The Greeks believed that gods and humans could mate and produce offspring with supernatural powers. These celestial children could expect great lives on earth followed by rich rewards in the afterlife. Likewise, the Egyptians declared all pharaohs to be gods who would bask in splendor with OSIRIS for all eternity. After death, they were promised a never-ending existence rich in banquets and festivals, with hundreds of slaves eager to fulfill their every desire.

In Christian usage, the elect are thought to be the only true recipients of JESUS' saving grace. They still require grace from the sacrifice of Christ to redeem them; however, they have been chosen from before time as its sole beneficiaries. *Institute of the Christian Religion*, a text composed in 1536, describes this theory of predestination and promotes it as an undeniable truth. All those who are not of the elect are damned, and nothing they do in life can change that fate.

Acceptance of the idea of the elect was thoroughly embraced by founders of Puritanism. Puritans immersed themselves in a complex system of laws, rituals, and ceremonies that they said identified them as God's chosen. They called themselves "communities of living SAINTS" who were unquestionably heaven-bound. Puritans also rejected every type of physical joy, renouncing alcohol, rich foods, dancing, ornate clothing, and other delights of the flesh. Denying themselves corporeal pleasures is symbolic of the fact that they are not of this world but of the next.

The Calvinists took the concept a step further, claiming that the elect could be easily identified among the living by their net worth. Founder John Calvin taught that God bestows favor upon his own, and therefore the rich and powerful are marked as "saved." Impoverished people, on the other hand, are damned in this world as well as in the afterlife. Their dismal state in life is simply an indication of the wrath they have incurred from the creator. The destitute are thus deemed "unworthy of charity," since God has no use for them in this life or the next.

Today, this concept has been abandoned by almost every belief system around the globe. Hinduism, Buddhism, Jainism, Christianity, Islam, and Judaism stress that one must embrace God and live according to divine law in order to be saved. Social status and wealth are trappings of this world that are meaningless in the afterlife. (In fact, they can often be a distraction that ultimately ends in damnation and misplaced allegiance.) Certain Eastern religions still contend that their holy men are destined for paradise; however, eternal joy is not limited to these clerics, and all have the opportunity to find unending bliss.

EL EZKERAH The *El Ezkerah* (Legend of the Ten MARTYRS) recounts the tale of revered Hebrew SAINTS who value their faith above all else. In the story, JEWISH HEAVEN is described as a place of study, discussion, and contemplation of sacred texts. In paradise, rabbis and scholars pass eternity reflecting on the wisdom of God's holy truth. ANGELS, including the messenger GABRIEL, answer questions about the mysteries of the universe and of the divine plan.

El Ezkerah extends the possibility of salvation to all believers who dedicate their lives to virtue. But the text holds a warning for those who dismiss heaven as nonsense, cautioning that "he who says there is no resurrection of the dead" will have no place in paradise.

ELIJAH Elijah is a Hebrew prophet of the Old Testament who is said to have been taken up to heaven in a fiery chariot. His name means "YAHWEH is God." Like the patriarch ENOCH and the VIRGIN MARY, mother of JESUS, Elijah is believed to have been assumed into heaven body and soul.

Elijah lived under the rule of Ahab and Jezebel, pagan monarchs who worshiped the god Baal. Elijah denounced this deity and preached allegiance to Yahweh. The Hebrew prophet challenged Ahab to a test to see which god was stronger. The men went to Mount Carmel and in front of onlookers prepared sacrifices to their respective lords. Elijah soaked his altar in water, so much that it formed deep pools. He then called upon Yahweh to send down his fire: "Then the fire of the Lord fell, and

Elijah entering heaven

consumed the burnt sacrifice, and the wood, and the stones, and the dust, and licked up the water that was in the trench" (Kings 18:38).

Ahab's priests were unable to perform the same feat, and Elijah declared victory. The crowd fell on its knees and begged Yahweh's forgiveness for their idolatry, then rose up and killed the priests of Baal. Ahab was forced to admit defeat; however, when Jezebel heard about what had happened, she sent assassins to murder Elijah. The prophet was forced into hiding, but God sent one of his protective ANGELS to care for him so he would not perish in his desert exile.

At great peril to his life, Elijah continued to spread the word of Yahweh and denounce those who rejected his holy teachings. To reward the preacher's loyalty and courage, Yahweh sent a celestial carriage to fetch Elijah to paradise. The man was walking with his pupil Elisha when the two beheld the miraculous sight: "And it came to pass, as they still went on, and talked, that behold, there appeared a chariot of fire, and horses of fire, and parted them both asunder; and Elijah went up by a whirlwind into Heaven" (2 Kings 2:11).

Centuries later, Elijah appears in the Garden of Gethsemane during the transfiguration of Jesus described in the New Testament. Some legends claim that Elijah will one day return from heaven to restore Yahweh's order on earth, perhaps during the epoch culminating in the LAST JUDGMENT. This belief is held by many Jews and Christians alike.

ELUCIDATION   A bucolic vision of medieval CHRISTIAN PARADISE is described in the monastic manual *Elucidation*. The text, distributed throughout Europe around the year 1100, envisions a restored Garden of Eden that will be given to the faithful in the afterlife. This earthly paradise will be re-created after the LAST JUDGMENT, at which time all people will be held to account for their lives. The saved will enjoy life eternal in this utopia where there will be no more pain, anxiety, hunger, or other human problems.

Elucidation presents a heaven of lush meadows, fragrant flowers, and indescribable beauty. Those inhabiting the garden will be naked, but there will be no shame, since this represents ultimate human purity. Paradise will be a realm of childlike innocence. Everyone will be equal, free of the class distinctions that were so central to life during the contemporary era. This vision of heaven was especially appealing to the poor, who endured incredible suffering, degradation, and abuse at the hands of the wealthy. *Elucidation* was written with the peasantry in mind, offering them some hope of joy so elusive in their earthly lives.

This heaven stands in sharp contrast to other traditional versions of Christian paradise, which feature a more urban setting. Many theologians, authors, and artists imagine the holy realm as a city of golden spires, crystal towers, and jeweled buildings encrusted with precious stones. Medieval peasants found this picture somewhat disturbing, suggesting a HEREAFTER designed to please the powerful ruling class that routinely treated the poor with cruelty and contempt. *Elucidation*, however, offers a rustic, natural heaven stripped of wealth and status symbols, which can be grasped by commoners, many of whom had no desire to ascend to a cosmopolitan afterlife. The peasantry enthusiastically embraced the natural paradise concept, and it remains a popular depiction of heaven.

ELYSIUM   The Elysium, or Elysian Fields, is the paradise of ancient Greek (and later Roman) myth. It is an earthly utopia where pure souls will enjoy feasts, dancing, and festivals for all eternity. Various legends place Elysium on the moon, below the earth, or within the kingdom of King Hades, lord of the dead.

The idea of a pleasant afterlife evolved slowly over the decades, replacing an earlier belief that all departed spirits would descend to a dreary, tedious existence in the bitter court of Hades. Philosophers and poets eventually revised this dismal myth, teaching that within the boundaries of Hades is a road that leads to a great paradise of unimagined delights. Only the most deserving souls, however, could find their way down that path to the Elysian Fields and escape the sorrows of underworld monotony.

Tombs dating to the fourth century B.C. show vivid depictions of this mythic paradise that awaited the righteous dead. Illustrations on MEMORIALS include images of great banquets, dancing, jeweled costumes, and vibrant celebrations. In the afterlife, the departed are shown attending wondrous feasts and enjoying stimulating companionship. The drawings illustrate a fantastic place of total fulfillment where happy spirits are eternally indulged.

Unlike CHRISTIAN PARADISE, DJANNA, JEWISH HEAVEN, and other religious paradises, souls in the Elysium do not dwell with the gods. The Greek immortals live on Mount Olympus, where no human could reside. From Mount Olympus the gods oversee earthly creatures, set epic challenges, and decide the fate of the lesser beings. (Some later works fused the two supernatural planes, suggesting that souls of the dead could spend eternity with the immortals. However, this notion was soundly rejected by most and was never truly assimilated into afterlife belief.)

The Elysian Fields appears in a number of classic works spanning the centuries. In Virgil's epic AENEID, Trojan War hero Aeneas journeys to Elysium to seek the advice of his deceased father. Virgil describes the realm as a "shining plain" where "souls take ease among the blessed groves." Later works of Western literature, including plays by Shakespeare and poems of Milton, make reference to the enchanted Elysium and its mystic powers. And the famous CHAMPS-ELYSÉES (Street of Paradise) in Paris is named for this mythic utopia.

EMPIRE OF JADE Chinese Taoists believe in an afterlife of bliss under the Jade Emperor, also known as Yuhang or "the August Personage of Jade." The Jade Emperor is god of the sky and lord of paradise. He is a celestial bureaucrat who keeps detailed records of every person's successive reincarnations and determines each one's fate in the next world. As overlord of all living beings, the Jade Emperor has the power to admit spirits into paradise or condemn them to further incarnations on the material plane.

The concept of the Empire of Jade evolved in China over the centuries as divergent philosophies and politics were mingled, resulting in a fascinating blend of Taoism, Buddhism, and bureaucratic procedures. The eclectic system embraces the idea of karma (collective consequences of good and evil deeds) and reincarnations and gives the reigning emperor control over the afterlife, dubbing him the "Son of Heaven." He is the only living mortal able to communicate with the Jade Emperor, lord of the dead. All others will have no contact with the Empire of Jade until after death.

of all living beings. These are deified mortals rewarded for their virtuous lives on earth with this elevated supernatural status. Now, as gods, they float through the heavens on clouds, enjoy great feasts, and dwell in unending happiness. Virtuous souls aspire to join them in the blissful Jade Empire.

Outside the palace is a fragrant garden decorated with an exquisite array of enchanted plants. Chief among these is the TREE OF IMMORTALITY. The peaches picked from this tree give their consumers life eternal (similar to the mystic PEACH trees of KHUN-LUN). Legend warns that mortals who try to steal these forbidden fruits will be dealt with harshly, as only Yuhang can decide who is worthy of enjoying the splendors of his Empire of Jade.

Chinese Taoist immortals,
Han Shan Shih-te painting. ART TODAY

When a person dies, the Jade Emperor reviews the account of the person's life and then renders judgment on the spirit. Yuhang holds court in a splendid palace aided by hundreds of servants, clerks, and attendants. His two primary assistants are Dongyue Dadi, who rules the East, and Dadi's wife, Xi Wang Mu, who oversees the West. Together they maintain watch over earthbound souls, noting who is doing good and who is doing evil. Their records will help determine whether the gates of the Empire of Jade are opened or barred to departed souls. Those who are deemed unworthy will be sent back to the earth for another attempt at purifying their spirits and making themselves worthy of paradise.

Within the Empire of Jade is the Palace of the Eight Immortals, the gods

EMPYREAN   The word *empyrean* has been used by both pagans and Christians to define paradise. In ancient usage, the term refers to a realm of supernatural fire and light. In Christian terminology, it means the "abode of the blessed and the ANGELS." Both uses, however, incorporate the image of the uppermost celestial plane, the summit of eternity and "highest reaches of heaven."

In modern interpretation, the word is used to describe an aspect of CHRISTIAN PARADISE, which centers solely on the spiritual quality of the afterlife. The empyrean is described as a luminous realm of radiance and joy, encompassing the beauty of every creation. Unlike the "opaqueness" of earth, the empyrean is pure light. It cannot be defined in physical terms, since it is above the bonds of material. The empyrean is the direct opposite of hell, which is utter and complete darkness.

Throughout the centuries, scholars and theologians have tried to describe this quixotic realm to the masses. In the Middle Ages, theologian THOMAS AQUINAS taught that after the LAST JUDGMENT, the saved would dwell in the empyrean in their GLORIFIED BODIES. These perfect physical forms would shine "seven times brighter than the sun," reflecting the divine light. Aquinas believed that all other creations (such as plants and ANIMALS) would separate into their four original elements: air, earth, fire, and water. The movement of all living beings would, at the end of time, forever cease.

Artists likewise have sought to represent the luminousness of heaven through innovations in CHURCH ART AND ARCHITECTURE. The most striking example is the proliferation of STAINED-GLASS WINDOWS in Christian churches during the era of Gothic architecture. Since they allow light to flood into the otherwise dark buildings, these portals (usually placed near the top of the vaulted cathedrals) produced a stunning allusion to the empyrean of paradise. The addition of brilliant colors and of scenes of the VIRGIN MARY, SAINTS, and other religious heroes suggested that the saved are illuminated from within, inhabiting physical forms that are somehow made entirely of light. Worshipers, seated below in dark pews, could not help but look up in awe at these dazzling windows that seemed to allow the living a glimpse of paradise.

The idea of the empyrean also is found in numerous works of fiction, most notably Dante's DIVINE COMEDY: THE PARADISO. The story tells of a mystic journey into the next world, which ends at the height of heaven. Dante reaches this pinnacle at the end of his trilogy, since the author views it as the ultimate fulfillment of humanity's desires.

ENLIL Enlil (also called Bel) is the master of heaven and creator of all living things according to Akkadian/Sumerian mythology. Ancient legend tells that Enlil, god of wind and storms, and fellow deity An, lord of the sky, routinely met to decide the fate of human beings. Over time, Enlil began absorbing An's importance and eventually became supreme. He then had exclusive power over fate in this world and in the next.

Some legends claim that Enlil once lived in paradise but decided he would prefer life in the material world. He descended to the earth and took up residence with his creatures. This blissful existence ceased, however, when the god became infatuated with a young girl named Ninlil whom he saw bathing in a stream. Overcome by her beauty and by his lust, Enlil raped the girl. The other gods, hearing of his vile deed, forced Enlil into the underworld and forbade him from ever returning to heaven or earth. (In some versions, Ninlil joins him there after discovering that she is soon to bear his child.)

The ancient Sumerians feared Enlil's ability to bring devastating storms and held frequent rituals to appease the god and beg for his divine protection. At his temple in the city of Nippur, worshipers chanted their belief that his domain of heaven was integrally connected to the land of the living. One prayer states: "Without lord Enlil, the great mountain, no cities would be raised . . . no high priest born. . . . The birds of Heaven would not nest on the wide earth."

After the Babylonian conquest, both An and Enlil were supplanted by MAR-DUK, the chief of the Babylonian pantheon. Enlil is also mentioned as the afterlife guardian in the *Epic of Gilgamesh*, an ancient poem about the exploits of a great cultural hero.

ENOCH Enoch is a hero of the Old Testament who is assumed body and soul into heaven through the power of the divine. According to both Hebrew and Christian tradition, Enoch was a virtuous servant of God who was much beloved by the creator. When Enoch's life was finished, the Almighty sent AUPIEL, the tallest of his ANGELS, to bring the patriarch directly to heaven so he would not have to suffer physical death. This event is recorded in the Bible: "And Enoch walked with God after he begat Methuselah three hundred years, and begat sons and daughters. And all the days of Enoch were three hundred sixty and five years. And he walked with God; and he was not; for God took him" (Gen. 5:22–24). (In some translations, the wording reads "he abode with God," but both variations are interpreted to mean that he entered paradise physically intact.)

Enoch is one of a select few who are believed to have been bodily transported to the joyous afterlife in Christian tradition. The others are ELIJAH, a prophet of the Old Testament, the VIRGIN MARY, mother of the Messiah, and JESUS, the son of God and redeemer of humankind. (Celtic/Christian mythology also places King Arthur in AVALON in both physical and spiritual form, where he is escorted after being mortally wounded in battle.) Many legends claim that these extraordinary figures will one day return to earth to fulfill profound destinies.

ER   The ancient Greek philosopher Plato's REPUBLIC includes a story called "Myth of Er," which describes the process of human life, death, reincarnation, and ultimate judgment. It is a fictional work of ESCHATOLOGY designed to inspire contemporaries to dedicate their lives to civic duty and selfless pursuits, similar to "SCIPO'S DREAM" written by fellow thinker CICERO.

According to the tale, Er is a valiant soldier who is killed in battle defending his homeland. His soul then travels with countless other departed spirits to a distant realm, where Er sees four chasms before him, two in the sky and two in the earth. Between the chasms are three judges who evaluate each soul and decide where it shall go. Just souls are directed into the right-hand opening in the clouds, while wicked spirits are forced into the left chasm in the earth. (Er is not judged but told to pay attention to what he is witnessing so he can tell others of his vision.) Out of the other portals, a steady stream of souls come forth, with very different tales to tell.

Those who have been through the passage in the sky emerge rejuvenated and bright, brimming with vibrancy. Their souls have been rewarded for living lives of virtue with rest, splendor, and joy in the afterlife. But spirits exiting the underworld are ragged and ravaged, with haunted eyes and trembling hands. These are the souls of people who were selfish in life, thinking nothing of their fellows. In the murky abyss of the dead, they have paid "tenfold" for their sins. With faltering voices, they tell Er that some spirits will never emerge, for their depravity merits eternal punishment in the supernatural torture chamber.

After spirits leave their respective chambers, they travel on to a place where the reincarnation cycle continues. Every soul is allowed to choose a new "mortal existence," either as a human or an animal. Some spirits choose well and return to a happy life on earth, but others make bad decisions that ultimately bring great suffering. One selfish man asks to be a tyrannical king, unconcerned about the penalty to be paid after death. The kind Orpheus, a folk hero who lost his beloved bride, returns in the body of a swan to a quiet existence of innocent grace and simple beauty. After making their decisions, each soul drinks from the River of Forgetfulness before going back, washing away all memory of the afterlife.

Recording all that he has seen, Er returns to his body, which has been placed on a funeral pyre. The mourners are amazed when the dead soldier sud-

denly jumps up and shares his extraordinary tale. Plato ends this story with a reminder that every person ultimately faces similar judgment, and that souls are neither good nor bad by nature but act virtuously or wickedly by choice. The philosopher admonishes all to prepare for this fateful day by denying their own desires and working instead for the common good.

ESCHATOLOGY   Eschatology is the branch of theology that concerns itself with "ultimate realities" and "last things," such as death, judgment, and the afterlife. The term derives from the Greek word *eschatos*, meaning "final, extreme."

Western eschatologists include Homer, PLATO, CICERO, SAINT AUGUSTINE, and THOMAS AQUINAS, all of whom wrote treatises on theories of human immortality. Works of these philosophers include exploration of the nature of damnation and salvation as well as the possibility of a LAST JUDGMENT that will take place at the end of time.

Eschatologists of the Eastern faiths study the mysteries of MOKSHA, KEVALA, and NIRVANA, concepts of spiritual paradise as "freedom from self" and mingling with the cosmic elements. These philosophers contemplate the methods by which humans can shed their "physical shell" and reach total "enlightenment" in the "highest reaches of the universe."

ETRUSCANS   The Etruscan civilization has been called the most "religious" society in history by many anthropologists. This largely unknown culture predates the Roman Empire, existing from around 800 to 200 B.C. and covering an area in Italy from Naples in the south to the Po Valley in the north. Details about the origins, language, and customs of the Etruscans continue to mystify historians; however, one fact is certain: They were obsessed with the afterlife and with notions of the ultimate fate of the human soul.

What little Etruscan text does survive (no literature has ever been recovered) is a collection of brief inscriptions related to funeral rites, magic, and religion. This Etruscan *Book of Fate and Death* reveals that its citizens believed that everything—from everyday life to political affairs—is predestined by the unseen forces of fate. These scattered texts also allude to a civilization rich in rituals. Etruscans offered animal sacrifices to their gods both to appease them and to seek favors. In some cases, humans were sacrificed, although records show that only captives and prisoners were used for these offerings. Etruscans also enjoyed elaborate games, parades, music, and even prize fights. All of these events were rich in ceremony and performed according to strict regulations.

The remains of most ancient Etruscan villages lay buried below modern cities, so few excavations have been done. However, many of these age-old towns have on their outskirts a necropolis—a city of the dead that mirrors the land of the living—carved out of rock. Some of these are quite elaborate and contain extensive illustrations of the afterlife. Etruscan MEMORIALS to the dead include colorful drawings of the world to come, complete with its banquets, games, feasts, and celebrations. Early decorations emphasize scenes of grand adventures the dead enjoy in the next world. Later pictures, however, became increasingly grim, tending to illustrate the horrors of hell rather than the splendors of paradise. The long journey the dead must make to the afterlife is another topic frequently depicted. Souls are shown making this passage by foot, on horseback, and sometimes by chariot.

Since the afterlife is believed to resemble life on earth, the wealthy and powerful could look forward to a far superior paradise after death than the common folk. Prominent citizens were entombed with succulent foods, jewels, works of art, and other luxuries. These would accompany the dead to the next realm, ensuring a pleasant afterlife of sensual indulgence. The poor, however, were interred in plain graves with little or no ornamentation. Etruscans believed that they would spend eternity serving the rich, or would simply cease to exist, possibly after suffering the tortures of the damned.

EVERYMAN *Everyman* is the most famous MORALITY PLAY ever written. The English drama, first performed around 1500, is derived from a Dutch production about the soul's judgment at the time of death and its possible sentences: salvation to paradise or damnation to hell. Its purpose is to make viewers conduct their own spiritual inventory and to inspire them to greater piousness.

The play opens as Death calls Everyman—representing humanity—to the afterlife to explain his sins and convince God that he should be allowed entrance into heaven. Everyman immediately panics, for he has squandered his life on petty pursuits, ignoring the teachings of JESUS and rejecting countless opportunities for grace. God appears and warns Everyman (and the audience) that those who live for their own pleasure "will become much worse than beasts" in the afterlife, while the virtuous soul will enjoy a "mansion" of "glory" in paradise.

Terrified, Everyman prepares for the long journey to the court of divine judgment. He asks his friends Worldly Goods, Beauty, Fellowship, and other lifelong companions to accompany him, reminding the personified abstracts that they have spent many years together. They all refuse, mocking his naïveté. During life, they have sworn allegiance to Everyman, but when the time comes for him to face possible damnation, these self-serving comrades abandon the foolish mortal. Worldly Goods laughs at Everyman's predicament, reminding him that "my love is contrary to love everlasting" and would clash with the sentiments of heaven.

Only Good Deeds agrees to accompany Everyman to the afterlife, although he is weak and languishing due to years of neglect. Too ill to make the journey, Good Deeds asks his sister, Knowledge, to escort Everyman to the hearing in his place. She agrees on one condition: The pilgrim must stop in the House of Salvation and bathe in the river Confession before continuing. Feeling his first glimmer of hope, Everyman happily submits.

After purging himself in the pure waters, Everyman discovers that Good Deeds has revived and will join him after all.

When Everyman arrives at the throne of God, he must admit that he is not worthy of salvation. He weeps over his foolishness and begs the Almighty for mercy. Fearing that the "day of doom" is upon him, Everyman pleads with God not to be thrown to the dark abyss. Good Deeds steps forward to testify on Everyman's behalf as Everyman slowly descends into the grave. One of the saving ANGELS then appears to tell Everyman he will be spared from hell because of his "singular virtue" and welcomes him into the "heavenly sphere." The play ends with a warning to the audience that not all human souls will be so fortunate. Viewers are left with the admonition, "Remember: beauty, wits, strength and discretion: they all at the last Everyman forsake." Faith in God and cooperation with his grace is the only sure way to attain CHRISTIAN PARADISE.

The five-century-old drama *Everyman* continues to be performed throughout the world. An updated version, *Jedermann*, was penned in 1911 by Austrian playwright Hugo von Hofmannsthal.

EZEKIEL Ezekiel, a Hebrew prophet who lived in the sixth century B.C., experienced astounding visions of paradise and of future cataclysmic events. These include foreseeing the resurrection of the dead and the LAST JUDGMENT that will occur at the end of the world.

Ezekiel describes the GLORIFIED BODIES, free of all imperfections, that the saved will enjoy in eternity. In one passage, the prophet recalls seeing the "Heavens open up" and describes the dwelling place of YAHWEH, the one true God: "So the spirit took me up, and brought me into the inner court; and behold, the glory of the Lord filled the house . . . And he said unto me, Son of man, the place of my throne, and the place of the soles of my feet, where I will dwell in the midst of the children of Israel for ever, and my holy name, shall the house of Israel no more defile" (Ezek. 43:5, 7).

Ezekiel's writings further describe HE-BREW PARADISE as a place of interaction between human souls and the Almighty. Other prophecies include visions of AN-GELS with "four faces," "four wings," and "the likeness of the hands of a man under their wings." In eternity, these creatures shall coexist with human spirits forever in the "house of the Lord."

FALL OF THE GIANTS The paradise of ancient Greek myth is depicted in Giulio Romano's *Fall of the Giants*. The mid-sixteenth-century fresco covers an entire room, spanning all four walls, the ceiling, and the floor. Even the door and windows are incorporated into the work. The effective result makes view-ers feel they are actually part of the scene and witnesses to the spectacular cataclysm.

Fall of the Giants shows an array of supernatural beings from Greek legends in a cloudy realm of laughter and cele-bration. Several divine inhabitants sit chatting and playing music, unaware that they are about to meet their doom. For in the opposite corner, the angry overlord Jupiter unleashes his wrath. His mighty arms smash the temple, bringing the columns of paradise crashing down. Standing inside the room, one has the distinct impression that the structure is collapsing around him. Romano's tumultuous composition offers an awe-inspiring glimpse into the Greek ELYSIUM and a frightening image of the destruc-tive power of the vengeful deities.

FALLEN ANGELS ENTERING PANDEMONIUM, THE John Martin's 1840 painting *The Fallen Angels Entering Pandemonium* is a vivid portrayal of the archangel MICHAEL leading the ANGELS in the battle for heaven and the damna-tion of Satan and his vile forces. The work depicts in flaming reds and blazing oranges the dark angel's rebellion against God and the descent of his demon army into a wretched abyss below.

At the center of the painting is the guided city of heaven, a beautiful palace of crystal domes and golden beacons. The spirit of God glows in a burst of sil-ver beams above the enchanted par-adise. The turquoise sky—Martin's only use of blue in the painting—is disturbed by a single bolt of lightning as scarlet clouds churn with the disturbance of the rebelling angels.

This achingly beautiful city is bounded by a river of raging fire. On the opposite bank is a harsh landscape of jutting rocks and broken cliffs, as if a tremendous earthquake has ripped the two regions apart. Unlike the gleaming metropolis of heaven, this cursed hell has no lights, no spires, no great buildings of polished marble. It is dark and desolate, illuminated only by the red glow of the molten river.

Scattered about the rocky cliffs are a myriad of fallen angels. Some shake their fists defiantly at the army of heaven that has defeated them. Others cower on the ground, weeping at their wretched fate. A few line the edge of the chasm, sorrowfully thrusting their spears upward. The majority, however, are amassed at the center of the abyss, cursing one another and beating their fists against the unyielding rock.

Martin drew inspiration for this work from St. John's REVELATION, the final book of the Christian Bible, which describes the war in heaven and the expulsion of the traitor angels.

FAMILY REUNION IN THE OTHERWORLD   One of the most prevalent modern themes of CHRISTIAN PARADISE is the belief in the REUNION of loved ones in the next life. This supernatural reward, the rejoining of family and friends who have died before, is poignantly illustrated in the painting *Family Reunion in the Otherworld* by Lee G. Richards. The picture shows a young couple and a child embracing an elderly man and woman gathered in a lush meadow. Every face shows boundless joy and grateful admiration, and each reflects an ageless elation that all pain and separation are now forever in the past.

This modern painting is a sharp contrast to the illustrations of the Christian afterlife from past eras. During the Middle Ages and the Renaissance, depictions of heaven focused almost exclusively on God, the VIRGIN MARY, JESUS, the ANGELS and SAINTS, and other religious heroes. There was also great emphasis on the ultimate joy of the BEATIFIC VISION, that is, seeing God face to face. The reuniting of family and friends separated by death was rarely shown (other than reunions involving prominent Christian figures). And in those few cases, the reunion was a minor component of the work, usually relegated to the perimeter of the painting or sculpture. Heaven was the province of the divine, not a meeting place for saved mortals, as indicated by the vast majority of CHURCH ART AND ARCHITECTURE dedicated to illustrating paradise.

But as Christianity mingled with humanism during the later years of the Renaissance, the notion of a reunion in the afterlife became increasingly popular. Attitudes about God shifted, and the Almighty himself was often entirely omitted from contemporary depictions of heaven. Replacing the absent deity were indications of more human delights to be enjoyed in eternity, including the concept of spending the ages with lost loved ones as depicted in Richards's *Family Reunion in the Otherworld*. The reunion theme remains popular, and is especially important in ideas of MORMON HEAVEN, which places great emphasis on the eternal family.

FAUST   The opera *Faust* by Charles Gounod is based on Part I of Johann

Wolfgang von Goethe's literary adaptation of the classic deal-with-the-devil story. Unlike most tales of the conceited doctor who sells his soul in exchange for great power, this version has a happy ending. For rather than being damned to the pits of hell, this Faust finds salvation and mercy awaiting those who repent of their sins and seek divine forgiveness.

Faust begins as the scholar, bored with his quest for knowledge, is contemplating suicide. He is roused from his dark despair by the sound of young voices outside his window singing a prayer. The demon Mephistopheles, sent to tempt Faust, offers to make the aging doctor young again so that he, too, may experience the long-forgotten joy of youth. Faust agrees and enters into the infernal bargain. In exchange for this mystic favor, Faust surrenders his soul to hell at the time of his death.

In his new and physically improved state, Faust determines to seduce the beautiful Marguerite, an innocent maiden who has caught his eye. After many attempts he manages to break down her resistance and robs the girl of her virginity. Marguerite's brother is outraged at the defilement of his sister and challenges Faust to a duel. But, through the intervention of the devil, the doctor overpowers and kills the lad. Faust then abandons Marguerite, shamed and pregnant with his child, to pursue more depraved carnal pleasures.

Eventually, Faust begins feeling remorse for his actions and seeks out the girl he has wronged. But by this time Marguerite has gone insane from the trauma and has murdered her illegitimate child. For this crime, Marguerite has been sentenced to death and quietly awaits her execution. Faust offers to help her escape prison, but she will have nothing to do with the plot so long as Mephistopheles is involved. She recognizes him as pure evil and calls on God for help. Exhausted and frail, Marguerite dies with the prayer on her lips. Mephistopheles declares that her soul is damned and must be delivered to hell, but a chorus of ANGELS intervenes. The gates of heaven open wide, and the angels carry Marguerite into paradise. Her faith in God has saved her. The divine emissaries suggest that Faust, too, should repent and beg forgiveness or else he will suffer a far darker fate in the world to come.

FAUST II   Johann Wolfgang von Goethe wrote the sequel to his classic FAUST story in 1832, not long before his death. He revives the characters for this continuation of the tale of a man who sells his soul to the devil in exchange for power, however *Faust II* lacks the passion and excitement of the original. It is a more wistful, sentimental treatment of supernatural matters that reflects the mellowing attitude of its aging author. In this literary follow-up, Goethe also transforms paradise into a distinctly feminine realm where the maternal instinct—and not the sacrifice of JESUS— brings about humanity's salvation.

Faust II opens with Dr. Faustus and his mistress, Gretchen, in a familiar predicament. They are facing damnation, the doctor for striking a bargain with hell and Gretchen for allowing herself to be seduced by the conniving scholar. The devil arrives to bear them off to the abyss when the VIRGIN MARY intervenes. She has taken pity on the pair (through Gretchen's supplications) and convinces God to declare Faust's contract null and void. The Queen of Heaven then sends a chorus of ANGELS to fetch the wayward spirits home to paradise.

Faust and Gretchen are then transported to the celestial plane where they discover the delights of salvation. Foremost among these is the REUNION of friends and family and the opportunity for love to continue and to grow. The doctor is thrilled to find that in heaven he can pursue knowledge for all eternity, for it was this intellectual curiosity that had led him to the devil's pact in the first place. Gretchen is more taken with the divine celebration of the angels (again exclusively female) as they sing and dance around the throne of God.

Overall, the paradise of *Faust II* is a realm of nurturing, gentility, and mercy. God the Father (as a masculine figure) is overshadowed by the ladylike qualities of the Virgin and her angelic peers. The play concludes with the blunt pronouncement that it is the "eternal feminine that draws man upward." For this reason (as well as the work's inherent inferiority to the original masterpiece), *Faust II* was derided by both religious scholars and dramatic critics upon its debut. But it remains important in the study of heaven as the work offers one of the few examples of a CHRISTIAN PARADISE with femininity as its defining characteristic.

FAVOLA D'ORFEO, LA   Claudio Monteverdi's opera *La Favola d'Orfeo* (The Fable of Orpheus) retells the legend of the man who braves the underworld in order to reclaim his dead bride. Orpheus is heartbroken when Eurydice, his young wife, is killed by the bite of a poisonous snake. Determined to retrieve her, Orpheus sets sail across the river Styx to the land of the dead in search of her.

Orpheus must overcome many obstacles in order to achieve this task. First, he charms the fierce gatekeeper Charon with enchanted music. The hero must then face Pluto (Hades in the Greek legend) and Prosperine (Persephone), king and queen of the underworld, to make his request. Pluto refuses to restore Eurydice, but Prosperine is touched by Orpheus's devotion to his lover. She convinces her husband to release Eurydice and let her return with Orpheus to the land of the living. But Pluto sets one condition: Orpheus must go first and Eurydice will follow him, but he must not look back. If Orpheus turns, he will lose his bride forever. Orpheus agrees, and the two begin the journey back to the upper world.

At first, Orpheus is jubilant to be leaving with his wife. But then he begins to have doubts. Is she really there? Has Pluto tricked him? What are the strange and frightening noises he keeps hearing behind him? Unable to resist any longer, Orpheus looks back to see if Eurydice is indeed following. But as he turns, the girl wilts and falls away. His doubt has sealed her doom. Eurydice is borne away by guardians of the underworld while an unseen force propels Orpheus back to the living, forever away from the one he loves.

In Monteverdi's operatic version, Orpheus is soothed by his father, the god Apollo. Apollo appears and offers to take his son to heaven, where he can write the story of their love in the stars. The two then enter the celestial orb, where Orpheus will be consoled by eternal visions of Eurydice's beauty.

La Favola d'Orfeo has distinct Christian overtones. Orpheus, like the Redeemer JESUS Christ, ventures to hell to reclaim his beloved. He then returns from the grave (albeit in Orpheus's case, unsuccessful in his mission) to take up a new, glorified existence. And the dramatic finale closely resembles Christ's ASCENSION to heaven to dwell in eternal joy with his father.

FIGHTING SULLIVANS, THE

The 1944 drama *The Fighting Sullivans* tells the true story of five brothers who truly personified the notion of brotherly love. During World War II, the Sullivan boys enlisted together and served on the battleship *Juneau*, shoulder to shoulder in patriotic duty. However, when one of them is confined to the ship's infirmary, the other four refuse to leave his side during the Japanese attack at Guadalcanal. As the boys struggle to save their brother, all five are killed in the bloody battle. The movie ends with a REUNION of the boys in heaven, where the five heroes march into the proverbial "white light" as the Navy theme song, "Anchors Aweigh," resonates triumphantly. Before departing to the HEREAFTER, the boys turn to smile, and wave, then

joyfully resume their supernatural adventure.

The film made an especially important statement about rewards for valor in the world to come. *The Fighting Sullivans* was released while World War II was still raging throughout Europe and Japan, and its "heaven scene" offered comfort to the thousands of Americans whose loved ones had been casualties of the war or who were currently fighting in distant lands. *The Fighting Sullivans* promoted the notion that mourning parents, grieving wives, and broken-hearted children would, in fact, see their heroic loved ones again in paradise. Such a message helped boost patriotic fervor as well.

The case of the five Sullivan brothers initiated a significant change in U.S. armed forces regulations. After the tragedy of losing an entire generation in one battle, family members were no longer permitted to serve in the same unit. As a lasting tribute to the valor of these men, the U.S. Navy also named a destroyer after them: the U.S.S. *Sullivan*.

FOLK PLAYS Folk plays—informal, often improvised dramas presented by common villagers (as opposed to professional thespians)—are the earliest known dramatic productions. Such "homemade" presentations are believed to predate written history itself, occurring years before the invention of record keeping. Initially, folk plays commemorated some cultural event such as a harvest festival, a New Year's celebration, or tribute to one of the gods. Over time they became a staple of entertainment and were routinely offered as amusement for the masses, eventually branching into distinct genres such as MYSTERY PLAYS and MORALITY PLAYS.

The first known folk plays date back to ancient Greek and Egyptian times, when tales of the afterlife kingdoms of OSIRIS and the ELYSIUM were translated into public performances. Other plays of the era emulated mysterious cult rituals and mystic funerary rites. Some productions claimed to contain magic and be capable of affecting audiences with supernatural powers, like conveying divine protection or bringing about a plentiful harvest. Such dramas were usually presented by priests or societies dedicated to the service of a particular deity.

Folk plays reached the height of popularity during the Middle Ages in Europe, when virtually every planting and harvest cycle was marked by a dramatic presentation of some kind. No carnival was complete without a performance, which usually moved throughout the crowd and solicited audience participation. Productions initially began with simple costumes and masks worn during the festival as participants ad-libbed their lines. Over time, these dramas became more organized, incorporating formal plotlines and distinct characters. Favorite topics included tales of King Arthur and the paradise AVALON, stories of underworld gods, and imitations of occult rituals. For some festivals, elaborate sword dances, fireworks, and other performance art were included to add pizzazz to the plot.

Unlike morality plays, folk plays were predominantly designed to entertain rather than educate the masses.

The vast majority of European folk plays included a death and resurrection sequence, focusing on magic and spells as well as Christian doctrines about immortality. (Some revisited the lives of the SAINTS, especially a village's patron, but these presentations were more cultural than religious.) Folk plays were typically presented during winter to offer a break in the monotony of dark days, frigid nights, and empty fields. Popular themes included harvesting, courtship and marriage (fertility), and other tenets of nature. The shows included heroes and fools offering their audiences action, comedy, and usually a happy ending.

Productions about Christian supernatural events, such as the LAST JUDGMENT, the creation of the world, and the life of JESUS, grew in popularity over the centuries. Heaven was depicted as a bright, light-splashed (via candles and lanterns) realm of white-robed ANGELS and somber saints. The VIRGIN MARY, mother of the Redeemer, was frequently accompanied by a celestial escort of cooing cherubs, adoring patriarchs, and other blessed souls. Her presence onstage would be marked with HYMNS and melodic strains. At the other end of the spectrum, satirical dramas poked fun at Christian heroes, depicting a paradise of wild-eyed zealots and restless angels with a taste for adventure rather than reverence.

European folk plays went into decline after the Protestant Reformation, when Puritan leaders denounced all drama as sinful, calling it the "work of Satan." In addition to protesting the "glorification of the occult," angry clerics were offended by the "comical" treatment of Christian ideas, especially the presentation of the devil as funny, even likable, in contrast to the often stern and rigid saints. Around the same time, professional theater in England and surrounding areas was blossoming. This new, highly polished dramatic movement had the support of the royalty and nobles of the era, and playwrights found them to be generous patrons. Thus, folk plays became less common in cities, although they continued to be popular in rural areas. Today, revivals of such free-form productions are staples of Renaissance fairs and other historical commemorative events.

Nutrition equated with "godliness." ART TODAY

FOOD NOVELTIES In contemporary American culture, visions of paradise are invoked to sell a wide variety of food novelties. Examples include specific brands (Chock full o' Nuts, that "heavenly coffee" and Celestial Seasonings Teas) as well as generic delicacies such as angel-hair pasta and heavenly hash ice cream. These succulent treats and others like them offer a taste of paradise on this side of eternity and tempt us into delicious indulgence.

Many food novelties use images of the great beyond in ADVERTISING as well. Hebrew National offers an ad campaign showing Uncle Sam savoring a tasty hot dog, while a voice-over claims the company must "answer to an even higher authority," referring to God himself. The accompanying visual depicts a billowy realm of "white light" shimmering above the humbled Uncle Sam. A radio advertisement for Chesa-

peake Bagel Bakeries describes a paradise where the blessed will be "wearing a bagel for a HALO." And Virginia Honey offers a more subtle suggestion: It packages its product in angel-shaped glass containers, implying that this is truly the nectar of the gods.

Traditional Christian holidays bring a seasonal deluge of confections alluding to paradise. Chocolates formed in the shape of ANGELS, boxes decorated with "heavenly hosts" and a star-filled cosmos, and even "inspirational fortune cookies" with biblical quotations fill Christmas stockings and Easter baskets. By mingling sweet sensations with notions of the afterlife, such products help remind true believers that the delights of paradise will overshadow earthly joys and offer pleasures beyond even the most delectable treats of this temporal life. They truly are a taste of heaven.

FOR HEAVEN'S SAKE The 1950 comedy *For Heaven's Sake* depicts the great beyond as a benevolent bureaucracy where ANGELS oversee earthly affairs. Written by the author of HERE COMES MR. JORDAN, this heavenly foray into human events stars Clifton Webb and Edmund Gwenn as a pair of celestial social workers dispatched to save the marriage of Broadway producer Robert Cummings and his long-suffering wife, Joan Bennett. But his obsession with the job, coupled with her waning interest, seems to spell doom for the angels' romantic plot.

After bumbling their way through the mission, Webb and Gwenn reveal the reason for their frantic efforts: The feuding couple has an as-yet unconceived baby waiting in heaven for Mom and Dad to get together. The angelic duo has come to earth on the child's behalf. In the end, angels and humans alike rejoice when the divine darling arrives, saving the marriage and providing a glimpse of paradise's currency of enduring love. The notion that heaven is a dwelling place of unborn humans as well as deceased souls is also explored in the 1987 drama MADE IN HEAVEN.

FORTUNATE ISLANDS Ancient Japanese mythology includes a verdant supernatural realm called the Fortunate Islands of Paradise. Souls dwelling in this enchanted garden enjoy eternal life free of hunger, pain, and sorrow. On the islands are three mountains, including the majestic Horai, the "seat of everlasting." A magical tree grows at the base of Horai with leaves of jade and branches of gold. The Fortunate Islands are also home to blessed ANIMALS that figure prominently in Japanese cultural legends, such as the tortoise and the crane. Delicious plums, nuts, and PEACHES more succulent than any fruit on earth grow in the rolling meadow, sustaining the islands' eternal inhabitants.

FOUR SAINTS IN THREE ACTS
One of the most bizarre theatrical productions of the early twentieth century is the enigmatic *Four* SAINTS *in Three Acts*. The opera, written by Virgil Thomson with English libretto by famed American author Gertrude Stein, was originally presented by "the Society of Friends and Enemies of Modern Music." A confusing mix of reverence and revelry, the free-form project offers a glimpse into heaven and a hint at the eternal mysteries that await the faithful in the afterlife.

Despite its title, *Four Saints in Three Acts* actually features more than a dozen saints, including Ignatius of Loyola, Teresa of Ávila, and Teresa of the Child JESUS. In one particularly convoluted scene, the two St. Teresas look through an enchanted telescope to the realm of CHRISTIAN PARADISE. When St. Teresa of Ávila reports seeing a gilded mansion, her counterpart asks, "how many doors and how many floors and how many windows" the palace has. The answer is left to the viewer's imagination, as the only reply is the rapture and exuberance on the saint's face. A vision of heaven is reprised at the finale, when the entire cast of saints assembles to rejoice in their eternal reward.

FRANCIS OF SALES, SAINT
(1567–1622) Italian bishop Francis of Sales concentrated much of his energies on conveying the complex doctrines of CHRISTIAN PARADISE to the common people. He sought to portray the HEREAFTER as a fulfilling realm of human delights without detracting from the significance

of being in God's presence. In numerous sermons and exempla, Francis assures his contemporaries that the saved do not simply sit motionless watching the BEATIFIC VISION; they interact with the Almighty. Redeemed souls will pass eternity expressing their boundless love for the infinite creator, while he in turn will reveal to them the mysteries of the universe.

One of the most poignant pleasures of Francis's depiction of paradise is conversation with JESUS, the Christian Messiah. Over the endless years, Christ will explain to each individual the depths of his suffering and "reveal great secrets" of divine history. The savior will also introduce souls in heaven to the SAINTS and ANGELS and to his beloved mother, the VIRGIN MARY, so that together they can contemplate the intricate puzzle that is the will of God.

Francis was equally intrigued with the concept of REUNION of friends and family in paradise. He was unsatisfied with SAINT AUGUSTINE's notion that although souls will recognize each other in the afterlife, they will be so focused on God that their relationships will be "absorbed" into an overall sense of mutual love. Breaking with tradition, Francis insisted that in paradise "friendships that were good in this life will continue into eternity" and that the blessed will love individuals to differing degrees corresponding to affection shared on earth.

During his lifetime, Francis often found himself at odds with the Calvinists, a strict Protestant sect that was prominent at the time in his diocese of Geneva. A great deal of his teachings on the nature of heaven resulted as a refutation of the cold, impersonal Calvinist concept of the ELECT, a doctrine that states that God has predestined a select few to dwell with him in eternal bliss; the rest (the vast majority of humans) are damned to everlasting hellfire. Francis often argued that the opposite is actually true: All souls are "predestined to glory" and bound for paradise. Only spirits who struggle against God's will and repeatedly reject his grace will descend to hell, and even these do so by free choice.

Francis of Sales was beloved throughout his lifetime for his gentle demeanor and quiet kindness. Because of his literary talent and ability to convey complicated ideas in simple terms, he has been named the patron saint of Roman Catholic writers. His 1608 *Introduction to the Devout Life*, a study in contemplative prayer, remains a classic religious work that is studied in monasteries to this day.

GABRIEL   Gabriel is one of the most prominent ANGELS in Jewish, Christian, and Islamic lore. He appears in numerous legends as a messenger of heaven and a guardian of paradise, delighting in his role as conduit between God and humanity.

In Jewish tradition, Gabriel is the "spirit of truth" who is sent to destroy the cities of Sodom and Gomorrah when the residents refuse to repent of their sins. Along with the archangel MICHAEL, Gabriel is the only angel named in the Hebrew Old Testament. He journeys to the human plane to protect the patriarchs, dispense divine justice, and slay the enemies of God. It is the angel Gabriel who comforts and shields the prophet DANIEL and assists him in interpreting his mystic visions.

According to Christian doctrines, Gabriel is the sacred emissary who delivers the message to the VIRGIN MARY that she has been chosen as the mother of JESUS the Messiah: "The angel Gabriel was sent from God unto a city of Galilee, named Nazareth, to a virgin espoused to a man whose name was Joseph, of the house of David; and the virgin's name was Mary. And the angel came unto her and said Hail, thou art full of grace, the Lord is with thee: blessed art thou among women" (Luke 1:26–28).

Some scholars believe he is also the angel referred to in the prophecy of REVELATION as the one who will blow the trumpet signaling the end of the world.

Muslim legends tell how Gabriel (called JIBRIL) dictated the KORAN to the prophet MUHAMMAD and helped the prophet decipher the sacred writ. Gabriel is thus the "angel of truth" of the Islamic faith. He dwells forever at the side of ALLAH, guarding the afterworld paradise DJANNA.

Gabriel is the second most frequently depicted angel (after the archangel Michael), appearing in thousands of works of literature, art, and even modern motion pictures. The celestial being is the "guardian of paradise" in Milton's

PARADISE LOST and in paintings by the Dutch master Rembrandt and by religious artist FRA ANGELICO. Allusion to Gabriel and his sacred mission features in the movies GREEN PASTURES, ALL DOGS GO TO HEAVEN 2, and THE HORN BLOWS AT MIDNIGHT. Gabriel even makes an appearance in an episode of the classic television series TWILIGHT ZONE about a dejected trumpet player seeking validation in an unfeeling world.

GAN EDEN The Gan Eden is the heaven of Jewish tradition. It is the mythical Garden of Eden, the earthly paradise of Adam and Eve, restored to its original splendor and promised to the faithful after the LAST JUDGMENT. The Gan Eden will be re-created on earth and will provide inhabitants complete fulfillment of both body and soul.

The concept of this natural haven of Adam and Eve elevated to supernatural status began evolving in the century preceding the birth of JESUS. Former tradition had taught a JEWISH HEAVEN of shadowy existence without real delight or joy. But scholars became increasingly convinced that YAHWEH, the heavenly Father, had designed a place where virtuous people who had been treated unjustly in life would be eternally rewarded. The glorious realm made for humanity— the original Garden of Eden—seemed a logical model for everlasting bliss. In the Gan Eden, the saved could experience complete spiritual and physical ecstasy in accordance with Yahweh's primary plan for humankind.

According to the Hebrew Midrash, the Gan Eden measures "800,000 years" at "10 miles per day." Within its massive grounds are five separate chambers, each designated for a specific group ranging from converts to Judaism to rabbis. The temple's rooms are decorated with crystal, silver, gold, and precious stones in accordance with the level of sanctity. In Gan Eden, blessed souls pass eternity studying the "mind of God" and marveling at its wondrous mysteries.

GATES AJAR The 1868 novel Gates Ajar by Elizabeth Stuart Phelps remains an important development in the secularization of paradise. Written when the author was just twenty-four years old, the book describes heaven as a village quite similar to the New England town in which Phelps lived. This depiction of the celestial orb exhilarated many and disgusted others, depending on the individual's opinion of late nineteenth-century Massachusetts. One contemporary critic, author Mark Twain, went so far as to denounce Phelps's paradise as a pathetic "ten-cent Heaven" in his own treatise on the afterlife, THE BIBLE ACCORDING TO MARK TWAIN. But for thousands of readers, Gates Ajar offered hope of an idyllic afterlife previously unimagined.

Gates Ajar broke new ground in American literature by blending the popular romance novel genre with supernatural philosophy. The story opens as Mary, a proper New England lady, learns that her brother has been killed in the Civil War. She is inconsolable until a recent widow arrives to reassure Mary that her beloved sibling is in heaven. The rest of the book features a debate on the nature of the afterlife and offers extensive descriptions of the eternal joys.

According to Phelps, the world to come is arranged much like a village from nineteenth-century America. It is filled with shops, libraries, restaurants, and museums where the saved pass many contented hours talking and attending social functions. It is a realm of simple pleasures with the REUNION of loved ones as the ultimate happiness. In heaven, all have GLORIFIED BODIES that bear no scars of human life. Everyone is forever beautiful, young, and healthy. And the emotional bonds of family and friends forged on earth are celebrated rather than dissolved. There is no perpetual adoration of God in Phelps's utopia, as she considers this too monotonous and unfulfilling a way to spend eternity.

Despite its critics, Gates Ajar sold hundreds of thousands of copies both in the United States and abroad. Many readers found this familiar depiction of an urban wonderland preferable to more traditional images of a spiritual heaven. The novel's success led to Beyond the Gates, published several years later. This "sequel" devoted itself exclusively to depicting a heaven where love endures beyond the grave. The dead occupy fine homes, coexist with ANIMALS and even get to meet deceased celebrities. Beyond the Gates, although not as commercially successful, was every bit as controversial as the original.

Gates Ajar also led to scores of copycat Victorian romances about love in the afterlife. Each volume was progressively more insipid and trite, and the genre finally collapsed upon itself. Readers found themselves resenting the notion that eternity is designed to please stuffy socialites and began rejecting the "New England village" concept of heaven. Ministers, too, were angered at the unceremonious dismissal of God from CHRISTIAN PARADISE and condemned the materialistic depiction of life in the next world. But the books fed the enduring curiosity about the afterlife and its vague promises of everlasting joy and furthered the debate over what precisely those joys will be.

GATHAS *Gathas* (meaning "song") is a book of the AVESTA, the sacred text of the religion of Zoroaster. This ancient Persian prophet taught that humanity is caught in an ongoing battle between two powerful deities: the benevolent AHURA MAZDA (later known as Ormazd) and Ahriman, his evil twin. The brothers are forever trying to influence human souls, Ahura Mazda by offering "the truth" and Ahriman through lies and deception. Humans who de   'their lives to obeying Ahura Mazda will depart to the BEST EXISTENCE after death, where they will be rewarded in a celestial paradise.

According to *Gathas*, when a person dies its soul remains by the body for three days. After this transitional period, the spirit departs the human plane and crosses CHINVATO PERETAV, (a perilous passage spanning the abyss of hell) that leads to ZOROASTRIAN HEAVEN. Zoroaster promises that he will send his ANGELS to guide virtuous souls safely across; however the corrupt will have no such protection. For them, the bridge will become "razor thin," and they will topple into a fiery pit of suffering. But Ahura Mazda's faithful are assured that the way will be wide and steady, and they will cross to the best existence waiting on the other side.

"GENESIS B" "Genesis B" is an adaptation of an old Saxon poem about the war in heaven that resulted in Lucifer's damnation. According to the poem (which borrows many notions from St. John's REVELATION), the ANGELS were the first beings created by God, and they reflected his magnificent glory. However, one vain angel named Lucifer considers himself to be God's superior, and he sets up a throne in the northwest corner of heaven and begins holding court. Lucifer manages to convince a number of his fellow angels to betray God and worship him instead. When the Supreme Being takes notice of this rebellion, he asks the rebels to reconsider their action. They haughtily refuse, blaspheming against their creator.

God then casts Lucifer and the his dark worshipers out of PARADISE. The rebellious spirits fall for three days and three nights, losing their angelic power and brilliance as they plummet into darkness. At last the fallen angels land in hell, a realm of despair that makes them ache for the light and beauty of heaven. Their cruelest torment is knowing they can never return to their former glorious existence and will never again look upon the face of the Almighty. Compounding this agony is the knowledge that lesser creatures—human beings—will one day enjoy the BEATIFIC VISION and spend eternity in paradise.

GENII According to the ancient Greek scholar Plutarch, a priest of the Temple of Apollo, genii are blessed human souls in an advanced state of spiritual development. The mission of the genii is to guide newly arriving souls into the highest reaches of heaven. Virtuous spirits eagerly respond to the genii and ascend to spiritual fulfillment, while self-serving souls refuse the offers of assistance. They must be reincarnated, perhaps hundreds of times, to purge their vices and admit the need to change. Such recalcitrant souls wander through time until they accept the help of the genii and dedicate themselves to spiritual improvement.

GERARDESCA Gerardesca, the Lady Tertiary of Camaldolese, offered thirteenth-century Christians a detailed vision of CHRISTIAN PARADISE as an urban jewel. According to her discourse, the saved could look forward to an afterlife in a world of landscaped parks, opulent palaces, and gilded castles. And the citizens of paradise all have designated places in this celestial society determined by the piety of their lives.

The city of Gerardesca's vision had three distinct areas: heaven proper, the seven castles of paradise, and the outlying network of minor fortresses. At the center of paradise is heaven proper, the dwelling place of the greatest Christian heroes. Within its boundaries reside the Trinity, the VIRGIN MARY, and the great-

est SAINTS and the topmost legions of ANGELS. Arranged around this focal point are the seven guilded castles, which house the lesser saints and angels. Three times a year, the palaces are visited by heaven's elite. All other saved souls (the vast majority of the blessed) dwell in the outlying areas of paradise. And though they live in the distant fortresses, these "lowly souls" have access to the city of God should they wish to pay tribute to the Almighty.

Gerardesca's heaven is a luxurious realm, encrusted with jewels and precious metals. The streets are paved with gold and dotted with all manner of gleaming gemstones. Lining these majestic boulevards are gardens of the most beautiful foliage imaginable. Buildings are decorated with banners of victory and shields bearing the Holy Virgin's symbol. The thrones of God, Mary, and the high-ranking angels are festooned with glitz. Around these thrones, the rest of the saved sit according to their celestial "rank," dressed in rich garments and singing the praises of the Lord. Gerardesca refers to this paradise as a realm "filled with ineffable jubilation and incomprehensible joy," reflected in the place's dazzling trappings.

GERTRUDE, SAINT (1256–1302) St. Gertrude was a mystic who experienced numerous visions of the supernatural during her lifetime. These extraordinary experiences began when she was just five years old, orphaned and left to the care of nuns. The apparitions intensified after Gertrude entered the convent, at which time she saw the souls of her departed sisters being escorted into heaven by beautiful ANGELS. She also witnessed many of her contemporaries being received in paradise by JESUS as his "spiritual brides" and crowned with gold and jewels.

In later life, Gertrude often fell into "trances" in which she conversed with the divine. These episodes became more frequent as her death approached. In one such instance, Gertrude was consoled by Christ and reassured that a great reward awaited her in the afterlife. He promised to lead her to a "Palace of Paradise" where she would be embraced by fellow SAINTS and angels. Her death would also be marked in heaven by a great celebration, which, Jesus explained, occurs whenever a soul is received into the celestial realm.

As part of her work in the convent at Helfta, Gertrude worked in the scriptorium decorating ILLUMINATED MANUSCRIPTS. During this time she had many mystic apparitions, which were later collected under the title *Revelationes* and published in 1289. She frequently discussed "divine truth" with fellow mystic MECHTHILD who had fled to Helfta after angering the local clergy, where the two became close friends. Due to her "extraordinary relationship" with the Lord and her legendary virtue, Gertrude was eventually canonized and is known as Gertrude the Great.

GHENT ALTARPIECE The *Ghent Altarpiece* is a masterpiece of oil painting and a grand accomplishment of Christian CHURCH ART AND ARCHITECTURE. The massive work was created during the mid-1400s by Jan van Eyck for the Cathedral of St. Bavo to show the grandeur of CHRISTIAN PARADISE. Through heavy use of gold and bright colors, van Eyck achieves a glorious vision of heaven that is truly inspirational.

The top portion of the altarpiece features a regal JESUS Christ dressed in a red robe trimmed with gold and wearing a papal tiara. The risen king is seated on the throne of the divine with his mother, the VIRGIN MARY, beside him. Mary is likewise adorned in splendor in royal blue garments and crowned with jewels, roses, and lilies. Nearby, the Christian hero John, bedecked in emerald robes, takes his place among the gallery of SAINTS. A contingent of ANGELS, with dazzling golden garments trimmed in velvet brocade, completes the vision. The celestial attendants play harps of gold in tribute to the Almighty and his faithful servants.

The lower panel of van Eyck's creation shows the created world, pale and rather dreary in contrast to the bril-

Van Eyck's masterpiece. ART TODAY

liance of heaven. Earth is a mix of olive and brown, with sparse use of bright color. However, this is not a realm of sorrow, for the people of this muted scene are shown rejoicing at the vision above. The *Ghent Altarpiece* invites members of the congregation likewise to turn their eyes—and hearts—toward paradise and dedicate their lives to the pursuit of heavenly citizenship.

GHOST   One of the biggest box office successes of 1990 was the "afterlife love story" *Ghost*. The film offers an intriguing blend of romance, suspense, and supernatural fantasy while exploring the notion of ultimate justice. *Ghost* also speculates on the power of the human soul to love from beyond the grave.

Ghost stars Patrick Swayze as a young banker who is killed in an apparent mugging in front of his horrified girlfriend, played by Demi Moore. As Swayze's mutilated body slumps to the ground, a brilliant "tunnel of light" appears before him and seems to beckon him to enter. But Swayze refuses to leave Moore's side, and the mystic portal disappears.

Unable to communicate with her or with any other living person, Swayze soon discovers other "lingering souls" in the dimension between life and death. These spirits can see and hear him but are unable to help him make contact with Moore. One old man tells Swayze he is "waiting for my wife," a cardiac patient about to expire, so he can escort the woman to the world beyond. Another teaches Swayze how to use his spiritual energy to move objects in the physical world. And a smiling girl strolling through the cemetery where Swayze's body is being buried motions him to join her on the path to paradise.

But Swayze is determined to solve the mystery of his murder and to protect Moore from suffering a similar fate. He soon learns that he was not the victim of random violence but was killed as part of a plot to steal his bank's security codes. One of his coworkers, a trusted friend, has engineered a complex money-laundering scheme and needs the codes to complete his illegal transfers. When the killer fails to retrieve the correct numbers from Swayze, Moore becomes the hit man's next target.

Eventually Swayze's spirit defeats his betrayer with the help of a psychic (played by Whoopi Goldberg) and saves Moore from the villains. With all his unfinished business resolved, Swayze is ready to depart to the afterlife. The proverbial tunnel of light opens once again, revealing a myriad of bright spirits linked hand in hand. Before joining them, Swayze turns to Moore and exclaims, "The love inside, you take it with you," and promises they will enjoy a REUNION in the HEREAFTER on some distant day. The rosy glow of divine souls envelops him as the saved welcome their new compatriot to paradise.

The afterlife depicted in *Ghost* is a distinctly modern interpretation of paradise. There is no indication of a BEATIFIC VISION or judgment by any God, only the companionship of ANGELS and cleansed souls. This portrayal of supernatural events also draws images from recent tales of NEAR-DEATH EXPERIENCES in which the "dead" person is typically drawn into a tunnel of light and filled with incomparable joy.

Ghost was written by Bruce Joel Robbins, who has penned a number of cinematic interpretations of the next world, including BRAINSTORM, JACOB'S LADDER, and MY LIFE.

GIFT NOVELTIES Consumers can purchase a diverse array of trinkets and toys reflecting images of paradise and its creatures. Examples range from necklaces depicting OSIRIS and his ancient pyramids to paperweights showing JESUS reigning in CHRISTIAN PARADISE. Retailers offer entire series of COLLECTOR PLATES showing supernatural scenes, running the gamut from pious reproductions of traditional masterpieces to whimsical collages of ANIMALS in the HEREAFTER. There is even a Cracker Jack prize that depicts a "heavenly" California Angels baseball player perched on a cloud and plucking a harp.

Among the best-selling lines of divine merchandise in recent times are items depicting ANGELS. These celestial beings can be purchased in the form of key chains, lapel pins, stickers, stuffed toys, Christmas ornaments, and figurines. Their images adorn everything from coffee mugs to T-SHIRTS. Many decorations for ANGELWARE are borrowed from classic works of CHURCH ART AND ARCHITECTURE, such as the cherubs of the SISTINE MADONNA.

Other items are adapted from stories about the celestial realm. *The Littlest Angel*, a classic of CHILDREN'S LITERATURE, spawned a number of gift novelties.

Fans of the story of a little boy's attempt to fit into the society of paradise can purchase snow globes showing the sweet child sitting perched in heaven (when shaken, a flurry of stars swirls around his divine cloud), cassettes adorned with images of paradise, and even dolls of the Littlest Angel. Similar examples can be found in MOVIE MERCHANDISING of such cinematic heavenly adventures as ALL DOGS GO TO HEAVEN and BILL & TED'S BOGUS JOURNEY.

Gift novelties with roots in Christian tradition also cover a wide range of interests, from the serene to the silly. A plaque that shows two quaint country homes side by side is accompanied by a passage from the Bible recalling that, "In my Father's House are many mansions," adding the sentiment, "I hope yours is next to mine!" A lighthearted set of "inspiration refrigerator magnets" includes one that reads, "Heaven will be perfect . . . no Mondays!" complete with picture of man slouching over a cup of coffee. And a wooden angel bears a card that says, "I'm just pretend. I'm nothing like the angels that heaven really sends," and ends with the reassurance, "Jesus is your shepherd, and heaven is your home."

Then there are the somber, serene gifts recalling paradise. The Franklin Mint markets a statue of Jesus patterned after Renaissance master Raphael's *Transfiguration*. The porcelain-and-resin reproduction shows Christ in his resurrected radiance, which is believed by religious scholars to depict the GLORIFIED BODIES all saved humans will inhabit in paradise. Franklin Mint's tabletop version offers a blue-robed Jesus floating amid the clouds, arms open as if about to embrace his divine father.

All of these items reveal humanity's hunger for glimpses of heaven. And such trinkets, whether serious affirmations of church doctrine or amusing offshoots of divine lore, help fill that need.

GILES OF ROME (1247–1316) Giles of Rome was a pupil of THOMAS AQUIN-AS, although his conclusions about the afterlife differed greatly from those of his teacher. While Aquinas envisions a THEOCENTRIC HEAVEN where all energies are concentrated on worshiping God, Giles portrays the HEREAFTER as a place of eternal social interaction. His great joy in the world to come centers on exchanging concepts and theories in a symposium that never ends.

Like the Roman orator CICERO, Giles believed that all saved souls, no matter what their national origin, would speak a common language and thus could communicate without difficulty. Free of any language barriers, souls in heaven could engage in endless discourse, probe the mysteries of the universe, and delight in knowledge for its own sake. Giles's works describe such an afterlife of intellectual rather than purely spiritual joys, a paradise for the curious mind. His works were at odds with the contemporary teachings of Christianity; however, scholars considered his conclusions "worthy of debate" and refused to condemn the theories. The concept of eternal social interaction has since become a popular component of CHRISTIAN PARADISE.

GIMLI Gimli (Gimle) is the heaven of later Norse mythology, combining elements of pagan VALHALLA with doctrines of CHRISTIAN PARADISE. It is a realm where Odin (sometimes referred to as ALFADIR), the creator deity, dwells for all eternity. Those who have pleased Odin are welcomed into Gimli, where they enjoy great banquets and revelry. And unlike Valhalla—which is reserved solely for heroes slain in battle—Gimli is the reward for all souls who have lived lives of virtue.

The PROSE EDDA, the epic of Norse myth, says that the "righteous shall dwell with Alfadir in the place of Gimli" while "the wicked shall go to Hell." The work describes Gimli as a fantastic castle replete with ballrooms, banquet halls, and lush gardens. Here, spirits are eternal guests in a luminous palace "more dazzling than the sun."

GISLEBERTUS The TYMPANUM RELIEF, carved above the doorway to the Cathedral of St. Lazare, in Autun, France, was produced under the leadership of French sculptor Gislebertus between 1125 and 1136. It shows the LAST JUDGMENT, the event prophesied in the Christian Bible when all will be eternally consigned to either heaven or hell. Carved depictions on this theme became a component of almost every Gothic cathedral erected in Europe during the Middle Ages. The compositions were usually situated over the church entrances so the images of salvation and damnation could serve as constant reminders to the faithful about their impending death and inevitable adjudication.

Gislebertus uses images from the Bible, Christian tradition, and ancient myth to create a unique portrait of CHRISTIAN PARADISE and its many joys. The work features JESUS, the Redeemer, as the judge who will review every soul that has ever existed. At Christ's left hand, demons weigh the good and evil deeds of souls on a scale similar to the one described in the Egyptian BOOK OF THE DEAD. As the demons go about their work, ANGELS try to tip the balance in favor of salvation. Those who have passed this test are admitted to paradise, and their faces are alight with jubilation.

This work is significant in a number of ways. First, Gislebertus draws images from a number of distinct sources rather than simply interpreting a church doctrine or text of the Bible. The tympanum relief also is one of the first artworks of the Middle Ages that can be positively attributed to its creator. The artist, whose style is denoted by abnormally elongated human bodies and the extensive use of ruffled textures to create depth, signed his composition. Gislebertus's work is therefore important not only in the study of afterlife beliefs but also in the advancements of art during this time. It is a testament to the prominence given to the Last Judgment during the era, especially in works of CHURCH ART AND ARCHITECTURE.

GLORIFIED BODIES Many myth systems and religious teachings from throughout the world include the concept of glorified bodies for the saved. These perfect human forms are beautiful, free of imperfection, and impervious to disease, injury, hunger, and aging. Some version of this notion are found in descriptions of heaven from tales of Norse VALHALLA, Native American HAPPY HUNTING GROUNDS, ancient Persian ZOROASTRIAN HEAVEN, Islamic DJANNA, and many others.

The theory of glorified bodies in heaven flowered under Christianity. Believers contend that in CHRISTIAN PARADISE, the saved will have physical forms free of all human imperfections and weakness. These idealized incarnations will never decay or corrupt. And they will have heightened senses, enabling the blessed to enjoy sensual as well as spiritual pleasures in the world to come.

Many Christian scholars (including THOMAS AQUINAS, author of the SUMMA THEOLOGICA) contend that these exalted bodies will approximate thirty-three, the age at which Christ died and was resurrected in his own glorified form. The Bible describes this reunion of body and spirit: "One star differeth from another in glory. So also is the resurrection of the dead. It is sown in corruption; it is raised in incorruption. It is sown in dishonor; it is raised in glory: it is sown in weakness; it is raised in power. It is sown a natural body; it is raised a spiritual body. There is a natural body, and there is a spiritual body as well" (1 Cor. 15:41–44).

St. Paul, author of the above passage, elaborates on this concept in a later letter to the early Christians: "For our conversation is in heaven; from whence also we look for the Saviour, the

Lord Jesus Christ: who shall change our vile body, that it may be fashioned like unto his glorious body, according to the working whereby he is able even to subdue all things unto himself" (Phil. 3:20–21).

St. John also refers to glorified bodies in the Book of REVELATION, describing them as one of the rewards bestowed on the faithful. The inhabitants of paradise will assume these bodies after the LAST JUDGMENT, when JESUS affirms the eternal fate of everyone. This will take place at the end of time when the earth will be destroyed.

Glorified bodies are also mentioned in COMPENDIUM OF REVELATIONS and in CITY OF GOD by SAINT AUGUSTINE, as well as countless other Christian works. According to the theories, glorified bodies are particular to humans since they are made in God's image and will differentiate the saved from the ANGELS in eternity. And since many of Christ's miracles involve healing, in heaven all people will enjoy the ultimate freedom from all bodily imperfections.

Because of this strong belief that in eternity the saved will have their bodies restored and exalted, persecutors and those hostile to Christianity often burned the bodies of MARTYRS in defiance of this doctrine. They contended that since the flesh had been reduced to ashes, no reunion of body and soul could ever take place. For this same reason, cremation of corpses was forbidden by the Christian church as sacrilegious, and no one who had been cremated could be buried in hallowed ground. (That ban has since been lifted, as scholars now contend that a God powerful enough to raise and reunite body and soul could just as easily transform ashes into a glorious form.)

GOLDEN LEGEND, THE The Golden Legend is a compendium of biographies of the SAINTS written in the thirteenth century by Jacobus de Voragine, the archbishop of Genoa. It details the lives of scores of heroes and MARTYRS and illuminates the joys awaiting virtuous souls in CHRISTIAN PARADISE. The Golden Legend contains stories about the VIRGIN MARY, mother of JESUS, SAINT CECILIA, Saint Thais, SAINT AUGUSTINE, and a host of early MARTYRS to the faith.

Though never officially sanctioned by the church, The Golden Legend had a dramatic impact on contemporary literature and art involving Christian themes. Symbols of paradise mentioned in the legendary text, such as the dove, the palm branch, and the rose, began appearing with great frequency in religious poems, HYMNS, paintings, and sculptures. Images from this writ were also incorporated into BOOKS OF HOURS designed to help struggling Christians draw closer to God. After the Protestant Reformation, however, The Golden Legend waned in popularity, denounced by Protestant authorities as "trite," "fanciful," and riddled with "unsubstantiated accounts."

GOOD THIEF The Christian Bible is devoted to the salvation of humanity; however, it lists but a precious few people who have actually been saved. One is LAZARUS, the allegorical blind beggar who is left to starve outside the gates of a callous nobleman's home. Lazarus is a gentle, God-fearing man who finds only pain and suffering in this world, but joy and peace in the next. On the other end of the spectrum, the Gospels describe the unlikely salvation of one of the criminals crucified with JESUS on Calvary. According to the account, two thieves are condemned to death alongside Christ. One mocks Jesus, saying, "If you are a king as you say you are, save yourself, and us!" But the second thief rebukes his companion for this insult and meekly asks Jesus' forgiveness: " 'Do you not fear God, seeing as you too are about to die? And we justifiably so, for we are guilty, but this man has done nothing wrong.' And he turned to Jesus and said, 'Lord, remember me when you come into your kingdoms.' And Jesus replied unto him, 'This day, you shall be with me in paradise' " (Luke 23: 40–43).

This simple phrase has led to a great deal of speculation regarding the nature of CHRISTIAN PARADISE. Religious leaders use this passage as evidence of Christ's profound mercy, for even at the point of death a sinner can find forgiveness and redemption. It has also been advanced as proof that the dead do not "sleep" in their graves until the LAST JUDGMENT (as Martin Luther taught) but face heaven or hell immediately after death.

Whatever deeper meaning may lie in this touching story, its literal interpretation has stirred the hearts of many. In order to achieve salvation, one need only ask Christ to be admitted to his kingdom. This act of faith is the cornerstone of every Christian denomination.

GORGIAS The ancient Greek philosopher Plato wrote several works regarding humanity's ultimate destiny, including *Gorgias*. *Gorgias* describes the judgment a soul undergoes at the time of death and details both the pleasures of the happy afterlife and the torments of the underworld.

According to the text, Plato believes that the "naked soul," stripped of all earthly trappings, is judged by the "divine" in the spiritual realm. Plato envisions a complex system of rewards and punishments facing the spirit after death. Virtuous souls ascend to higher levels of fulfillment, whereas petty and self-centered spirits are condemned to purge their iniquity through a varying degree of tortures.

GOTTSCHALK OF HOLSTEIN The late twelfth-century German mystic Gottschalk of Holstein gave great attention to describing CHRISTIAN PARADISE to his contemporaries. According to his vision, heaven is the ultimate utopia, a peaceful city set with carefully sculpted gardens, sapphire streams, and bountiful orchards. The saved inhabit neatly arranged houses in paradise, which line crisp, geometric avenues. Surrounding this celestial city are jeweled walls, as strong and protective as they are beautiful. Within heaven's boundaries, blessed souls enjoy social interaction similar to village life on earth.

This depiction of paradise differs sharply from other portraits of heaven. *ELUCIDATION*, a text written a century before Gottschalk's time, describes paradise as a natural wonderland of vegetation, rivers, and simple beauty. The work rejects urban heaven, asserting that such material splendor is in conflict with the divine will. SAINTS, the book claims, should be naked as they were at the time of their creation, rather than robed in linen and silks. Gottschalk found this notion ridiculous and pointed out that God created the world—and everything in it—for humanity's use and enjoyment. Therefore, a paradise featuring "worldly goods" would be the ultimate fulfillment of the Almighty's plan.

Other contemporary preachers taught that in paradise there would be no materials at all, whether natural or cosmopolitan. Heaven, they claimed, is a purely spiritual realm where the saved are completely absorbed in the BEATIFIC VISION. Dwelling in God's presence is the one true joy; thus neither garden nor city is necessary for happiness. Many doctors of the Christian church, including SAINT AUGUSTINE, teach such an eternity, although Augustine allows for the *possibility* of pleasures beyond looking upon the face of God.

Gottschalk advanced his theories in direct opposition to these more esoteric depictions. He considered such bleak images of the eternal reward to be unappealing—even incomprehensible—to the masses. His paradise of linear streets, gilded gates, and "modern" splendor could be easily envisioned and embraced by both peasants and royalty alike.

GREAT DIVORCE, THE Acclaimed modern author C. S. Lewis once lamented that the great Christians who fought the Crusades or suffered to end slavery and other contemporary evils were gone, leaving a generation of mediocre mediators. "It is since Christians have largely ceased to think of the otherworld," he wrote, "that they have become so ineffective in this." He thus devoted much of his career to illuminating the faith of JESUS, from philosophical treatises such as *Mere Christianity* and *The Problem of Pain* to imaginative fiction works like *The Screwtape Letters* and the Chronicles of Narnia series. His *Great Divorce*, a stylized refutation of WILLIAM BLAKE's *Marriage of Heaven and Hell*, takes up the subject of the afterlife, depicting a HEREAFTER where every soul gets not what it deserves but what it craves.

The story opens in a dreary "grey town," where cantankerous spirits engage in a never-ending battle of insults and injury. A few weary residents gather at a bus stop awaiting a celestial vehicle that will take them on a trip to paradise. For some, it will be a day-long outing that will result in further bitterness toward self and society. For others, it will serve as the first step in finding salvation.

After a bumpy ride (really a "float") to loftier realms, the bus arrives in a verdant meadow more beautiful than any earthly vale. Lewis calls this the "Valley of the Shadow of Life." On the lush plain are majestic ANIMALS: "unicorns . . . white as swans," "velvet-footed lions," and scores of dogs, cats, and horses that have accompanied their owners to paradise. There are beings in this realm, too, lovely, luminous creatures dazzling to behold. In contrast to the murky, transparent "ghosts" of "grey town," these heavenly residents are "solid-people" and the ANGELS, "flaming spirits." One blessed spirit explains that "Heaven is reality itself," so the dimension of the divine is a physical as well as spiritual place. When the ghosts complain that walking through the meadow is painful, they are assured that "it will hurt at first" since "reality is harsh to the feet of shadows," but eventually they will "thicken" if they persevere.

The narrator of *The Great Divorce*, a man dreaming about the afterlife, witnesses several ghosts enjoying REUNIONS with departed loved ones. For every passenger who has journeyed from hell there is a corresponding Solid Person sent to invite the damned to remain in heaven. "Be happy and come with me," offers each magnificent soul; travel to the distant mountains of "Deep Heaven," where "you will see the face of God." Most of the ghosts, however, are more interested in complaining about their current circumstances than in improving them. Accepting the divine invitation would mean putting aside self-obsession, and they are not willing to do so. This, laments one of the Solid People, is the true tragedy of damnation: It is a choice embraced by many, even in the face of eternal joy.

Some do choose to make the difficult pilgrimage to the mountains and are assisted by the Solid People as well as powerful angels. Though they "cannot carry" new arrivals to their destination, the welcoming spirits offer a shoulder to lean on and a sturdy arm to hold. For redeemed souls who accept the celestial assistance to "leave that grey town behind," the dismal place was merely a sort of PURGATORY rather than hell. These spirits, who will remain eternally in heaven, have now purged themselves of the last residue of sin and can journey, unencumbered, to the highest levels of paradise.

In the text, Lewis poses several questions to the supernatural messengers through his characters. One asks if the saved can meet celebrities and heroes in heaven, noting that many on earth gleefully anticipate meeting history's elite in the afterlife. The celestial escort laughs at this notion, noting that "fame in this country and fame on Earth are two quite different things." He further explains that the vast majority of people who were idolized as living humans are anonymous in paradise, blending in with the millions of saved souls who have done nothing to particularly distinguish themselves in God's eyes. On the other hand, great parades and celebration often surround those whom few had ever heard of during the living years, virtuous souls who led quiet lives of extraordinary devotion. They are the heroes of heaven.

The author also brings up a common philosophical dilemma: How can the saved enjoy paradise if their loved ones are languishing in hell? The emissary of heaven responds that the damned have chosen their state, freely and willingly rejecting God and all his comfort, and will not reconsider. The Almighty will not save any soul against its will, but neither will he let "the makers of misery" inflict their agony on the saved by polluting paradise with misplaced pity. Thus the residents of heaven will recognize justice inherent in the divine plan and will not grieve for those who seek to "blackmail the universe" with their self-inflicted sorrow.

Lewis explores the nature of paradise further in his nonfiction works *The Problem of Pain*, *Miracles*, and *Mere Christianity*. He notes that all his ideas are simply "guesses" designed to "arouse factual curiosity about the details of the afterworld." He is quick to remind readers that if his speculations about the splendor of heaven are not true, "something better will be."

GREEN PASTURES, THE *Green Pastures*, the 1936 film adaptation of Marc Connelly's Pulitzer Prize–winning play, stirred great controversy and debate on its premiere. The movie recounts several episodes from the Bible through the perspective of contemporary "Negroes" viewing the happenings from heaven. Critics charged that it enforced negative stereotypes and insulted black Americans. Southern theater owners boycotted *Green Pastures*, objecting to the all-black cast and most especially the depiction of God as an African-American. Its supporters (acclaimed author Graham Greene among them) countered that the film's purpose is to elicit empathy for the injustice and oppression that black citizens had suffered over the centuries and to emphasize the unique relationship they have to biblical heroes who were likewise abused.

Green Pastures stars Rex Ingram as "de Lawd," a kind, genteel God who views his creations as beloved children. The film opens with a note from the pro-

ducers explaining that this project seeks to convey "that humble reverent conception" that since all humans are made in the image of the Almighty, he can accurately be portrayed as a member of any race. Paradise, too, can be portrayed as a reflection of particular desires, and in *Green Pastures* heaven is a "fish fry" picnic held in a lovely bucolic meadow. From this lofty realm, God and his ANGELS watch history unfold on earth, with less than pleasing results. Sorrowed by what he sees, "de Lawd" pays a number of visits to his faithful and his fallen.

After witnessing the sin of Adam and Eve, Cain's slaying of his brother Abel, and other atrocities, Ingram decides he must make his first journey to the earth to set things right. He leaves the beloved angel GABRIEL (played by Oscar Polk) "in command" of heaven and travels below to ask humans why they do not respect their divine father. Ingram is saddened to hear that most consider the Almighty to be "a God of wrath," stern and cold, who has lost his influence over humankind. At first he responds by declaring that he will abandon his children. But he is moved to pity by the unquestioning faith of many of his followers and at last concludes that "God must suffer too" and sends his son to carry the "heavy burden" of redemption.

Green Pastures depicts biblical heroes as well as metaphorical sinners. The watchers above view Noah on his ark, the courage of Joshua at the Battle of Jericho, and the martyrdom of the holy prophets by allies of Satan. Ingram goes in person to escort the soul of the patriarch Moses to paradise, a land he declares "a million times nicer than the Land of Canaan!" The spirits of Abraham, Isaac, and Jacob, now adorned in splendor, routinely appear before Ingram to remind the Almighty that despite the many sins of humanity, humans can indeed be pious and devoted to their heavenly Father.

Along with imaginative interpretations of religious events, *Green Pastures* also features several traditional components of paradise. White-winged angels ride clouds and lean on the PEARLY GATES as they enjoy their picnic. Through a Sunday school class, the film addresses the questions: Will there be ANIMALS in heaven? What do angels do all day? And, the most sublime speculation of all, what does God look like? Throughout the film, the comedy-drama is punctuated with beautiful HYMNS sung by the heavenly choir, praising "de Lawd" and extolling the pleasures of the afterlife. The result is a unique portrait of CHRISTIAN PARADISE that reminds believers that God made all races and fervently desires their happiness in this life and the next.

GREETING CARDS There are literally hundreds of "heavenly" greeting cards currently available, with new entries arriving daily. Such lofty communiqués allow friends and loved ones to exchange sentiments that go beyond the ordinary; they are, by virtue of their supernatural allusions, "divine." And whether they celebrate good news or seek to take the sting out of tragedy, this assortment of celestial greeting cards calls to mind a more perfect place where joy is unceasing.

Many cards offer whimsical caricatures of the blessed afterlife with puns or clichés about paradise. One example declares, "Our friendship was made in Heaven—they do good work there!" Another card of this type depicts a sky full of puffy clouds, shooting stars, and smiling cherubs. Inside, the message reads, "Congratulations! What heavenly news!" Other "divine greetings" mix a particular theme with images of paradise, such as a St. Patrick's Day card containing a poem about the blessings of the Irish, noting that "they keep company with ANGELS and bring a bit o'Heaven to earth."

Certain occasions lend themselves to heavenly metaphors. Birth announcements, for instance, often note that the new arrival "comes straight from heaven." These baby cards are usually accompanied by illustrations of smiling angels. Christmas cards are likewise perfect conduits for divine images since the holiday itself is about the joining of heaven and earth. A typical card shows a band of celestial spirits cavorting in star-filled skies, its message declaring, "Have a heavenly Christmas!" The Salvation Army distributes its own divine holiday greetings to those who donate to the annual kettle drive. These miniature greetings contain biblical quotes about CHRISTIAN PARADISE, uniting the notion of helping others on earth with the promise of "treasure in heaven."

Sympathy cards also invoke familiar icons of paradise. A condolence greeting from Hallmark describes the mystic

An assortment of "heavenly" greetings

journey parting souls take on their way to eternity. According to the text, when a person dies, an angel is dispatched to take the spirit "by the hand" and lead it down "the shining path" to a "place of light and love" where it will find eternal joy. A similar sympathy notice from American Greetings promises mourners a REUNION in heaven, where loved ones will "meet again in eternity."

The recent rise in popularity of angelic images on GIFT NOVELTIES has produced a deluge of notepaper, cards, stickers, and other stationery products incorporating graphics of these celestial beings. Now a prominent component of ANGELWARE, angel greetings have become so popular that there are now en-

tire lines of such cards offering a vast array of sentiments. One series, Heaven's Unofficial Greetings (H.U.G.'s), features supernatural guardians performing various kindnesses and conveying light-hearted messages.

Hallmark also has its Heavenly Collection, a line of cards covering wedding wishes to birthday greetings and everything in between. Entries in this series use various illustrations of paradise ranging from whimsical sketches of cloud-dancing angels to reverent reproductions of classic religious works. Abbey Press, a gift company specializing in Christian products, offers "inspirational" Easter cards that show glimpses of the promised paradise. They feature pictures of angel-filled skies; luminous meadows of ethereal beauty, and other divine imagery. Inside the greetings, verses from the Bible's Book of REVELATION and the four Gospels about the splendor of that eternal reward provide spiritual refreshment.

In a society that often seems hostile to religion and notions of God, these cards provide an outlet for soulful sentiments. And they offer hope—to both senders and receivers—that there is a "bigger picture" for humanity that includes citizenship in blessed eternity.

GREGORY THE GREAT (540–604) Gregory the Great, also called Gregory I, was the first monk in Christian history to be elected pope. Born of a wealthy Roman aristocracy, Gregory was more interested in spiritual riches than in material prosperity. After rejecting his life of luxury and joining a religious order, Gregory gave his vast fortune to the poor and dedicated himself to the faith of JESUS. He eventually wrote a clerical guide called *Pastoral Rule* that was used in monasteries for centuries.

A talented writer with a flair for the fantastic, Gregory penned numerous works concentrating on the nature of heaven and hell in a text entitled *Dialogues*. This collection of "discussions" between him and a deacon (standing in for SAINT PETER) focuses on miracles, doctrines, articles of faith, and other canons. *Dialogues* also offers numerous accounts of people who claimed to have "died" and visited the afterlife before being revived, making the text an important source of VISION LITERATURE of the period.

The pontiff is also credited with saving Rome from a devastating plague by calling on the powers of heaven. According to the legends, Gregory invoked the archangel MICHAEL when a horrific plague raged through Rome in 590. The newly elected pope led a massive procession through the streets of the city to ask for divine relief from the seemingly unstoppable sickness. When the assembly reached the tomb of Hadrian, a sacred place, Michael descended from heaven in response to the people's cries for help. The angel waved his fiery sword, then returned it to its sheath, symbolically signaling that the plague was over. Gregory and his followers were so grateful for this angelic intervention that they built a chapel at the site that stands to this day.

Among his other accomplishments, Gregory I is credited with dispatching a contingent of missionaries who converted Britain to Christianity and with strengthening the authority of the papacy throughout Europe. He has since been declared a Doctor of the Church, and the Gregorian chant is named in his honor. St. Gregory the Great's feast is celebrated on September 3.

GUY NAMED JOE, A Spencer Tracy stars as a World War II pilot killed in action in the 1943 film A *Guy Named Joe* (a reference to the slang that a "Joe" is a "good guy"). Unable to enjoy paradise due to "unfinished business" back on earth, Tracy leaves the company of ANGELS and returns to help his distraught love (played by Irene Dunne) overcome her grief and try to love again. In the process of mending her broken heart,

Tracy also helps save the life of fellow fighter pilot Van Johnson.

The heaven presented in *A Guy Named Joe* is a bustling realm of social interaction, bureaucracy, and celebration. In paradise, souls from all ages strike up new friendships or enjoy REUNIONS with departed loved ones. One contemporary British reviewer claimed this dynamic presentation of the world to come took the "sting" out of death by portraying a "good, busy, hearty HEREAFTER." This cinematic afterlife is also a place of tenderness and mercy, where the powers above take an avid interest in helping those on earth find happiness.

A Guy Named Joe was remade by Steven Spielberg in 1989 under the title *Always*. This glossy update features Audrey Hepburn as an angel in her final earthly role.

GWENVED   Gwenved is an ancient paradise believed to derive from pagan Celtic teachings. According to the old legends, human souls go through numerous incarnations, each time purging themselves of some inborn evil. Spirits who perfect themselves then eventually ascend to Gwenved, the "White Heaven," where they will be rewarded with eternal rest and great earthly pleasures.

H

HALO   The halo is a common artistic symbol used to indicate a citizen of CHRISTIAN PARADISE. Deriving from the Latin word for "clouds," halos were originally used in portraits of God and the ANGELS, then later extended to the Christian Redeemer JESUS, the SAINTS, patriarchs, MARTYRS, and Christ's mother the VIRGIN MARY. Those deemed worthy of this supernatural crown are shown with a brilliant ring of light above their heads. Luminous crowns of glory were replaced in later works with halos of gold, silver, or other precious metals.

At one time, the shape of the halo had specific significance to artists. Triangular halos adorned only God the Father, while his son Jesus often had a cruciform. Mary, the saints, and angels were given circular halos. A square halo indicated that the person shown was still living at the time the work was created (but sainthood was expected of this holy individual). Hexagon-shaped halos meant that the figure was a personification of some abstract notion such as piety, honesty, or wisdom. Over the years this shape-based system was abandoned, and all blessed souls were crowned with circular bands of glory.

During the Renaissance, artists began omitting halos altogether. In an era that emphasized the human joys of paradise over its divine rewards, these holdovers from medieval times seemed old-fashioned, even silly. Garments, possession, and accessories were used to convey the heavenly citizen's role or level of sanctity. The Virgin Mary, for example, often holds a PEACH, representing immortality. John the Baptist frequently appears wrapped in animal skins, since he lived as a hermit in the wilderness while on earth. Clerics wear their orders' vestments in paradise, and nuns their traditional habits.

In modern usage, halos are used to indicate dedication to virtue and strength of character. ANIMATED CARTOONS often depict angelic "consciences" complete with wings and halos, battling their demonic horned and pitchforked counterparts. Product ADVERTISING likewise adds a golden disk over items deemed beneficial to humankind, such as reduced-fat snacks or low-calorie sweets. Contemporary places of worship sometimes use halos in works of CHURCH ART AND ARCHITECTURE to convey a sense of brilliance and spiritual glory.

Deriving from the image of a luminous unearthly glow, the *halo* has become a modern meteorological term meaning a ring of light that surrounds the moon, sun, or other heavenly body, caused by light reflected in ice crystals in the atmosphere.

HANNELE'S ASCENT INTO HEAVEN

German playwright Gerhart Hauptmann offers a bittersweet vision of paradise in his 1893 drama *Hannele's Ascent into Heaven*. Combing elements of naturalism with a strong spiritual belief, Hauptmann creates a sad tale of a poverty-stricken child whose every day is a bitter struggle for survival. Unable to overcome the unrelenting onslaught of sickness, hunger, and despair, young Hannele finally succumbs. She perishes in a holy deathbed vision, seeing a compassionate JESUS reaching out his hand to her. The Savior welcomes her into his kingdom of CHRISTIAN PARADISE, promising that her time of suffering is over forever.

In Hauptmann's view, heaven represents both a comparison and a contrast to peasant life in late nineteenth-century Europe. The contrast is obvious: Heaven offers the happiness and security so sorely lacking in Hannele's life. And paradise holds the promise of unending joy, a marked difference from her current existence of perpetual sorrow where every day brings new agonies. The comparisons are more subtle. Most notable is the purity and innocence of Hannele herself, a luminous child whose inner beauty buoys the spirits of all around her. She personifies paradise, inspiring hope of something better that is yet to come.

Hauptmann's later works—which eventually won him the Nobel Prize for Literature in 1912—incorporate further interpretations of supernatural themes, although none more poignant than *Hannele's Ascent*.

HAPPY HUNTING GROUNDS

Many Native American tribes (especially of the western prairies) equate paradise with the Happy Hunting Grounds. These are lush supernatural fields laden with delicious fruit and herds of buffalo. In the Happy Hunting Grounds, everyone dwells in harmony and respects all other creatures. It is a realm of communal bliss and perpetual joy.

According to beliefs of the Cherokee, Algonquian, and Iroquois, spirits departing to the next world need to prove their worthiness to enter such a haven. They must demonstrate loyalty, kindness, or courage before ascending to this great beyond. One of the key ways spirits can show their benevolence is by intervening on behalf of the living. Members of the tribes therefore often ask the assistance of deceased spirits in sending a bountiful harvest or defeating enemies on the battlefield. Souls who comply are rewarded with admittance to the Happy Hunting Grounds, where they continue to watch over the affairs of their people.

References to the heaven of Native American belief appear in numerous SHORT STORIES, films, and other works of fiction. In Disney's 1953 animated feature *Peter Pan,* the villainous Captain Hook threatens to drown an Indian princess for refusing to aid his wicked schemes, warning, "There is no path through water to the Happy Hunting Grounds." This mythic place of eternal repose is also described in *Will I Go to Heaven?,* a contemporary work of CHILDREN'S LITERATURE, as an ongoing picnic replete with buffalo burgers, smiling ANIMALS, and peace pipes. And a scene in the 1990 film *Young Guns 2* depicts a "spirit horse" sent to carry the soul of a dying Indian (played by Lou Diamond Phillips) to his eternal reward.

HARDROCK CAFÉ Known for its lavish decorations focusing on the American pop culture music scene, the Hardrock Café restaurant chain has truly deified the "gods of rock'n'roll." Nowhere is this more apparent than in its Orlando, Florida, location, which adapts traditional CHURCH ART AND ARCHITECTURE to the café's unique format. The decor of Orlando's Hardrock is designed as a grand cathedral, patterned after baroque Christian churches of centuries past complete with ceiling frescoes, relics of the "SAINTS," and STAINED-GLASS WINDOWS of the genre's top icons.

The restaurant's vaulted ceiling portrays the hierarchy of contemporary music's biggest stars. Reminiscent of the patchworks scenes of MICHELANGELO's Sistine Chapel mural, the restaurant's collage features images of Mick Jagger and the Rolling Stones, the Beatles, Buddy Holly, and other legends of the art. Stained-glass windows depict Elvis Presley (complete with "crown of glory") and Chuck Berry, a patriarch of modern music. These and other famous faces are shown floating through the pastel sky like harmonious ANGELS, strumming their instruments and joining in the "heavenly choir."

HAWAIKI People of eastern Polynesia believe in a paradise called Hawaiki, which means "our homeland." At the time of death, the spirit leaves the body and begins a long pilgrimage toward Hawaiki. The road is beset by many dangers. Common folk almost never survive the journey and usually perish along the way. But the souls of chieftains, warriors, and other powerful humans can easily reach Hawaiki, where they become immortal. Survivors of the dead can help ensure safe passage by performing funerary rites in the name of the deceased and by making offerings to the gods.

HEART AND SOULS The 1993 comedy *Heart and Souls* combines the Eastern concept of transmigration of souls with the modern notion that spirits cannot enjoy paradise while they have "unfinished business" left on earth. The film stars Robert Downey Jr. as young man whose soul is "shared" by four departed spirits who died in a bus accident on the night he was born. Unable to find rest in the afterlife, this marooned quartet quietly inhabits Downey's body, until they realize that they can prevail on the man to conclude matters for them and help them move on to the next world.

Downey is, understandably, reluctant to let these disembodied souls posses his body in order to conduct their affairs. But it is clear that *he* will have no peace until they are exorcised, and this seems to be the only way to send them to the next realm. By the film's conclusion, all four manage to say good-bye to lost loves, comfort their orphaned children, and realize unfulfilled dreams. And they manage to save Downey's soul in the process. Having come to terms with earthly life, the deceased quartet ascends to a billowy, luminous heaven for a long-awaited celestial celebration.

HEAVEN CAN WAIT A 1978 update of the 1941 comedy HERE COMES MR. JORDAN, the modern tale *Heaven Can Wait* recounts the supernatural adventures of a football hero struck down in his prime. Warren Beatty plays a professional quarterback destined for greatness who is "taken" from his body by overanxious ANGEL Buck Henry, convinced that Beatty is about to suffer a very painful death. Henry then leads him to a celestial "way station" where he is told to board a shiny white jetliner headed for his "ultimate destination." Beatty protests that his time has not yet come, and the argument escalates to the point that angelic supervisor "Mr. Jordan" (played by James Mason) must intervene.

Mason checks the "records" (a ledger reminiscent of the "Book of Life" mentioned in REVELATION and discovers that Beatty has in fact arrived fifty years too early. The embarrassed novice "escort" admits that he snatched Beatty's soul prematurely and offers to return him to earth. But it's too late: Beatty's best friend has had him cremated. The distraught man then scatters the ashes, whispering, "I hope they got the best football team in America in heaven, and hope God makes you first string." Unwilling to give up his destiny (to be starting quarterback in the Super Bowl), Beatty begins searching for a suitable "replacement" body to live out his remaining years.

Heaven Can Wait incorporates a number of themes familiar to afterlife films. Several sequences allude to "tunnels of light" and other components of NEAR-DEATH EXPERIENCES in which clinically dead people visit the HEREAFTER, then revive to tell the tale. The movie also features angels as caretakers of human beings, a sentiment shared in IT'S A WONDERFUL LIFE and THE HORN BLOWS AT MIDNIGHT. And in a twist on "making amends" return-to-life movies such as HI HONEY, I'M DEAD and HEART AND SOULS, *Heaven Can Wait* offers a story in which the divine powers must correct their mistakes rather than demand that humans atone for their errors.

HEAVEN: THE ULTIMATE COMING ATTRACTION

Actress Diane Keaton explores concepts of the HEREAFTER in her 1987 documentary-style film *Heaven: The Ultimate Coming Attraction*. The movie blends lay notions of heaven, religious interpretations of the afterlife, and vintage film clips depicting the world to come. Keaton notes, "I think everyone has a shot at heaven," and offers this compilation as encouragement to viewers curious about eternity.

Opinions on what might await human souls on the other side of the grave run the gamut from seeing "the Lord God Almighty" to going to a place much "like New York, Chicago, or Miami." One woman looks forward to having "much better bodies" in the next realm, while another envisions "ANGELS flying around" a restored Garden of Eden. Controversial boxing promoter Don King makes a cameo appearance, affirming his belief in heaven and in God's mercy. A giggling girl remarks that "God is like Groucho Marx, constantly playing tricks on us."

Along with these somewhat convoluted snippets, *Heaven* features heavy emphasis on themes common to CHRISTIAN PARADISE. Many of those interviewed express belief in a REUNION of loved ones in heaven. There is likewise frequent reference to enjoying the BEATIFIC VISION and to inhabiting GLORIFIED BODIES throughout eternity.

Some participants describe being involved in supernatural events, including NEAR-DEATH EXPERIENCES and visits with the divine. One man claims firsthand knowledge that Christ is living in London "in a Pakistani community" where he is readying himself for "an international press conference" to announce his plan for humanity. Most, however, provide more lucid—and reasonable—comments concerning the mysteries of the human soul.

Balancing these views are comments by nonbelievers who consider the notion of heaven to be ludicrous. A frustrated dissenter, representing the atheist viewpoint, repeatedly shouts, "Can you *prove* that heaven exists?!," refusing to entertain the possibility of an afterlife without some scientific evidence. An equally exasperated minister replies that the Bible offers all the proof he needs and that God's word should be sufficient.

Movie footage used in *Heaven* includes clips from THE GREEN PASTURES, A GUY NAMED JOE, and other cinematic depictions of the world to come. But these scenes are inserted randomly with seemingly no rhyme or reason, more to fill time to illustrate a specific belief. Overall, *Heaven* provides no conclusions and endorses no particular doctrine. However the film does show the diversity of humanity itself, indicating that the mind of God is endlessly creative and suggesting that paradise will be likewise engaging.

HEAVENLY KID, THE

Lewis Smith plays a soul caught in LIMBO in the 1985 comedy *The Heavenly Kid*. After being killed in a car accident while drag racing, Smith is refused entrance to paradise since he has wasted his life and shirked his responsibilities. Meanwhile, back on earth, his pregnant girlfriend has borne a son who turns out to be a shunned loner with few prospects for a happy future. In a last attempt to prove himself worthy of heaven, Smith returns to the land of the living to help his now-teenage child resolve his mounting dilemmas.

One of the major weak points of *The Heavenly Kid* is the depiction of paradise as a haven for self-righteous tyrants obsessed with their own inherent superiority. Rather than a realm of mercy and forgiveness, the heaven of this film serves as a forum for demeaning others. It also flounders because Smith's hair, clothes, and expressions are decidedly 1950s: He looks like a clone of *Happy's Days*'s Fonzie. But the accident that took Smith's life supposedly occurred in the late 1960s when American fashion was tie-dyed shirts and bell bottoms, not black leather jackets and white cotton T-shirts. The combination of petty paradise and incoherent chronology makes *The Heavenly Kid* seem anything but divine.

Sealing its doom at the box office, *The Heavenly Kid* was also compared to the classic musical CAROUSEL, with which it could not possibly compete. Both had similar plotlines regarding wayward fathers who must return from the dead to help their children in order to gain entrance to paradise, and *Carousel* was vastly more artistic, imaginative, and appealing.

HENRY, SAINT One of the most bizarre afterlife legends involving a Christian saint concerns St. Henry, the tenth-century emperor and husband of St. Cunegund. According to the tale, Cunegund wished to consecrate herself body and soul to God and begged her husband to respect her wishes. In deference to her piety, Henry agreed, and both took vows of chastity on their wedding day. Over time, however, Henry began to suspect that his wife was having an affair with a corrupt confessor. He confronted her with his accusations, and when she denied them he slapped her and called her a liar. At that moment, the sky opened and JESUS cried out that his mother, the VIRGIN MARY, knew that Cunegund was still a virgin and had never even entertained lustful notions. Henry wept and begged for forgiveness from both his wife and the savior.

Upon his death, however, Henry was still haunted by the memory of his wicked treatment of the virtuous Cunegund. As he lay dying, he saw a "host of vile demons" coming to bear his soul to hell. He begged the intercession of St. Lawrence, whom he credited with helping him win great victories on the battlefield. St. Lawrence then appeared and approached the "scales of divine justice" (similar to those of the pagan OSIRIS) and placed a dish of gold on them, tipping the balance in favor of Henry. Seeing this, the demons cringed away, and Henry's soul escaped to PARADISE.

Cunegund then entered the convent and remained chaste for the rest of her life. She eventually died and joined her husband in heaven, where the two enjoyed a great REUNION at the throne of God. St. Henry's feast is celebrated on July 15.

HEREAFTER The term *hereafter* has become virtually synonymous with heaven in modern usage. It originally derives from biblical references to the next life and prophecies of things not yet seen. In the Book of REVELATION, the Christian Redeemer JESUS instructs St. John to: "Write the things which thou hast seen, and the things which are, and the things which shall be hereafter" (Rev. 1:19).

Following this directive, Jesus describes to the evangelist the wonders that will occur at the end of the world, including the impending LAST JUDGMENT, the damning of the wicked, and the celebration of the saved in paradise. The term *hereafter* has since become a secular expression referring to the pleasant afterlife.

HERE COMES MR. JORDAN The 1941 film *Here Comes Mr. Jordan* is based on the premise that even in heaven, mistakes are made. In this case, one overzealous guardian ANGEL (referred to as "Heavenly Messenger #7013") takes the soul from a young boxer (played by Robert Montgomery), certain that the man is about to suffer a brutal death. He then delivers the spirit to PARADISE, a billowy realm of puffy clouds and misty smoke. But when Montgomery arrives in the afterlife, he insists that his departure from earth was premature. Supervising angel Mr. Jordan (played by Claude Rains) checks the records, and sure enough, Montgomery is not scheduled to arrive in paradise for another fifty years.

To right this celestial wrong, Rains offers to return Montgomery to his body but is thwarted when the he discovers that the boxer's remains have been cremated. His only other option is to find Montgomery a new body to inhabit for the remainder of his lifespan. Montgomery reluctantly agrees and goes about selecting a new carcass to inhabit.

Here Comes Mr. Jordan won the 1941 Academy Award for Best Original Story and Best Screenplay. Its creators went on to produce FOR HEAVEN'S SAKE, the tale of two angels who descend from paradise to help a troubled couple save their marriage. *Here Comes Mr. Jordan* was remade in 1978 by Warren Beatty under the title HEAVEN CAN WAIT.

HERMES Hermes (called Mercury in Roman mythology) is the Greek god who escorts souls to the land of the dead. He is the son of Zeus and Maia. In some legends, he also helps judge spirits to determine their fate in the afterlife. His role is similar to that of the Egyptian ANUBIS, who conducts departing souls to the next world and aids OSIRIS in sentencing them.

The deity Hermes appears in a variety of ancient texts, such as Virgil's AENEID and Homer's *Odyssey*. He is sometimes called the god of commerce, science, and invention, as well as the protector of travelers in strange lands. This association with safe journeys helped secure Hermes as the escort of spirits to the afterlife.

HIGH PLAINS OF HEAVEN The High Plains of Heaven is the paradise of Japanese belief. According to ancient legends, it is a land of abundant fruit and sweet rivers where souls enjoy unending bliss. Over the years, notions of the High Plains of Heaven have been mingled with other stories involving Buddha and reincarnation. Many now consider the High Plains of Heaven to be a place of temporary respite where spirits rest before rejoining the ongoing life cycle.

HIGHWAY TO HEAVEN Michael Landon created, wrote, directed, produced, and starred in *Highway to Heaven*, the 1980s television series about wandering "probationary ANGELS" helping humanity. Landon plays a celestial adjunct dedicated to helping lost souls find their way back to God. (The character is patterned according to EMANUEL SWEDENBORG's concept that virtuous humans transform into angelic form in the afterlife.) But before being admitted into PARADISE, Landon must fulfill his mission of assisting others on the road to salvation.

In each episode Landon travels to a new location to convince others to give peace, love, and understanding a chance. The show opens with a shot of heaven, symbolized by a turquoise sky rippled with a blanket of white clouds, a dazzling burst of sunshine at its center. Landon quietly emerges from the proverbial "tunnel of light" to drift toward yet another bankrupt farmer, impoverished widow, or ill child. Along with the serious message about human decency, scripts are also peppered with lots of tongue-in-cheek

references to the HEREAFTER. Landon often quips that "my boss" (God) is generous, patient, and wise. And the angel himself performs small miracles in the completion of his missions, such as making food appear in an empty refrigerator or undoing a lock without a key.

Highway to Heaven aired weekly from September 1984 to August 1989, when Landon ceased production due to health problems. Throughout the show's five-year run, Landon was careful to prevent his series from becoming overly preachy or saccharine, even lambasting his own past theatrical efforts. The most notable was the October 1987 episode "I Was a Middle-Aged Werewolf," a wry parody of Landon's 1957 cinematic debut *I Was a Teen-age Werewolf*. By laughing at his own works, Landon promotes his message that paradise is a realm of genuine joy and laughter, not a somber realm of cold worship and colorless adoration.

Highway to Heaven is similar to such films as IT'S A WONDERFUL LIFE and FOR HEAVEN'S SAKE, which portray angels on divine missions to help their earthly brethren.

HI HONEY, I'M DEAD During the late 1980s and early 1990s, films about the afterlife and the endurance of human relationships beyond the grave enjoyed immense popularity. This obsession with supernatural adventures produced such theatrical releases as GHOST, BILL & TED'S BOGUS JOURNEY, MADE IN HEAVEN, HEART AND SOULS, and *Switch*. Encouraged by this trend, Hollywood began producing made-for-television movies with similar afterlife themes.

Hi Honey, I'm Dead, which aired in 1991, stars Kevin Conroy as an arrogant, self-absorbed real estate developer who dies suddenly and finds himself in the HEREAFTER. Heaven in this drama is a rather mundane way station where a soul's actions are reviewed before judgment is rendered (reminiscent of the courts of the Egyptian OSIRIS or Asian YAMA). For Conroy, the decision is not good: He is sentenced to return to earth to atone for his pettiness and vanity. He reincarnates in the body of a "working stiff" (played by Curtis Armstrong) and begins trying make amends to his wife (Catherine Hicks) and son (Joseph Gordon-Levitt) for years of neglect and abuse. Assisting him in this task is comedian Paul Rodriguez as a wisecracking ANGEL assigned to help Conroy make the transition from pompous nihilist to loving family man.

Hi Honey, I'm Dead presents a whimsical look at the afterlife, buoyed by notions of mercy and second chances. Similar films that focus on the next world as a place for "making amends" include CAROUSEL, *THE HEAVENLY KID,* and *HEART AND SOULS.*

HILARY OF POITIERS, SAINT
(born ca. 315) St. Hilary of Poitiers, a Doctor of the Church, French bishop, and influential writer on theology and philosophy, had a unique brush with heaven that almost cost him his own life. According to one legend, Hilary begs God to take his wife and daughter up to heaven to spare them life's cruelty and pain. The two soon die, and Hilary is accused of their murders.

In another tale, Hilary helps King Clovis and the Franks defeat the invading Aryan hordes of Alaric. Years after his death, the courageous Hilary appeared to Clovis with an army of ANGELS he called the "Lord's hosts" and vowed to help Clovis "deliver thy foes" and triumph over them. Using this as a battle cry, the Franks rallied and repelled the Aryan forces. King Clovis dedicated the victory to Hilary and demanded that homage be paid to the saint. Hilary's feast day is celebrated on January 14.

HILDA, SAINT
(614–680) St. Hilda, a seventh-century Northumbrian princess, dedicated her life and her considerable fortune to "living the word of JESUS," the Christian Messiah. She became abbess of Whitby Abbey and assisted countless souls in drawing closer to God. According to the legends, Hilda is so holy that upon her death, the woman's pristine soul was borne into heaven by a legion of ANGELS, similar to the ASSUMPTION of the VIRGIN MARY.

Hilda remains a venerated saint in the Roman Catholic church. Her feast day is celebrated on November 17.

HILDEGARD OF BINGEN
(1098–1179) Born in medieval Germany, Hildegard of Bingen was a quiet, intelligent girl who knew at a very young age that she wanted to live out her life as a nun. She entered the convent while still in her teens and quickly gained a reputation as a powerful mystic. Even in her youth, she experienced visions and offered prophecies of the future. This supernatural ability drew extensive notori-

ety, and she was often called the "Sibyl [priestess/seer] of the Rhine." These episodes would continue until her death in 1179. She used these as inspiration for scores of poems, sermons, HYMNS, and a MORALITY PLAY.

While in the convent, Hildegard spent the majority of her time in deep prayer and mediation on the mysteries of the divine. During these prayer sessions, she occasionally saw troubling images of hell as well as beautiful apparitions of paradise. In her book *Nosce Vias Domini* (Know the Ways of the Lord), or *Scivias,* she recounts twenty-six supernatural visions and the images that came to her while in the trancelike state.

In her writings, Hildegard describes heaven as a royal court where the SAINTS are dressed in "garments of silk." Each is adorned in splendor according to his or her merits, and all are gathered around the throne of the divine. The ultimate joy of PARADISE is the BEATIFIC VISION; the blessed are enraptured with looking on the face of God. Hildegard envisions the Almighty as a brilliant, radiant disk surrounded by nine concentric circles of ANGELS. (This image bears striking similarities to the beatific vision described in Dante's DIVINE COMEDY: THE PARADISO.)

Because of her reputation as a mystic, Hildegard was constantly sought by popes, nobles, and kings to give advice on matters of religion and politics. She traveled extensively throughout the Rhineland and founded several convents and abbeys. During these travels, Hildegard made many enemies by reprimanding corrupt clerics and unjust monarchs who were treating the poor

unfairly. She further upset church authorities by allowing a man who had been excommunicated to be buried on sacred ground. But the virtuous woman insisted that he be given a Christian burial, noting that only God is able to judge the state of his soul accurately.

Although Hildegard was never officially declared a saint, she is still highly revered in areas along the Rhine. Pope John Paul II has called her an "outstanding saint," and recordings of her hymns and musical compositions continue to be popular throughout the world.

"HILLBILLY HEAVEN" Country-Western singer Marty Robbins offers a touching tribute to his departed colleagues in his 1993 song "Hillbilly Heaven." The lyrics recall a wondrous dream in which the singer "sees" a host of deceased country performers enjoying paradise. Robbins recites a litany of country singers and celebrities and is thrilled with the prospect of enjoying a REUNION of his beloved idols in the world to come.

According to the lyrics, Robbins is standing at the PEARLY GATES when the deceased patriarch of country music, Hank Williams, pulls up in a limousine. Williams then takes Robbins on a tour of "Hillbilly Heaven," where the two speak with a variety of past stars. Robbins greets some of his heroes, such as Patsy Cline, and checks on acquaintances who have recently died. He remarks with great joy that among the blessed are "Keith Whitley" and "Reba McIntyre's band," noting that "they were all friends of mine."

Before returning Robbins to the realm of the living, Williams offers the young singer some advice on maintaining happiness while achieving fame. The elder then bids Robbins good-bye and heads off for his one true delight: performing in concert for the divine.

HOLY TRINITY The composition *Holy Trinity* is the focal point of the Church of St. Johannes Nepomuk in Munich, Germany. The massive cathedral was designed, built, and decorated by brothers Cosmas Damian Asam and Egid Quirin Asam between 1733 and 1746 next to the family's grand estate. The purpose of this architectural marvel was to present the glory of heaven to the masses. Inside the church are numerous examples of CHURCH ART AND ARCHITECTURE including lavish paintings and intricate carvings of supernatural beings, most notably the polychrome woodwork *Holy Trinity*.

This imaginative piece features a carving of the Godhead suspended from the ceiling above the high altar. The positioning of the Father, Son, and Holy Spirit represents their eternal place at the center of heaven. Each figure is carved in painstaking detail. God the Father is presented as an elderly patriarch, JESUS Christ as a vigorous youth, and the Holy Spirit as a magnificent bird. The three originate from the same base to show their unity as one God in three persons.

The ceiling immediately behind this sculpture is covered with a painted interpretation of heaven. A chorus of adoring ANGELS swirls in rapt attention in the background praising the master. Light from an unseen source illuminates the composition, creating the illusion that the *Holy Trinity* is glowing from within. Churchgoers cannot help but lift their gaze to this amazing spectacle and ponder how much more luminous and beautiful true paradise must be. The *Holy Trinity* mixed-media composition remains one of the most compelling depictions of the BEATIFIC VISION ever created.

HORN BLOWS AT MIDNIGHT, THE Jack Benny stars as one of heaven's most famous ANGELS in this 1945 comedy about celestial matters. Benny plays an aspiring trumpet player in the "Paradise Coffee" radio orchestra, who falls asleep in the studio one night and dreams he is the archangel described in the Bible's Book of REVELATION. According to the text, an angel sent from above will blow GABRIEL's horn to signal the end of the world and set in motion a series of cataclysmic events culminating in the LAST JUDGMENT. In his dream, Benny assumes the role of this divine emissary.

The heaven of Benny's dream sequence is a bureaucracy that resembles a typical government office, complete with huge file cabinets, endless red tape, and photo IDs. In paradise, Benny serves as a trumpet player in the massive choir of angels, before the "Director of Small Planet Management" summons him for a special mission. He is told that earth has become totally "out of hand" and that the celestial guardians have been told to "slap it apart." The planet's destruction will occur after Benny blows "the first four notes of the Judgment Day overture" with his enchanted horn. The "chief" of operations then dispatches him to the Hotel Universe via a mystic elevator to complete his task.

In the film, Benny and others make frequent JOKES about the nature of heaven. One character examines a one-dollar bill and remarks how happy George Washington will be when they return to tell him about seeing his picture on the currency. Benny laughs about being admitted through the PEARLY GATES as reward for his virtue and musical talent. And when the angel sits in with a dance hall band, the tune they play is a jazzed-up version of the Christian HYMN "Swing Low, Sweet Chariot," which anticipates a divine escort into paradise. There are also jokes about conveying messages to SAINTS and to biblical heroes upon returning to the great beyond.

One of the prominent themes in *The Horn Blows at Midnight* is the notion that in heaven human souls are elevated to angelic status and can earn rewards for successfully completing celestial missions. This concept has been advanced by such philosophers as EMANUEL SWEDENBORG and WILLIAM BLAKE, both of whom taught that in paradise humans become angels and can ascend to higher levels of spiritual fulfillment. The "divine reward" system has also received fictional treatment in such television shows as HIGHWAY TO HEAVEN and in the movie IT'S A WONDERFUL LIFE.

HOURI The houri are beautiful maidens promised to the faithful in DJANNA, Islamic heaven. According to the KORAN, the sacred text of Islam, in paradise the saved will receive the favors of these "dark-eyed virgins" whose beauty surpasses that of any creature on earth. Each man will receive seventy-two houri, who will fulfill all physical and spiritual needs. These lovely beings will be forever young and attractive and have no other purpose than to serve their masters.

HYMNS Songs of reverence and supplication to supernatural beings have been part of religious rituals for centuries. They are especially significant in funerary rites, as they are believed to send the deceased to the next realm with respect, celebration, and holy fear. Ancient civilizations sang about the unknown wonders of the great beyond, extolling the virtues of OSIRIS, ENLIL, and YAMA. AVESTA, the sacred book of the prophet ZOROASTER, dedicates much of its centuries-old text to GATHAS (songs) praising AHURA MAZDA in ZOROASTRIAN HEAVEN. And since the founding of Christianity, countless SAINTS have penned beautiful songs describing God in his glorious heaven. The practice of "making a joyful noise unto the Lord" persists.

Modern hymns describe every aspect of CHRISTIAN PARADISE. Standards such as "In the Sweet By and By," "Shall We Gather at the River," and the "Glory Song" all expound on the varied pleasures of eternity. A hymn dating back to the early 1700s by Isaac Watts declares:

There is a land of pure delight
Where the saints immortal reign
Infinite day holds back the night
Where pleasure replaces pain.

Sheet music from a hymn about
Jesus Christ's arrival in paradise

In America, lyrical interpretations of
paradise often reflected social conflicts.
The Civil War led to the writing of
"Battle Hymn of the Republic," which
equates the wartime violence of Union
troops with the "second coming" of JESUS,
an event prophesied in REVELATION. According to the lyrics, "mine eyes have
seen the glory of the coming of the Lord"
to destroy the wicked (slave owners) and
escort the blessed (northern troops) to
heaven. The very institution of slavery
likewise produced a deluge of spirituals,
songs written and sung by the oppressed
slaves and their descendants anticipating
justice in the world to come. Victims of
this Supreme Court–sanctioned atrocity
looked toward a utopia where all people
would indeed be considered equal. Until
the Dred Scott decision was overturned,
death was the only thing most black
Americans had to look forward to.

Since dying meant finding freedom,
the notion of heaven became a popular
topic for musical speculation. The song
"Sit Down" describes a newly arrived
soul's excitement at entering the HERE-
AFTER. Its lyrics tell of a man so entranced
by the lovely SAINTS and beautiful ANGELS
that he is unable to sit still. His celestial
welcomers encourage him to relax, but all
the happy spirit wants to do is "to look
around." The verses ask and answer a variety of questions, ranging from inquiries
about biblical heroes to a request for a
meeting with the Almighty. Another traditional spiritual, "God's Trombones," describes Jesus sending Death down from
heaven on a winged stallion to fetch the
souls of the saved into paradise.

Other American hymns about the
afterlife seek to translate the concept of
eternity into more mainstream terms.
The perennial favorite "Amazing Grace"
attempts to convey the vast sense of eternal life. Its lyrics explain that "when
we've been there ten thousand years" we
still have "no less days" to worship the
Almighty "than when we first begun."

Some songs anticipate specific pleasures of paradise, such as "Yes, I Shall
Arise," which describes the BEATIFIC VI-
SION. The words of this hymn joyously
describe the long-awaited time when "I
shall gaze upon the loveliness of God
forever more." Similar songs express
elation at the prospect of dwelling with
the saints, angels, and the VIRGIN MARY,
mother of Christ.

Perhaps the most common theme relating to Christian paradise is the sense of
"coming home." Many Christians look
forward to a grand REUNION in heaven

with lost loved ones. This sentiment is reflected in hundreds of hymns. "Out of Darkness" proclaims that the Almighty loves "to take His people home" where believers will be "claimed by Christ as God's own." The time-honored classic "Oh God, Our Help in Ages Past" echoes this belief, calling the divine realm "our shelter from the stormy blast and our eternal home" where the blessed will live forever in harmony.

Because of their allusion to heaven, hymns are frequently used as background music for films about the afterlife. Examples range from the poignant classic the *GREEN PASTURES* to the offbeat documentary *HEAVEN: THE ULTIMATE COMING ATTRACTION* to the modern comedy-drama *MICHAEL.*

Page from an illuminated manuscript
ART TODAY

ILLUMINATED MANUSCRIPTS

Artistic interpretations of heaven have been appearing on illuminated manuscripts for millennia. The earliest of these highly decorated texts date to approximately 2000 B.C., when Egyptian scribes adorned their religious writings with images of OSIRIS, ANUBIS, the judgment of the dead, and the complex afterlife of the pharaohs and aristocracy. These first editions were etched on papyrus rolls and eventually were replaced with ornate parchment scrolls. The detailed decorations helped illustrate intricate supernatural doctrines and gave the largely illiterate masses a glimpse at paradise.

Christian illuminated manuscripts began appearing around the sixth century. They began in the Byzantine style, a form of Greek with oriental influence resulting in dazzling pictures and ornate type styles. Early Christian versions—usually texts of the Bible or stories of the lives of SAINTS—were painted individually by hand on vellum, and the tiny pictures of heaven, hell, and religious events were dubbed "miniatures." The books had intricate borders of ivy, delicate patterns, or majestic flowers. Each edition took months, sometimes even years, to complete and led to the creation of monasteries dedicated exclusively to studio arts. Creating illuminated manuscripts became a talented monk's life work.

Like the ancient examples, Christian illuminated manuscripts first emerged in Egypt and Syria where the artform had been around for centuries. But it was not until the practice spread to Eastern Christendom and finally to Italy and Western Europe that these one-of-a-kind creations reached their zenith. The greatest artists spent their lives penning BOOKS OF HOURS for wealthy patrons and high officials. With their lavish illustrations of heaven and perfect rows of religious text, books of hours were as important to worship as traditional liturgical texts. A typical edition employed heavy use of gold and bright colors to convey the "glory of the divine."

As new religions emerged and literary trends progressed, the practice of creating highly decorated texts spread. By the ninth century, editions of the Islamic KORAN and Hindu BHAGAVADGITA incorporating extravagant pictures became popular throughout the regions where these religions were practiced. The faithful were enthralled with images of Islamic DJANNA and of legendary Indian paradises contained on the pages.

The custom of creating these handmade masterpieces largely died out in the sixteenth century due to the advent of engraving. New printing methods meant that hundreds of copies could be produced from the same original, making inexpensive editions available to the masses. Some wealthy patrons continued to commission individual books, but monasteries dedicated to creating illuminated manuscripts began disappearing. The invention of the printing press killed off illuminated manuscripts altogether by the eighteenth century. Today, surviving examples such as LES TRÈS RICHES HUERES DE DUC DU BERRY offer a look at the stunning artwork that helped shape generations of afterlife belief.

IMMORTALITY OF THE SOUL Religious scholar Henry More penned *Immortality of the Soul* in 1659. The book is a collection of poetry, prose, and essays about heaven. Included in the text are references to Christian doctrines, ancient mythological beliefs, and legendary heroes such as Dido and Aeneas, the ill-fated lovers from Virgil's epic AENEID. *Immortality of the Soul* also features descriptions of ANGELS and their glorious celestial celebrations.

More's overall conclusion is that the souls in PARADISE enjoy exclusively spiritual joy. He rejected the notion of GLORIFIED BODIES, claiming that there would be no material existence in the next life. Heaven's pleasures are purely intellectual delights. *Immortality of the Soul* includes lengthy descriptions of celestial ecstasy resulting from pursuing knowledge, communicating with past philosophers, and speculating on the divine.

Both human and angelic spirits are described as ethereal beings who "sing, play and dance" metaphorically. According to More's viewpoint, there is no great garden or gilded city in the clouds, only a realm of luminous spirituality where humanity's higher nature will find true fulfillment.

INKOLWE The Bazela of Zaire believe that after death spirits take their place in a hierarchy of ancestors. Inkolwe (firstborn) were the first men to die and thus having been dead the longest are the highest order and have inhabited this

AFRICAN PARADISE since its creation. The society of the next world mirrors life on earth: Each person has duties and roles similar to those enjoyed while living. There is much respect and admiration of the Inkolwe among both the living and the dead, since only the most deserving souls are elevated to this lofty status.

INTERROGATION OF THE DEAD
Thought it is not an official doctrine, many Muslims believe in the interrogation of the dead. This is the time of the soul's judgment and sentencing in the afterlife. The myth of this divine accounting is believed to be derived from the teachings of Zoroastrianism, which predominated Persia in the days before Islam.

According to tradition, after a person is buried and all mourners have left the graveside, the ANGELS MUNKAR and NAKIR come to examine the dead person's soul. They pose a series of questions to the departed; "Who is God?" "What is his word?" and "Who is his prophet?" The righteous soul responds that "ALLAH is the Lord God, Islam is the true religion, and MUHAMMAD is God's true prophet." Upon hearing these answers, the angels open the gates of DJANNA (heaven) and allow safe passage.

Infidels, however, are unable to respond correctly. After having lived empty lives set against the will of Allah, the souls are weak and confused and do not have the truth within them. They are deposited at the gates of hell, where the angels and all who are just abandon them.

The heat and pestilence of the underworld come up to claim these souls, crushing them in their graves.

The interrogation of the dead is denounced as heresy by some Muslims, since the KORAN clearly states that every person's acts are accurately recorded in the Divine Scrolls. These are Allah's own records, which will be read at the time of judgment. Since such flawless accounts are kept, there is no need to rely on an interrogation to determine who is saved and who is damned.

IRENAEUS, SAINT (ca. 125–202)
Irenaeus served as the bishop of Lyons. He was a Christian philosopher who sought to explain the joy of paradise in human terms. According to his theory, heaven is the compensation one receives for enduring injustice in this lifetime. In his version of paradise, humans have every material and spiritual need fulfilled, and there is no more pain of any kind.

Irenaeus's conclusions about the nature of heaven were based heavily on his unpleasant experiences at the hands of anti-Christian authorities. He survived numerous attacks by pagan forces (most notably Roman soldiers) and spent much of his adult life in hiding. During this time, countless Christians were tortured and killed for refusing to renounce their faith in JESUS Christ. Many were burned to ashes or thrown to the lions to mock the Christian concept of a LAST JUDGMENT at which time the body and soul are believed to be reunited. Irenaeus reassured his followers that in the next world, all would be more than re-paid for the years stolen from them by their persecutors.

The bishop of Lyons enumerated his theories in AGAINST HERESIES, an exten-sive treatise about the afterlife. His work asserts that all matter is good, since it is created by God, and therefore paradise is a place of great material reward. In heaven, humans receive eternal life rich in sensual delights. Irenaeus described the rewards of paradise not as an eleva-tion to higher spiritual plains but rather the ultimate natural existence.

ISIS   Isis is the Egyptian sister-wife of OSIRIS, the lord of the dead. She is men-tioned throughout the BOOK OF THE DEAD as a devoted and loving mistress of Osiris and a powerful afterlife force. Many of the prayers and incantations in the text focus on finding joy in the next world through Isis's benevolence. In some leg-ends, Isis has the power to restore the dead to life and to protect the living from harm. She can also summon the sun god RA from heaven to aid her in her en-deavors.

An ancient myth describes how Isis's brother Set kills Osiris and scatters his mutilated corpse throughout Egypt. Isis then gathers all the pieces, binds the corpse with linen strips, and restores her husband to life through enchanted incantations. (Osiris is the first Egypt-ian mummy; future pharaohs were buried similarly wrapped with shredded cloth to win his favor in the afterlife.) She then joins Osiris in the underworld, helping him judge souls and mete out

punishments and rewards in the world to come.

Isis became one of the most revered deities of ancient myth. Great festivals in her honor marked the planting and harvesting of crops, as she is also identi-fied with fertility. The goddess is some-times compared to the VIRGIN MARY, mother of the Christian Messiah JESUS. Both women have been called "lady of heaven" and are said to have mystic abilities. Isis is also featured in Mozart's opera, THE MAGIC FLUTE.

ISLAMIC HEAVEN, see DJANNA.

ISLE OF THE BLEST   has been used by several cultures to describe the paradise of the next world. Greek mathemati-cian Pythagoras refers to an Isle of the Blest located in the moon. Souls must soar there after purging the residue of life on earth, but they are hindered by evil intermediaries who try to destroy the spirits. Only by performing magic rites and rituals during one's lifetime could a soul preserve itself from these dark forces.

Both Plato and CICERO also described an Isle of the Blest lying somewhere be-yond the stars. Plato's theory is that the physical body weighs down the soul, and that at death, the soul is free to ascend to the heights. The pure spirit becomes stronger as it rises, eventually arriving in paradise. There, it takes up existence in the "realm of ideas" (but not with the gods, who inhabit a separate haven). Souls were free to return to the earth to visit loved ones or observe human events.

Isle of the Blest is also the name of the joyful island of supernatural delight from Briton legend, derived from the ancient Celtic paradise TIR NA N'OC. Like many other versions of heaven, the Isle of the Blest is thought to be located in the west, linked to the place of sunset. It is a realm of beautiful flowers, celestial music, and everlasting feasts. ST. BRENDAN supposedly visited the Isle of the Blest during his mystic sailing adventures.

ISRAFEL Israfel (burning one) is the ANGEL of the Islamic faith who will announce the LAST JUDGMENT, when ALLAH will call all human souls to account for their lives. Though he is not mentioned by name in the KORAN, Islam's holy book, tradition describes Israfel as the guide of MUHAMMAD who gave the prophet a tour of DJANNA, the garden paradise. The story tells that after three years, the angel JIBRIL then dictates the Koran to Muhammad before returning him to earth. Other legends claim that one of the delights of heaven is the sweet music played by Israfel.

Israfel is also the patron of music. As he sings HYMNS to Allah, from his breath come millions of radiant angels who also give perpetual honor to the Almighty. According to some legends, departed human souls can find eternal rest in the horn of Israfil, where they will pass the aeons joining in this adulation.

The angel is immortalized by Edgar Allan Poe in his POETRY. Poe declares in one of his works that Israfel "has the sweetest voice of all God's creatures."

IT'S A WONDERFUL LIFE Frank Capra's 1946 classic film *It's a Wonderful Life* unites heaven and earth in this portrait of a "hometown boy" who needs a little help from above. The movie opens with a scene of the HEREAFTER, depicted as a cloudy realm of SAINTS and ANGELS. The voices of these celestial beings discuss the case of George Bailey (played by James Stewart), a kindhearted businessman who has been beset by bad luck on this snowy Christmas Eve. Heaven is being inundated with prayers for the man, all of them begging God to intervene. In answer to these requests, Joseph (foreman of the angels), assigns the hapless Clarence Oddbody (played by Henry Travers) the task of rescuing Stewart. If Travers succeeds, he will be promoted to "angel, first class" and win his long-awaited wings.

It's a Wonderful Life then launches into a flashback of Stewart's life, beginning with the rescue of his drowning brother when both were boys. The next section of the film follows the misadventures of Travers and his charge as the angel tries to convince Stewart that suicide is not the answer to his problems. Viewers then share the happy ending, when Christmas bells ring out, signaling that somewhere in paradise an angel has just gotten his wings.

This perennial holiday favorite offers imaginative insights into the workings of heaven. According to the film, good souls do indeed ascend to paradise after death, but once there they must *earn* their way into the ranks of angels. (This is an afterlife reminiscent of the teachings of EMANUEL SWEDENBORG, who taught that all virtuous humans transform into angels in the next life.) Conflict, uncertainty, and failure are still a part of the afterlife, as Travers is described as having been "unsuccessful" in achieving his objective on past missions. And perhaps must touching, *It's a Wonderful Life* concludes that every prayer made by the living reaches the ear of God in his heavenly home.

During the half century since its initial (and financially disappointing) theatrical release, *It's a Wonderful Life* has become an American icon. Scenes from the film have been incorporated into a vast array of GIFT NOVELTIES, COLLECTOR PLATES, and commemorative MOVIE MERCHANDISING. The movie also continues to inspire numerous parodies, including a *SATURDAY NIGHT LIVE* version in which "lost footage" reveals a violent ending for the film's villain (originally played by Lionel Barrymore). The beloved angel was also revived for a less-than-spectacular made-for-cable movie *Clarence*. In this sequel, the celestial guardian returns from heaven and risks his beloved wings to help save another "lost soul."

Jacob's vision of a ladder to heaven. ART TODAY

ings of paradise with God's material creation: "And he dreamed, and behold a ladder set up on the earth; and the top of it reached to heaven, and behold the ANGELS of God ascending and descending unto it. And behold, the Lord stood above it, and said, 'I am the Lord God of Abraham, thy Father'" (Gen. 28:12–13).

After awakening from this dream, Jacob is shown the land he and his heirs are to claim as their own, which God refers to as "the gate of heaven." Images derived from this biblical passage have been incorporated into a variety of GIFT NOVELTIES, such as COLLECTOR PLATES depicting the astounding vision.

JACOB Jacob is a Hebrew hero of the Old Testament who has a vision of a LADDER that extends between earth and heaven. According to his apparition, the two realms are connected by a mystic passage that unites the celestial be-

JACOB'S LADDER The 1990 film *Jacob's Ladder* offers a glimpse of the peaceful heaven that awaits souls after death. The surreal tale involves the often baffling misadventures of a Vietnam War veteran Jacob Singer (played by Tim

Robbins) who has endured psychological as well as physical damage on the battle-field. After returning "to the world," his life spirals into a convoluted tangle of hallucinations, paranoia, and disturbing memories as he struggles to maintain his sanity. Robbins is continually haunted by dark images of grisly battles, a lost love, and the young son who died in an accident years before the war.

Sifting through the maelstrom of despair, Robbins eventually concludes that he is inextricably caught up in some sinister government experiment. Those around him begin mysteriously disappearing, often in violent "accidents." Every time he comes close to finding answers, something goes horribly wrong. At last he seems to have found confirmation of his dark suspicions, but this knowledge does not alleviate his sense of detachment. But Robbins is freed from this seemingly hopeless quagmire by departing for heaven after a "final moment" when everything suddenly makes sense. His salvation invokes many traditional symbols of paradise, including a REUNION of loved ones and the proverbial STAIRCASE into eternal peace.

Jacob's Ladder conveys the message that each person's afterlife fate is based on perspective. Those who "are scared to die" are damned by memories too painful to surrender and suffer having "devils tearing your life away." However, people who have made peace with themselves will find that the devils are actually "ANGELS freeing you from the earth" and aiding the transition to eternity. With this in mind, Jacob's Ladder devotes a fair amount of attention to

the idea of home. Characters long to go home; they ask one another, "Where is your home?" and the more chilling, "Am I home?" Not surprisingly, the film's resolution is set in Robbins's house, the sanctuary he returns to after withstanding emotional, psychological, and physical assault. From this comfortable repose, he ascends to the tranquil "eternal home" that offers joy, acceptance, and, most of all, the elusive feeling of peace.

The screenplay for Jacob's Ladder was written by Bruce Joel Rubin, author of the love-beyond-the-grave story GHOST; MY LIFE, a poignant tale of a man facing terminal cancer; and the sci-fi afterlife exploration BRAINSTORM. Rubin originally intended to show graphic scenes of both heaven and hell in Jacob's Ladder; however, such visions were omitted in favor of more subtle allusions. Director Adrian Lyne softened the supernatural images into mere suggestions of the divine and the infernal to imply that salvation and damnation are specific to each individual. The ambiguity is central to the tension that follows Robbins as he tries to make sense of his situation, and it makes the eventual resolution that much more profound.

JESUS Jesus (meaning "God saves") is the Messiah of the Christian faith who is responsible for opening heaven to all humankind. He has a dual nature, being the son of God, the divine Father, and of his human mother, the VIRGIN MARY. By offering himself as the sacrifice to atone for the sin of Adam and Eve (and therein the sins of all humanity), Jesus redeems every soul and enables each

Christian Messiah Jesus by Jan van Eyck
ART TODAY

person the opportunity to attain eternal salvation.

The New Testament of the Bible describes the life and works of Christ of his first followers. A great orator and wise teacher, Jesus uses parables to explain the beauty and splendor of CHRISTIAN PARADISE, frequently invoking images of a WEDDING FEAST, "lost lambs" returned to safety, a fruitful garden, and a "mansion" with many rooms. But according to Christ, the ultimate joy of the next world is the BEATIFIC VISION, that is, being able to look upon the face of the Almighty. During his Sermon on the Mount, he tells his flocks: "Blessed are they who are pure in heart: for they shall see God" (Matt. 5:8).

During his time of teaching, Jesus also instructs his disciples on how to pray to the heavenly Father. When asked what words should be used for such supplications, Christ dictates the LORD'S PRAYER (also known as the Our Father), which reveals a great deal about the nature of paradise. The prayer confirms that

the divine creator has a plan for all people, and that cooperating with that plan is the only way for humans to be truly happy. Virtuous behavior will "deliver us from evil" and bring about a truly harmonious existence "on earth as it is in heaven."

But his most important feat is serving as the "lamb" to be sacrificed "for the sins of mankind." Jesus is eventually arrested for spreading subversive ideas and for "blaspheming" against YAWEH and is sentenced to death on the cross. He accepts this dire fate willingly, telling his father in heaven, "Not my will but thine be done." According to Christian doctrine, Jesus is put to death on Passover just before the start of Sabbath (now referred to as Good Friday). Even as he was dying, Jesus spoke of paradise and promised to deliver the GOOD THIEF who was crucified alongside him into eternal joy.

After Christ's death, the Gospels tell that the Lord "descended into hell" to liberate the souls of the patriarchs who could not ascend to heaven until Jesus' sacrifice opened its gates. Three days later, he returns from the dead, vibrant and radiant, in the prototype of human GLORIFIED BODIES. Christ then spent the next forty days preaching, instructing his disciples, and explaining the mysteries of the faith. When this time was up, Jesus made a "glorious ASCENSION" into heaven after promising believers to "prepare a place for you, and I will come again and receive you to myself."

Since the first days of Christian belief, followers affirm that the only way to heaven is through Jesus. No amount of good deeds, sacrifices, or other offerings will win salvation. This is reiterated throughout the New Testament: "For whosoever shall call upon the name of the Lord shall be saved" (Rom. 10:13), "For as in Adam all die, even so in Christ all shall be made alive" (1 Cor. 15:22), "Jesus saith unto him: I am the way, the truth and the life: no man cometh unto the Father, but through me" (John 14:6).

The Bible also claims that Jesus will return to earth once again at the end of the world. St. John's REVELATION, a collection of divine prophecies, foretells a "second coming of Christ" that will immediately precede the LAST JUDGMENT. At this time the world will be destroyed, and every human soul will be called before the throne of God to answer for the actions of his or her lifetime. Those judged worthy will enjoy eternity in a glorious "new heaven and a new earth," while the wicked who have rejected Christ will be cast into a "lake of everlasting fire."

Over the past two millennia, Jesus has inspired countless works of art, literature, POETRY, and other creative endeavors. His image is found in CHURCH ART AND ARCHITECTURE throughout the world. He has been called the most "influential person in the course of human history," and his followers number in the hundreds of millions. For people throughout Christendom, notions of paradise begin and end with the words of Jesus Christ.

JEWISH HEAVEN The concept of a paradise in the afterlife has undergone many changes during the history of Judaism. Originally, early Hebrews believed that the dead departed to Sheol, a dark, sullen pit of quiet monotony. Souls existed in Sheol as weak, faded beings known as shades. Their existence was devoid of any pain or pleasure; it was merely a pale lingering. Writings dating to around 700 B.C. refer to the murky underworld as a "land of gloom and deep darkness."

Later, however, rabbis began teaching a concept of rewards in the afterlife. The prophet Isaiah describes a mystical realm where the "eyes of the blind shall see," the "ears of the deaf shall be opened," and "the lame shall leap" for joy, forever free of pain. This great land is "down the way of holiness," where, "The ransomed of the Lord shall return, and come to Zion with songs and everlasting joy upon their heads: they shall obtain joy and gladness, and sorrow and sighing shall flee away" (Isa. 35:10).

Other Hebrew patriarchs, such as King David, looked forward to a paradise where loved ones would enjoy an eternal REUNION. After the death of his infant son, David consoled himself with the notion that "he will not return to me, but I shall go to him" in the next world. The prophet EZEKIEL likewise describes a glorious otherworld where the saved will live with one another and with God himself. He describes this BEATIFIC VISION, noting that the "Son of Man" assures his beloved "I will dwell in the midst of the children of Israel forever."

In the second century before Christ, new ideas about a LAST JUDGMENT and a system of final rewards or punishments began to spread. This crystallized into the concept of GAN EDEN, the paradise created for Adam and Eve before they sinned against God and were banished, now restored to its original splendor. Souls of the faithful who had led moral lives could look forward to enjoying eternity in this garden, which would be located on earth after the end of the world.

Lore and legends have elaborated on the official teachings regarding paradise. The Jewish tale EL EZKERAH (Legend of the Ten MARTYRS) says that more is required for salvation than simply living a decent life. In order to be saved, one must also actively believe in the world to come: "All of Israel shall have a portion in the world to come, except he who says there is no resurrection of the dead."

The story further describes a paradise of intellectual enlightenment where souls spend eternity discussing sacred teachings and studying the holy texts. In this heaven, there will be no dissent, since all truths will have been revealed to humankind. Another Jewish folktale, this one about ANGELS determining the fate of newborn babes, has been adapted into the modern CHILDREN'S LITERATURE work *Dybbuk: A Story Made in Heaven*.

JIBRIL Jibril is the Islamic equivalent of the Christian angel GABRIEL, the celestial emissary of paradise. His name means "messenger of God." According to Islamic legend, the angel Jibril took MUHAMMAD, founder of Islam, on a tour of the paradise DJANNA. Jibril stayed with Mohammed for three years, showing the prophet the many joys of heaven. Jibril also instructs Muhammad on the "order of paradise" and tells him how one can grow holy enough to look upon the face of ALLAH.

JIHAD The term *jihad* is Arabic for "struggle," and in modern usage the word refers to a "holy war." This originally applied to the battle to extend Islamic-held territory; however, it has since become synonymous with fighting religious wars, including committing acts of terrorism. According to the Islamic religion, soldiers who die in service to ALLAH go directly to DJANNA, a garden paradise.

A true jihad can be of the "pen," the "tongue," or the "sword." MUHAMMAD, founder of Islam, called the latter the "lesser jihad" and encouraged followers to try to win the hearts and minds of infidels (nonbelievers) rather than simply defeat them militarily. But the ultimate purpose of the jihad is not conversion but conquest of new lands to consecrate to Allah. Traditionally, soldiers fighting the jihad are forbidden to participate in "treachery," "mutilation," and the "killing of children." In modern practice, however, many religious zealots believe that the "defense of Allah" justifies virtually any action no matter how extreme.

Those who lose their lives in a jihad are called SHADID, or MARTYRS. They ascend immediately to Djanna where they are welcomed as great heroes and are rewarded with feasts and celebration. Jihad warriors are also given HOURI, beautiful "dark-eyed maidens" who fulfill their every carnal desire.

JIZO BOSATSU Jizo Bosatsu (called Ti Tsang in Chinese Buddhism) is the deity in Japanese Buddhism who gives comfort to the dead. He is depicted in artworks as a Buddhist monk with a shaved head who bears a staff in one hand and a precious gemstone in the other. His role is to set followers on the path to NIRVANA, the ultimate bliss of collective consciousness. Jizo Bosatsu also has the power to release souls from hell and allow them to be reincarnated and continue the life cycle.

Worship of Jizo Bosatsu dates back to at least 850 B.C. Japanese Buddhists have developed an intricate array of prayers, mediations, and offerings designed to win his help in the afterlife. Jizo Bosatsu is also the guardian of children and is revered by parents hoping for his paternal protection.

JOKES Heaven has served as a source of humorous inspiration from time immemorial. The realm of the blessed routinely makes its way into comedic presentations by a wide variety of performers. Among these are *Tonight Show* host Jay Leno, who offers the recurring character Beyondo, a disembodied head that floats across the set spouting humorous quips about the afterlife. Stand-up comedian Jeff Foxworthy presents a parody of paradise in his act as well. He cautions audience members, "If you think heaven is a lot like Daytona Beach, Florida, you might be a redneck."

The HEREAFTER likewise lends itself to innumerable cocktail party jokes about the rewards—and perils—of the world to come. Typical jests of this type involve religious icons of CHRISTIAN PARADISE such as the PEARLY GATES, SAINT PETER, ANGELS, and the "book of life" described in REVELATION. Many also involve celebrities or politicians trying to secure a place in eternity. Other favorite characters include SAINTS, historical heroes, and even nefarious villains who have ascended to the divine realm. A typical example:

> *Microsoft CEO Bill Gates died and was met at the Pearly Gates by St. Peter. St. Peter told him, "You've been such an influential person on earth, I'm going to let you decide where you want to spend eternity. Which do you want to see first, heaven or hell?" Gates, a bit surprised, said, "Show me heaven first," so St. Peter took him to paradise. There, Gates saw saints and angels sitting on clouds plucking at harps. It was pretty, but also rather dull. "Okay," said Gates, "now I'm ready to see hell." So St. Peter brought him to the abyss, which Gates was amazed to discover looked just like a beach resort. There where people playing volleyball on the sand, ice-cold drinks, and even a pit barbecue. "No offense," said Gates, "but I want to stay here! Heaven is just too boring!" "Suit yourself," replied St. Peter. Then in a flash he was gone.*

A few weeks later, St. Peter thought he'd better go check on Bill Gates, so he descended to the inferno where he found Gates chained to a flaming rock. "So," he asked Gates, "how's everything going?" "Are you kidding!?" shouted Gates, "what happened to the hell you showed me where everyone was having such a great time?" "Oh," answered St. Peter, "that was just the demo version!"

Humorous depictions of heaven have also been mainstays of television shows like SATURDAY NIGHT LIVE and *Kids in the Hall*. And similar jests of paradise have made their way into ANIMATED CARTOONS, COMICS, and ADVERTISING campaigns.

K

KAILASA, MOUNT Mount Kailasa is the "paradise of Shiva," located in Tibet. At the foot of the mountain is the mystic "Palace of Opulence," a regal court of indescribable beauty. Its peak is believed to be the center of the universe. On Mount Kailasa, gardens abound with beautiful flowers and delicious fruit, superior to the best harvests of earth. All life in this enchanted realm is sustained by waters of the "everlasting river" of replenishment. Deceased Hindus might be rewarded with respite at Mount Kailasa for virtuous lives before rejoining the reincarnation cycle and continuing the quest for MOKSHA, ultimate enlightenment.

KATMIR Katmir is an enchanted dog of Islamic legend, believed to be one of the ANIMALS that dwells in DJANNA, the tropical paradise. Though Katmir is not named in the KORAN, Islam's holy book, the text does include a passage about a canine guard that protects the friends of ALLAH. Katmir is also mentioned in the legend of the SEVEN SLEEPERS as the dog that watches over a band of youths fleeing religious persecution.

KENYA, MOUNT Mount Kenya is believed by local tribes to be the location of AFRICAN PARADISE. The mountain reaches "into the heavens," where God oversees the events of human history. Good and pure souls, favored by the divine Father, are believed to ascend Mount Kenya after death. From atop this great summit, spirits of the dead watch over and protect their descendants, anticipating a great and final REUNION in the afterlife.

Mount Kenya, believed by some to be the portal to paradise. ART TODAY

KEVALA Kevala is the highest "stage of knowledge" of the Jain faith, and souls who attain kevala dwell in eternal bliss. It is similar to the Buddhist notion of NIR-VANA and the Hindu MOKSHA, in which the ultimate goal is to dissolve the "self" in favor of "enlightenment." In order to ascend to the kevala state, a soul must make its way through five "pathways to liberation" before finally becoming omniscient. Making sufficient progress usually entails many lifetimes, and most souls will therefore undergo a lengthy cycle of birth, life, death, and rebirth before reaching kevala.

Souls who achieve kevala are called siddhas, meaning "perfect ones." Their spirits soar to the "height of the universe" where they remain forever. Unlike the paradises of Judaism, Christianity, and Islam, these blessed spirits pass eternity motionless and without physical pleasures. The greatest delight according to Jainists is the shedding of the body and the transformation into a "free soul" stripped of all individual characteristics.

KHUN-LUN Khun-lun is the Buddhist paradise and place for "spirits of the blessed." Within this mystic realm grow the "fruits of immortality" in a splendid, ever-fertile garden west of the "Moving Sands." The enchanted land is ruled by Hsi Wang Mu, called the "royal mother of the western paradise." She was once a hideous beast; however, she was eventually transformed into a "gracious spirit" and given rule over Khun-lun.

Hsi Wang Mu lives in the Palace of Khun-lun, which is protected by a golden rampart encircling the royal estate. On the grounds are a Magic Fountain, a Lake of Gems, and the grove of Enchanted PEACH Trees. The fruit of these trees takes three thousand years to ripen, and those who eat these peaches will thus live for three millennia. At the end of this time, they eat again to perpetuate their immortality.

Once every three thousand years, coinciding with the harvest of the Enchanted Peaches, the gods gather at Khun-lun on Hsi Wang Mu's birthday for the "Great Feast of the Immortals." During the festivities, each deity consumes one of the magic fruits. The festival also includes a grand celebration of song and dance and a buffet of culinary delights.

KI-AGPGA-POD According to the Tupi Indians of Brazil, after a person dies, the body remains intact for three days, then its heart develops into a ki-agpga-pod. This is a small, humanlike creature that grows at an accelerated rate until it finally becomes large enough to break out of the dead heart. The ki-agpga-pod then ascends to the heavens through the aid of a patobkia (magic man), where it will soar through the skies forever.

While this is happening, the corpse's eyes become a pabid, "spirit of the man," and dwell in the land of the dead. In this murky afterlife the pabid could engage in sexual intercourse with ancient deities, bear spirit children, and continue in an existence that closely parallels their earthly life.

KINTU Kintu is a figure of African Ugandan myth, similar to the Christian

Adam, who was the first man and father of the human race. Kintu and his wife, Nambi, could travel between heaven and earth and consort with the gods. But during one sojourn, Nambi's brother Death followed his sister from heaven to earth and began claiming the lives of Kintu's children. The two could not defeat Death, although they were able to force him to live underground, where he remains an ever-present threat to all humankind. After suffering at Death's hands, souls are believed to return "to the sky" to enjoy a restful afterlife.

KORAN The Koran (Qur'an) is the Islamic holy book, similar to the Christian Bible and Hebrew Torah. Koran means "protect, save, find peace," and the text

Page from a 1911 illuminated Koran. ART TODAY

is designed to help humans find comfort in the afterlife. It was dictated to the prophet MUHAMMAD by the angel JIBRIL (GABRIEL), from a "perfect copy," which remains in paradise.

The Koran promises that all those who keep the word of ALLAH (God) will be rewarded with eternal life in DJANNA, a magnificent paradise. In Djanna, the saved dine on delicious food, sip fine wine and enjoy carnal pleasures forbidden during earthly existence. The greatest joy, however, is dwelling in the presence of Allah, the "all-merciful Father" who loves his children beyond human understanding.

The Koran also foretells a cataclysmic LAST JUDGMENT that will occur at the end of the world. When this occurs the earth will be destroyed, and the souls of all who have ever lived will be summoned before the throne of the Almighty. Allah will then review each person's life and pronounce divine sentence, allowing his faithful entrance into Djanna but condemning infidels (nonbelievers) to annihilation.

In addition to describing the realm of Allah and foretelling future events, the Koran lists articles of faith that all believers must accept. Among these are the five "essential truths": (1) Allah is the omniscient deity; (2) ANGELS are divine creatures made by Allah; (3) the "revealed books" are the divine word of Allah; (4) the prophets, especially Muhammad, are divinely inspired; and (5) all souls will face a Last Judgment. These doctrines are not debatable.

The Koran was instrumental in spreading Islam throughout the Arabic world. Believers carried copies of the book with them, preaching the word of Allah and extolling the virtues of the prophet Muhammad. In just a few years, the new religion supplanted the ancient faith Zoroastrianism and likewise dispelled the notion that human lives are ruled by blind fate. The work also helped to shape moral standards of millions (it specifically forbids the then-common practice of murdering infant girls) and completely transformed contemporary Arabic society. Today, the Koran remains sacred to millions of Muslims throughout the world and represents the promise of eternal paradise.

KOTLUWALAWA Kotluwalawa is the Hopi Indian "village of the dead." This mystical land lies beyond the Lake of Whispering Waters somewhere in the west. Similar to the LAND OF SUNSET, Kotluwalawa is a lush meadow with plentiful game shielded by beautiful mountains where all dwell together in peace. Departing spirits are said to journey to Kotluwalawa to find eternal repose.

KOWALSKA, M. FAUSTINA
(1905–1938) Helena Kowalska, a woman of great piety and devotion to the Christian Redeemer JESUS, experienced numerous supernatural visions during her short lifetime. Among these were images of heaven, hell, and PURGATORY.

Kowalska was born in Poland in 1905 and entered the convent at nineteen, taking the name Sister Mary Faustina as her religious title. She suffered from chronic ill health and was unable to per-

form "active" works of charity, so she decided to devote her life to contemplation of Christ's divine mercy. As part of her work, Kowalska kept a detailed diary of her daily prayers titled *Divine Mercy in My Soul*. She worked on the book until her illness advanced to the point that she could no longer continue writing.

Contained in that diary, published in the United States in 1987, are numerous accounts of contact with supernatural beings. Kowalska transcribes prayers dictated to her by Jesus and records seeing ANGELS praising God in PARADISE. She also reports seeing the VIRGIN MARY as an "unspeakably beautiful" woman arrayed in glory. And Kowalska beholds the BEATIFIC VISION and looks with awe on "the glorious face of the Lord."

Among her more uplifting experiences, Kowalska visits a place of sorrow where souls burn with "longing for God." Jesus informs her that this is the realm of purgatory, a "prison of suffering" where spirits cleanse themselves before ascending to heaven. Spirits in this intermediate place are comforted by the realization that their agony is only temporary and that they will one day dwell in the presence of God.

In contrast to the visions of pain and suffering, Kowalska alludes to the "indescribable joys" of paradise. She proclaims, "Death destroys nothing that is good," and reassures readers that virtuous souls take their holiness with them to eternity. Anticipating her own demise, Kowalska writes: "I look forward with joy to the last stroke the Divine Artist will trace on my soul, which will give my soul a unique beauty that will distinguish me from the beauty of other souls. . . . On that day, for the first time, I shall sing before heaven and earth the song of the Lord's fathomless mercy."

In *Divine Mercy,* Kowalska continually stresses the fact that God wants every human soul to be united to him in paradise. She encourages all to surrender themselves to his will, for only this will bring happiness in this world and the next. The last entry in her diary, written as tuberculosis overtook her, shows calm acceptance of whatever lies ahead, since Kowalska is confident that Jesus wants only the best for his children. "I see that clearly" are her final written words.

Kowalska died at age thirty-three and is being considered as a candidate for sainthood in the Roman Catholic church.

K'UNLUN, MOUNT Mount K'unlun is the nine-level realm according to Chinese Taoist belief, the counterpart to the Buddhist KHUN-LUN. At the summit of Mount K'unlun are the "gates of paradise" through which blessed souls pass on their way to everlasting bliss. Like Khun-lun, this enchanted land is ruled by Hsi Wang Mu, the "queen mother of the west." In Taoist stories, she has power over fate, mortality, and human destiny in this life as well as the world to come.

One legend claims that Hsi Wang Mu has a magic potion that allows mortals to ascend to heaven without having to die first. Stories about quests to "steal" or "purchase" this enchanted elixir abound. In some tales, Hsi Wang Mu sells her potion to wealthy rulers and aristocrats (equating divine favor with material riches) or to extraordinary "holy men." Emperor Huang-ti and the Toaist patriarch Huai-nan are among those whom the queen has favored with her powerful tonic. Some were able to procure enough of the elixir from Hsi Wang Mu to deliver their entire families to paradise in this manner. Humans who try to trick or rob Hsi Wang Mu are dealt with harshly, and their souls are forever barred from entering paradise.

LADDER One of the most prevalent symbols of heaven is the ladder. Representations of this image are found in cultures from across the globe and in all epochs of time. The "bridge to paradise" is typically shown slanted diagonally with one end in earth and the other reaching into the skies. Ladders to the divine realm figure into stories of AFRICAN PARADISE, Hebrew tales of the prophet JACOB, illustrations of CHRISTIAN PARADISE, and a variety of other afterlife references.

In Christian tradition, metaphorical ladders into eternity frequently figure into works of literature. Dante's DIVINE COMEDY: THE PARADISO describes the levels of heaven being linked by a mystic ladder. Likewise, the COMPENDIUM OF REVELATIONS uses the symbol to con-

Illustration of a ladder to paradise for
Dante's *Paradiso*. ART TODAY

nect the physical "garden of paradise"
with the spiritual realm. And legends of
SAINTS such as SAINT CRISPIN involve
ladders between the land of the living
and the HEREAFTER.

LAKE MACHIRA Lake Machira is the
"enchanted water" paradise of the Carib
of South America. Departed spirits
travel to the mystic pool where they are
swallowed by "grand serpents" who take
them to a realm of sheer delight. In this
"land of every pleasure," souls enjoy
great feasts, dancing, and revelry that
never ends. Because of this myth, the
Carib consider all lakes and pools of still
water to have magical powers.

LAND OF THE MOON Native American Inuits believe that virtuous souls
travel to the Land of the Moon where

they find eternal rest. According to the
legend, pure spirits rise to this mythic
paradise after death, while wicked souls
descend to Adlivun, which means "those
beneath us." Adlivun lies at the bottom
of the ocean, a place of sheer darkness,
while the Land of the Moon is forever
bright and lively. Blessed souls ascend to
this luminous paradise via a magic "river
in the sky."

LAND OF SUNSET The Land of
Sunset is the realm of the dead found in
Native American myth. Admission to
this paradise is not selective; virtually all
spirits go there after death. It is a fertile
hunting ground laced with sweet rivers,
plentiful orchards, and pleasant weather.
In the Land of Sunset, all people are
equal, and there is no conflict, sorrow, or
pain.

The Land of Sunset is so-called because it is in the west, somewhere beyond the horizon of the setting sun. The
beautiful colors of the sky at dusk are
said to spill over from this mystic land
to remind the living of their departed
loved ones.

LARES Souls of the benevolent dead
become lares (lords) and remain in the
family home according to Roman myth.
The lares protect the household and ensure that the bloodline does not die out.
Lares familiaris watch over individual
families, *lares compitales* preside at cross-
roads to protect travelers, and *lares
praestites* guard cities and villages. To
win the continued favor of these deified
spirits, the living offer them prayers and

gifts of food and wine. Lares are also revered at elaborate festivals in their honor held throughout the year.

The *lares'* evil counterpart are the larvae, wicked spirits that are restless and vengeful in the afterlife. Unlike the lares, who continue to participate in the community and receive praise and adulation, larvae are despised beings, blamed for all manner of personal and collective misfortune. Special rituals can banish these dark souls but not destroy them, forcing the larvae to prowl the earth for fresh victims.

LAST JUDGMENT The concept of an impending last judgment, a supernatural adjudication in which all human souls are sentenced in the afterlife, appears in belief systems across the globe and throughout history. Since its first appearance more than four thousand years ago, this doctrine has become prominent in Judaism, Christianity, Islam, and even in some Eastern faiths that place heavy emphasis on reincarnation. Thousands of artworks, including examples of CHURCH ART AND ARCHITECTURE as well as secular compositions, reflect the various interpretations of the Last Judgment that have evolved over the centuries.

Ancient Egyptians believed that the dead are tried in the Hall of OSIRIS, ruler of the otherworld. Aided by the jackal-headed ANUBIS, Osiris weighs each soul's heart against the "feather of truth" to determine its appropriate afterlife fate. Spirits could boost their chances for reaching paradise by studying the BOOK OF THE DEAD and arming themselves with information necessary for finding peace. Most Egyptians believed that judgment would occur immediately after a person's death, although some accounts indicate that time does not exist in eternity so chronology in the court of Osiris is meaningless.

The earliest records of a Last Judgment that would take place at the end of the world are found among the teachings of Zoroaster (Zarathustra). The prophet, who lived about 600 B.C., taught that when a person dies, the soul remains by the body for three days. After this time, it journeys to CHINVATO PERETAV, the "Bridge of the Separator," to give an account of its actions to the deity AHURA MAZDA. Virtuous souls could easily cross the razor-thin bridge to paradise. Wicked spirits, however, would tumble into a wretched abyss where they would suffer until the earth is destroyed in an apocalyptic battle between the forces of good and evil. The righteous would ultimately win and would dwell forever in eternal bliss, while damned spirits would be annihilated.

This first sentencing would be followed at "the end of time" by a final judgment. After the prophesied battle, previously condemned souls could still be saved and allowed entrance into ZOROASTRIAN HEAVEN by rejecting "the lie" of Ahriman. Those who refused to abandon their vile ways would be eradicated from existence.

Early Hebrew records indicate a similar doctrine, referred to as the "Day of the Lord." The exact date of this im-

Medeival Christian depiction of the
Last Judgment according to Revelation
ART TODAY

pending cosmic upheaval is unknown, so believers are cautioned to be ever prepared. (Some records indicate that biblical heroes had been told by God when this will happen; however, they were forbidden from revealing the secret to others.) And unlike the Zoroastrian Last Judgment, the damned will not be destroyed but will be sentenced to everlasting punishment. Saved souls will be rewarded with eternal bliss in JEWISH HEAVEN.

In Islam, the Last Judgment is called the "Day of Decision." At this time, all souls will be "awakened" and judged by ALLAH. Those who have embraced his truth will be welcomed into the garden paradise of DJANNA. Infidels (nonbelievers) will burn to annihilation through the fire of their own evil. But the blessed will savor the delights of heaven for all eternity, wearing "bracelets of gold" and drinking fine wines at a never-ending banquet in Allah's court. The doctrine of the Last Judgment is an article of faith that all Muslims must accept in order to be saved.

The Christian concept of the Last Judgment derives from the prophecies in St. John's REVELATION. This graphic work describes the end of the world, the coming of an "antichrist," final apocalyptic battles, and the resurrection of everyone who has ever lived. When these events come to pass, the mysteries of humanity will be revealed, and all secrets will be laid bare. Humans will be given GLORIFIED BODIES that remain forever free of imperfections. And each person will be called before JESUS, the Christian redeemer, to give an accounting of his or her life: "And I saw the dead, small and great, stand before God: and the books were opened: and another book was opened, which is the book of life: and the dead were judged out of those things which were written in the books, according to their works" (Rev. 20:12).

Controversy exists in many religions over whether souls will be judged twice—once on death and again at the Last Judgment—or will "sleep" until they are sentenced at the end of time. Martin Luther, leader of the Protestant revolt, believed that there would be no adjudication when a person dies and that virtually all people would be judged only once after the destruction of the earth. Other Christian scholars refute this theory, citing the story of the GOOD THIEF in which Jesus tells the dying man "this day you will be with me in paradise." Similar dissent exists in Jewish and Islamic belief regarding trial in the afterlife. One thing most agree on: The Last Judgment will occur, and only those who have properly prepared themselves will ascend to paradise.

LAST JUDGMENT ART The theme of a LAST JUDGMENT, a belief that all human souls will be raised and called forth to account for their lives, has been a prevalent topic for artwork around the world. In some religions this event is prophesied to take place at the end of the world; in others it occurs constantly as a deluge of souls travels through the life cycle. And from millennia-old MEMORIALS of the ETRUSCANS to modern compositions by such masters as WILLIAM BLAKE, this prophesied adjudication has inspired some of the most profound religious creations in history.

Ancient compositions show the judgment before King OSIRIS, Egyptian lord of the dead. The first such illustrations can be found in the BOOK OF THE DEAD, a text of magic spells and incantations designed to help souls enjoy a pleasurable afterlife. Typical drawings depict Osiris and his aid ANUBIS determining the fate of departed souls in the Hall of Justice. Similar images have also been found on the walls of tombs and on scrolls dating back millennia.

In Asian cultures, departing souls are shown appearing in the court of YAMA, the mythic magistrate of the dead. Most pictures depict the stern deity holding court while cowering spirits beg for mercy. Followers of the ancient prophet Zoroaster portray a kinder, gentler adju-

dication in the ZOROASTRIAN HEAVEN before the benevolent god AHURA MAZDA. And Islamic portraits of the judgment before ALLAH (heavily influenced by the earlier teachings of Zoroaster) show the Almighty sorting the wicked from the blessed in the world to come.

Artworks inspired by notions of the Christian Last Judgment have proliferated over the past twenty centuries and account for hundreds of examples of CHURCH ART AND ARCHITECTURE. Most of these illustrations derive from passages of St. John's REVELATION, the book of the Bible that describes the end of the world. Revelation contains graphic details about the destruction of the planet, the raising of the dead, and the separating of the saved from the damned. JESUS, the Christian Redeemer, is the divine judge who pronounces sentence on the souls of all humankind in many of these compositions.

The *Last Judgment* fresco of the Church of St. George Voronet in Romania, created about 1550, covers the entire west wall above the chapel entrance. It shows God at the center with the twelve apostles seated around him, six on each side. They in turn are flanked by adoring ANGELS. Below the celestial choir is a row of SAINTS, followed by blessed souls and other religious heroes. The work employs extensive use of gold, so much that the work almost seems to glow. This creates a striking image of eternity and serves as a powerful incentive to live by Christian doctrines.

Without question, the most famous and critically acclaimed *Last Judgment* was painted by the Renaissance master

MICHELANGELO for SAINT PETER's Cathedral in Rome. The massive work took five years to complete, going through several versions before the artist was finally satisfied with the results. Michelangelo, intrigued by humanism that enveloped Europe during the mid-1500s, incorporated into his work images from Greek and Roman myth as well as symbols of CHRISTIAN PARADISE. This caused great controversy at the time of painting's unveiling. Many decried Michelangelo's *Last Judgment* as "blasphemous," since it depicted Jesus as clean-shaven (pagan gods were without beards, but Christ had always been portrayed with facial hair) and seething with anger. Others objected to the nudity of the damned. Overall, contemporary clerics and worshipers alike considered it "unfit" and "improper" for a religious setting.

Michelangelo was not the only painter whose creativity resulted in condemnation by church officials. The *Last Judgment* by Flemish master Peter Paul Rubens was removed from the altar of a Bavarian church because authorities deemed it "irreverent" and "disrespectful." Unlike previous depictions of paradise, Rubens's work did not show a THEOCENTRIC HEAVEN where all attention is focused on the Almighty but rather a bustling afterlife of social interaction. His paradise, in their estimation, gives too much emphasis to the REUNION of loved ones and not enough to the BEATIFIC VISION. In short, the saved are depicted paying more attention to one another than to God. Clerics of the time found this absolutely unacceptable and demanded it be moved elsewhere.

During the High Middle Ages, illustrations of the Last Judgment were so popular in Christendom that they were not confined to churches and religious houses. Rogier van der Weyden painted a dazzling *Last Judgment* for the Hôtel-Dieu in Beaune, where it is still displayed. This fifteenth-century masterpiece offers heaven as a blaze of gold with a crimson-robed Christ at its center. The Messiah is flanked on either side by angels adorned in flowing white linen. A further contingent of celestial escorts guides the saved through the gates of paradise to the NEW JERUSALEM, a city of golden spires and jeweled courtyards.

Speculation about the impending Last Judgment continues to fire the minds of artists. Modern painters often incorporate images of nuclear annihilation, the Nazi Holocaust, and other recent atrocities into their works. These horrific scenes provide a stark contrast to the promised delights of the world to come.

LAZARUS   In a parable designed to warn against self-righteousness and hypocrisy, JESUS, founder of Christianity, describes heaven as a place of comfort for even the poorest and most wretched. The story of Lazarus describes a destitute blind man who slowly starves outside the palace of Dives, a callous nobleman. Eventually the pauper dies, and his soul is taken to paradise. But when death comes for Dives, the once-mighty lord is damned to hell for his heartless disregard of his fellow human beings: "And it came to pass, that the beggar died, and was carried by the ANGELS into Abra-

Lazarus starves while the rich feast.
ART TODAY

ham's bosom: the rich man also died, and was buried; And in hell he lift up his eyes, being in torments, and seeth Abraham afar off, and Lazarus in his bosom" (Luke 16:22–23).

This image of heaven as a realm of comfort for those who suffer in this world quickly became central to concepts of CHRISTIAN PARADISE. Unlike the ancient Greek and Egyptian myths, Christ taught a paradise open to the common person rather than an afterlife reserved for the rich and powerful. There was also a tendency among contemporary Jewish leaders to consider themselves "favored" because of their status and to criticize and condemn the peasantry. The parable of Lazarus angered and insulted them and threatened to erode their authority.

The story of Dives and Lazarus also broke with earlier "maps" of the next world. Ancient notions of the afterlife drew no real barriers between regions of joy and places of gloom. But in Jesus' parable, Dives asks Abraham to send water to quench his burning thirst, and Abraham replies that a "great gulf" separates the two worlds, so that none can pass from one to the other. Thus the afterlife of Christian tradition is separated into distinct chambers designated for either reward or punishment, and no in-teraction is possible. This concept of eternal segregation of the saved and the damned persists to this day.

LEWU LIAU The Ngaaju of Borneo believe that souls of the dead journey to Lewu Liau, a place of fertile fields and plentiful game where the air smells of summer flowers. Here, spirits enjoy a REUNION with loved ones and dwell eternally in paradise.

LIBANZA Libanza is the sky god and lord of the dead according to the Upotos of the Congo. The son of the first gods, Libanza is the hero of many tales of AFRICAN PARADISE. One story tells how he often quarreled with and even killed his kin. After such an incident, Libanza climbs a tree that reaches to the heavens, where he has a terse REUNION with the deceased spirits of family members he had defeated. Some accounts claim Libanza had the power to restore the dead to life and took pity on his brethren. He resurrected them, only to have their fighting resume and intensify.

In other legends Libanza is the supernatural escort who delivers departing souls to paradise. The moon is Libanza's boat; it picks up spirits of the dead and ferries them to his eternal kingdom. In the afterlife, human souls become luminous and transform into stars visible in the night sky. They watch over the living, begging Libanza not to let the sky collapse and destroy those on earth.

Libanza is also said to be responsible for bringing death to humankind. Legend tells that he once called all the people of the moon and the people of the earth to his court. The moon people came right away, so he rewarded them with two days each month to rest, after which they would return more dazzling then before. But the people of the earth tarried, angering Libanza. When they finally arrived, he decreed that all humans would die and then "return to me" in the next world.

LILIOM   Hungarian author Ferenc Molnár's 1909 story *Liliom* depicts paradise as a place of final reckoning, a realm of justice tempered with mercy. The story follows the misadventures of handsome cad Liliom as he marries Julie, an innocent servant girl, panics when she announces she is pregnant, then is killed in a botched robbery attempt. When Liliom's soul ascends to the afterlife, the "eternal judges" offer him one last chance to redeem himself. The man agrees to return to earth to "help" his family. However, when he visits his widow and now-grown daughter, Liliom realizes that he is unable to change his errant nature. But by accepting his faults and cautioning his child against making similar mistakes, Liliom ultimately finds peace.

Molnár's tale of resolution in the afterlife has enjoyed numerous adaptations over the years. The 1930 fantasy film *Liliom* stars Charles Farrell as the Budapest carnival worker who is killed in a fight and ascends to paradise. But Farrell is too restless to enjoy heaven and feels out of place among the saved. Dissatisfied with the blessed afterlife,

Farrell returns to earth to make sure his beloved wife and family are faring well in his absence. Director Fritz Lang emphasizes the "trial in heaven" aspect in his 1935 French version. Lang's interpretation casts Charles Boyer as a rogue who dies and must prove he is worthy of paradise.

The most successful American adaptation of *Liliom* is Rodgers and Hammerstein's Broadway musical CAROUSEL, a standard of modern theater. Molnár's work has likewise inspired a number of theatrical failures, such as the ill-fated PINK JUNGLE and the critically disparaged film HEAVENLY KID.

LIMBO   Limbo is a realm of Christian legend that is not an official doctrine but is believed by many to exist. It is an intermediate dimension for souls of unbaptized children and other "innocents" who still have the taint of original sin and therefore cannot ascend to heaven. Some accounts also describe limbo as the "holding cell" where the patriarchs and virtuous awaited redemption. Since only JESUS could open the gates of heaven, worthy souls who died before Christ's crucifixion could not enter paradise. They, like the spirits of children, went to this place of earthly happiness and peace.

Limbo offers most of the pleasures of CHRISTIAN PARADISE with one notable exception: Souls in this realm cannot enjoy the BEATIFIC VISION. Their only sorrow is being unable to look upon the face of God. However, most scholars believe that after the LAST JUDGMENT, limbo will be emptied and all souls therein will be welcomed into heaven.

In Dante's *Divine Comedy: The Inferno*, Limbo is the antechamber of hell and contains the souls of virtuous pagans. These spirits do not suffer any torture, but they must remain forever outside the divine realm, their only solace being fine companionship and social interaction.

LIVING END, THE   *The Living End*, a 1977 novel by Stanley Elkin, provides a distinctly unappealing picture of the HEREAFTER. According to his work, paradise is "like a theme park" of golden spires, jeweled streets, and glimmering towers. But far from the awe-inspiring portraits of traditional CHRISTIAN PARADISE, Elkin's eternity is a place of pettiness populated with jealous SAINTS and discontented ANGELS. *The Living End* is particularly insulting to the VIRGIN MARY, who is reduced to the role of celestial nanny to children ripped from their parents to please a tyrannical God.

In addition to housing multitudes of dour spirits, Elkin's heaven is used to tease and torture the damned. On their way through the afterlife, all souls are given a quick glimpse of paradise. For condemned spirits, the image of paradise's beauty "induced sadness, rage" that intensifies over the eons. This is indeed ironic, as those "lucky" enough to be allowed into God's city are as miserable as their damned counterparts. Overall, *The Living End* satirizes common beliefs about ESCHATOLOGY, attempting to take the sting out of death by presenting a parody of the afterlife that, according to Elkin, is laughable.

LOA   Spirits of the dead can become loas according to Haitian voodoo. A loa is a deified human soul that becomes godlike in the afterlife. As a loa, the spirit can travel by thought, influence village affairs, and even take possession of a living person. In the "abode beyond," loas must be respected and revered by the living in order to maintain a happy existence. Those who are not shown proper reverence will visit their anger upon those who offend them.

LORD'S PRAYER   The Lord's Prayer, also called the Our Father, is one of the few prayers of the Christian faith dictated by JESUS himself. When asked how the "children of God" should address the Almighty, Jesus tells them to use these words:

> *Our Father, who art in Heaven,*
>   *hallowed be Thy name.*
> *Thy kingdom come, Thy will be*
>   *done, on earth as it is in Heaven.*
> *Give us this day our daily bread,*
>   *and forgive us our trespasses*
> *As we forgive those who trespass*
>   *against us.*
> *And lead us not into temptation,*
>   *but deliver us from evil.*

In addition to instructing Christians on paying homage to the heavenly father, the simple yet powerful prayer reveals a great deal about the nature of CHRISTIAN PARADISE. In the text, believers ascertain an afterlife where they will dwell with God the Father in a realm of perfect harmony, enjoying this BEATIFIC VISION. The words also promise a dimension of perfect bliss where the divine will is respected, dissolving all human conflict. And the Lord's Prayer depicts an ethereal "kingdom" where souls will take their place in the eternal court of the Supreme Being.

The Lord's Prayer remains immensely popular among Christians of many denominations and is used in religious services throughout the world. Modern artists have set the words to music, further inculcating the sacred text into Western popular culture.

M

MADE IN HEAVEN The 1987 film *Made in Heaven* depicts paradise as a place for saved souls as well as a "waiting room" for persons as yet unborn. It stars Timothy Hutton as a man who dies trying to save a child from drowning. After ascending to paradise for this virtuous act, Hutton falls in love with the lovely Kelly McGillis. Their romance is just beginning to blossom when McGillis is dispatched to earth in the body of a newborn baby. Distraught at losing her, Hutton convinces his guardian angel (Debra Winger) to allow him to reincarnate as an infant so he can find his love in the land of the living. Winger reluctantly agrees, [giving the couple thirty years to meet and fall in love. If Hutton

is unsuccessful at winning McGillis's heart by his thirtieth birthday, he must return to heaven alone.

The joys of paradise in *Made in Heaven* reflect images of CHRISTIAN PARADISE. Saved souls have the ability to travel by thought, they enjoy social interaction with family and friends, and they have endless hours to spend in levity and conversation. There is no God presiding over eternity; however, human souls are befriended by benevolent ANGELS who aid them in making the transition to life eternal. *Made in Heaven* also features an imaginative twist on the REUNION theme, showing souls—separated by birth rather than death—finding each other in the temporal plane.

MAGIC FLUTE, THE *The Magic Flute*, Wolfgang Amadeus Mozart's last completed opera, offers an operatic allegory of the afterlife, incorporating ancient images of paradise. It was written and first produced in 1791 for a pedestrian audience, as Mozart was at the time considered an outcast from "decent society." Critics of the day condemned *The Magic Flute* as "pagan" and "blasphemous"; however, it was immensely popular with the people. The "uneducated peasants" found it truly mesmerizing.

Set in ancient Egypt during the reign of Ramses I (about 2000 B.C.), the opera was dazzling and exotic to eighteenth-century peasants, many of whom had never heard of the age-old gods before. And the story, which follows the exploits of two mortals seeking to enter the realm of OSIRIS and ISIS to learn the secrets of the supernatural, was engaging and adventurous, in contrast to the stodgy, static royal productions of the day. *The Magic Flute* introduced them to ideas of blessed eternity far different from their familiar CHRISTIAN PARADISE.

Mozart's opera simulates passage through the next world, from hell to paradise. His heroes must endure trials by fire, divine judgment, and a host of supernatural challenges. Aiding the courageous souls are protective figures reminiscent of ANUBIS, the eternal escort who guides human spirits into the Hall of Osiris. *The Magic Flute* also invokes passages from the Egyptian BOOK OF THE DEAD, offering charms, spells, and incantation to shield people from dangers of the unknown and help them reach paradise.

Over the two centuries since its debut, *The Magic Flute* has become one of the most popular operas in the world and is now hailed as "an operatic masterpiece" of fine music, creative plot, and fascinating supernatural imagery.

MAHABHARATA The *Mahabharata* is a massive Indian epic poem, written in Sanskrit and dating back to around 400 B.C. It describes a power struggle that ends in heaven. The *Mahabharata* details a war between the virtuous Pandava brothers and their rivals, the Kauravas, as they fight for control of the kingdom of Dritarashtra. After a lengthy battle, the Pandavas are successful, but they ultimately choose spiritual development over material gain and renounce their royal status. The five brothers then enjoy a joyous REUNION in paradise after dedicating their remaining years to pious devotion and charitable works.

The *Mahabharata* contains a dialogue known as the BHAGAVADGITA between the Hindu god Krishna and one of the Pandava brothers. In this text, the doctrines of Hinduism and its underlying philosophy are summarized and explained. Over the centuries, other legends and essays of India have been added to the *Mahabharata*, making it a virtual treasure trove of Indian culture, history and literature. Millions of Hindus derive their images of afterlife bliss from this age-old writ.

MAN AND SUPERMAN The 1905 drama *Man and Superman* by George Bernard Shaw includes a play within a play called "Don Juan in Hell." This dream interlude (which is often performed independently) is a foray into the afterlife that paints paradise as a dull realm of "boring" SAINTS and tedious pleasures. In contrast, the damned enjoy a "Merry Hell" dynamic with activity.

In Shaw's work, salvation and damnation are simply a matter of perspective. This notion, explored in depth by artist/philosopher WILLIAM BLAKE, suggests that some souls would find paradise insufferably monotonous and would welcome condemnation to the feisty inferno. This cavalier attitude toward divine matters caused considerable controversy when the play premiered on the European stage. Shocked critics decried the drama as "blasphemous," prompting some proprietors to demand that the author include a "disclaimer" in the show's program. The London Royal Court Theatre required Shaw to justify his unconventional work in writing and distributed his explanation to all patrons. The author, both amused and perturbed at this "censorship," grudgingly complied, and his lengthy exhortation is included in many publications of *Man and Superman*.

"Don Juan in Hell" has only four characters: legendary ladies' man Don Juan; the lovely and virtuous Dona Ana; Ana's father, Don Gonzalo, the commandant of Calatrava who was killed by Don Juan in a duel over Ana's honor; and the demon Lucifer, lord of hell. The play opens as Don Juan, a longtime resident of hell, welcomes the recently deceased Dona Ana to the afterlife. Horrified at the thought that she has been damned, Ana insists that a mistake has been made and that she belongs in heaven. An elaborate debate about the nature of heaven and hell ensues, eventually drawing the attention of Lucifer and of Ana's father who is visiting from paradise.

During this dialogue, Shaw's characters deride heaven as "dull and uncomfortable" while extolling the wonders of hell, called "the home of honor, duty, justice and the rest of the seven deadly virtues." Don Juan denounces the saved as weak and complacent, and even Ana's father says of the underworld "the best people are *here!*" The citizens of paradise, in contrast, are the "dullest dogs" of honor, "not beautiful, but decorated." Angered at this declaration, Ana reminds her father

that he lost his life defending her virtue and is himself a man of great esteem. The commandant coolly responds that he did not enter the duel out of love or devotion but because he feared what people would think of him if the did not do his "duty" by protecting his daughter's reputation.

Don Juan, on the other hand, reveals that it was not lust but an insatiable thirst for spiritual fulfillment that caused his constant philandering. Desperate to find some "deeper meaning" in life, he went from woman to woman in a futile search for this knowledge. Human love could not satisfy such a soulful ache. Now in hell, his attempt to unravel the mysteries of life is further frustrated. He laments that although he suffers no physical agony, the underworld "bores me beyond description, beyond belief." In Shaw's estimation, hell is a place of gratification, whereas heaven is a realm of contemplation. Meditation before God, a fate the superficial commandant finds unbearably boring, would be ultimate bliss for Don Juan.

At the conclusion of this act, Lucifer tells Don Juan that there is nothing keeping him in hell, and if he truly wishes to ascend to heaven he is free to go. Bewildered at this claim, Don Juan departs for the realm of the blessed. The commandant, on the other hand, elects to remain in hell, the "palace of pleasure," and joins Lucifer for a tour of the abyss. Ana, disgusted with both men, decides that no one could find happiness in such a "backwards" eternity with its seemingly nonsensical criteria for salvation. Audiences are left to ponder the point as the dream sequence abruptly ends.

The French drama AUCASSIN ET NICOLETTE offers a similar depiction of the world to come. In the play, starcrossed lovers vow they would rather suffer together in the depths of hell than languish in a celibate heaven filled with "dull" saints

MANES   Manes are the benevolent spirits of Roman myth who preside at MEMORIALS and watch over the dead. Romans worshiped these "blessed ghosts" as gods. Over time, manes (called *di manes,* meaning "sacred dead") were differentiated from familial spirits (*di parentes,* "dead of the family") and were worshiped at separate cultural festivals such as Feralia and Lemuria.

During late February, the Feralia (Festival of the Manes) was celebrated with feasts, rituals, and ceremonies to cleanse the dead. By paying homage to these immortal spirits, the living consoled themselves that their deceased loved ones where at peace. Grand monuments were dedicated *dis manibus sacrum* (sacred to the divine dead) during the festival. Manes are also mentioned in Virgil's AENEID as deified spirits.

MANSIONS OF THE SUN   Favored Inca souls are believed to ascend to the Mansions of the Sun, a great paradise. The most honored regions of this heaven are reserved for nobles, priests, and brave warriors. In this luminous realm, the blessed enjoy complete spiritual fulfillment and sensual gratification. The Inca worship the sun and consider the defining characteristic of paradise its eternal brilliance. Evil souls, however, are damned to an arid realm of suffering veiled in perpetual darkness.

MARDUK   Marduk (Merodach) is the chief deity and master of heaven in Babylonian mythology. The *Epic of Creation,* written around 1000 B.C., tells how Marduk formed the earth and the heavens and defeated evil spirits of destruction. During an apocalyptic battle with the wicked Ti'amat, Marduk is wounded, and from his blood, spilled on the clay soil of the new world, humankind sprang forth. Despite his injury, Marduk is able to kill Ti'amat. (The story bears some similarities to the Christian tale of a war in heaven between Satan, enemy of God, and the archangel MICHAEL.)

As the Babylonian empire spread during the two millennia B.C., Marduk often replaced gods of conquered peoples, such as the Sumerian ENLIL and the Assyrian Bel. During the early days of Judaism, Hebrew prophets warned that it is not Marduk, but YAWEH, who reigns supreme and holds the fate of the universe in his hands. Jeremiah foretells the destruction of Babylon, declaring: "Declare ye among the nations, and publish, and set up a standard; publish and conceal it not: say Babylon is taken, Bel is confounded, Marduk is broken in pieces, her idols are confounded, her images are broken in pieces. For out of the north cometh a nation against her" (Jer. 52:2–3).

In other myths, Marduk is the deity of calm over chaos. Great festivals were held in his honor to celebrate the new year, signaling the end of the old and the beginning of the new. During these ceremonies Marduk was worshiped as the "absolute ruler of heaven" and guardian of souls in paradise.

MARISHITEN Marishiten is the queen of heaven of Japanese Buddhist myth. She is often portrayed with three faces, two serene and one fearsome, and with eight willowy arms. A courageous deity worshiped by soldiers, Marishiten has power over the moon, stars, and sun. Many believe she has the ability to protect the living as well as provide comfort to souls in the "otherworld."

MARTYRS Those who give their lives in the service of religion are called martyrs, derived from the Greek *martys* meaning "witness." Because of this act of reverent bravery, martyred souls ascend directly to heaven. The term was first used to refer to followers of JESUS, the Christian Messiah, who refused to renounce their faith even in the face of death. Saint Stephen is called the "first Christian martyr," as the Bible tells how Stephen was stoned for angering a gathering of Jews and other nonbelievers: "When they heard these things [condemnations], they were cut to the heart, and they gnashed their teeth. But he [Stephen], being full of the Holy Ghost, looked up steadfastly into heaven and saw the glory of God, and Jesus standing on the right hand of God. . . . Then they cried out with a loud voice . . . and cast him out of the city and stoned him" (Acts 7: 54–55, 57–58).

Following this event, the Acts of the Apostles records "a great persecution against the church" by Roman authorities that would continue for centuries. Over the next twenty centuries, enemies of Christianity have used cruel torture, threats of death, and horrible executions to try to obliterate the religion. In most cases the plan backfires when victims go to their deaths with great enthusiasm, confident of their salvation. Sixteenth-century French martyr Anne du Bourg met her demise with typical elation, telling her captors that "six feet of earth for my body, and the infinite heavens for my soul is what I soon shall have."

Sir Thomas More, beheaded by King Henry VIII for refusing to bless the infamous king's divorce and remarriage, faced his death with the same unflinching courage. He chided his executioner, asking, "Please do not chop my beard in two, *it* has not committed treason!" Some stories claim that the axman began to weep at the prospect of executing such a virtuous man. More consoled him with the cheering words, "You send me to God."

The victims of this and subsequent religious persecutions are considered great SAINTS and heroes of CHRISTIAN PARADISE. Martyrs are memorialized in works of CHURCH ART AND ARCHITECTURE throughout the world. And according to REVELATION, a collection of prophecies regarding humanity's ultimate destiny, those who have "died for the testimony of Christ" will be handsomely rewarded in the next world. One passage describes how "them that were slain for the word of God" will be given white robes to symbolize their virtue.

After a "season of rest," these shining souls will have "places of honor" at the "eternal WEDDING FEAST."

The concept of martyrdom occurs in other faiths as well. In Islamic tradition, those who die in a JIHAD (holy war) are called SHADID. These brave souls are immediately delivered to the paradise DJANNA, where they enjoy special favors in the court of ALLAH. Hebrew lore includes EL EZKERAH (Legend of the Ten Martyrs), a tale of faith that transcends fear.

MA TSU P'O Ma Tsu P'o is the "lady of heaven" of Chinese Taoist belief, similar to the Japanese Buddhist MARISHITEN. Like her counterpart, Ma Tsu P'o is worshiped by seafarers and warriors hoping for her assistance in "calming the skies" and providing favorable weather conditions. When Jesuit missionaries came to China in the sixteenth century, they likened Ma Tsu P'o to the VIRGIN MARY, mother of JESUS and Queen of heaven in Christian tradition. The women are believed to dispense favors both in this world and the next.

MECHTHILD OF MAGDEBURG (ca. 1207–1290) One of the most enigmatic figures of medieval ESCHATOLOGY is the German mystic Mechthild of Magdeburg. The controversial "holy woman" describes numerous "visions" of heaven in her book *Das Fliessende Licht der Gottheit* (Flowing Light of the Godhead). The work is a compilation of poems, allegories, meditations, and "accounts" of her supernatural apparitions written over two decades, spanning the years 1250–1270. Her book was distributed throughout Christendom and is believed to have influenced Dante, who includes allusion to Mecthild in his *Purgatorio* (PURGATORY).

A self-proclaimed "seer" of supernatural activity, Mechthild claimed to have visited the court of the divine on many occasions during her lifetime. Based on these "travels," she describes a CHRISTIAN PARADISE separated into various locales, each distinct in appearance and function. Critics have had trouble discerning what portion of her writings represent actual visions and which are merely speculation or outright fancy; however, the images contained in *Flowing Light* had a widespread impact on her contemporaries. Many considered the book to be a verbatim diary of Mechthild's experiences and accepted every word as gospel truth.

Mechthild's journey in *Flowing Light of the Godhead* begins in the "earthly paradise," a lower realm that is hidden somewhere on earth. Here, she meets the Old Testament patriarchs ENOCH and ELIJAH. The two men, although virtuous and devoted to God, cannot ascend farther since they died before JESUS Christ opened the gates of heaven after his crucifixion. This first circle of the HEREAFTER is a lush garden of fragrant flowers, sweet rivers, and gentle winds. In addition to housing the spirits of those who lived in the era before Christ, this dimension is the dwelling place of righteous souls not pious enough to dwell in the presence of the Almighty.

Next in ascending order are ten "domes," with every level indicating a greater "degree of sanctity." This config-uration had once been completely in-habited by the ANGELS. However, after the rebellion in heaven (in which the archangel MICHAEL defeated Lucifer), the "vile" spirits were cast into hell. The spaces they left are now awarded to human souls. Those who die without facing severe challenges (such as infant children) and the "moderately virtuous" are relegated to the lower domes, while the SAINTS are given loftier spots. MAR-TYRS fill the eighth level, the apostles the ninth, and "holy virgins" (such as Mechthild herself) the tenth and high-est layer, which is closest to God. The VIRGIN MARY, mother of Jesus, is fore-most among these blessed women.

Atop these domes is the pinnacle of paradise, referred to as the "Third Heaven," consisting of the "palace of the Trinity" and what Mechthild calls "Christ's bridal chamber." This highest level is reserved for "holy virgins" who have lived lives of chastity, dedicating themselves body and soul to the Lord. In the afterlife, the blessed maidens (who usually reside in the tenth dome) are in-vited into the "bridal chamber" to enjoy "union" with Christ. Virgins are also the only souls given the BEATIFIC VISION, en-abling them to witness the majesty of God fully and with complete understand-ing. (The rest of the saved experience a lesser "vision" of the divine, appreciating his beauty in human terms but unable to fathom the spiritual magnificence.)

Mechthild also claims that during a particularly intense supernatural appari-tion, she was kissed by the Son of God, and the physical contact left her feeling "elevated above the angelic hosts." For such pure and "untouched" women, the delights of heaven would more than compensate for the carnal pleasures for-sworn on earth.

Throughout all levels of paradise, the saved are clothed in rich robes reflecting their status in the "divine court." The holiest of saints also receive special jew-elry and robes as part of their reward. God Himself awards crowns to extraordi-nary souls who have endured grueling trials for the sake of their faith.

Mechthild also describes in *Flowing Light* the realm of purgatory, where spir-its purge themselves of the "stain of sin" before proceeding to paradise. It is a place of sorrow tempered with hope, for the souls in this intermediate place know that they will one day look upon the face of God. Spirits in purgatory are also filled with a sense of justice, for they see clearly the ugliness of their sins (no matter how minor the offense) and are eager to cleanse themselves of the taint. Only after purging all residue of sin are these souls willing to take their places in heaven.

Due in part to her insistence that vir-ginity is the one true measure of holiness, Mechthild's writings have never been sanctioned by Christian leaders. Many, in fact, have dismissed her *Flowing Light* as "fanciful delusion" and even "self-aggran-dizement." Contemporary clerics decried the woman as wicked and forced her to flee her hometown and take sanctuary in the convent where SAINT GERTRUDE was prioress. However, Mechthild remained the subject of much devotion for decades after her death. Her notions of eternal rewards inspired many young girls to "take up the cloth," with its inherent vow of chastity promising a lofty status in the world to come.

MEDIEVAL DRAMA   After the last public theatrical performance was held in Rome in A.D. 533 drama in Europe ceased production for almost four centuries. It was not until the tenth century, when Roman Catholic church officials began presenting religious plays, that performers returned to the stage. These dramas, versions of Christian MYSTERY PLAYS, began as amateurish interpretations of such supernatural events as the war in heaven led by the archangel MICHAEL, the resurrection of JESUS and the LAST JUDGMENT. Scenery consisted of painted booths representing the earth, heaven, hell, PURGATORY, and other settings. Actors simply moved from one booth to the next as the plot unfolded, with much narration to fill in the gaps. From these meager origins, medieval drama emerged as a dominant force in European culture.

Early medieval plays were strictly overseen by church officials. These passion plays offered dramatizations of lives of SAINTS, MARTYRS, AND THE VIRGIN MARY and adventures of ANGELS such as GABRIEL, Michael, and RAPHAEL. But by the late 1300s, most public dramas were produced by craft guilds dedicated to theatrical arts. Some of the most powerful scenes involved tales of the afterlife, and competing crafters were constantly trying to outdo one another. Special ef-

fects added pizzazz to the plays, with the more elaborate productions featuring fireworks, explosions, and crude pyrotechnics.

But this shift in emphasis from religion to entertainment led to problems with Christian officials. Clerics disapproved of the "edited" plots as they strayed ever further from biblical accounts and offered more "speculative" treatments of supernatural mysteries. Christian leaders were concerned when crowds became more enraptured with scenes of Satan and hell than with less spectacular images of God and PARADISE, worrying that this glamorization of damnation would erode their authority and take the sting out of their dire warnings.

Eventually, public presentations branched off into several different areas. Mystery plays continued to treat aspects of the supernatural but with ever-increasing emphasis on the occult, fairies, magic spells, and other subjects frowned on by church hierarchy. Christian authorities began funneling their efforts into MORALITY PLAYS, dramas that adhered strictly to the teachings and events of the Bible. Allegories showing the necessity of virtue such as the classic EVERYMAN also received church approval.

FOLK PLAYS, a less polished version of theater, also became increasingly popular throughout Europe. These dramas, usually free-form efforts using amateur players, often moved through the crowds during festivals and centered on some particular event (harvest) or person (the village's patron). Unlike morality plays, the point of these performances was to entertain rather than educate.

Medieval dramas also began the evolution of theater, which resulted in the rise of such literary geniuses as William Shakespeare, Christopher Marlowe, and a host of European dramatists.

MEFISTOFELE   Arrigo Boito's 1868 opera *Mefistofele*, like Charles Gounod's *FAUST*, is based on Johann Wolfgang von Goethe's 's classic story of deals with the devil. However, Boito's version is unique in that it traces events from the point of view of the demon Mefistofele, sent to tempt Dr. Faust into selling his soul, rather than from the doctor's perspective.

The opera opens as Mefistofele is visiting the "hosts of Heaven" and makes a wager with the Almighty. He bets that he can corrupt Faust, a pious scholar, and convince him to renounce Christianity. God accepts the challenge, and the demon immediately appears to Faust with a bevy of delights. Mefistofele first makes the doctor young again, and the two then embark upon an orgy of sexual escapades and occult rituals. After indulging in all manner of carnal pleasures, the devil takes Faust to ancient Greece to sample the favors of the sensuous Helen of Troy.

At first, Faust revels in this wanton excess. But when Margherita—a young maiden he seduced, impregnated, and then abandoned—despairs and drowns their infant child, the doctor is moved to pity. Before he can atone for his cruelty, Margherita dies and is carried to heaven by compassionate ANGELS. Faust is unable to forget her and spends the rest of his days regretting his bitter bargain with hell.

By the opera's end, Faust has become obsessed with Margherita and detests himself for what he has become. He utters a forlorn prayer and waits to die. Touched by his words, God forgives the wayward scholar and sends a chorus of cherubim to console him. They shower Faust with roses as the celestial gates appear and open to allow him entrance to heaven. Mefistofele, enraged at this act of mercy, has no choice but to return empty-handed to the inferno. Unlike his human counterparts, the demon is unwilling to reject his evil and embrace goodness and therefore will never again know the joy of paradise.

MEMNOCH THE DEVIL Anne Rice's 1995 novel *Memnoch the Devil* details a war for the allegiance of Lestat, the glamorous New Orleans vampire. Satan, renamed Memnoch in Rice's work, describes himself as "the Archangel and Accuser of God" who is more concerned with human salvation than is the Almighty. Determined to prove himself more compassionate than the creator, Memnoch takes the vampire on a guided tour of heaven, hell, and human history in an attempt to endear Lestat to the devil's cause.

The heaven depicted in Rice's book is a luminous realm of dazzling "archways, towers, halls, galleries, gardens, great fields, forests, streams." It is populated with human souls and ANGELS, whose joy is so complete it makes a sound resembling laughter. Paradise is a great mingling of diverse beings, "ever enhanced and enriched by new souls from all quarters of the world" bearing "garments of all different kinds." Social interaction in heaven includes embracing, kissing, talking, and laughing. Blessed souls partake in "a great and final gathering," the ultimate REUNION of loved ones in eternity.

While in heaven, Lestat also sees a vast display of "books and scrolls" containing the mysteries of the universe. They lay open, inviting the curious to read and learn. Beyond this is a celestial observation deck where the saved can view the earth "in all its ages," from the ancient days of Mesopotamia to modern times and beyond. Watching over the human world is God, a being of light beautiful to behold, with "his face perfectly symmetrical and flawless, his gaze intense."

But *Memnoch the Devil* takes a bizarre turn when it is revealed that God is not particularly interested in the eternal fate of human souls. Lestat learns that Memnoch was once a glorious angel in heaven's court before he angered the Almighty and was cast to the earth. After this expulsion, Memnoch travels to hell and dedicates himself to bringing human souls to paradise from Sheol, a bitter realm of gloom for departed souls. God is quite uninterested in this crusade. Hearing this, Lestat suspects that Memnoch is lying or perhaps deluding himself about God's supposed indifference. In either case, he is reluctant to take the word of the devil on matters of divine truth.

Within her convoluted philosophical venture, Rice conjures afterlife images from a variety of cultures. She compares JESUS to the Egyptian OSIRIS, refers to the angels MICHAEL and URIEL, and likens paradise to the sketchings of WILLIAM BLAKE. *Memnoch the Devil* also culls the descriptions of NEAR-DEATH EXPERIENCES, speculating on the "tunnel of light" so often connected to such mystic visions. The result is a perplexing mix of pseudophilosophy that manages to present an appealing heaven while portraying a distinctly distasteful Supreme Being.

MEMORIALS   Many cultures believe that the way a person is buried and memorialized has a direct impact on that soul's pleasure in the afterlife. Some peoples, including the Romans and Greeks, thought that those who were not given proper funerary rites could never reach paradise. Such spirits would be damned to spend eternity wandering the "ghost realm" in search of elusive peace. Numerous African tribes equate respect of the dead with the soul's afterlife fate and therefore pay great homage to their deceased loved ones. Similarly, medieval Christians believed that bodies must be buried in sacred ground in order to ascend to heaven and would make sure their family members received the requisite rites and ceremonies.

Ancient Chinese tombs dating back to before 1000 B.C. often include stone "guards" posted near the graves. The statues depict fierce soldiers charged with protecting the deceased and aiding souls in reaching the joyous afterlife. One recently discovered site revealed a deep funerary pit containing eleven elaborate royal grave sites. In addition to the bodies of the eleven rulers, archaeologists found the remains of hundreds of dogs, horses, and servants sacrificed to serve the emperors in the next world. Scientists estimate that just to move the dirt involved in creating such as massive structure must have taken at least seven thousand man-hours of labor.

The ancient Egyptian pyramids were likewise magnificent feats of architectural accomplishment. Each towering edifice contained dozens of rooms and a maze of "secret passageways" to prevent grave robbers from looting the gold, jewels, and foodstuffs entombed with the pharaoh for his use in the afterlife. Most also included chambers for animals and servants—who were buried alive—to serve their king in eternity. Even the triangular design of these grand tombs was intended to do more than simply commemorate past rulers. The Egyptians believed that the pyramids served as divine "steps" that would lead the regal spirits to paradise.

The ETRUSCANS dedicated vast amounts of creative energy to memorializing their dead. Most cities were bounded by a necropolis, a replica of the village believed to be inhabited by departed spirits. The walls of these structures were decorated with murals showing an afterlife of banquets, jeweled goblets, and great celebrations (although later illustrations tended to show the horrors of hell rather than the pleasures of paradise). Similar graphics adorn fourth-century B.C. Greek SAR-COPHAGI. The art discovered on these ancient memorials depicts blessed ELY-SIUM where the dead gather at an eternal festival of social delights.

In Islamic culture, the TAJ MAHAL is among the most elaborate and well-known monuments to the dead. The beautiful complex, with its smooth domes, elegant spires, and intricate gardens, was erected by seventh-century emperor Shah Jahan in memory of his young bride. After losing his love soon after their wedding, the distraught widower demanded a memorial be built in her honor. Years of planning and design went into creating the Taj Mahal, much of it devoted to "simulating paradise." The walls of the beautiful palace even feature inscriptions from the KORAN (Islam's holy book) regarding DJANNA, the blessed realm of the Almighty.

Followers of JESUS, the Christian Messiah, often memorialize their dead with passages from the Bible describing CHRISTIAN PARADISE. Gravestones typically include biblical references to heaven, pictures or statues of ANGELS, or allusions to a REUNION in eternity. Common epitaphs include such phrases as "together forever," "joined in paradise," and "never to part again." These affirmations of belief in a "life in Christ" after death remain prevalent.

In contemporary American culture, victims of certain types of deaths are frequently memorialized in specialized tributes. Fallen police officers, firefighters, and other civic heroes are remembered in ceremonies to commemorate their ultimate sacrifice. Likewise, soldiers killed in battle are routinely honored with public procession and services.

'Tis Better to have
Them Say, "There he Goes"
Than, "here he Lies".

A World War I memorial card imagines fallen
heroes in a better place.

mystic realm dwell in eternal bliss and find enlightenment with Indra, the "lord of paradise."

In the BARDO THODOL, the Tibetan Book of the Dead, Mount Meru is called the "site of worship" where ancient sages gathered to ponder the mysteries of the cosmos. Many scholars believe that this is how the mountain came to be associated with heaven and eventually declared the site of eternal paradise.

MESSIAH The *Messiah*, an oratorio celebration of the life of JESUS Christ, was written by George Frideric Handel in 1742. Composed in three sections, the work traces the plan of human salvation from Old Testament prophecies about the coming Redeemer to the birth of Christ to his sacrifice on the cross and subsequent resurrection. The most famous movement of the *Messiah* is the "Hallelujah Chorus," reminiscent of the choirs of ANGELS who sing eternally at the throne of God.

This musical masterpiece infused the age-old biblical stories with dynamic energy and intangible beauty. Handel also greatly advanced the development of European chorus singing with this piece by replacing traditional Latin text with the vernacular. By using English lyrics that could be understood by audiences, Handel created a grand religious production that was aesthetically pleasing as well as truly inspirational.

In addition to the *Messiah*, Handel wrote a number of works inspired by the lives of SAINTS and patriarchs. These include *Ode for* SAINT CECILIA's *Day* as

And people lost to drunk-driving accidents, AIDS, cancer, violence, or other "untimely deaths" are often memorialized through events (such as fund-raising drives) or awareness programs designed to bring some positive good out of tragedy. These and similar tributes offer comfort to mourners, intimating that the deceased are "in a better place" where all pain has forever ceased.

MERU, MOUNT According to ancient Hindu legend, the paradise SWARGA is located atop Mount Meru, the "shining mountain." It is believed to lie at the center of the universe, directly above the Himalaya mountains. Spirits in this well as compositions celebrating Old Testament heroes Joshua, Esther, and Sampson. A prolific composer, music scholars note that "one edition of his complete works fills a hundred volumes." Many of Handel's compositions are still performed, although his *Messiah* remains his crowing achievement.

METHODIUS, SAINT (died ca. 870) Saint Methodius is a hero of the Greek Orthodox church who (legend claims) converted an entire nation with his compelling painting of the LAST JUDGMENT. According to the story, word of Saint Methodius's artistic talent spread along the Danube, where he was working as a Christian missionary. His reputation piqued the curiosity of Borgias, a pagan king of Bulgaria, who asked the young cleric to paint a grand mural in his banquet hall where he entertained guests. Methodius filled the wall with images of SAINTS and ANGELS, demons and the damned, and a magnificent JESUS pronouncing sentence on legions of souls. The portraits of heaven and hell were inspired by REVELATION, bringing to life fantastic images of the dazzling NEW JERUSALEM. The celestial city was more splendid than anything Borgias had ever imagined, let alone seen.

When the picture was unveiled, the king was so overcome by the work he implored Methodius to educate him on this unknown faith. He was mesmerized by the beautiful paradise and longed to enter this mystic place. After listening to the descriptions of the blissful afterlife and the way to reach this realm, Borgias was immediately baptized and declared Christianity the official religion of Bulgaria. He then invited Methodius and his fellow missionaries to preach to the masses and facilitated their efforts to spread the gospel. Within a few decades of this event, the entire kingdom had converted to the faith of Christ.

Saint Methodius is revered by artists throughout the world. His feast day is celebrated on May 11.

MICHAEL The 1997 film *Michael* stars John Travolta as a restless ANGEL who descends to earth to relish the delights of cigarettes, Motown music, and "one-night stands." A winged wonder, Travolta claims to be none other than MICHAEL the archangel, the celestial warrior who battled Satan and forced the rebel angels into hell. He relishes repeating his war stories, excitedly describing how he prevailed in the face of demons who "came at me from every angle of heaven . . . as a hundred mouths, open and stinking with decay!"

Now on an earthly vacation, Travolta embodies many angelic qualities despite his more human appearance. He defends the weak, protects the vulnerable, and comforts the sorrowing. Pragmatic but optimistic, the heavenly visitor explains that although he "can't change the nature of the world," he is able (as are all angels) to perform "small miracles" for the benefit of humankind. And unlike his human counterparts, he truly recognizes and appreciates God's handiwork in simple things. In this quiet and offbeat way, Travolta gives viewers a glimpse of heaven.

Michael also incorporates familiar SYMBOLS of heaven into the film. The most significant is the WEDDING FEAST, a prominent biblical image of paradise. Travolta and his human companions are aided in changing a tire by a pair of newlyweds, who then join them at a makeshift party in a roadside diner. The celebration involves a buffet of pie, followed by joyous singing and dancing. As the revelers sample slice after slice of tasty pastry, Travolta's date coos that at times like these, she knows "God is in heaven and all is right with the world."

In a touching final scene, Travolta and the soul of a deceased friend dance through the streets of Chicago, unseen by human eyes. "Let's go home," they decide, and they depart for heaven, still dancing and laughing as they go.

Michael the Archangel engraving by Martin Schongauer. ART TODAY

MICHAEL THE ARCHANGEL The archangel Michael (whose name means "like God") is the most prominent ANGEL in Judeo-Christian lore. He is the celestial protector of heaven who appears in artworks and literature from Jewish, Christian, and Islamic cultures as well as in numerous secular compositions.

In Hebrew legends, Michael is credited with writing some of the Psalms and visiting biblical heroes to inform them of coming events. Christian tradition describes Michael as the brave warrior who defends paradise from an attack of rebel angels. According to the *Book of* REVELATION, Michael rallied the faithful against Satan and his minions and forced them out of paradise: "And there was a war in heaven: Michael and his angels fought against the dragon; and the dragon fought and his angels and prevailed not" (Rev. 12:7–8).

Religious scholars throughout history have been fascinated with the archangel Michael. He has been given an array of titles and credited with numerous supernatural feats. SAINT BASIL called him the "Prince of All Angels," while THOMAS AQUINAS referred to Michael as the leader of the lowest choir of heavenly spirits. His assistance was invoked by Pope GREGORY THE GREAT in 590 to end a terrible plague that had been decimating the population. Islamic texts refer to Michael (Mika'il) as a mediator who will "implore the pardon of ALLAH" (God) and seek mercy for sinners.

In 1886 Pope Leo XIII had a horrific vision of the future in which Michael played an important role. According to the account, Leo collapsed and was feared dead by the cardinals with whom he had been talking. However, the pontiff suddenly bolted upright, declaring that he had witnessed an encounter between God and Satan in which the devil vowed to viciously attack the church (and humanity in general) during the twentieth century. The fiend swore he would wage his most violent war against the forces of goodness. Upon awakening, Leo wrote a prayer begging the assistance of Michael in this conflict, since the angel had already demonstrated his ability to defeat Satan's vile schemes: "Saint Michael the Archangel, defend us in battle! Be our protection against the wickedness and snares of the devil. May God rebuke him, we humbly pray, and do thou, Oh Prince of the heavenly host, by the power of God, thrust into hell Satan and all the other evil spirits who roam the earth seeking the ruin of souls."

By papal decree, this prayer was recited at the close of all Catholic masses. A similar prayer, invoking Michael as the "Most glorious Prince of the Heavenly Army," is used in rites of exorcism to cast out demons and preserve human souls from "the princes and powers and rulers of darkness." And the centuries-old offertory chant from the Mass for the Dead asks that "the standard-bearer Michael conduct [the souls of the dead] into the holy light, which thou did promise of old to Abraham and his seed."

The archangel is mentioned in numerous religious works, including the Bible, KORAN, Talmud, and DEAD SEA SCROLLS. He is called the "leader of the Sons of Light" and "defender of paradise." Michael also appears in such secular fiction classics as Dante's DIVINE COMEDY: THE PARADISO, Milton's PARADISE LOST and scores of works of POETRY. And the title character of the 1997 film MICHAEL is offered as a modern incarnation of the ancient hero.

Because of his role as protector and defender of the virtuous, Michael is often depicted holding an unsheathed sword. Roman Catholic doctrine refers to him as the patron of police officers and soldiers, and his intercession is sought on behalf of all those who are oppressed.

MICHELANGELO

(1475–1564) Michelangelo Buonarroti has been called the "greatest artist of all time" by art scholars from across the world. This Renaissance genius mastered a variety of media during his illustrious career, creating classic works of sculpture, oil painting, fresco, charcoal sketching, and even architectural design. His creations have prompted many to describe the artist as "divine." Among his great compositions are numerous depictions of GOD, ANGELS, the VIRGIN MARY, and heaven itself.

Though Michelangelo's father, a mayor and critic of artistry, discouraged his son from pursing a career in art, the boy's talent was quickly recognized by influential patrons in his hometown of Florence, Italy. At age fourteen, Michelangelo was invited to live and study with the powerful Medici family, where he quickly emerged as the most gifted artist in the guild. During this time, he spent his days in the company of intellectuals who were fascinated with the resurgence of Roman and Greek mythology and who were increasingly criticizing Christianity as stern and repressive. Michelangelo, a devout Roman Catholic, found himself caught in this debate, and his works reflect these differing influences.

Like many artists of the time, Michelangelo was intrigued with anatomy, and he dissected corpses to learn the wonders of the human form. He believed that the soul is equally beautiful and directly reflects the majesty of the creator. As early as age sixteen, he began producing works based on both pagan mythical creatures and sacred religious doctrines, eventually blending them in his later masterpieces. In 1527, Protestant armies of the heretic Martin Luther unleashed a nine-month reign of terror that deeply affected Michelangelo. During that time, Luther's forces committed rape, murder, vandalism of churches, and all manner of atrocities. This brutal attack on Catholicism forced Michelangelo to reexamine his own beliefs, and ultimately he emerged more devoted to his Catholic roots than ever.

Word of his abilities spread, and the artist was approached to paint the ceiling of the Vatican's Sistine Chapel. At first Michelangelo argued that the commission should be given to the master Raphael, whom he considered to be a superior painter. Michelangelo saw himself as a sculptor and preferred working in this medium. Eventually he acquiesced to Pope Julius's request and spent the next four years working on the Sistine Chapel ceiling. The completed mural, which is more than 130 feet long, includes scores of religious heroes and patriarchs, biblical stories, and events in Christian history.

One of the most famous sections is "The Creation of Adam." This panel depicts God the Father as an elderly gentleman with white robes and a long beard. He is leaning down from heaven to touch, and thereby bestow life on, Adam, his new creation. God is supported by two wingless angels, one male and one female, who flank him in a crimson aura. The Father's face is loving, paternal, strong. (This painting has spawned numerous adaptations, including an 1887 ADVERTISING campaign for Williams Shaving Products. The ad shows Michelangelo's art above text reminding buyers "Adam was created *without* a beard" and suggesting that heaven prefers clean-shaven men.) Other scenes show God in heaven creating plants, light and dark and other facets of the firmament. In each image, the Almighty is surrounded by gracious angels in billowy purple clouds.

During his tenure in Rome, Michelangelo also painted a magnificent LAST JUDGMENT scene behind the altar of SAINT PETER's Cathedral. The massive work, which mingled images of the Greek underworld Hades with CHRISTIAN PARADISE, reveals the artist's growing obsession with the afterlife. The composition took seven years to complete, occupying Michelangelo from 1534 to 1541, and caused quite a stir when it was finally unveiled. Clerics were offended by the clean-shaven Christ (resembling the pagan Apollo) and by his stern, almost vengeful countenance. Other critics objected to Michelangelo's decision to portray souls as naked beings stripped of all earthly possessions. Such nudity, they claimed, had no place in a church.

Another frequent subject for the artist was MEMORIALS to nobles, popes, and royalty. The skilled sculptor brought his talent for showing the grandeur of paradise to these stone monuments. Before his death, Michelangelo also completed architectural plans for the dome of St. Peter's Basilica, which was later finished and remains one of Europe's most imitated structures.

MILKY WAY The constellation Milky Way has been called the "cradle of heaven" by many cultures. Ancient Greek beliefs held that the path to eternity led to the stars, where blessed souls would take their place in the cosmos. Priests of Apollo taught that after death, purified spirits become stars and watch over humanity for all eternity. For the Egyptians, the Milky Way serves as the road to paradise and departing point for the "boat of the sun god RA."

The Milky Way figures into notions of AFRICAN PARADISE as well. The Dagba of Central Africa believe that the Milky Way is in fact the remnants of a mystic rope that once linked heaven and earth. It had been a passageway so that humans could visit the "upper world" and socialize with the gods. However, the gods eventually became angry with humankind for constantly disturbing them with

requests and complaints about life on earth. Exasperated, they destroyed the radiant cord and scattered its pieces across the sky, creating the Milky Way. Now, humans can ascend "to the skies" only upon death, from which there is no return.

MILLENNIUM The millennium refers to the Christian concept of a thousand-year epoch of peace and harmony that will immediately precede the LAST JUDGMENT and will usher in the eternal reign of God. The millennium is foretold in St. John's REVELATION: "And he laid hold on the dragon, that old serpent, which is the Devil, and Satan, and bound him a thousand years, and cast him into the bottomless pit, and shut him up, and set a seal upon him, that he should deceive the nations no more, till the thousand years should be fulfilled" (Rev. 20:2–3).

Believers who have rejected evil "shall be priests of God and of Christ, and shall reign with him a thousand years." After that time, Satan will be loosed, and JESUS will preside over the Last Judgment, when all human souls will be summoned to give an account of their lives. The just will be rewarded with beauty and wisdom the likes of which "neither eye has seen, nor ear has heard, nor mind has imagined" in heaven. But those who have embraced sin will be "cast into a lake of fire."

When these events come to pass, the earth will be destroyed, and the NEW JERUSALEM will appear. In this enchanted realm, humans will dwell with ANGELS, and sin, suffering, and war will cease to exist. The saved will spend eternity in the "house of the Lord."

MIRROR WORLD African Congolese believe that spirits depart to a mirror world that closely resembles earthly life, only in reverse. In this mystic plain, spirits, called MIZUMU, rise at night and sleep during the day, plant in the autumn and harvest in the spring, etc. This paradise is "white" and the world is "black," with a rainbow connecting the two. Community life continues much as it had among the living, and social status remains the same. The image of the mirror world bears many similarities to other concepts of AFRICAN PARADISE, such as the CITY IN THE SKY and SKY VILLAGE.

MIZUMU In the Congo, it is believed that departed spirits live on as mizumu in a MIRROR WORLD similar to earthly life. After death, the mizumu remain close to their homes, as they still need food, shelter, companionship, and other creature comforts. However, life as mizumu is far superior to mortal existence. Mizumu spend their time dancing, drinking, and enjoying great feasts. The sounds of mizumu drums and celebrations can be heard by putting an ear to the ground, especially during the dark of the moon.

The mizumu have the power to harm the living, especially if they are not paid proper respect by their surviving family members. Childhood deaths, illness, and droughts are often thought to be caused by angered spirits in retribution for such offenses. In order to pacify the mizumu, rituals and offerings of food (and in rare cases even human sacrifice) are paid to the departed tribespeople.

MOKSHA Moksha is the ultimate spiritual destiny of Hinduism, similar to the Buddhist NIRVANA and the Jain KEVALA. It is literally "liberation" from samsara, the continuing cycle of reincarnation. Souls who devote their "living energies" to meditation can achieve moksha upon death rather than be returned to the earth in another body. Instead of reincarnating, the spirit dissolves as an individual entity and joins the collective cosmic essence, as "a drop of rain joins the ocean." Liberated souls thus spend eternity "as one with the universe," considered the perfect state of spiritual bliss.

MONICA, SAINT (332–387.) An early SAINT in the Christian church, Monica had frequent visions of heaven during her lifetime. She often discussed them with her son, SAINT AUGUSTINE, a great philosopher and Doctor of the Church. The two would pass hours contemplating paradise and often experienced spiritual ecstasy, becoming so focused on the divine they temporarily lost touch with the physical world. St. Monica was convinced that the greatest imaginable pleasures on earth "could not compare with the joys of that eternal light."

During one especially powerful incident, the mother and son sat in the Garden of Ostia envisioning heaven. Both became enraptured with this overwhelming vision. When the apparition was over, St. Monica expressed her eagerness to shed her human body and ascend to that sacred realm. Her son agreed that the joys of paradise indeed surpassed the greatest delights imaginable on earth. Less than two weeks after the vision at Ostia, St. Monica died with Augustine at her side.

Monica was canonized a saint in the Roman Catholic church and is considered the patroness of married women. Her feast day is May 4.

MONTY PYTHON'S THE MEANING OF LIFE   The British comedy troupe Monty Python takes a stab at ESCHATOLOGY in its 1983 film *Monty Python's The Meaning of Life*. The film strings together a number of sketches that probe humanity's most compelling question: What is this life all about? Preoccupied with irreverent jabs at organized religion and stomach-churning scenes of cascading body fluids, writers Graham Chapman, John Cleese, Terry Gilliam, Eric Idle, Terry Jones, and Michael Palin offer little insight into the eternal mystery. However, the final segment, set in the Great Beyond, does illustrate a rather unconventional image of paradise.

After eating tainted salmon mousse, a gathering of dinner party guests is approached by Death, personified as a hooded figure carrying a scythe. After convincing the reluctant souls that they are indeed deceased, he orders them to accompany him to the afterlife. Still protesting their fate, the couples drive "spirit cars" to the HEREAFTER, where they discover that heaven resembles a luxury hotel. After "checking in" at the celestial front desk, the couples are seated in the hotel's grand ballroom just as the floor show begins. In the production, singers extol "every day is Christmas" in heaven, as the saved gobble down Steak Diane and Chicken Kiev. The film then shifts to a montage of surreal images and whimsical clips, concluding with a parody of the Queen Mum mundanely revealing "the meaning of life."

Famed British reviewer Leslie Halliwell succinctly sums up *Monty Python's The Meaning of Life* as "a series of sketches in questionable taste" that provide humor rather than illumination regarding humanity's ultimate destiny.

MORALITY PLAYS   In the 1300s, church officials decided that MYSTERY PLAYS, dramas that often included notions of CHRISTIAN PARADISE, hell, and other religious doctrines, were becoming too secular. Clerics felt that the plays titillated rather than terrified audiences with lavish hell scenes and conversely made paradise seem downright boring. Concerned with the effect this was having on the faithful, religious leaders banned the offending productions and replaced them with their own dramatic presentations. These new dramas, called morality plays, adhered strictly to biblical text and official Christian dogma. Relating tales of legendary SAINTS and MARTYRS as well as stories from the Bible, each play's sole objective was to inspire the audience to greater holiness.

Common themes for these dramas

included the war in heaven, the creation of the earth, the prophesied apocalypse, the LAST JUDGMENT, and splendors of paradise. Personified abstractions such as Lust, Gluttony, and Avarice were common villains who fought Obedience, Honesty, and Purity in these cautionary tales. Theatrical sets included elaborate fuming hellmouths and billowy heavens, brightened with extensive use of gold and brilliant white.

The most famous morality play is EVERYMAN, first produced around the year 1500. This English drama depicts the soul's journey to the afterlife and eventual judgment before the Almighty. The title character, a typical human, is called before the throne of God and must prove himself worthy of salvation. If he fails, he faces eternal damnation to a fiery pit of torture. Everyman enlists the aid of numerous virtues, confesses his sins, and ultimately is admitted to heaven not by merit but by the grace of God. His redemption is announced by grand ANGELS who happily tell audience members that virtually all humans can ascend to paradise if they put their faith in JESUS.

Morality plays went into decline around the seventeenth century, when professional writers and performers began producing theatrical works. Many localities continued presenting religious dramas about their patron saints, usually as part of some traditional festival. Over the years, these shows too became increasingly secular, focusing on cultural rather than religious events, and eventually died out altogether. Today, revivals of morality plays are enjoyed for their historical importance rather than their inspirational content.

MORMON HEAVEN   The Church of Jesus Christ of Latter-Day Saints, also known as the Mormon church, has a distinct concept of the afterlife that differs greatly from traditional CHRISTIAN PARADISE. The religion was founded by Joseph Smith a controversial figure who claimed to have received a series of divine visions beginning around 1820. In one of these, the angel MORONI told Smith he was to become the "first prophet" of JESUS' new earthly church. This angelic messenger then gave Smith gold plates written in the "language of Heaven," which he deciphered into the Book of Mormon. The mystic golden tablets were then borne back to paradise, where they would remain for eternity.

According to Smith's teachings, humans exist prior to their earthly lives as "spirit children" in heaven, but they forget this celestial life when they are incarnated. Once on earth, they grow in understanding before death moves them to the next stage of development, the "spirit world." This realm is not itself heaven but a place for further spiritual growth before "the resurrection" (LAST JUDGMENT), at which time the saved will enter eternal bliss.

Paradise offers both natural splendor—such as fragrant flowers, majestic mountains, and crystal streams—and created treasures as divine rewards. Physical delights include houses of gold, jeweled streets, and sculpted fountains. While in this intermediate place, souls try to "teach" and "convert" the dead who have not accepted the "truth of Mormon" during the living years.

Married Mormons wishing to continue their marital relationship for all eternity must participate in a special ceremony while still alive. A husband and wife can "seal" their marriage on earth, thereby ensuring that their family will remain intact in the afterlife. Otherwise, souls not "sealed" to each other can remarry in the next realm and procreate more "spirit children." (Writings explain that these celestial offspring will populate "other worlds" as well as provide future earthlings.) Those who have sealed marriages can also become "godlike" in eternity, an aspiration no single person can ever achieve.

Mormons also believe in the baptism of the dead. This doctrine states that people can christen their deceased relatives by proxy, literally by naming the individual and then washing in the baptismal pool. In this way, followers can "redeem" the souls of their deceased loved ones and even ancestors from generations back. Thus all can enjoy a REUNION in heaven, even those who never heard of or accepted the Mormon faith while alive.

Once in Mormon heaven, the saved can ascend to different realms of glory, the greatest of which is a "renewed Earth." In this lush garden paradise, human souls can become gods themselves, enjoying "the highest glories of eternity." Smith claimed to have seen visions of this "New Eden" during his lifetime and offered them as powerful witness to his followers.

Mormonism was dismissed as a pass-ing cult when it first appeared on the American scene. Founder John Smith was not considered credible, since he had been arrested for such varied crimes as necromancy, bank fraud, and even involvement in an attempted political assassination. He provoked further condemnation by declaring that his followers did not have to obey U.S. laws and that he himself was the ultimate arbiter of right and wrong. Smith was eventually murdered by an angry mob, and his critics believed the Church of Mormon would die with him.

But Mormonism found new life under the direction of Brigham Young, a vivacious, eloquent man with great leadership abilities. He succeeded Smith as head of the Mormon church in 1844 and moved the flock from Smith's native New York to Utah to avoid religious persecution. President Fillmore was so impressed with Smith he appointed him governor of the territory (a post Smith subsequently lost for refusing to renounce polygamy). In 1890 Young revamped the church's policies and helped elevate Mormonism to the level of respectability, winning thousands of converts with the new reforms.

Today, the Mormon church is in full compliance with national law and thus has become an accepted religious denomination. Its temple in Salt Lake City and the National Temple in Washington, D.C. (designed to reflect the splendor of paradise), annually welcome thousands of pilgrims and visitors alike.

MORONI Moroni is the angel who delivered the "gospel of the new REVELA-

TION" to Joseph Smith according to the Church of Jesus Christ of Latter-Day Saints, also known as the Mormons. The legend states that Moroni brought to young Smith a set of gold plates written in "the language of Heaven" that contained the completion of the Bible. When Smith had finished deciphering these with Moroni's help, they were taken back to paradise, where they remain today. A statue of the majestic angel marks the site where this miraculous event occurred, just outside Palmyra, New York.

MOST RIDICULOUS DIALOGUE
Italian dramatist Ruzzante offers a sardonic view of the afterlife in his play *Most Ridiculous Dialogue*, penned around 1537. In the work, a deceased man gives a description of two "otherworlds" that await beyond death. The first is a gleaming realm for the virtuous, where active souls "eat, drink, and do whatever they like." This paradise is a perfected version of earthly life where every desire is met. But it is without the BEATIFIC VISION.

God dwells in the second heaven, a deist-centered orb for "world renouncers" who want nothing to do with the sensual delights of the flesh. These "holy souls" consider themselves above such carnal pursuits. Spirits ascending to this realm do not eat (they are used to fasting), do not drink (they have rejected alcohol as intrinsically evil), and never even *think* about sexual gratification. All these souls want is to occupy themselves with contemplation of the Almighty, a task that supplies "all their bliss."

Ruzzante depicts the heavenly Father as fading from importance in the grand scheme of eternity, as more and more souls aspire to the carnal heaven and consider his realm insufferably boring. Human paradise, the author suggests, is fast overtaking the "divine reward" as the populist ideal. God's creatures are more interested in indulging in sensual pleasure than in contemplating the eternal mysteries in this work that satirizes both notions of CHRISTIAN PARADISE.

MOVIE MERCHANDISING Movie merchandising has become a major industry, often accounting for significant revenues in addition to a film's ticket sales. Toys, trinkets, and other related items also provide added ADVERTISING for movies, and even films that do not fare well at the box office can generate huge profits through licensing fees. This trend is evident in the host of movie merchandising products related to motion pictures about the blessed afterlife.

The holiday classic IT'S A WONDERFUL LIFE was recently released as an "anniversary re-issue," accompanied by a deluge of promotional tie-ins. These include COLLECTOR PLATES, Christmas ornaments, posable dolls, porcelain figures, trading cards, and even reproductions of the original script. The vast majority focus on the bumbling but lovable Clarence, the ANGEL who watches over George Bailey from heaven before coming to his aid on a critical Christmas Eve.

One of the biggest sellers for this and other movie promotions is the T-SHIRT, often printed with a scene from the film or the title graphics. Such "wearable posters" spread awareness of

Various promotional tie-ins to afterlife films

the film during its initial run and provide ongoing advertisement for the video release. Many studios sell "advance copy only" and "staff" T-shirts to help give the project a push into the marketplace. Makers of the ANIMATED CARTOON feature ALL DOGS GO TO HEAVEN 2 released several such shirts, each with art showing the film's angelic canine hero complete with wings and HALO.

Similar items have tie-ins to other afterlife films. These include fast-food give aways incorporating characters from *Casper the Friendly Ghost*, "novelized" scripts for OH, HEAVENLY DOG, and even a breakfast cereal commemorating BILL & TED'S BOGUS JOURNEY. The animated adventure *All Dogs Go to Heaven* has been reformatted into a COMPUTER GAME in which children can read the story, play games based on the film, and print movie graphics. For consumers, such promotional items help keep the "magic" of a favorite movie alive even after the screen has gone dark.

MUHAMMAD (ca. 570–632) Muhammad (Mahomet, Mohammed, Muhamed) is the prophet of Islam (which means "surrender to God and find peace") and founder of the Muslim religion. According to his accounts, Muhammad traveled to DJANNA (heaven) on the back of the BORAK, an enchanted beast. While in paradise, the prophet witnessed the splendors awaiting those who are faithful to ALLAH, the divine creator. On this mystic journey he is also given the text of Islam's holy book, the KORAN.

Nineteenth-century lithograph of
Muhammad teaching at Medina

The angel GABRIEL (JIBRIL) takes
Muhammad on a tour of paradise that
ends in the "7th Heaven," the dwelling
place of Allah. Here the prophet is
surrounded by blinding light that em-
anates from a golden cloud. Touched by
Muhammad's faith and courage, Allah
dictates to him the words of the Koran
and instructs him to return to earth and
spread the sacred word. Muhammad transcribes the text and begins evangelizing
Medina (City of the Prophet). He later
returned to his hometown of Mecca in a
triumphant crusade. Mecca remains the
seat of Islamic faith and the "holy city"
that all devout Muslims must face as they
recite their daily prayers.

MU MONTO Mu Monto is a hero of
Siberian mythology who journeys to the
realm of the dead looking for a horse he
had sacrificed to the gods. Determined
to retrieve the beast, Mu Monto travels
due north until he comes upon an enchanted rock that seals the passageway
to the afterlife. He lifts the stone and
shouts "Come!" into the murky hole. A
black fox emerges and escorts Mu
Monto into the next world.

In the land of the dead, Mu Monto
sees the rewards and punishments meted
out according to each soul's worth. Spirits who have suffered on earth are richly
compensated in the next world. Mu
Monto recognizes a poor woman who is
now robed in regal garments, dining at a
lavish banquet. He also sees spirits of formerly infirm children laughing and playing free of all disease. Evil souls, on the
other hand, are tortured for their sins.
Unfaithful wives are lashed to thorny
bushes, greedy landowners are dressed in
flea-infested rags, liars have their lips
sewn shut with wire. Mu Monto then returns to his village, telling all of his mystic journey and encouraging them to live
well in order to enjoy a peaceful afterlife.

MUNKAR Munkar (Monker) is one of
the ANGELS of Islamic tradition who in-
terrogate the dead to determine if the
soul is worthy of DJANNA (heaven). Together with NAKIR, Munkar travels to the
grave to ask the deceased, "Who is the
one true God?" Spirits who answer,
"ALLAH, and MUHAMMAD is his prophet,"
prove themselves deserving of salvation.
However, souls who do not know the correct response or who give a wrong answer
are abandoned to "monstrous beasts" who
tear at them for eternity. These damned

souls suffer until the LAST JUDGMENT, when they are called before Allah to explain themselves. At this time, spirits of all believers are shown mercy and admitted to heaven. Infidels (nonbelievers) are be annihilated for their refusal to accept the truth.

MY LIFE The 1993 drama My Life explores various notions of the afterlife through the fearful eyes of a terminally ill executive (Michael Keaton). Angry, embittered, and trying to shed his blue-collar past, Keaton fearfully faces death while at the same time his wife, played by Nicole Kidman, prepares for the birth of the couple's first child. This dual study of life's beginnings and endings was written by Bruce Joel Rubin, whose treatments of the supernatural include the films BRAINSTORM, JACOB'S LADDER, and GHOST. In My Life, Rubin links people's fear of dying to a lack of philosophy, ignorance of spiritual matters, and the failure to live "an examined life."

My Life follows Keaton as he seeks a cure for his body, determined to beat death and prove the fatalistic doctors wrong. He tries a number of experimental medical treatments that do nothing to stop the progress of his cancer. Refusing to abandon hope, Keaton goes to a "Chinese healer" (played by Haing S. Ngor), hoping "for a miracle." After examining Keaton, Ngor suggests that it is not his body but Keaton's soul that requires healing. The spiritualist further recommends that Keaton makes peace with his past to avoid carrying "so much anger into the next life." And though the cancer is growing out of control, Keaton "until that last moment" still has time to change.

During his visits to Ngor's rather unorthodox clinic, Keaton has visions of a dazzling "tunnel of light" often associated with NEAR-DEATH EXPERIENCES. Ngor explains that these images show that Keaton is purging himself of the "poison" of "anger, very old and very deep" that is more dangerous than the encroaching tumors. Bewildered by Keaton's sudden interest in ESCHATOLOGY, his superficial coworkers suggest that he "stop contemplating the afterlife and enjoy *this* one." But Keaton finds himself continually drawn to Ngor and the comforting "source of life" he sees in his mysterious apparitions.

My Life also probes the role of God in determining the course of human events. The movie includes several scenes in which Keaton's character prays for various favors, ranging from "make the circus be in my backyard" to "let me live long enough to see my child." There are also allusions to the SAINTS and the VIRGIN MARY, shown prominently during a marriage ceremony (connoting the WEDDING FEAST, a common metaphor for paradise). As Keaton stands with the groom at the altar, STAINED-GLASS WINDOWS depicting ANGELS and a painting of the mother of JESUS emblazoned on a field of gold shine around him. Images of the CHRISTIAN PARADISE soften the prospect of departing the mortal world.

Rubin's film also uses the analogy of a roller coaster ride to symbolize Keaton's transition from shallow business executive to introspective husband and father. At one point, Keaton tells his wife that as a child he had "learned the meaning of the word *fear*" when he agreed to accompany his cousin on the wild ride. Thirty years elapse before he tries again, braving the amusement park's Serpent on "death day," the date the doctors had said he would not live to see. And though he courageously completes the raging course, Keaton refuses to let go of the safety bar and abandon his fears and embrace the new sensations.

This scene is revisited in the film's finale, as a dying Keaton breathes his last. After making peace with his estranged family, his neglected wife, and finally himself, Keaton quietly expires. His spirit, now free of the diseased body, has learned to let go and surrenders itself to whatever unknown destiny lies ahead. The scene dissolves to a shot of a vital, vibrant Keaton alone on a roller coaster that climbs to a lofty, sun-drenched summit. Just before plunging downward, he throws up his hands and laughs, unafraid. The car dips and turns, then catapults Keaton into the proverbial "white light" where peace awaits his weary soul.

Rubin dedicated his soulful and touching *My Life* to his mother, Sondra Rubin, who also appears in the film. The movie is a homage to the woman who taught him that "dying is a hard way to learn about life" and showed him how to appreciate this world before departing to the next.

MYSTERY PLAYS Mystery plays are a diverse body of dramatic works. Productions range from plays patterned after Egyptian funerary rituals to Christian performances about the nature of the afterlife. Pagan dramas usually focus on mystic ceremonies and magic spells that promise to help departing souls find pleasure in the next world. The most common of these are plays about OSIRIS, the ancient Egyptian judge of the dead. During the productions, men dressed in ceremonial garb stand in pits (representing the land of the dead) while animals are offered as sacrifice. The blood of the beast is poured over their bodies, purifying their spirits and enabling them to reach paradise.

Christian mystery plays focus on supernatural events, such as the creation, the life of JESUS, and the prophesied LAST JUDGMENT. Originally written in Latin (the language of the Roman Catholic church), these dramas were designed to communicate complex doctrines to the mostly illiterate peasantry. As mystery plays became more popular, performers began presenting them in the audiences' native languages to increase their appeal to the masses. The vast majority were based on passages from the Bible and were produced by local churches, usually to commemorate some important event or SAINTS' feast days.

Mystery plays routinely presented CHRISTIAN PARADISE as a lofty realm bounded by clouds where white-winged ANGELS flitted serenely about the stage. Jesus, the VIRGIN MARY, and other religious heroes made frequent appearances, usually attempting to intervene on behalf of humanity. These residents of paradise were for the most part serious, intense, and humorless. Human welfare was the prime motivation of the blessed in these dramas, often resulting in characters who were simply too good to be true, or at least too virtuous to be empathetic.

Performers quickly began recognizing that scenes of hell and demons were vastly more popular than depictions of stodgy heaven, and so the netherworld began crowding out paradise. God's abode, envisioned as a pious place of averted eyes and hushed tones, was viewed by audiences as dreary, dour, and unappealing. Hell, on the other hand, was populated with dynamic "merry souls," rogues, and scoundrels who made jokes, flatulated, and encouraged audiences to join the fun. The underworld was also seen as a realm of magic and enchantment filled with playful fairies and exotic heroes of pagan myth. Compared with static existence in paradise, damnation seemed far more exciting than salvation to God's somber realm.

Many clerics worried that the glamorization of hell and corresponding devaluation of heaven would have an adverse effect on their efforts to save human souls. Spurred by this fear, mystery plays were banned altogether by the thirteenth century, when church officials declared them wicked "works of Satan" designed to corrupt humanity. The offending dramas were replaced by MORALITY PLAYS, which were written, staged, and performed under strict scrutiny of religious leaders. These new productions emphasized education over entertainment and were designed to teach moral lessons and affect behavior. Morality plays, under the watchful eye of the church, were the only dramas presented throughout most of Christendom for the next several centuries.

The evolution of MEDIEVAL DRAMA into a profession rather than a pastime undercut the popularity of all "amateur" productions. However, revivals of mystery plays continue.

N

NAKAA   Nakaa is the lord of paradise of Micronesia's Gilbert Islands. He watches over human souls and determines who is worthy of a pleasant afterlife. According to the legends, Nakaa sits at the entrance to the spirit world, holding an enchanted net. When islanders die, their spirits must pass Nakaa in order to enter paradise. Virtuous souls are allowed to continue, but Nakaa uses his net to catch and detain wicked spirits. Myths vary on where the spirit world is located. In some versions, it is a beautiful island in the sky; other variations place paradise under the earth, accessible only by a secret pathway that leads to eternity.

NAKIR   Nakir (Nakeer) is one of the "blue-eyed" black Islamic ANGELS charged with examining the dead to determine the soul's fate in the afterlife. When a person dies, Nakir and MUNKAR journey to the tomb and command the deceased to sit upright for the examination. They quiz the spirit on its knowledge of ALLAH and MUHAMMAD. If the soul is able to give accurate answers, it is taken to DJANNA, Islamic paradise. Spirits unable to respond correctly are cast into hell to be gnawed on by huge beasts until the LAST JUDGMENT. At this time, faithful souls (even the wicked ones) are forgiven and restored to heaven. Nonbelievers, however, are tortured until they are eradicated from existence.

NATS Burmese myth claims that deceased souls travel on to a spirit world, where they become nats. These supernatural beings retain their human qualities, remaining good or evil as they had in life. Nats have the power of astral projection and can travel anywhere simply by wishing to do so. They can be contacted through spiritualists called nat-kadaw, or appeased by offerings and special rituals. Each year, the nat Thagya Min descends from the heavens to honor the beginning of the Burmese New Year, and this event is marked by a great festival.

NEAR-DEATH EXPERIENCES Despite a recent boom in the popularity of such accounts, near-death experiences, or NDEs, are not new to the twentieth century. For centuries scribes have recorded supernatural adventures experienced by everyone from peasant farmers to bishops and kings. These fantastic tales reached a high point during the Middle Ages, when VISION LITERATURE regarding the afterlife dominated Europe. Accounts from such famous sources as the Venerable BEDE recounted visits with ANGELS, conversations with SAINT PETER, and tours of heaven, PURGATORY, and hell.

Most of these stories shared common elements. They invariably involved someone who is believed "dead"

but who later revives with an extraordinary tale to tell. While on this metaphysical journey to the next world, the "spirit" is usually escorted by a heavenly guide such as an angel or SAINT. And the majority included witnessing both the horrors of the damned and the delights of the saved, the images of which inspired the person to live a life of virtue in preparation for "dying" again.

Such incredible tales of astral travel have inspired great artworks over the centuries. In his ASCENT INTO THE EMPYRIUM, fifteenth-century master Heironymous Bosch shows a proverbial "tunnel of light" through which departed spirits enter heaven. Some of the souls pause at the entrance, perhaps considering a return to the land of the living. (This image has since become identified with modern NDEs.) Three hundred years later, artist WILLIAM BLAKE's *Soul Hovering Above the Body* depicted a spirit leaving the flesh to venture among the unknown. Some scholars believe that this work was inspired by the mystic artist's own out-of-body experiences.

In modern times, the advance in medical techniques has led to an explosion in reported NDEs, since it is no longer uncommon for patients declared clinically dead to be revived. More and more of these people are claiming to have visited another realm while undergoing this process. In 1975, Dr. Raymond Moody collected more than 150 such contemporary accounts in *Life After Life*. The work coined the term *near-death experience* and brought the phenomenon international attention.

Suddenly, people from all walks of

life began coming forward with similar stories about "visiting paradise" and seeing supernatural creatures. This prompted Dr. Kenneth Ring to conduct quantitative research on the data. He came to several conclusions about NDEs and published his own book, *Life at Death*, in 1980. His work states that religious belief has little or no bearing on the details of reported NDEs, that women are more likely to have an NDE after a prolonged illness whereas a sudden injury results in more male NDEs, and that people who have never heard of the phenomenon are actually *more* likely to have some sort of "afterlife" adventure than those who are familiar with NDE accounts.

Both of these authors, as well as many others specializing in the field, report common elements that recur from person to person. NDEs routinely involve astral projection, being "outside one's body," seeing the "tunnel of light," enjoying a REUNION with loved ones, and experiencing an overwhelming sense of peace. Many also report seeing their lives flash before them, sometimes as a continuous awareness, like a filmstrip. Other times, this is described as a sort of stop-motion slide show, in which different episodes from life appear one after another.

Some revived patients report meeting JESUS or angels in the next dimension. Often the "dead" person is given comfort or information "on the other side," such as reassurance that health conditions will improve or confirmation that a loved one is in heaven. A few even claim to have met God and talked with him about life, truth, and philosophy. And in rare instances, people experiencing NDEs report having seen celebrities such as Marilyn Monroe and Elvis Presley in paradise, while others swear that beloved ANIMALS accompany their owners to heaven. In all of these cases, the NDE concludes with the "otherworld" beings convincing the newcomer to "go back" and resume life on earth.

Reporting NDEs has in recent years become a cottage industry. Betty J. Eadie's 1993 *Embraced by the Light*, based on a heavenly out-of-body experience she claims to have had two decades prior, remained on the best-seller list for months. The former professional hypnotherapist recounts how she "died" during a hysterectomy on November 19, 1973, then left her body and entered paradise She calls this place the "glorious life beyond" and describes it as a land of unbelievable beauty and unconditional love. Her tale also contains vivid descriptions of mingling with angels, greeting departed friends, and meeting Jesus himself.

According to Eadie, the trip to heaven began with a murky, dark tunnel that led to a brilliant world of light. Beyond this passage lay a radiant landscape of mountains, waterfalls, and lush gardens. Disembodied souls floated freely, laughing and talking, while angels swirled through the skies. And Jesus, robed in blinding "white light," spoke softly, telling Eadie that "it is not yet your time." On hearing this, Eadie returned to her body and to her life in Seattle, Washington, forever changed by the mystic adventure.

Eadie recalls other supernatural encounters in *Embraced*. She claims to have seen heaven during a previous illness in her childhood. Her first visit to the great beyond occurred at age eleven when she was suffering from double pneumonia. At the high point of her fever, Eadie awoke to find herself being "held and rocked by a beautiful man of light." She cheerfully remembers, "I played with his beard." Soon after this divine encounter, the girl fully recovered.

The release of *Embraced by the Light* touched off contentious debate among religious scholars, spiritualists, and skeptics of Eadie's story. Critics dismiss the account as either a hallucination brought on by medication and anesthesia or an outright hoax. Most criticism resulted from the author's refusal to provide any medical records of her experience, or even to name the attending doctor or the hospital where she "died" in 1973. Her response to these requests was simply, "I don't have those facts." Doubters find her reluctance suspicious and manipulative, casting further aspersions on her "trip to heaven" story. However, for many readers, the book offers a credible account of what awaits human souls in CHRISTIAN PARADISE.

Not all NDEs are as pleasant as those described by Moody, King, and Eadie. Dr. Maurice S. Rawlings, a renowned cardiologist with "no significant religious beliefs" was stunned in 1977 when a patient he was trying to resuscitate sud-

denly shrieked, "Don't stop! Don't let me go back to hell!" Rawlings began studying what he terms "negative NDEs" and has compiled the findings in his own book, *To Hell and Back*, published the same year as Eadie's *Embraced*. His work is filled with dark excursions to the realm of the damned.

NDEs have also inspired a number of films, such as WHITE LIGHT and BRAIN-STORM, and they are satirized in the comedy BILL & TED'S BOGUS JOURNEY.

NEHALENNIA   Nehalennia is the Germanic goddess of death and escort to the afterlife. Ancient pagans attributed her with the power to deliver departing souls to a place of peace and eternal rest. Nehalennia's symbol is a rat, which also is associated with death because of its reputation as a notorious carrier of lethal plagues.

NEW JERUSALEM   New Jerusalem refers to an urban concept of heaven. Unlike the simple, natural paradise described in such texts as ELUCIDATION, the vision of New Jerusalem conjures images of golden spires, gilded walls, and jeweled mansions. As early as the ninth century, verbiage of such a cosmopolitan court became part of the monks' chant as they envisioned CHRISTIAN PARADISE.

The concept of a dazzling holy place has its origins in the Hebrew Old Testament, in passages that anticipate a glorious city of unending joys. Later, in the Christian Book of REVELATION, St. John describes a "new heaven and a new earth" that will be guilded in gold and jewels. He declares: "And I John saw the holy city, new Jerusalem, coming down from God, out of heaven, prepared as a bride adorned for her husband. And I heard a great voice saying 'Behold, the tabernacle of God is with men, and he will dwell with them, and they shall be his people, and God himself shall be with them, and be their God'" (Rev. 21:1–3).

In this prophecy, St. John also speculates on the SIZE OF HEAVEN, declaring it to be "twelve thousand furlongs; the length and the breadth and the height of it are equal," approximately 1,500 cubic miles. This "measurement" has since become the topic of contentious debate among clerics and critics alike.

Christian scribe St. Paul also describes a city "whose builder and maker is God" in his writings. One of his letters to the early Christians offers followers citizenship in the eternal "city" of paradise, a "heavenly Jerusalem" where they will dwell with God in "the innumerable company of ANGELS." This image is a sharp departure from other notions of paradise as a bucolic garden of natural wonders, where lush meadows, crystal streams, and fragrant flowers abound.

NIRVANA Nirvana is orthodox Buddhist paradise, the equivalent of the Hindu MOKSHA and Jain KEVALA. The origin of the word is in dispute; however, linguists believe it is a combination of *nir*, meaning "without," and *vana*, "the wind." Together, nirvana suggests the placid surface of a pond on a

Buddha in Nirvana, twelfth-century sculpture
ART TODAY

windless day: still, uninterrupted, deep. Such will be the state of souls in the vast cosmos after final "enlightenment."

In order to reach nirvana, Buddhists must dissolve all individuality and join the collective good. After the cessation of self, spirits are free to unite with the eternal force. This is done through intense meditation on the divine truth, self-denial, and quiet reflection.

Ancient texts describe the "death of Buddha" and his passage to nirvana. According to the tales, when Siddhartha Gautama, the founder of Buddhism, died, his pure soul departed the prison of material and joined with the spirit of the cosmos: "When the Lord attained Nirvana . . . there was a great shaking of the earth, terrifying and frightful, and the drums of the gods sounded."

Followers of the great Buddha hope to enjoy the same fate. However, for most souls, this will involve numerous cycles of life, death, and rebirth. The reincarnations will continue as spirits try to rid themselves of imperfection so they too can enter nirvana.

NISE-E Nise-e are "likeness paintings" popularized during the Kamakura period (twelfth century) in parts of Asia. They often depict supernatural mysteries, such as the splendors of paradise and the torments of hell. Such divinely inspired nise-e typically show souls dwelling with the gods in great palaces or beautiful gardens, wearing luxurious robes and glittering jewels. Text describing the scene usually accompanied the hand scrolls, offering details about the picture. Many nise-e survive in Asian temples and provide examples of CHURCH ART AND ARCHITECTURE of the afterlife.

OBATALA Obatala is lord of the sky and ruler of the AFRICAN PARADISE of the Yoruba. He is the second son of the sky god OLORUN and founder of the Yorubas' first city Ifé. According to the belief, in the next world Obatala rewards those who have lived virtuous lives with peaceful existence in a beautiful village. Those who are wicked in life, however, are punished, sometimes by becoming slaves or by physical torture. The Yoruba myth differs from many other African concepts, as it emphasizes behavior over ancestor worship in determining a soul's afterlife fate.

ODIN Odin is the "all-father" of Norse myth, the supreme being who reigns in VALHALLA, paradise of fallen warriors. Legends tell that soldiers who are killed in battle are taken to the Hall of the Slain where they feast at Odin's banquet every night. By day, the brave spirits engage in fierce gamesmanship before returning at sunset to the table of paradise. Tales of Odin are included in the PROSE EDDA and in the epic "BALDER DEAD."

OGIER Ogier, a hero of the Charlemagne legend cycle, is among the souls dwelling in the paradise of AVALON. He is a Danish hero taken hostage by the invader Charlemagne, but he eventually returns home to ascend the throne of Denmark. In some versions, Ogier has been favored since birth by magic fairies who protect and strengthen him. Other tales claim that he defeated a giant and fought off forty men at once. But he is best known for his dispute with Charlemagne over a battle between the two men's sons, which was resolved by a heavenly messenger.

Ogier's son and Prince Charlot, Charlemagne's heir, had been lifelong friends. But the two erupted in an explosive argument over a game of chess. Charlot lost his temper and killed Ogier's son with a blow from the heavy chessboard. Ogier then demanded that Charlot be executed, but Charlemagne refused to punish him at all. The enraged Ogier joins the army of Charlemagne's main rival but is eventually captured and put on trial for treason. He repeated his demand that Prince Charlot be executed, otherwise he would remain an avowed enemy of Charlemagne's court.

But an ANGEL descended to tell Ogier to forgive Charlot, as is God's will. Ogier, fearing that if he rejected this order he would lose his soul and thus never be reunited with his son in paradise, agreed. He and Charlemagne renewed their friendship, and Ogier left Charlot's punishment to divine justice.

After this, Ogier set sail to conquer new territories for France. But on his voyage he encountered a mystic castle that disappeared into the mist each morning. While exploring the strange land, Ogier also met Morgan le Fay, half sister of the legendary King Arthur. She fell in love with him and gave him a magic ring that granted him eternal youth and a crown that caused him to forget his former life. Ogier then joined her in AVALON, where he enjoyed the company of past heroes. Like King Arthur, legends claim that Ogier will remain in this paradise until some distant day when he will return to earth to restore his kingdom.

OH, HEAVENLY DOG!   The 1980 comedy, *Oh, Heavenly Dog!* offers a comedic plotline reversal of another afterlife take, YOU NEVER CAN TELL. In the 1951 film, a murdered dog returns to life in human form to find his killer. However, in *Oh, Heavenly Dog!* Chevy Chase stars as a man who is killed, then comes back as a canine in a search for justice.

Paradise in this movie is portrayed as a celestial government bureacracy, where deceased souls, clad in white hospital gowns, wait in long lines for their afterlife accommodations. Case-

worker ANGELS speak in abbreviations; they refer to NTT ("natural termination time"), IDEF ("intermediate destination evaluation facility"), and the divine UR ("ultimate reward"). God is never seen, although there are allusions to the "boss" who oversees this realm.

Although humorous, this heaven is hardly happy. The angels bemoan the lackluster crop of souls that have been arriving lately. One dour case worker complains he hasn't seen any SAINTS "since the sixteenth century." He laments that modern spirits are mediocre, complacent, undistinguished. These MM (marginal material) souls must be sent back to earth for an FAA (final assessment assignment) to determine whether they will be elevated to paradise or damned to hell.

Chase, a morally neutral man who never distinguished himself as good or evil, is charged with returning to solve his own murder or face immediate damnation. The only problem is that heaven has only one body available for this assignment: that of a mongrel dog "about to hit by a garbage truck." Feeling that he has no choice, Chase assumes the canine identity and begins sniffing out the killers.

Far from being a wondrous place of joys, the afterlife in *Oh, Heavenly Dog!* is a bleak way station totally lacking in compassion or appeal. Ultimately, Chase himself decides to remain in the mutt's body rather than return to the officious, impersonal HEREAFTER.

OLELPANTI   Native American mythology of the Wintun includes belief in Olelpanti, a paradise of peace and rest. At one time, Olelpanti was a place of renewal where mortals could go to bathe in the waters of immortality and grow young again. It could be reached by a stone LADDER between heaven and earth, so humans could ascend and descend at will. But the trickster god Coyote soon convinced Olelbis, the ruler of Olelpanti, that people would be "more fulfilled" by welcoming new generations (having children) and parting with elders (dying) than by constantly renewing their own lives. Olelbis agreed, and so Olelpanti became a haven for departed souls.

OLORUN Olorun is the "god of space and the heavens" of Nigerian Yoruba mythology. He dwells in the spirit world, relegating human affairs to his son OBATALA. In Olorun's eternal home, the good are rewarded for their virtue, while the wicked are punished for their sins.

ON LOVE French chaplain Andreas wrote *On Love*, a satirical "manual of courtly love and romance" around 1180, a time when the French aristocracy was riddled with hypocrisy. While clerics preached chastity from the pulpit, members of France's ruling class bragged about their sexual conquests. Many of these self-proclaimed adulterers routinely entertained Christian officials and attended Sunday services in order to placate their consciences.

On Love offers the perfect compromise: Humans who keep their virtue intact while living can ascend to a paradise of unlimited physical gratifica-

tion. In his text, Andreas depicts heaven as of a dormitory of "bridal beds" where valiant knights choose their tender lovers before indulging in carnal pleasures. Unlike traditional descriptions of CHRISTIAN PARADISE, *On Love* envisions a utopia of silk, satin, and sensuality. God has been replaced by the "King and Queen of Love," who oversee this ongoing orgy. Andreas's work mocks a monarch who teaches Christian values but himself indulges in every type of sexual perversion.

In a final statement about delayed gratification, Andreas implies that most people would rather enjoy lust on earth than spend eternity in a "chaste" paradise. The delights of heaven, he laments, will never have the mass appeal of a "lusty liaison."

"ON THE HEAVENLY JERUSALEM"
Thirteenth-century Italian scribe Giacomino of Verona offers his view of the HEREAFTER in his poem "On the Heavenly Jerusalem." The work greatly elaborates on the concept of a NEW JERUSALEM first described in St. John's Book of REVELATION. According to Giacomino, the pleasures that await the saved are more beautiful than anything imagined on earth; every house is "a work of art," with palaces of "rare marble" dotted with "blue and gold" ornamentation. This vision was especially appealing to the peasantry who spent their earthly lives in squalor.

Giacomino's work became a standard depiction of CHRISTIAN PARADISE and was used by clerics throughout Christendom to entice believers to lead virtuous lives. It inspired numerous sermons, exempla, and other treatises on the cosmopolitan afterlife.

ORCUS Orcus is the Roman equivalent of the Greek Hades, the realm of departed souls. It is also the name of the god of death who is frequently depicted as a reaper harvesting grain. The kingdom of Orcus contains a frightening chamber for wicked souls as well as a more pleasant paradise for the favored. Virgil's AENEID mentions the "Gates of Orcus" through which spirits must pass on the way to ELYSIUM. Inside this enchanted place spirits enjoy dancing, singing, and great festivals.

OSA Osa is the lord of heaven according to myths of the Edo. In his realm of AFRICAN PARADISE, there is no disease, famine, or pain of any kind. His wicked enemy, Osanoha, created sickness and death and brought it to humanity through trickery and deceit. Determined to undermine Osanoha, the benevolent Osa offers shelter to humans, providing them with a haven of rest and harmony. He watches over spirits in this life and welcomes them into paradise in the next.

OSANNA OF MANTUA (1449–1505) Dominican nun Osanna of Mantua claimed to have had many visions of heaven during her lifetime. While enjoying these supernatural escapades, she met heroes of the Bible as well as SAINTS of the early Christian church.

In one vision, St. Paul and Simeon escort Osanna to the "throne" of God, where the Almighty receives her with an affectionate kiss and deep embrace. Osanna and JESUS conduct a great discussion about the lives of such mystics as THOMAS AQUINAS, CATHERINE OF SIENA, and Mary Magdalene. On another "visit," she meets St. Dominic on his feast day and takes part in his celebration. In her most poignant and personal experience, Osanna "sees" a friend, living miles away, die and be elevated to paradise on the wings of ANGELS.

OSIRIS Osiris is the ancient Egyptian lord of the dead and judge of souls in the afterlife. The deity is based on a historical figure, the first pharaoh who, after death, is said to have become ruler of the world beyond. According to the legend, Osiris's jealous brother Set murders the pharaoh and chops his corpse into pieces, then scatters them throughout the land. Osiris's sister-wife ISIS gathers the pieces and binds them together with strips of cloth, creating the first mummy. Enraged by Set's behavior, the gods restore Osiris to life and allow him to return to Isis. But Osiris decides instead to journey to the land of the dead, where he will rule for all eternity.

Osiris figures prominently in the BOOK OF THE DEAD. The text contains numerous spells, rituals, and incantations designed to curry favor with Osiris in the next world. Early accounts claim that only wealthy lords and powerful statesmen will enjoy eternal pleasure in the House of Osiris. However, over the centuries, the hope of a pleasurable afterlife was extended to the peasantry as well.

Egyptian lord of the dead Osiris. ART TODAY

Osiris is aided in the afterlife by ANUBIS, the jackal-headed deity who serves as guardian of the dead. Anubis escorts departing souls to the Hall of Osiris, then reviews the record of the person's actions. Before determining the spirit's fate, Osiris weighs the deceased's heart against the "feather of truth" to see how honest the soul has been. If the scales tip in favor of virtue, the spirit will find its way to paradise. However, if the scales reveal the spirit as wretched, it will be consumed by monsters or left to die a "final death." The scribe THOTH (son of Osiris) records the verdict in his sacred annals.

Osiris remains one of the most in-triguing otherworld gods ever studied. Over time, aspects of this Egyptian ruler were mingled with Greek and Roman deities, resulting in the hybrid deity SER-APIS. He appears as a pagan lord of hell in Milton's PARADISE LOST, and his temple is the setting for Mozart's opera the MAGIC FLUTE. The rituals of Osiris have served as the basis for MYSTERY PLAYS, which reenact ceremonies of his cult of the dead. Modern authors have likewise in-cluded him in SHORT STORIES about the world beyond.

OTHERWORLD The Celts believe in a paradise called the Otherworld, a "puri-fied and elevated" earth. It is the dwelling place of the gods (there are literally scores of deities, each with specific duties, re-sponsibilities, and powers). Only a thin metaphysical barrier separates the two realms, so the living and the dead can communicate with one another. Druid priests taught that the gods could invite a living soul to the Otherworld (usually for sex) and that humans could enter by force, stealth, or trickery.

The Celtic tales of this and other myths were rarely written down. Most stories passed by word of mouth from generation to generation, always with great awe and respect. Most modern knowledge of Celtic culture is derived from records kept by the Greeks and Romans about this mystic people. Such accounts are somewhat "contam-inated," however, often mingling their own beliefs with myths of the Celts. Celtic/Christian legend is likewise blended, adapting the Otherworld into the paradise of AVALON.

OUR TOWN Thorton Wilder wrote *Our Town* in 1938, and the play has since become an American classic. The story depicts a small New England town around the turn of the century. In the play, the village of Grovers Corners and its quirky inhabitants live, die, and take their place in the afterlife. The drama focuses on the characters Emily Webb and George Gibbs as they weave intricate webs of love and loss within their seemingly simple lives.

After wedding her beloved George, Emily eventually dies in childbirth while delivering a baby girl. The final scene shows Emily in the HEREAFTER, where deceased souls sit quietly watching the world. She enjoys a REUNION with the brother she lost years ago and other friends among the dead. In paradise, the "stage manager" (a metaphor for God), allows Emily the opportunity to revisit her past. She chooses not a great adventure or outstanding event: Emily's wish is to sit at the kitchen table and chat with her mother, savoring the time they can spend "together again." Before returning to the other world, Emily finally realizes that there is greatness in the most insignificant moments, as long as love exists.

Wilder's theme is simple: The delights of paradise exist all around us, and each person determines his or her own happiness. Human pleasures can be as simple as the sound of "clocks ticking" or the dazzling display of "mother's sunflowers." Finally seeing the beauty of her lost life, Emily asks the stage manager if anyone, while living, comprehends the grandeur of "the earth." He softly replies that "SAINTS and poets" are the only ones who come close.

Wilder's afterlife has also been analyzed as a sort of PURGATORY. In this interpretation, his somber hillside is a realm for coming to terms with earthly life before making the transition into the afterlife. Recognizing the taken-for-granted splendors of life is essential to moving on to the spiritual plane. In this scene, characters experience both joy and sorrow, a sort of "growing pain" as spirits pass to the next world. Souls do not leave the world behind but outgrow it.

PALACE OF THE IMMORTALS Chinese Buddhists believe that worthy souls not immediately returned to earth through reincarnation are sent to the Palace of the Immortals, a lush repose where all human desires are fulfilled. It is located on an enchanted island, protected by stern oceans over which only the purest of souls can pass. In addition to serving as a resort for departed souls, the palace is the eternal dwelling place of the gods.

The Palace of the Immortals is described as a luxurious pagoda tended by Fu-Hsing, the god of happiness. Ancient artifacts—including plates, scrolls, and murals—show blessed spirits feasting and celebrating in paradise. In this mystic realm, the immortals travel by cloud, gently soaring through the heavens. Stories tell of mystic trips made to distant lands, faraway fields, and even the undersea kingdom. Human souls might enjoy such adventures in the Palace of the Immortals before reincarnating in another life-form.

PARADISE Paradise, meaning "protected land," is a common synonym for heaven. It appears in hundreds of myths, religious texts, artworks, poems, and other media. Paradise can refer to a supernatural haven of glory, or to an earthly realm of delights such as the Garden of Eden. Different religions and cultures have their own versions of paradise, such as AFRICAN PARADISE, BUDDHIST PARADISE, CHRISTIAN PARADISE, DJANNA (Islamic heaven), JEWISH HEAVEN, SWAHILI PARADISE, TIAN (Chinese Paradise), and ZOROASTRIAN HEAVEN.

PARADISE FOUND *Paradise Found* was written by John Milton in 1671 as a sequel to his classic epic PARADISE LOST. The follow-up continues the adventures of humanity after being expelled from the Garden of Eden. After the sin of Adam and Eve, Milton traces biblical events through the emergence of the Hebrew prophets as they foretell the coming of JESUS, the Messiah. From above, God protects his human creatures and promises to welcome them "home" to his eternal kingdom.

As in his first book, Milton's heaven is a place of light and radiance, where ANGELS enjoy the BEATIFIC VISION as they sing, dance, and celebrate their union with God. *Paradise Found* focuses on the life of Jesus as he begins his mission, prepares for his crucifixion, and is tempted by Satan in the desert. It ends

triumphantly, as Christ harrows hell and delivers the souls of the just to paradise, opening the gates of heaven to all humanity. Milton invites readers to live their lives according to the sacred words of Jesus in order that they, too, might ascend to CHRISTIAN PARADISE.

PARADISE LOST Seventeenth-century English author John Milton wanted to write a Christian epic in the style of Homer's *Iliad* and Virgil's AENEID. After years of struggling with the concept, he wrote the allegorical *Paradise Lost*, a dramatic retelling of the war in heaven, creation of hell, and the fall of Adam and Eve in the Garden of Eden. The book introduced a new writing style, dubbed "grand style," to English literature and changed the way future books were written. This new format incorporated traditional verbiage with expressions, terms, and phrases from languages across the globe.

Paradise Lost describes a THEOCENTRIC HEAVEN where all activity centers around God, the object of eternal adoration in the vast EMPYREAN. The ANGELS, including MICHAEL, GABRIEL, and URIEL, worship at the throne of the Almighty, singing HYMNS and declaring his glory. These celestial beings wear brilliant HALOS, soar on magnificent wings, and play harps of gold. Milton explains that their main activity is to celebrate God, the "Fountain of Light," from whom all other creations spring.

But all is not well in Milton's tale. There is a great war in heaven, the rebellion described in the Bible's REVELATION in which Satan and his forces try to overthrow the heavenly father, "and prevail not." Under the leadership of the archangel Michael, the rebellious spirits are cast into hell and barred from paradise forever. Milton takes up the story at this point, offering his own speculation on what transpires next. In *Paradise Lost,* God then decides to create man to "repopulate Heaven" and fill the places left vacant by the lost angels.

But the Almighty decrees that humans, like angels, must have free will and be allowed to choose whether they will do his will. Otherwise, the new creatures would be mere puppets whose devotion would be meaningless. The angels are delighted when Adam and Eve are formed in paradise (the earthly garden of delights) and journey from heaven to visit them. Gabriel guards the gates of paradise with a fiery sword, keeping the human children safe. Michael, Uriel, and Raphael likewise pay visits to their physical compatriots during the course of the poem.

However, harmony between the shared realms does not last. Satan, determined to "punish" God by causing his new creation to sin, leaves hell to prey upon Adam and Eve. As he prowls the spiritual world, he passes LIMBO, then sees, with great sorrow, the grand STAIRCASE that leads to heaven. Milton likens this to the LADDER of JACOB's supernatural visions. Atop the beautiful stairwell are PEARLY GATES fashioned of gold and encrusted with diamonds. Satan longs to return to this mystic splendor, yet he knows he will never again be admitted into God's presence. So he turns instead to the earthly paradise, where Adam and Eve sleep in innocent bliss.

Through trickery and deceit, Satan is able to convince the pair that God is a "great Forbidden" who wants to subjugate and control them. They defy the Father's orders and eat the fruit he declared off-limits, bringing about their expulsion from paradise. Sadly, the angels descend to tell Adam that he must leave this utopia and venture into a world filled with pain, sadness, and struggle. Before leaving, Michael takes him to the summit of paradise and shows Adam the future of humanity. The man and his angelic guide observe the foreshadows of Noah, Abraham, Moses, and finally JESUS Christ. Michael assures Adam that the Messiah will "defeat Sin and Death," the allies of Satan, and restore humanity to heaven.

Paradise Lost also describes the coming LAST JUDGMENT, when Jesus will call all people "forth from their graves" to answer for their lives. The just will be embraced and delivered to eternal rejoicing, whereas the evil and indifferent will be cast into hell. During this time of adjudication, the universe will be purged through consuming fire. Heaven and Earth will burn away, and a "new Heaven and a new Earth" will emerge for the enjoyment of the saved. Ancient pagan gods of death, such as the Egyptian OSIRIS, will take their place among the damned, having made pretense to being divine.

Milton's epic ends as Adam and Eve leave paradise to make their way into the unknown world. And though they have lost their beloved homeland and alienated themselves from God, the book has a happy ending. For the two vow to work together, sharing each other's joys and sorrows, forging a new home in the wasteland. And they go with the promise that heaven will one day be theirs and that Eve "bears the seed" that will one day flower in divinity, with the long-distant birth of Jesus Christ.

Not long after *Paradise Lost*'s publication, a friend asked Milton "what happens next?" Intrigued by this question, the author penned PARADISE FOUND in 1671, describing the further supernatural events of human history.

PARADISE OF BIRDS SAINT BRENDAN, a legendary adventurer, visited many mystic places during his supernatural travels, including the Paradise of Birds. According to the story, Brendan's men were becoming dejected and anxious after many years at sea. Just as they begin to despair, they come upon "a beautiful island of flowers, herbs and trees" and head for its shores. They give thanks to God for this place, and as their prayer rises the men notice a tree so full of white birds that "hardly a leaf could be seen." The sound of the birds singing their sweet song is "like the noise of Heaven" to their ears. So overcome by this lovely spectacle, Brendan falls to his knees and exclaims, "Father above, what is this place?" Hearing this, one of the birds flies down and explains the mysteries of the isle.

The bird tells Brendan that the flock was once a band of ANGELS, but they rebelled against God and joined Lucifer's thwarted coup. Since they have

sinned, they can no longer remain in heaven; however, the merciful Lord cannot bear to cast them into hell. So he transformed them into birds and placed them on this island to "sing praises" and rejoice. Brendan and his men spend the Easter season in this paradise, listening to the birds chant the psalms and coo vespers and morning prayers.

Before returning to the trees, the bird also tells Brendan that he and his men are destined to sail for seven years before coming to the "Land of Promise." The sailors sadly listen to the prophecy of the birds, then set sail after Pentecost, determined to fulfill their mystic quest.

PATALA Patala is the name for a collection of Hindu underworlds designed to help souls find ultimate enlightenment. Though they are considered to be places of "trial," many underworlds of Patala actually offer sensual indulgence and carnal fulfillment rather than punishment. Spirits pause in Patala before rejoining the reincarnation cycle and progressing on toward "surrender of the self," the ultimate blissful state known as MOKSHA.

PEACH The peach is one of the most enduring SYMBOLS of heaven and of eternal life, appearing in depictions of paradise from across the globe. Peaches are among the enchanted fruits growing in the Chinese Taoist EMPIRE OF JADE, the Japanese FORTUNATE ISLES, and the Buddhist KHUN-LUN. They are also the fruit of the TREE OF IMMORTALITY, and all who eat these magic peaches will live eternally in bliss. Many folk heroes also have connections to the lucious fruit. These include the Japanese Momotaro (meaning "son of the peach"), who is sent to earth by the gods in a huge ripe peach. The child is raised by an elderly childless couple and eventually defeats a fierce demon and inherits the beast's vast fortune.

The succulent fruits are frequently mentioned in legends about DJANNA, the heaven of Islam, as well as tales of CHRISTIAN PARADISE. Renaissance painters often portrayed the VIRGIN MARY, mother of the Messiah JESUS, beneath a peach tree or sometimes holding the fruit. Because of its ancient association with immortality, the peach became a religious symbol of salvation and of the joys of paradise.

PEARLY GATES One of the most common Western SYMBOLS of heaven is the pearly gates. In contemporary usage, the term is synonymous with paradise. It derives from biblical passages that compare the pearl to a saved human soul. The glorious pearly gates are mentioned in THE HORN BLOWS AT MIDNIGHT and are featured in countless COMIC BOOKS, ANIMATED CARTOONS, television shows, movies, and other works of art.

The Bible calls the pearl "precious" and of "great value." Sinners are likened to the grain of sand inside an oyster, itself worthless and indistinct. But the grace of God envelops the human soul, layering it with beauty and opulence, creating a unique treasure. This image is extended to the entranceway of paradise, with the very gates of heaven proclaiming this mystery and bespeaking the grandeur of the Almighty.

PETER, SAINT Saint Peter is one of the original twelve apostles, the first followers of JESUS who helped found the Christian church. He was originally named Simon, and he and his brother Andrew were fishermen working with two other brothers, James and John. The men had embraced the prophecies of John the Baptist who claimed that a "Messiah" was coming whose "sandal strap I am not fit to loosen." When Simon meets Christ, Jesus invites him to become a "fisher of men," and thus Simon becomes the first apostle. Andrew, James, and John soon follow. Later, Jesus changes Simon's name, appoints him head of the disciples, and gives him the power to forgive sins in the name of God: "Thou art Peter [the rock], and upon this rock I build my church; and the gates of hell shall not prevail against it. And I will give unto thee the keys of the kingdom of heaven: and whatsoever thou shalt bind on earth shall be bound in heaven: and whatsoever thou shalt loose on earth shall be loosed in heaven" (Matt. 16:18–19).

Due to the images of this passage, St. Peter is often depicted as the watchman of the PEARLY GATES who greets and directs incoming souls. In his role as gatekeeper of the eternal city, St. Peter appears in countless works of CHURCH ART AND ARCHITECTURE, literature, paintings, plays, and films. He is credited with dictating the apocryphal

French thirteenth-century stained-glass image of St. Peter. ART TODAY

Vision of Saint Peter, and legends of his mystic powers are recounted in THE GOLDEN LEGEND.

In modern culture, the celestial greeter is incorporated into countless JOKES, COMICS, CARTOONS, ANIMATED CARTOONS, ADVERTISING, and T-SHIRTS. His feast is celebrated on June 29.

PHAEDO   The ancient Greek philosopher Plato, a follower of PYTHAGORAS, wrote his *Phaedo* as a homage to his beloved idol Socrates. It describes Socrates' last hours, as the sage prepares his body for death and his spirit for the afterlife. Written from the perspective of Phaedo, one of the witnesses to the philosopher's death, the work offers a tender depiction of the departure for paradise. In the drama, Plato explores notions of social justice, truth, logic, and immortality.

The *Phaedo* is set in prison, where Socrates, convicted of "corrupting the youth of Athens" with his unconventional ideas, awaits his execution. Just before his sentence is to be carried out, the philosopher calls his followers around him to speculate on what might loom beyond the grave. He speaks without fear of his upcoming "pilgrimage" to "another place" where "the soul and her mansions" will find great ecstasy. Socrates' disciples are moved to pity by his courage, but he assures them that no tears are necessary; he is confident that he will find only joy and peace in the next world.

The *Phaedo* calls the human soul "the very likeness of the divine." Humans who pollute this divinity with evil are reincarnated as "asses" and other lowly "beasts," while virtuous souls ascend to new heights. According to the philosophies of Plato, this drifting of the soul from existence to existence enables the spirit to grow and develop, learning new truths with each incarnation. When the spirit has elevated itself to the point where no further purification is necessary, then it is liberated forever of the body, which he calls a "shell," to become a "free spirit" without limitation. Socrates, according to the *Phaedo*, is bound for such glory after being condemned by small-minded cretins incapable of comprehending this cosmic mystery. The drama ends as the grief-stricken Phaedo, having witnessed Socrates' death, declares that the executed teacher "was the wisest and justest and best" man he has ever known. His joy in eternity is assured.

PI   The pi is the symbol of heaven according to ancient Chinese belief. It is a circle with a space in the middle to allow "lightning" to pass through that dates back three thousand years to the Chou dynasty. It is used in rituals involving the "Son of Heaven," the presiding emperor who is believed to be divine, in invocations of the "powers of paradise." The pi represents the perfect being of TIAN, Chinese paradise.

PIERS PLOWMAN   William Langland's allegorical poem *The Vision of William Concerning Piers the Plowman* (known simply as *Piers Plowman*) mixes Christian doctrines, contemporary social commentary, and supernatural speculation in a powerful cautionary tale. The fourteenth-century piece became widely distributed in the mid-1500s, when *Piers Plowman* became standard reading throughout Europe. The lengthy work, which has since become a classic of English literature, traces the creation of the world, the sin in the Garden of Eden, the sacrifice of JESUS, and the opening of paradise to all. In the narrative, Langland also denounces the religious hypocrisy of his time and condemns clerics who use their position for personal profit rather than for God's work.

Piers Plowman describes a dream in which the narrator meets Jesus Christ, represented as a gentle farmer. During the encounter, he also is approached by virtues and vices personified and talks with the ANGELS GABRIEL and MICHAEL. Seeing the confusion that surrounds mankind, Piers Plowman (Christ) offers to escort his contemporaries to the dis-

tant Tower of Truth (heaven) that lies down a path fraught with obstacles. He asks only that before they embark on the journey, all work together to help cultivate his fields. The plowman is saddened when most not only refuse this request but also abandon the quest for paradise in favor of their own petty pursuits.

The story of *Piers Plowman* beseeches readers to dedicate their lives to God and cooperate with the divine plan. And though this may mean sacrifice on earth, the reward will be great in paradise.

PILGRIM'S PROGRESS

English preacher-turned-author John Bunyan's *Pilgrim's Progress* was published in 1684, when his country was in the grip of religious intolerance and persecution. Under a vicious religious repression enacted by Queen Elizabeth I, subjects belonging to any religion other than the Church of England were stripped of their land, imprisoned, and often executed. Refusing to renounce his faith, Bunyan spent more than a decade in jail while the struggle for England's soul raged outside the prison walls.

During his incarceration, Bunyan witnessed a wide range of horrors as his fellow prisoners were beaten, starved, and forced to live under the worst possible conditions. Those who became ill were left to die among the filth while the British regents insisted this atrocity was the will of God. Throughout this time, Bunyan pondered the question of the purpose of life and the ultimate fate of the immortal soul.

Bunyan, who believed that he had been visited by ANGELS and other mystic creatures since early childhood, was haunted by the theories of John Calvin, a prominent Puritan scholar. Calvin taught that only the ELECT would ascend to paradise; the rest (the majority) had been predestined to suffer eternity in hell. But how, Bunyan wondered, could a person know if he or she was among the saved? Bunyan contemplated this mystery and tried to reconcile it with one of his most striking supernatural visions in which God asked him, "Wilt thou leave thy sins and go to Heaven, or have thy sins and to Hell?" This profound question, and his conflicts over the concept of predestination, preoccupied Bunyan for the rest of his life.

A catharsis of these various episodes, Bunyan became obsessed with creating a cautionary tale about human destiny. The result was *Pilgrim's Progress*, a Puritan allegory that follows the story of Christian (representing humanity), a decent man who is disgusted by the sinfulness he sees all around him. Christian begins fearing that his hometown, the "City of Destruction" (the world), is about to incur divine wrath and decides to flee. The virtuous man picks up a heavy sack (sin) and sets off on a pilgrimage to the "Celestial City" (heaven), where he can dwell eternally with the "king" of divine glory.

The journey will not be an easy one; Christian must overcome a number of obstacles if he is to reach paradise. These include people (such as the personifications Ignorance and Hypocrisy), places (Slough of Despond and Difficulty Hill), and even the biblical demons Apollyon and Beelzebub who will try to keep Christian from reaching his goal. But he has allies, too, including his friend Faithful who agrees to accompany Christian on the difficult quest. He will also be aided by ANGELS, called "Shining Ones."

Christian and Faithful begin their journey, praying for perseverance in the looming trials. Things go well at first, and the two are cheered by thoughts of the Celestial City. But tragedy strikes when the pilgrims are arrested and charged with disrupting commerce by refusing to purchase "worldly goods." The evil "Lord Hate-good" sentences them to death for this crime, and Faithful is beaten, pierced with blades, and finally stoned to death. His soul ascends to paradise to join the legendary MARTYRS for Christ. Christian is able to escape and continues on, alone and desolate without his companion.

After much struggle, Christian comes to the town of "Vanity Fair," where he meets a man named Hopeful who is also weary of the world's wickedness. The two become friends, and Hopeful happily joins Christian on the road to the Celestial City. So the journey continues, with still more tests and travails that must be overcome.

Finally, Christian and Hopeful arrive at the base of the divine mountain. The "Shining Ones" help the men climb the steep slope (an image symbolic of the LADDER to heaven) and deliver them to the jewel-encrusted gates of the Celestial City. Over the entrance, the happy pair sees a sign written in gold that reads: "Blessed are they that do His commandments, that they might have the Right to the Tree of Life, and may enter in through the gate into the city."

They are greeted by the patriarchs Moses, ELIJAH, and Abraham, who present their request for sanctuary to the king. Recognizing Christian and Hopeful as his faithful followers, the king allows them into the Celestial City, with its massive towers and streets paved with gold. Christian and Hopeful are given "garments of shining gold" and invited to join the SAINTS in praising the Almighty. The bells ring joyously, joined by the voices of the saved, in a magnificent and eternal symphony in CHRISTIAN PARADISE.

Due largely to its simple style and forthright tone, *Pilgrim's Progress* was an immediate success. The work captured the imagination of the common person (at that time the population was barely literate) and was far more lively and understandable than typical literature of the day, written for the intellectual elite. Contemporary religious scholars criticized *Pilgrim's Progress* as ridiculous and simple-minded, but the masses loved it. Bunyan had hit his target audience: poor, humble Christians hungry for ideas they could embrace. By putting complex religious doctrines and philosophical concepts into an entertaining and easily grasped story, Bunyan had produced a classic that would appeal to peasants of his native England as well as generations of believers throughout the world.

Bunyan's work was so popular that within a few years of its publication, *Pilgrim's Progress* had been translated into more than a dozen languages and distributed all over Christendom. In response to the book's popularity and to many requests from readers, Bunyan wrote a sequel, *Pilgrim's Progress Part II*, which details the struggle of Christian's wife, Christianna, and their children to reach heaven despite the allure of evil.

PINK JUNGLE, THE The *The Pink Jungle*, a Broadway-bound musical that never reached the New York stage, offers a pseudofeminist update of Rodgers and Hammerstein's CAROUSEL, which itself is based on LILIOM. Written in 1959, the muddled play cast Agnes Moorehead as president of a cosmetics firm who is more concerned with market share than spiritual development. After dedicating her life to shady deals, avaricious profits, and sarcastic one-liners, Moorehead dies and arrives at the PEARLY GATES, only to be sent back to earth for one last chance at redemption. Her mission is to perform a single "act of decency" designed to help someone besides herself.

Moorehead decides to concentrate her efforts on helping a naive, kind-hearted hairdresser (played by Ginger Rogers) achieve success. At first, the departed mogul tries to manipulate company matters so that Rogers will be promoted to the post left vacant by Moorehead's death, but she ultimately chooses instead to help Rogers find true love. *The Pink Jungle* ends as Moorehead is admitted to paradise for convincing Rogers to devote herself to her man rather than pursue a career.

Unlike *Carousel*, *The Pink Jungle* had few redeeming features and died just three months after its San Francisco premiere. The combination of poor script, ludicrous plot, and preachy-love-is-better-than-money message made it immediately forgettable, while *Carousel* continues to be performed on stages throughout the world.

PLEASING EXPLANATION   The 1504 book *Pleasing Explanation of the Sensuous Pleasures of Paradise* offers an interpretation of the physical joys of CHRISTIAN PARADISE. According to the text, in the afterlife the saved have GLORIFIED BODIES that never age, degenerate, or feel pain. These reconstructed forms feature heightened senses that make food taste better, music sound sweeter, and magnificent sights appear even more lovely.

Pleasing Explanation further elaborates on the REUNION of loved ones in the world to come. The author calls this "one of the greatest joys of Heaven," especially for parents who have lost children in infancy. Now, with perfected bodies and free of the constraints of time, they can pass eternity enjoying one another at a celebration that knows no end. For many sixteenth-century Christians, this paradise of human delights was much more appealing than a perplexing heaven of "divine contemplation" and the BEATIFIC VISION. And many of these "earthly pleasures" remain components of modern views on the realm of the saved.

POETRY   Heaven has been the province of poetry from time immemorial. From the ancient Babylonians to our modern masters, poets have probed the eternal shores for inspiration, enlighten-ment, and answers. These lyrical looks at the divine run the gamut from short sonnets to epic poems such as the AENEID, the PROSE EDDA, and Dante's DIVINE COMEDY: THE PARADISO. Heroes of heaven, from Zoroaster to JESUS to ALLAH, have likewise appeared in innumerable poetic works. And common SYMBOLS of heaven, such as the STAIRCASE, PEARLY GATES, mountains, a jeweled city, and the WEDDING FEAST, are feature in countless examples of supernatural speculative poetry.

Poetic works also help trace the evolution of ESCHATOLOGY though history. A medieval poem titled "The Dream of the Rood [Cross]" offers a portrait of CHRISTIAN HEAVEN as pictured in the Middle Ages. It describes the vision of a man "sunk in slumber" who finds the cross upon which JESUS was crucified. The enchanted rood speaks, telling the tale of Christ's death and the glory of his resurrection. Dumbstruck, the man falls to his knees before the now-bejeweled cross, praying for the grace necessary to attain salvation:

> Bring me where is great gladness
>   and heavenly bliss,
> Where the people of God are
>   planted and established forever
> In joy everlasting.

He begs to know the unspeakable joy of the SAINTS in the "heavenly home" beyond the grave. The writer also invokes images of the VIRGIN MARY, ANGELS, and MARTYRS as residents of paradise.

Several centuries later, the poet

Novalis wrote his 1797 "Song of the Dead" in tribute to his dead fiancée. Its words praise her pure soul now in paradise, a place where "no tears" are shed, and lovely spirits are "absorbed in blissful contemplation" of the divine. Edgar Allan Poe offers a similar love-beyond-the-grave theme in his "Annabel Lee," which recalls a love so pure "the winged seraphs of Heaven coveted her and me." A heavenly remembrance by Henry Wadsworth Longfellow declares that the stars are "the forget-me-nots of the Angels," ever growing in the "infinite meadows of Heaven." All these poems anticipate a grand REUNION in paradise with lost loves.

Not all poems take so reverent a tone toward eternal bliss. Lord Byron describes paradise as an orgy of the flesh in "If That High World." According to his work, lovers enjoy an endless rendezvous free from the hazards of jealous husbands, gossiping communities, or condemning clergy. He likewise mocks the Christian notion of the BEATIFIC VISION as tedious and insufferable in "The Vision of Judgment." The satirical lyric bemoans a bleak HEREAFTER where God's creatures complacently repeat their endless routine:

> The angels all were singing out of
>   tune,
> And hoarse with having little else to
>   do,
> Excepting to wind up the sun and
>   moon,
> Or curb a runaway young star or
>   two.

Other artists try to find middle ground, blending their own ideas of heaven with traditional religious concepts. Poet Emily Dickinson, raised in a strict Calvinist family, rejects the harsh paradise of her parents in favor of a gentler afterlife. Dickenson envisions of realm of quiet tranquillity where sadness will be obsolete. But she resists the belief that heaven is a place of "eternal rest," chiding that it would be impossible to work out the logistics of "so many beds" to accommodate the dead.

The eighteenth-century mystic and philosopher WILLIAM BLAKE defined his own concepts of the hereafter, then adapted these notions into a number of poetic works. Among these are the *Songs of Innocence and of Experience*, which depict the joys and sorrows of the human soul. "The Lamb" and "The Divine Image" mix traditional Christian concepts with improvisational images about death, salvation, and God. Blake further likens angels to the "creative spirit," inspiring humans to produce great works of the imagination.

Many poems about the blessed afterlife have been developed into HYMNS extolling the delights of paradise. Among the most enduring is a piece by Robert Lowry:

> Shall we gather at the river
> Where bright Angel feet have trod:
> With its crystal tide forever
> Flowing by the throne of God?

This song of praise remains a standard in American Christian worship service.

And the realm of the divine continues to inspire works of poetry even in what is often considered a "secular" society.

POIMANDRES   The *Poimandres* is a Christian book written around A.D. 200 in the very early days of Christianity, which discusses beliefs regarding the afterlife. The unknown author claims that at time of death, a pure soul goes through seven "spheres of heaven" and eventually joins a chorus praising God. To prepare for this journey, the living must renounce material things and contemplate beauty and divine truth.

This work influenced many religious scholars, including SAINT AUGUSTINE who taught that total union with God is the ultimate joy of heaven. After studying *Poimandres* and pondering the supernatural mysteries, Augustine concluded that human souls could experience no greater delight than basking for all eternity in the BEATIFIC VISION. This sentiment was later echoed by such diverse philosophers as SAINT THOMAS AQUINAS, Martin Luther, and WILLIAM BLAKE.

POLE STAR   The Pole Star is the pivot point of the Aztec universe and encompasses the realm of the dead. Thirteen doomed realms revolve around it: one for each known planet, the moon, sun, clouds, lightning, rain and heat. Below the earth are nine underworld regions with the Land of the Dead at the very bottom. These material dimensions complete the divine balance and keep the universe in motion around the Pole Star.

Legends abound about the nature of

Jade and brass Aztec mosaic shows a playful sun god as lord of paradise.

this place of the dead. In some versions it is a peaceful place where people live in skeletal form with all social conventions of earthly life. Other stories claim a possibility (though rare) of being reincarnated after a brief stay within the Pole Star. And some accounts call the "world of the dead" a region of rest where the dead "sleep" forever.

Later records of the Aztec offer detailed descriptions of a four-part underworld, with each chamber corresponding to direction of the compass. Eastern paradise is reserved for warriors who die in battle, humans offered as sacrifices to the gods, and explorers or tradesmen who die in foreign lands. These souls depart to the "place of sunrise," to dwell forever with the sun god. To the south is TLALOCAN, the realm for those whose deaths are related to water, such as victims of drowning, floods, or swamp fevers. These souls go to a tropical garden of perpetual warmth that is free of pain and sorrow.

Women who die in childbirth journey to the "distant sunset" of the west, where they become "companions of the Sun" in the paradise TAMOANCHAN. They are rewarded for giving their lives for their children and are highly respected and honored by their survivors. Most souls, however, are destined to descend to Mictlan, a subterranean place of quiet gloom in the north.

Some records indicate a separate paradise for the souls of infants, young children, and other innocents called CHALMECACIVATL. It is a land of great earthly pleasure and natural happiness, similar to the Christian LIMBO. Chalmecacivatl is believed to be a hybrid of Aztec notions mingled with teachings of the early Spanish missionaries who brought Western religion to the region.

POLYGNOTUS (ca. 480–450 B.C.)

Polygnotus was a Greek artist who painted extensive murals involving ELYSIUM, the blessed realm of the dead. Tragically, all his works have been lost; however, literature of the era describes his compositions. This secondhand record—combined with images on contemporary MEMORIALS—provides the only knowledge the modern world has of ancient Greek portrayals of the afterlife.

Polygnotus's works decorated shrines of Apollo and provide some of the earliest examples of Western CHURCH ART AND ARCHITECTURE depicting the realm of the dead. The illustrations showed blessed spirits reclining at banquet tables, dancing, and enjoying games in paradise.

POTEAU-MITAN Haitian voodoo rituals employ the use of the poteau-mitan, a carved wooden pole reminiscent of the biblical staff of Moses. It is used to represent the spiritual world, with heaven at the top and hell at its base. Between these is the land of the living, and through the poteau-mitan departed souls can communicate and even travel from realm to realm. Believers summon LOAS, or defied souls of the dead, to follow the poteau-mitan on this supernatural journey. They descend the pole and inhabit special containers called govis that house the loas during the sacred ceremonies.

PRITI LOKA Though the Hindu religion teaches that humans are continually reincarnated, many believe that those who have lived especially pious lives are given a respite in Priti Loka. This is a realm of paradise free of pain, conflict, and suffering where spirits can rest before assuming another incarnation. Residence in Priti Loka must be temporary, since there is no opportunity for spiritual development in a place without sorrow. Spirits therefore cannot move from Priti Loka to enlightenment: they must resume mortal existence in order to achieve MOKSHA, the ultimate spiritual goal.

While in Priti Loka, the devout enjoy REUNION with deceased friends and family members and exchange ideas with other virtuous souls. This knowledge then helps them progress as they take on new earthly lives on the path toward moksha where the self is dissolved so the spirit can join the collective conscience.

PROM THEMES   Every year, high schools across America host elaborate dances called proms, each with a particular theme designed to attract attendees. Among the most popular motifs are those that associate the annual event with the great beyond. Common examples include decorations invoking images of Celtic AVALON, the ancient ISLE OF THE BLEST, and Greek ELYSIUM.

Comparisons to paradise imply that youthful patrons—soon to be dispersed by graduation—can look forward to a REUNION where friendships will be renewed. A recent perennial favorite motif is "STAIRWAY TO HEAVEN," inspired by the 1971 Led Zeppelin classic song. This theme conveys the notion that these almost-adults are on their way toward some grand, almost mystical, destiny. Decorations typically include classic and contemporary SYMBOLS of the divine, such as the STAIRCASE, LADDER, and glittering stars.

PROSE EDDA   The *Prose Edda*, an example of epic POETRY involving the afterlife, was written by Snorri Sturluson around the year 1200. Snorri designed the *Prose Edda* as a "guidebook" for writers trying to emulate the Viking "scald" style of literature. It is broken into three parts: The *Gylfaginning*, which describes the Norse gods, the *Skaldskaparmal*, detailing expressions and images of the era, and the *Hattatal*, an original poem based on historical heroes. The *Prose Edda* also includes Snorri's commentary and extensive body of Nordic and Icelandic myth.

Today, the most significant section of the *Prose Edda* is the first section, which serves as the source for much modern knowledge of the Norse pantheon. Snorri includes elaborate descriptions of the gods and their mythic adventures and retells legends from past centuries not found elsewhere. Among these is the legend of VALHALLA, the Nordic "Hall of the Slain." In Valhalla, fallen warriors enjoy feasts, games, and revelry for all eternity. Courier spirits called VALKYRIES, daughters of the god ODIN, visit battlefields to gather soldiers' souls and take them to the distant paradise. A passage in the *Prose Edda* states: "Odin . . . chooses for his sons all those who fall in combat. For their abode he has prepared Valhalla."

In addition to providing important cultural information, the *Prose Edda* has been the source of inspiration for numerous literary works, including Matthew Arnold's "BALDER DEAD."

PSYCHOPANNYCHIA   John Calvin (Cauvin, Chauvin), French philosopher and founder of the Calvinist religion, offers his notions of heaven in the treatise *Psychopannychia*. Calvin had been educated a Roman Catholic during the early 1500s but was disturbed by the rampant corruption and hypocrisy he witnessed among the clerical ranks. He rejected the "authority of the Holy See" (pope) and proclaimed that the Bible alone holds the answers to questions on faith and morals. Using this sole source, Calvin wrote several works on ESCHATOLOGY, including *Institutes of the Christian Religion* and *Psychopannychia*.

The latter work explains that death

"frees" a soul from its human shell so it can proceed to the afterlife. Members of the ELECT (those predestined for salvation) can then form a pleasing, although incomplete, union with the divine. True and complete union cannot be achieved until the LAST JUDGMENT, which will occur when the Christian Messiah JESUS returns and the earth itself is destroyed. At that time, every soul that has ever existed will be called forward to give an account of its life. Those judged worthy will then ascend to CHRISTIAN PARADISE where they will enjoy the BEATIFIC VISION for all eternity. The rest—a vast majority of humanity—will be cast into "everlasting fire."

Calvin incorporated these ideas into his own church founded in Geneva in 1541. His Reformed church led to Protestant breakaway sects such as the French Huguenots, the Scottish Presbyterians, and the Dutch Reformed church. His works also had a major influence on Puritanism in England and its colonies.

PULOTU Pulotu (Putoto) is the Western Polynesian land of the dead according to mythology of the Tonga. This "light-filled" realm is inhabited by spirits of the wealthy, the priests, and heroes; commoners are not admitted to this blissful paradise. In Pulotu, souls enjoy earthly pleasures such as banquets, dancing, and games.

PURE LAND Buddhists of Japan teach a Pure Land that awaits good souls after death. By praying to the god Amida (Lord of Light) on their deathbeds,

Japanese Buddhists believe that they can be born into a realm free of pain, frailty, and human failings. Here in this Pure Land, they peacefully await the Final Enlightenment, when all will be purged of flaws and absorbed into the blissful consciousness of NIRVANA.

In other legends, the term *pure land* often refers to temporary paradises such as SUKHAVATI, a resting place where souls pause before rejoining the reincarnation cycle. These regions are also sometimes referred to as the "high plains of heaven," where "sweet rivers" and "fruitful orchards" await the virtuous. Enchanted PEACHES grow in the pure lands, and a single bite of these luscious fruits grants immortality.

PURGATORY Purgatory is the transitional realm where human souls prepare to enter heaven. It is a sort of spiritual anteroom for spirits not wicked enough to be damned but not pure enough to ascend directly to paradise. Belief in purgatory is especially prevalent among Roman Catholics, who define it as the "place wherein souls who have died in the state of grace expiate their sins." Numerous SAINTS, including Lucia dos Santos and M. FAUSTINA KOWALSKA, have received supernatural visions of this mystic dimension.

Specifics regarding purgatory differ with various cultures. The ancient prophet Zoroaster taught that spirits who die with the "stain of sin" will face a final "trial" in the afterlife. He referred to a "molten river" and a perilous chasm through which all must pass on the way

Angels Freeing Souls from Paradise,
Tiepolo, Italy. ART TODAY

to paradise. Those with taint of wickedness will have their evil burned away before entering ZOROASTRIAN HEAVEN as they navigate these obstacles. These challenges do not offer a "second chance" for salvation but rather aid in the final preparation for audience with the divine. Irrevocably vile spirits will be destroyed long before reaching the flaming river and monster-infested pit.

The Roman Catholic church first explored the concept of a purgatorial realm and found it "worthy of credence" during the Middle Ages. Since that time, the nature of purgatory has been debated by religious scholars. Most agree that it is a place of purging, where the soul is cleansed of its last residue of sin. This description derives from St. Paul's letter to early Christians, in which he states: "If any man's work shall be burned, he shall suffer loss: but he himself shall be saved; yet so as by fire" (1 Cor. 3:15).

Critics, however, claim that St. Paul's words are metaphorical and refer to the "fire" of salvation itself. This saving grace has been secured by the sacrifice of JESUS Christ, and thus no individual afterlife penance is required.

Renowned Protestant author C. S. Lewis wrote that "our souls *demand* Purgatory" and would not want to go into glory smelling of sin but choose to be purified first. He notes that purgatory is not a place to atone for sin, since this has been done by Christ's crucifixion. Instead he views it as a dimension for having the "scars" of iniquity removed from human souls. The modern author elaborates on this idea in THE GREAT DIVORCE, a fictional speculation on what awaits human souls in the world beyond.

Contemporary philosopher Peter Kreeft calls purgatory "Heaven's kindergarten." In his *Everything You Ever Wanted to Know about Heaven*, Kreeft describes a transitional realm where souls learn of the glories they are about to see in paradise. Once through, the saved will be ready to advance into eternal joy with God. He notes that in purgatory, spirits experience joy as well as sorrow, witnessing firsthand how the Almighty brings beauty from ruin, triumph from tragedy. Humans do not simply observe this divine truth but participate in it, readying themselves for the ultimate beauty: restoration to their divine Father.

In Roman Catholic tradition, the VIRGIN MARY is sometimes called the Queen of Purgatory. Her intercession is believed to help shorten the time a spirit must spend there before proceeding to heaven. Numerous prayers, including the Catholic rosary, invoke her assistance in speeding spirits on to paradise from this celestial way station.

Purgatory appears in many works of Western literature, foremost among these as a book in Dante's afterlife trilogy called the *Purgatorio*.

PYTHAGORAS (ca. 500 B.C.) Greek philosopher and mathematician Pythagoras believed in a great paradise he called the ISLE OF THE BLEST. According to his theories, this enchanted realm exists on the dark side of the moon. After death, human spirits fly toward the isle and must overcome wicked interlopers who try to thwart their ascent. Souls can overcome these obstacles by performing certain magic rituals while alive, which would shield them from the power of the "dark forces."

Residence in the Isle of the Blest is only temporary according to Pythagoras's theories. He believed in the transmigration of souls, contending that the spirit is indestructible and goes through many "life-forms" on its endless journey. With each new incarnation, a soul gains knowledge, experience, and understanding before traveling on to another realm. After reaching perfection, "pure spirits" could transcend physical bonds permanently and dwell forever in the "limitless expanse" of space.

RA Ra (Amon-Ra, Re) is the Egyptian sun god who is mentioned extensively in the BOOK OF THE DEAD. The ancient text contains rituals and rites to appease him and curry his favor in the world to come. According to the belief, Ra rose in the morning in an enchanted boat.

His journey continued across the sky, and in the evening—when the earth is dark—Ra traveled to the underworld dispensing food, comfort, and encouragement to the dead. His very presence soothes deceased spirits as they negotiated the perils of the afterlife and seek repose in heaven. The "blessed" of Ra reside in SEKHET-AARU, one of the stops on the god's daily journey through the cosmos.

In some legends, Ra is the supreme deity and head of the Egyptian pantheon. Many early rulers claimed to be the sons of Ra or even his human incarnation. At the height of the god's cult worship, the high priests of Ra had power surpassing that of the pharaohs. They could "mark" a spirit or invoke the anger of the deity against those who angered or offended them, and such tainted souls would then be barred forever from paradise.

Ra lost prominence during Egypt's sixth dynasty, when the god OSIRIS (a historical figure believed to have been deified after his murder) was hailed as ruler of the land of the dead. ISIS, Osiris's sister-wife, placed a magic spell on Ra that transferred many of his powers to her husband. In the ensuing years Ra faded from importance, although he continued to serve as a comforter to departed spirits in the court of Osiris.

RAM Ancient Persian mythology describes the ram, sacred angels who deliver souls to paradise after death. The ram are incorporated into tales of ZOROASTRIAN HEAVEN, appearing as escorts who shepherd souls across CHINVATO PERETAV to the blessed afterlife.

These celestial guardians are featured in numerous works of fiction of the region as well.

RAMAYANA *The Ramayana* is a Sanskrit epic poem written by the Hindu scholar Valmiki around 350 B.C. It tells the tale of the hero Rama, who is actually the incarnation of Vishnu, second in the Hindu pantheon only to the creator Brahma. In response to pleas from the childless King Dasa-ratha, Brahma gives the man a magic potion that will impregnate his wives with divine children. Four sons are born to the king, including Rama, the "favored of the gods."

In the text, Rama battles demons, accomplishes heroic feats, and marries Sita, a beautiful princess. After the death of his father, a dispute erupts over who should ascend the throne. Dasa-ratha had wanted Rama to be king, but the mother of one of Rama's brothers insisted that her child inherit the crown. The brothers eventually agree that Rama will be banished from the kingdom for fourteen years but will return after that time to rule. But during Rama's exile, his beloved Sita is kidnapped by the evil Ravana who is overcome by the woman's unspeakable beauty.

Rama pursues Ravana and engages him in a series of battles. The enraged Rama enlists the help of a legion of mystic "warrior monkeys" who eventually help him capture and kill Ravana. Reunited with his bride, Rama begins to suspect that while in Ravana's house, Sita shared his bed. He asks her if she was intimate with Ravana, and Sita emphatically denies the charge. Even the gods testify on her behalf. But his doubts persist, as do rumors throughout the kingdom that the Rama has been shamed. Unable to put thoughts of Sita and Ravana out of his mind, Rama sends his wife into exile, where she gives birth to Rama's twin sons.

Almost two decades pass when at last the boys, now in their late teens, visit Rama's kingdom without realizing that the ruler is in fact their father. Rama sees and recognizes them and knows immediately that they are his children. Ashamed of his mistrust, he begs Sita to return to his side. She journeys to his kingdom only to be "received into the earth" as Rama watches, horrified. He asks the gods to end his life, too, as he is unable to continue without the wrongly accused Sita.

After much deliberation, Rama renounces his rule and goes to the Sarayu, a river believed to have enchanted waters. As he submerges, he hears the voice of Brahma calling him to paradise. Rama joins Brahma in heaven, where his broken heart receives comfort and his spirit finds eternal rest.

The poem is attributed to the sage Valmiki, with whom Sita is said to have spent her many years of exile. During that time, she reportedly recounted the events of Rama's life to the author, who then filled in the gaps by consulting other witnesses. His 24,000-stanza *Ramayana* is believed to be based on a historical figure, later embued with divine qualities. It has served as the inspiration for such diverse works as the 1575 *Ramcaritmanas* The Mindpool of the Deeds of Rama) to the contemporary orchestral piece *Ramayana* by American composer Bertram Shapleigh. Hindu poet Tulsi Das's sixteenth-century retelling of Rama's adventures is the most widely read of all Hindu works, often dubbed "North India's Bible." The ancient *Ramayana* remains popular in India and is the basis for an annual cultural celebration called the Ramlila.

RAP MUSIC   Images of paradise have become a standard component of rap, a style of music denoted by metered measures, short lines of rhyming lyrics, and artistic improvisation. The art form began as a blend of verse, simple tunes, and social messages and soon evolved into highly specialized entertainment. Called a "modern form of POETRY," rap has emerged from the harsh streets of the inner cities to become one of the most popular forms of music in America today.

Rap was initially brought to the mainstream by M. C. Hammer as an innovative mix of slick lyrics, dance beats, and self-expression. Even at this early stage, notions of divine truth and spiritual speculation were intrinsic to rap music. Hammer's 1990 hit "Pray" warns that even the rich and celebrated must answer to God, who provides sustenance in this world and salvation in the next. Hammer proclaims, "I have to pray just to make it" through every day, and the singer suggests that his fans do likewise.

Hammer's perky dance tunes soon gave way to "gangster rap," which reflected many of the artists' violent backgrounds. Lyrics boil with threats, hatred, and cries for vengeance. But when several of its biggest stars were murdered in the streets, rap music revealed a softer side. The next wave of songs pondered the fate of the deceased performers. Suddenly, singers who had once belted out ballads about bullets and bloodshed were raising their voices in hope, describing a peaceful afterlife where pain is obsolete and joy is eternal.

In 1995, artist Tupac Shakur was murdered by a rival gang. Ironically, his previously completed music video for "I Ain't Mad at Cha" depicts the singer in heaven meeting his heroes and preaching "forgiveness" of violent criminals. The scenes of the HEREAFTER include many common SYMBOLS of paradise, including billowy clouds, white pillars, and brilliant light. One line mourns the deaths of "all my homies who never made it home," while the song itself is dedicated to "all the people who lost a loved one this year." In a tragic irony, Shakur's own family would be among those mourners within months of the song's release.

Shakur's death was quickly followed by the loss of another rap musician. In a 1997 tribute to slain star Notorious B.I.G., colleague Puff Daddy tells his fallen friend, "When this life is over, I'll see your face." His "I'll Be Missing You" is a poignant expression of sorrow, brightened by a belief in the REUNION of loved ones in paradise. One lyric proclaims "I know you're in Heaven, smiling on us" and waiting in the world beyond to "open the gates for me."

Master P expresses similar sentiments in his "I Miss My Homies." Haunted by visions of brutality against his brethren, the singer finds solace in knowing that his friends "are in a better place," where he hopes to see them again. Like the previous musical eulogies, his song is reminiscent of Christian HYMNS, soothing and somber with a simple spiritual beauty.

Rap music continues to offer interpretations of paradise both in lyrics and in images from its music videos. These televised clips feature such prominent symbols of heaven as the STAIRCASE, tunnel of light, and satin-robed ANGELS.

RAPTURE   Rapture refers to a Christian belief in coming of JESUS Christ on earth, when the saved will be transported bodily to heaven. It is derived from the Latin *rapture*, meaning "ecstasy." St. Paul alludes to such a future event in a letter to the early followers of Christ: "Behold, I show you a mystery; We shall not all sleep, but we shall all be changed. In a moment, in the twinkling of an eye, at the last trump: for the trumpet shall sound, and the dead shall be raised incorruptible, and we shall be changed. For this corruptible must put on incorruption, and this mortal must put on immortality" (1 Cor. 15:51–53).

The "sleep" is translated as a metaphor for death, and thus not all will die but will be swept into heaven while still alive. Another passage of the Bible foretells that "two men shall be plowing in a field" when the LAST JUDGMENT begins. One will be taken to paradise body and soul, whereas the other "shall be left standing" as darkness and destruction overtake the earth. Belief in the Rapture remains prevalent, especially among born-again and charismatic denominations.

RAPTURE, THE   Evangelical Christianity, the MILLENNIUM, and concepts of CHRISTIAN PARADISE are probed in *The Rapture*, a 1991 supernatural drama. The film stars Mimi Rogers as a restless, world-weary woman who tries to escape the tedium of her life through wanton sexual escapades. This, too, soon becomes unsatisfying, and she moves on to a new obsession: charismatic Christianity. Rogers joins a congregation that believes that the end of the world and the LAST JUDGMENT are imminent and that total surrender to God is necessary to attain salvation. Believing she has been "called to the desert" to "meet JESUS," Rogers departs for the arid wilderness to await the foretold RAPTURE.

Devotion becomes obsession as Rogers's sole focus after her "awakening" is to "be with God in heaven." But when the "deliverance" she has convinced herself is coming fails to materialize, Rogers takes matters into her own hands. She concludes that she must kill herself and her young daughter so the two can ascend to paradise together. However, after shooting the child, Rogers is unable to kill herself, certain that suicides are immediately damned. Her fervor turns to loathing, and she begins to despise the divine Father she once so adored. When at last she must declare her allegiance to the Almighty, Rogers says she cannot love a God who "causes so much pain."

Much of the imagery in *Rapture* comes straight out of the Bible's Book of REVELATION. As the cataclysmic events prophesied by St. John the Evangelist unfold, the movie offers scenes of the Four Horsemen of the Apocalypse, the destruction of the earth, and the long-awaited "rapture of the faithful." The film's final sequence takes place just outside the NEW JERUSALEM, across the river of eternity. From the barren plain, Rogers looks to the eternal city and gasps, "It's beautiful." She enjoys a REUNION with her lost child but finds that she has love in her heart only for the girl, not for the God who made her. Rogers wants no part of his eternity.

Like the heaven in C. S. Lewis's GREAT DIVORCE, the paradise of *Rapture* must be freely chosen by each individual soul. God will not force anyone to be saved, a mystery Rogers is left to ponder "forever."

RASHNU Rashnu (Rash, Rast) is one of the ANGELS of justice according to the ancient Persian religion of Zoroastrianism. The celestial judge, assisted by the angel Astad (guardian of the sixty-fourth gate of paradise), Rashnu weighs the good and evil acts of the departing spirit three days after the person's death. If the balance of the "golden scales" tips in favor of salvation, the soul is delivered into ZOROAS-TRIAN HEAVEN. However, if the spirit's wickedness weighs down the scales, it is left to cross the perilous CHINVATO PERE-TAV (Bridge of the Separator) without diving protection.

Rashnu bears similarities to the ancient Egyptian OSIRIS and to the Islamic angels NAKIR and MUNKAR (which are believed to derive from Astad and Rashnu.)

REPUBLIC *The Republic* is a classic of Western literature written by Plato, who also wrote the PHAEDO. It is a dialogue exploring the nature of justice both in this life and the next. In the text, Plato's hero Socrates describes the "perfect society" where all work together for the good of the whole. The *Republic* also takes up the concept of rewards and punishments in the afterlife.

Plato was fascinated with ESCHA-TOLOGY and sought to unravel the mysteries of life, death, and immortality of the human soul. He believed that spirits would live forever, but he rejected the notion that the dead would have physical bodies in the next world. According to his theories, the soul is a "prisoner of the flesh," and death frees it to ascend to loftier realms. His afterlife is a purely spiritual dimension of intellectual delights where those who have lived virtuous lives find true happiness. Plato also teaches reincarnation as a reward for souls who grow "restless" in the afterlife and as a means for "developing" petty, self-serving spirits.

Contained in the *Republic* is the allegorical "Myth of ER." In this story, the hero Er travels to the land of the dead to witness life beyond the grave. He then returns with a tale of judgment, reward, and retribution and with a strong message about civic duty.

REUNION One of the most pervasive concepts of paradise throughout the world and across time is the belief that souls will be reunited with loved ones after death. This notion has been advanced by the ancient philosopher CI-

CERO, by Hebrew prophets of the Old Testament, and by scholars describing CHRISTIAN PARADISE. The reunion theme is also embraced in many versions of AFRICAN PARADISE as joining the circle of long-deceased ancestors.

Cicero taught that the ultimate joy of the afterlife is being restored to family and friends separated temporarily by death. In the Old Testament, the patriarch David laments that his dead son "shall not return to me" but "I will go to him" after death. And an elaborate sta-tue over central portal of Notre-Dame Cathedral depicts a loving couple holding hands in paradise. The joy of afterlife reunion is similarly described on MEMORIALS that promise souls will be together in paradise.

Not all religions have accepted the concept of heaven as a place of great social interaction. Protestant cleric Martin Luther soundly rejected the notion that the saved will enjoy the company of loved ones in the world to come. He taught a THEOCENTRIC HEAVEN, offering the sole splendor of contemplating the nature of God for all eternity. According to Luther, no other joy necessary. In fact, his version of CHRISTIAN PARADISE includes no interpersonal relationships of any kind—the only union is with the Almighty.

In contemporary secular culture, the theme of being rejoined to family and friends has become a common topic of RAP MUSIC and SHORT STORIES speculating on spiritual matters. It is also featured in modern films regarding the next world, including THE FIGHTING SULLI-VANS, GHOST, JACOB'S LADDER, and MADE IN HEAVEN.

REVELATION One of the most fascinating texts of the Christian Bible is the Book of Revelation. Written by St. John the Evangelist in the first century A.D. the book describes many cryptic events that will transpire at the end of time. Among these is the MILLENNIUM, a thousand-year era of peace, the RAPTURE during which the pious will be taken directly into heaven, and the LAST JUDGMENT, when every soul that has existed since the dawn of time will be received into paradise or cast into hell. Revelation has been called by modern scholars "the quintessential study on ESCHATOLOGY."

Revelation also contains specific descriptions of what awaits the saved in CHRISTIAN PARADISE. John depicts a jeweled realm of gold, rubies, and diamonds in the city of NEW JERUSALEM. At its center is a glorious throne where God presides over his creation. ANGELS, patriarchs, and MARTYRS celebrate his divinity with rousing HYMNS and blaring trumpets. During this vision, John "sees" into heaven and beholds a huge multitude of souls "impossible to count" enjoying the BEATIFIC VISION. The crowd is composed of members of "every race, tribe, nation and language": "Therefore are they before the throne of God, and serve him day and night in his temple: and he that sitteth on the throne shall dwell among them. They shall hunger no more, neither thirst any more; neither shall the sun light on them, nor any heat. For the Lamb which is in the midst of the throne shall feed them, and shall lead them unto living fountains of waters: and God shall wipe away all tears from their eyes" (Rev. 7:15–17).

A preacher's "time line" chronicling the events foretold in St. John's Revelation. ART TODAY

One of the most hotly debated parts of John's description of paradise is the measurements he includes to convey its area. He puts the SIZE OF HEAVEN at "12,000 furlongs square" (about 1,500 cubic miles). This has been cited by critics who claim that the saved would have to be "stacked like cordwood" to fit into such a relatively limited realm. Christian scholars counter that such discourse is ridiculous, since the number was offered simply to give a sense of grandeur to St. John's contemporaries. True heaven, religious leaders agree, knows no boundaries.

Images in Revelation have inspired numerous works of CHURCH ART AND ARCHITECTURE, POETRY, plays, SHORT STORIES, movies, and other creative endeavors. Examples range from Milton's classic PARADISE LOST to the modern film RAPTURE.

ROHUTU Rohutu is the realm of the dead of Leeward Islands. For the wealthy and elite, it is a paradise with air "like sweet perfume." Peasants, however, will find Rohutu foul and unappealing since legends equate status on earth with pleasure in the afterlife.

SAINTS People believed to dwell in paradise as a reward for particularly virtuous lives are known as saints. The term covers holy ones of Jewish, Christian, Islamic, Jain, and Hindu lore. Highest among these pure souls are the MARTYRS, those who make the ultimate sacrifice by dying for their faiths. Many believe that saints have the power to intercede for the living and can help other souls reach heaven through prayers before the throne of God.

Christian saints are referred to as the "church triumphant" who now dwell with God in paradise. Their mediation helps souls of the living, or "church militant," in the war against evil. These pious heroes are often represented in works of CHURCH ART AND ARCHITECTURE, including frescoes, sculptures, paintings, and STAINED-GLASS WINDOWS. Saints' images are designed to help inspire the faithful to greater holiness and remind all of their ultimate spiritual destiny.

Intense debate erupted over the veneration of saints during the Middle Ages, when many Protestants objected to the practice of "praying to the dead." They claimed the practice had no basis in scripture and was therefore "contrary to the word of God." Catholic scholars took up the matter formally at the 1563 Council of Trent. After much deliberation, the religious leaders decreed that the living most definitely *should* "invoke the saints," as the blessed deceased are still part of the church, separated only temporarily by death. The living ask one another to pray for certain causes, they argued, so it is logical to extend those requests to our "deceased brethren" who have "preceded us to heaven."

In Muslim tradition, a wali is a "saint" who performs some extraordinary act of devotion to ALLAH. These members of the "spiritual elite" founded monasteries and other sacred brotherhoods dedicated to finding the "shining path" of divinity. Walis dwell in DJANNA, the paradise of Islam, and intercede for the living at the throne of the Almighty. Each wali is said to be imbued with special graces that can serve as "mystic channels" for others to find truth, overcome obstacles, and receive the favor of Allah. The power of the walis increases after death, so burial plots of these saints draw pilgrims and devotees wishing to show their respect and gain favor.

Followers of Jainism believe that all souls are called to become saints. This is accomplished by living according to a set of behavioral ethics similar to the Judeo-Christian Ten Commandments. In order to attain KEVALA, the optimal state of spiritual enlightenment, a person must adhere to the following rules: "(1) never intentionally extinguish a life; (2) never lie or give false account; (3) never steal; (4) never be unchaste in thought, word or action; (5) refuse to accumulate wealth beyond basic needs, give any excess to the common good; (6) avoid people and places of temptation; (7) limit the amount of personal possessions held at any given time; (8) protect the self from foreseeable evil; (9) engage in meditation; (10) practice self-sacrifice; (11) dedicate some time to monastic living; and (12) donate alms to a monastic community."

By striving to meet these goals, believers in the Jain faith can hope to be rewarded with a "motionless afterlife at the summit of the universe," the religion's concept of sainthood.

In modern cultures, respect for those who have suffered persecution, lived devout lives, and renounced personal gratification in favor of helping others remains strong. This is evident in the examples of such revered contemporary icons as Mahatma Gandhi, Mother Teresa of Calcutta, and Martin Luther King Jr. People of all religious faiths acknowledge the immense contributions of these steadfast heroes. And many traditional Christian saints remain in the public arena as cultural mainstays. These include St. Patrick, St. Valentine, and SAINT PETER, recognized "keeper of the keys to the kingdom" of heaven.

SANDALPHON Sandalphon (Sandalfon) is the angel believed to carry prayers from humans directly to God. The Hebrew Talmud says his head "reaches to heaven," and he is often referred to as the "tall angel." He likewise appears in Islamic legend as well as in works of literature and POETRY. Henry Wadsworth Longfellow calls him "Angel of Glory, Angel of Prayer."

Sandalphon is also believed to have influence over conception of children, being able to determine if the child will be a boy or a girl. For this reason, his intercession is frequently invoked by infertile couples and pregnant women.

SAN HSIEN SHAN The San Hsien Shan are the Three Mountains of the Immortals of ancient Chinese myth. They are actually three islands in the Eastern Sea, Fang-chang, Ying-chou, and P'eng-lai. Souls dwelling in the tropical paradise of San Hsien Shan attain immortality by feeding on a divine plant with supernatural powers. In some accounts, this mystic vegetation is a PEACH tree that produces enchanted fruits that allow humans to live forever.

SARCOPHAGI Sarcophagi are stone coffins commonly used in ancient societies. The more elaborate examples feature carvings that depict the afterlife and its many delights. Ancient tombs from Greek, ETRUSCAN, and Egyptian civilizations often depict images of the dead enjoying great feasts, participating in games, or mingling with the gods in the next world. The MEMORIALS frequently include images of the gods Hades and Persephone, OSIRIS and ISIS, ANUBIS, and other otherworld deities.

SATURDAY NIGHT LIVE NBC's long-running comedy series *Saturday Night Live* has used the afterlife as a source of humor for more than two decades, poking fun at salvation and damnation alike. Guest stars are routinely sent to the HEREAFTER where they encounter all manner of hilarious adventures in eternity. Most concentrate on notions of CHRISTIAN PARADISE and lampoon everything from ANGELS to the Almighty in often irreverent depictions of the realm of the blessed.

In a send-up of grocery store tabloids, *Saturday Night Live* offered a cover story promising to reveal whether the recently deceased Gloria Swanson went to heaven or to hell. A photo of the star was alternately shown "flying" into paradise and plummeting into the inferno. This was followed by an enthusiastic declaration: "I want to know!"

A 1987 sketch casts John Larroquette as a departed soul arriving in paradise, where a celestial greeter welcomes him. Larroquette begins asking the angel to reveal to him the mysteries of his own life, such as, "What's the dumbest thing I ever did?" and "Who had a crush on me I didn't know about?" His spiritual guardian admonishes him, "You don't really want to know. You couldn't stand it!"

Several seasons later, an overworked JESUS (played by Phil Hartman) descends from heaven to ask guest host Sally Field's overly devout character to stop her constant praying over insignificant matters. He explains that God hears and answers every prayer, and her unceasing supplications about "not burning the pot roast" and getting stains out of her husband's work clothes are occupying a great deal of the Almighty's time. The Redeemer politely suggests that she reserve her divine requests for vital affairs and see to the everyday trivialities herself.

The show also parodies NEAR-DEATH EXPERIENCES in a skit that sends cast member Chris Farley to paradise. In the sketch, Farley is a "superfan" obsessed with his beloved Chicago Bears football team. After suffering a heart attack, his "spirit" travels down the proverbial "tunnel of light," and Farley enjoys a REUNION with departed relatives, all of them superfans. Finally, Farley comes face to face with God, who bears an uncanny resemblance to former Bears coach Mike Ditka. Through the use of edited sports tapes, Ditka-god repeats, "This one isn't over

yet, this one isn't over yet," as Farley's spirit plunges back to the temporal plane. Revived, the superfan vows to become more devoted than ever to the Windy City's gridiron heroes.

Saturday Night Live continues to spoof heaven in JOKES, sketches chiding ADVERTISING, and skits regarding the eternal mysteries.

"SCIPIO'S DREAM" Roman consul and orator CICERO penned several works regarding the joys of paradise, including "Scipio's Dream," contained in his *De Republica*. The SHORT STORY tells the tale of a civil servant who envisions the afterlife (referred to as the ISLE OF THE BLEST) as a place where friends and family will enjoy a great and eternal REUNION. In the dream, Scipio's happiest moment comes as he embraces his long-dead father, knowing that they will never again part. They have until the end of time to share each other's compnay.

Cicero's image of the HEREAFTER as a forum for fellowship and social interaction permeated Western thought for millennia and continues to be a component of modern notions of heaven. CHRISTIAN PARADISE offers the saved a chance to mingle not only with their kin but also with a litany of SAINTS and ANGELS in the world to come. And though some scholars (such as SAINT AUGUSTINE) downplayed the concept as "insignificant" compared to the ecstasy of the BEATIFIC VISION, eternal reunion had undeniable appeal. At a time when infant mortality rates were astronomical and the average lifespan was less than five decades, the idea that heaven would reunite lost loves was eagerly embraced. Cicero's "dream" was shared by the masses and would be revisited by students of ESCHATOLOGY henceforth.

Cicero's promised paradise is the reward for those who dedicate their lives to others through military service, political advocacy, or charitable works. His main goal in writing "Scipio's Dream" was to encourage philanthropy, although the author no doubt firmly believed in his vision of the world to come. A similar sentiment that social responsibility is essential for rest in the afterlife is expressed in Plato's "Myth of ER." Middle English genius Geoffrey Chaucer also uses the story in his 1380 *Parliament of Fools*, a parody of contemporary politics.

SEKHET-AARU   Ancient Egyptian mythology includes the paradise Sekhet-aaru, the fragrant "fields of grain." It is an enchanted island where departing souls feast on the daily harvest of sweet barley and savory wheat while waiting for the Sun god RA to make his visit. Favored spirits dwell eternally in Sekhet-aaru. In later legends, the island becomes part of the kingdom of OSIRIS, the judge of the dead and overlord of the afterlife.

SEMITIC HEAVEN   Semitic heaven predates the Hebrew religion and was eventually replaced by concepts of JEWISH PARADISE. The Semites envisioned a realm of monotonous quiet where souls will dwell forever. This place is called Sheol. In early texts, Sheol is free of pain and torture; however, spirits in Sheol are weak, faded, and lethargic. The dead had no communication with the realm of God or with the ANGELS, although the living could contact both the divine upper world and the underworld through enchanted rituals.

Over time, this gloomy dimension became increasingly identified as a subterranean realm of punishment for evil-doers. The souls of pious humans were thought to receive comfort and rest in the afterlife, perhaps in the "bosom of Abraham." Semitic tradition also began teaching a possible REUNION in the next world where those parted by death would be restored to one another in eternity.

SERAPIS   Serapis is a Greco-Egyptian variation of OSIRIS, god of the dead, incorporating traits and powers of Greek underworld deities as well as those of Osiris himself. There is some disagreement over the time and origin of the cult of Serapis, but most scholars agree that the hybrid god was manufactured by Greek and Egyptian rulers to unite the two cultures after the conquest by Alexander the Great. Eventually, Serapis was also absorbed into Roman mythology as a powerful lord of the afterlife. Temples dedicated to Serapis drew worshipers of Greek, Egyptian, and Roman backgrounds, all invoking the same deity in hopes of finding joy in the next world.

SEVEN SLEEPERS   A medieval legend of both Islam and Christianity, the Seven Sleepers are young MARTYRS who surrender their lives rather than renounce their faith. According to the story, the men hide themselves in a secluded cave while a fierce religious persecution sweeps the nation. Protected by ANGELS, the men fall into comalike sleep and spend the next several centuries suspended in the cavern. Soon after they awaken, they perish and are escorted to paradise as a reward for their loyalty.

The tale of the Seven Sleepers appears in numerous books, including religious texts and fictional works. In the KORAN, the Islamic equivalent of the Christian Bible, the seven are guarded by a fierce beast who watches over the steadfast men. Although unnamed in the text, some believe that this animal is the legendary canine KATMIR, a mystical dog who is beloved of ALLAH. (Katmir is one of the ANIMALS believed to dwell in paradise.)

An Arabic fictionalized version of the drama titled *Ashab al-Kahf* tells that the young men actually lived for three centuries, sustained by the will of Allah. They are finally killed hundreds of years after their flight but are immediately transported to the garden paradise of DJANNA. A great celebration greets them as all heaven celebrates their fine example.

In the Christian legend, the seven men are hiding from the infamous Emperor Decius, whose vicious persecution of the early church entailed torture, mutilation, and throwing Christians to the lions. The seven men, all sons of wealthy families, refuse to renounce JESUS, the Messiah, and are threatened with a variety of punishments. They escape to the sanctuary of a cave in the wilderness and plan to remain there until Decius's ferocious rule ends. Exhausted from their flight, they fall asleep and remain unconscious for almost 230 years. They die soon after reviving, and their bodies are taken to a grand cathedral for interment. The seven are honored as exemplary martyrs and soon become heroes of early Christianity.

Around 1800, the German author Wolfgang von Goethe (author of "the quintessential FAUST story") took up the subject in his poem "The Seven Sleepers of Ephesus." Goethe mingled elements of both the Islamic and Christian versions of this legend, adding his own religious beliefs and mythic images. He includes the angel GABRIEL as the guardian who escorts the boys to heaven after their long slumber.

Despite the enduring popularity of the Seven Sleepers story, it has been declared "unworthy of credence" by Christian officials. Most scholars conclude that the tale is probably based on fact, but that the fragment of truth has been highly embellished over the years, rendering the entire account incredible. Church leaders do, however, praise these men—whether real or imaginary—who made the supreme sacrifice for their faith and suggest that all believers should be prepared to do likewise.

SHADID The Shadid are MARTYRS of the Islamic faith, religious crusaders who lose their lives in defense of their beliefs. According to the legends, anyone dying in a JIHAD (holy war) is forgiven all sins and taken immediately to DJANNA (Muslim paradise). The Shadid are the "blessed of ALLAH," the supreme deity of Islam.

SHEEN, FULTON Fulton Sheen was one of the most beloved Roman Catholic bishops of the twentieth century. A great speaker and inspired writer, Sheen offered many eloquent treatises on the joys of CHRISTIAN PARADISE and the criteria for salvation. The bishop frequently took up the subject of the nature of heaven and the BEATIFIC VISION, putting complex doctrines in simple terms that could be understood and embraced by the masses.

Determined to convince Christians that paradise is not a boring realm of monotonous worship but a dynamic mingling with divine grandeur, Sheen wrote: "It is the mystery of the Trinity which gives the answer to our quest for our happiness and the meaning of Heaven. Heaven is not a place where we find the fullness of all fine things which slake the thirst of hearts, satisfy the hunger of starving minds and give rest to unrequited love. Heaven is the communion with perfect Life, perfect Truth and perfect Love."

This, according to Sheen, is the true ecstasy of the afterlife: the contemplation of God and his infinite goodness. He joins such acclaimed Catholic scholars as SAINT AUGUSTINE and THOMAS AQUINAS in concluding that the greatest pleasure of eternity is basking in the "light of the Godhead." Sheen's works have inspired a generation of clerics and continue to be cited in discussions of paradise and its mystic rewards.

SHORT STORIES The nature of paradise has long been an inspiration to writers offering their speculations on the great beyond. Ancient artists etched their images of paradise onto clay pots and carved them into SARCOPHAGI, creating grand tales to accompany their illustrations. Afterlife deities OSIRIS and ISIS, BEL, ODIN, SERAPIS, ANUBIS, and others appear in these stories found on MEMORIALS of their respective cultures.

During the Middle Ages, theorists—still dealing with largely illiterate audiences—presented their notions of paradise in the form of MYSTERY PLAYS. These dramas drew on ancient mythic images as well as Western concepts of CHRISTIAN PARADISE. Such secular productions were eventually supplanted by MORALITY PLAYS presented by church officials and based on sanctioned doctrines of the supernatural realm. They featured the escapades of SAINTS, ANGELS, and other religious heroes forging their way from the mortal plane to the eternal reward.

In modern times, short stories reflect the pluralism of contemporary society, and heavenly ideas run the gamut from traditional religious images to highly imaginative metaphors of the "great beyond." Sci-fi master Ray Bradbury off-ers "The Third Expedition" (part of the *Martian Chronicles*), in which a team of American astronauts lands on Mars only to find it populated with their deceased loved ones. Thrilled yet unsettled by the sudden REUNION with lost family and friends, the crew asks, "Is this Heaven?" They are told by the Mar-tians that this is a "second chance" after death. The incredulous spacemen are also warned that "God's good to us" and it would not be wise to pry into his mystery. But paradise turns suddenly sour when the men realize—too late—that they have been lulled into a trap baited with their own dearest wishes and darkest fears.

Jewish author Isaac Bashevis Singer describes legends of paradise in his 1964 "Short Friday," a tender story about a reverent couple called to heaven by the angel DUMA on the eve of the Sabbath. An elderly couple is just sitting down to Sabbath supper when the celestial emissary arrives to transport them to eternity. The dazed man and woman give an account of their lives, and the angel rejoicingly transports them to paradise on his magnificent "flapping wings."

Stephen King, most famous for his horror masterpieces, takes up the subject of a pleasant afterlife in a number of his short stories. In "The Reach," part of his *Skeleton Crew* anthology, King paints the next world as a place of joyful reunion with deceased loved ones, where the "dead love" as they did in life. Touching in its simplicity, devoid of any religious or theological message, the story leaves an impression of comfort and consolation. King's afterlife is a familiar place where all blessed souls will be welcomed into the circle of friendship.

Literary interpretations on heaven and its joys have also been adapted into teleplays for such programs as TWILIGHT ZONE and *Way Out*. TWILIGHT ZONE MAGAZINE likewise offered a forum for presenting fictional works on humanity's ultimate abode.

SIDRET-EL-MOUNTEHA The Sidret-el-Mounteha is an enchanted tree that grows at the pinnacle of DJANNA, Islam's paradise. The magnificent plant has branches of emerald, and on its leaves are written the names of every living human being. During Ramadan, Islam's holy season, the leaves bearing the names of all those who are going to die in the upcoming year fall to the ground. As Arab traders introduced the religion of Islam to northern Africa, the Sidret-el-Mounteha evolved into the CEDAR TREE OF THE END, a legendary plant of AFRICAN PARADISE.

SIGNORELLI, LUCA   (1441–1523) Fifteenth-century Tuscan painter Luca Signorelli broke with tradition by depicting CHRISTIAN PARADISE as a realm of human vibrance and sensuality rather than a place of gentle, muted beauty. His LAST JUDGMENT at the Cathedral of Orvieto features the saved as muscular, voluptuous physical specimens unashamed of their nudity. And while Signorelli's ANGELS are robed in flowing full-length garments, the men and women of paradise stand naked before the Almighty. (Due to complaints from shocked patrons, loincloths were later added to cover the offending anatomies.) Heaven, according to Signorelli's vision, is the realization of ultimate beauty for both body and soul.

The artist inherited the Orvieto project from another Christian painter, FRA ANGELICO, who provided illustrations for the vault above the altar then abandoned the project. Unlike his predecessor and other painters of the era, Signorelli wanted to show the Last Judgment as a process rather than an event. He accomplishes this by depicting scenes described in REVELATION on separate walls of the cathedral, culminating in the BEATIFIC VISION of God in his glory. His series includes frescoes detailing the *Appearance of the Anti-Christ, Resurrection of the Flesh,* and *Damned Consigned to Hell.*

Signorelli's *The Coronation of the* ELECT also provides a truly stunning representation of human salvation. This composition offers achingly beautiful men and women receiving golden crowns from their celestial guardians. Other angels are shown playing instruments, dancing, and welcoming their mortal friends. (These celestial attendants are robed in majestic garments, unlike their sword-wielding counterparts in *Damned Consigned to Hell,* who are dressed in full body armor.) Awestruck souls, some of them kneeling, watch the glorious spectacle and await their own induction into eternity.

Art scholars have declared Signorelli's works to be great achievements in realism, comparable to the compositions of MICHELANGELO. However, Signorelli distinguishes himself as a master in using elongation of limbs to create compelling images that seem truly unearthly. His paintings are among the finest products of the Renaissance era in Christian art and remain stunning achievements in CHURCH ART AND ARCHITECTURE.

SIN EATER Medieval Christian families tried to guarantee their acceptance into heaven by hiring a sin eater—usually a destitute waif or wanderer—to "consume" the evil of the recently deceased. Mourners would place a loaf of bread or pitcher of milk on the fresh corpse, believing it would absorb the inherent sin and its requisite punishment. This would then be eaten by the hired man (women were never used as sin eaters). By taking this dark communion, the sin eater also agreed to accept the guilt and burden of the departed's transgressions. The deceased soul would thus be cleansed and could ascend immediately to paradise.

Some towns had professional sin eaters who would be called to the deathbed along with the family priest. In other areas, it was believed that the sin eater must be a complete stranger with no ties to the dead person. Families who could not afford to pay the fee sometimes offered tainted food and drink to beggars, surreptitiously "poisoning" them with the "sins." People bearing grudges also tried to feed the "sin" to their enemies, confident that this would blight their souls.

Christian officials frowned on this practice for a variety of reasons, not the least of which that it mocked the very notion of salvation. Admittance to heaven, they claimed, is contingent on the will of God and the mercy of JESUS. A soul could be purified only through prayer, penance, and the sacraments, not by some magic ritual. Due to this objection and growing skepticism of the process, sin eating eventually died out.

SISTINE MADONNA   The *Sistine Madonna*, a breathtaking accomplishment of religious art, was painted by Renaissance master Raphael in 1513. The rich oil painting shows the VIRGIN MARY in heaven holding the infant JESUS. Behind her is an ocean of ANGELS, followed by layers of SAINTS including St. Barbara, the patroness of a peaceful death. As the enraptured souls watch, Mary and Jesus float on clouds as they prepare to welcome a new soul into CHRISTIAN PARADISE.

The lower portion of the painting shows the coffin of Pope Julius II (for whom the artwork was commissioned) as the pontiff awaits burial. Green velvet curtains part to reveal the supernatural vision above. Perched on Julius's casket are two chubby cherubs musing about the scene. They are calm, almost mirthful, as they ponder the great mysteries of human salvation. One looks to the skies while the other rests his chin on his folded hands, waiting patiently for the pope's soul to depart for heaven.

In recent days, the pair of cherubs has become a popular illustration for ANGELWARE. Their image adorns magnets, key chains, COLLECTOR PLATES, and a host of GIFT NOVELTIES.

SIZE OF HEAVEN   For centuries, critics and clerics have debated notions of the size of heaven. A reference in REVELATION puts the blessed realm at approximately 1,500 miles (a "furlong" times 12, an important biblical number). Such a place would stretch from Canada to Florida, New York City to Santa Fe, and would tower for miles into the sky.

Atheists often ridicule this literalist version of the size of heaven, chiding that the saved would be crammed in like sardines in such a relatively small area. Gene Kasmar of Minnesota Atheists wrote a 1994 letter to the editor of the Christian publication *Nation* proclaiming that using logic and arithmetic, he had concluded that even if only "two in every billion" people were saved, paradise would have been "filled" around 1930.

Of course, Christian scholars counter this by reminding nonbelievers that the reference was offered by St. John to give his contemporaries some concept of a vast paradise. The dimensions he gave made a great impression on these early followers of JESUS and conveyed the sense of grandeur. Philosophers further argue that God, being omnipotent, could easily expand the perimeter of paradise to accommodate an infinite number of souls and GLORIFIED BODIES. Thus trying to "limit" the number of souls who could be saved is ludicrous.

SKY VILLAGE   The afterlife of many African myths is quite similar to life on earth, except that it takes place in the sky. The belief is that when a person dies, the soul simply ascends to a lofty village, and existence picks up where it left off before the demise. The specifics of this theory vary from tribe to tribe and region to region, but most agree that in the sky village, people recognize friends and family, have all their needs met, and do not suffer any pain or illness.

The Kongo of Zaire believe that the sky village is a mirror of our world, a place where people rise at night and sleep during the day. The heaven is white, whereas the earth is tainted black from evil. A red rainbow connects the two realms. All other aspects of existence are roughly the same on both sides, following the white-red-black cycle. (Birth is white, life is red, death is black. Dawn is white, midday is red, nightfall is black, etc.)

In Mozambique, the Tonga tell legends about visits between the world below and the CITY IN THE SKY. In the most popular tale, a young girl breaks her water jar and shouts out for help. The people in the sky village respond, sending down a rope that the girl climbs to reach the celestial realm. She immediately recognizes many who have died and renews old friendships. When it is time for her to return to the lower world, a kind woman offers to let the girl pick out a baby to take with her. There are two: one wrapped in white, the other in red. The girl wants the red baby, but a wise ant tells her that this is a mistake. She selects the white-wrapped baby instead.

The girl is greeted with great joy when she returns home. Fellow villagers gather to hear her stories of the mystic realm and to admire the beautiful baby. The girl's sister becomes quite jealous and takes her own trip to the upper plain. But she is ill-behaved and rude, angering all she meets. When she leaves, she demands that she be allowed to take the red baby home with her.

The ant tries to warn her, but she kicks it away. When the red baby is placed in her arms, her flesh vanishes and she becomes a skeleton. The bewitched baby is a trick, designed to weed out unworthy visitors. The envious sister's bones fall to the ground in a white rain on her village, a warning to others.

The concept of a sky village bears similarities to other notions of AFRICAN PARADISE in which generations enjoy a REUNION above. This belief is also likened to the Congolese idea of a MIRROR WORLD for departed spirits.

SOUL OF ST. BERTIN CARRIED UP TO GOD The painting *Soul of St. Bertin Carried Up to God* by fifteenth-century Dutch master Simon Marmion reflects many components of CHRISTIAN PARADISE. It shows two white-robed ANGELS carrying a small wrapped linen up to the skies, past a rush of dark stormclouds. Within the linen is a glowing, naked figure representing the saint's pure soul. Heaven is depicted as a circle of light with God at its center seated on a gold throne. The deity is regally outfitted in red robes and a gold crown and is holding a gold scepter. All of paradise centers on the BEATIFIC VISION, the "glory of heaven."

Marmion's work is significant in that it not only depicts heaven but also illustrates the process of dying. According to the artist's interpretation, human spirits depart for eternity under the protection of a celestial escort. With the assistance of celestial brethren, mortal souls are elevated to immortality through the luminous mercy of the divine will. In paradise, humans and angels alike celebrate forever the radiance of the Almighty in his eternal courtyard of splendor.

SOVI   According to Slavic folklore, Sovi originated the custom of cremating the dead in order to assure them a peaceful afterlife. A thirteenth-century Russian tale describes the death of Sovi's son and the attempts made by the family to put the spirit to rest. When the child dies, his father buries the body on the family estate, but the boy cries out that he is being devoured by maggots. Sovi digs up the body and places it in a hollow tree, but the child then complains that insects are constantly stinging him. He is in misery.

Finally, Sovi gathers a pile of deadwood and burns his son's body on a great funeral pyre. Once the corpse is consumed in flames, the spirit of Sovi's child is released and suffers no more pain. Before departing, the boy tells his father he is "as a babe in the cradle," free of suffering and without a care in the world. The liberated soul soars to the heavens in bliss. Satisfied that his son is finally at peace, Sovi then spreads the word that bodies should be cremated rather than interred or entombed. Any other method will result in great agony for the deceased.

SPIRIT WORLD   *Spirit world* is a generic term used by many cultures to refer to the blessed realm of the dead. It is found in legends of AFRICAN PARADISE, in Native American tales of the HAPPY HUNTING GROUNDS, and in myths and religions from across the globe. In the vast majority of cases, the term

connotes a realm of tranquillity where human souls continue to enjoy a peaceful existence.

STAINED-GLASS WINDOWS
Stained-glass windows are a common component of CHURCH ART AND ARCHITECTURE used to convey the beauty and glory of CHRISTIAN PARADISE. Designed to show the luminous opulence of heaven, windows frequently depict JESUS, the VIRGIN MARY, SAINTS, and ANGELS. The light passing through the colored glass creates an impression of shining souls illuminated from within. This is a dazzling contrast to bleak images of hell, which is believed to be "opaque" and incapable of conducting light.

Stained-glass windows began emerging in popularity around the twelfth-century. They replaced traditional stone

Fourteenth-century stained-glass window shows the archangel Michael weighing souls in the afterlife. ART TODAY

walls—dark and gray—with brilliant panels of vivid colors. The windows symbolically joined the living worshipers to dead saints and vicariously put the faithful in the presence of the divine.

The artistry of a church's stained-glass windows was a matter of great pride, so members of the congregations frequently donated material, artistic skills, and money to ensure that the church was the most beautiful building in the area.

Rose windows became popular during the high Middle Ages. These contain small "petals," each with a particular scene or color. Together, the individual portions figure into larger pattern, extending the notion that all of Christ's followers, whether alive or in heaven, are interconnected and belong to one mystical body. Rose windows became powerful tools for expressing this concept of the COMMUNION OF SAINTS, a complex doctrine that was often hard for the illiterate masses to fathom.

Some of the most elaborate examples of stained-glass windows are in the world-famous cathedral of Notre-Dame, the American Shrine of the Immaculate Conception, and the National Shrine. These fragile wonders continue to grace Christian churches and have also been incorporated into GIFT NOVELTIES, ANGELWARE and COLLECTOR PLATES of divine inspiration.

STAIRCASE One of the most common SYMBOLS of ancient, medieval, and contemporary heaven is the staircase. Images of celestial stairways appear in myths ranging from the Egyptian pyramids (designed to suggest a stairway leading into the world beyond) to New Age encounters with "heavenly spirits" ascending the cosmos.

According to the teachings of Islam, heaven and earth are connected by a "stairway of light." When a person dies, one of ALLAH's divine ANGELS is sent down the stairs to guide the soul to DJANNA, a great paradise. Worthy spirits travel quickly up the stairs to take their places at the throne of the Almighty.

The image is also found in Christian tradition. A passage in the Bible refers to a supernatural conduit between the land of the living and the realm of the divine: "Hereafter you shall see heaven open up, and the angels of God ascending and descending upon the Son of man" (John 1:51).

The heavenly staircase has been adapted into Christian HYMNS regarding paradise. Sarah F. Adams incorporates this symbol into her "Nearer, My God, to Thee":

There let the way appear
Steps unto Heaven.

Her work further states that upon death, God will dispatch "ANGELS to beckon me" home to paradise.

Because of its connection to heaven, the staircase has likewise been used in modern ADVERTISING campaigns. A recent ad for Orville Reddenbacher popcorn depicts a staircase stretching into the clouds. At the top, the departed spirit's life is reviewed before divine sentence is pronounced.

Modern theatrical productions about the great beyond have updated and elab-

Cherubs descend the heavenly staircase to confer their blessings on the United States.

orated on the proverbial staircase. The British film STAIRWAY TO HEAVEN transforms it into a massive white escalator to paradise. In BILL & TED'S BOGUS JOURNEY, a comedic supernatural adventure, huge white steps lead to the throne of God. And in the Broadway disaster CARRIE: THE MUSICAL, the finale is set on a mystical stairway to eternity.

Derivations of the stairway metaphor have become part of the American vernacular. God is "the man upstairs" of a popular phraseology. The image has also been translated into GIFT NOVELTIES illustrating the world to come.

"STAIRWAY TO HEAVEN" The rock music group Led Zeppelin achieved artistic immortality with its 1971 song "Stairway to Heaven." Coauthors Robert Plant and Jimmy Page produced an innovative blend of mythic icons, religious inferences, and cryptic images set to an ethereal tune. Musicologist Chuck Eddy, whose book *Stairway to Hell* focuses on heavy metal music, told *Rolling Stone* magazine that he views the ditty as "the marriage of hard rock and corny medievalism." Led Zeppelin's tune has since become a fixture of "countdown" programs and PROM THEMES across the country.

Of the song, Page says he is ever "searching for an ANGEL with a broken wing." He calls the tune "a milestone" for his band, although he has since become so tired of it he has repeatedly referred to "Stairway" as "that bloody wedding song." Despite such disparaging remarks from one of its writers, "Stairway to Heaven" remains the most requested song at radio stations nationwide almost three decades after its release.

For a generation of the "spiritually homeless," the song "Stairway to Heaven" means many things: mockery of religious hypocrisy, New Age imagery, mysticism, and romanticism married to vague notions of the divine. It also contains numerous SYMBOLS of paradise dating back centuries: a mystical place in "the West," beyond the horizon, a "spirit crying for leaving," a glittering realm of "gold," a mysterious "lady" who "shines white light," a "new day" dawning for humanity. And the STAIRCASE itself is one of the most common images of heaven in both ancient and contemporary art and literature.

Over the past three decades, "Stairway" has been declared the "best song of all time" and the "ultimate rock classic" by experts throughout the industry. It has been chided in films such as *Wayne's World* and has spurned innumerable parodies, including the classic "She's Shopping at 7–11."

STAIRWAY TO HEAVEN This 1946 British film recounts the tale of a World War II Royal Air Force pilot, played by David Niven, who travels to paradise to contest his "date of termination." Niven had been "ready to go" when his time came, but he survives what should have been a fatal plane crash when the ANGEL sent to escort him to the afterlife loses Niven in a dense fog. The dashing soldier then falls in love with a beautiful American WAC (Kim Hunter) and finds new reason to live. So when the "angel of death" finally catches up with him, Niven refuses to go, telling the messenger he has missed his opportunity.

A battle begins, with Niven fighting to keep body and soul together. His spirit must face an "appeal before the high court" of heaven to determine whether he must surrender his soul. Meanwhile, doctors have determined that he needs immediate brain surgery to repair damage done during the plane crash. Niven's chances of survival, even with medical intervention, are not good. The climactic supernatural hearing occurs during Niven's risky operation, and only a divine reprieve can save him.

The paradise portrayed in *Stairway to Heaven* is a massive configuration of souls of every race, nationality, and culture. Quakers mingle with Chinese foot soldiers, each group distinguished by traditional garments. In heaven, many languages are spoken, but the saved understand one another without need of interpretation, sharing a common bond that transcends such barriers. The great heroes of history are present too: PLATO, Socrates, Solomon, Abraham Lincoln, and Caesar Augustus are among the blessed. And travel between the land of the living and the realm of the dead (located at the center of the MILKY WAY) is conducted via a huge white escalator, a modern version of the ethereal STAIRCASE.

The celestial trial offers further interesting commentary on the world to come. A spiritual "prosecutor" argues that Niven's "time is up" and so he must "by law" take his place among the dead. Niven's lawyer (played by Roger Livesey) counters that love must take precedence over law in this case, since it was the "mistake" of the eternal messenger that has resulted in this dilemma. Livesey offers as evidence a silver tear brushed from the cheek of Niven's paramour, a drop that bespeaks volumes about "love, friendship, truce" between the two soldiers from opposite sides of the world. Unable to reach a verdict, the heavenly jury journeys to earth to see the lovers for themselves to determine which side should prevail.

On earth, Hunter and Niven are asked to "prove" their love for each other. Niven is asked, "Will you die for her?" and he declares, "Yes!" without hesitation. Then Hunter offers to "take his place on the balance sheet," allowing him to live on by surrendering her own life force. At this Livesey declares victory, claiming, "Nothing is stronger than love!" The judge (a richly robed metaphor for God) agrees, stating, "Love *is* heaven, and heaven is love." With that, Niven's soul is returned to earth and his life extended for decades, after which he is promised a REUNION with his new celestial friends.

STATIC Keith Gordon wrote and starred in the 1985 independent film *Static*, the tale of an out-of-work mechanical genius who invents a device for "watching" heaven. The quirky technician pieces together a machine that, when hooked up to the television set, allows viewers a peek at the HEREAFTER. At first his friends are thrilled to hear about this mystic accomplishment, until they realize that no one else can see the divine images Gordon claims are dancing across the screen.

In the end, *Static* says more about alienation than salvation, although it does help define paradise as a place where each individual's desires are completely fulfilled. Reviewers compared it to the fairy tale "The Emperor's New Clothes," blurring the line between cold reality and self-delusion. The implication is that paradise, in this world if not in the next, is what each individual makes it.

SUKHAVATI Sukhavati (PURE LAND) is a concept of Chinese and Japanese Buddhists. It is a place free of pain, hunger, and human weakness. Belief in Sukhavati was established by Buddha Amida, the "Lord of Light," to give respite to "deserving" souls. In this en-chanted world, fragrant lotus flowers bloom in lush gardens. Some estimates claim that this Pure Land extends for more than ten miles.

Sukhavati is one of many temporary paradises in which virtuous spirits are rewarded before being returned to the reincarnation cycle. While reposing in Sukhavati, the blessed enjoy beautiful foliage, jeweled trees, and sweet waters. They are lulled by the musical sounds of "gentle rivers" and "whispering winds" that run through this tropical heaven.

SUMMA THEOLOGICA The *Summa Theologica* is the consummate masterpiece of SAINT THOMAS AQUINAS, left unfinished at the time of his death in 1274. The massive work expounded and reiterated much of what SAINT AUGUSTINE had said of CHRISTIAN PARADISE almost a millennium earlier. Aquinas uses sacred scripture, theology, and traditional doctrines to support his theories. The *Summa Theologica* has been hailed the ultimate work on Christian philosophy and ESCHATOLOGY. Its text describes the historical events of JESUS' crucifixion and resurrection and the salvation of humanity in metaphysical terms.

Heaven according to the author exists in contemplation, not action. In paradise, the saved enjoy the BEATIFIC VISION and bask eternally in the presence of God Ultimate joy is not material fulfillment but intellectual stimulation: a saturation with the divine. No physical delight or material reward can compare to the sublime elation of pondering the nature of God throughout eternity.

Like many of his colleagues, Aquinas thus concludes that though other pleasures are *possible* in paradise, they are unnecessary. God alone suffices.

The theories contained in *Summa Theologica* have been sanctioned by the Roman Catholic church and are taught in religious institutes throughout the world. Aquinas's ideas have also influenced many Protestant sects and formed the basis for Martin Luther's notion of a THEOCENTRIC HEAVEN.

SUMMERLAND   Summerland is the paradise of modern New Age spiritualists. It is a purely spiritual realm with no material properties, and all delights are intellectual and emotional. The name began appearing around 1850, when the philosophies of EMANUEL SWEDENBORG and his American counterpart Andrew Davis were gaining popularity. They rejected the notion of GLORIFIED BODIES and physical pleasures in the afterlife in favor of a purely ethereal dimension.

Some believers contend that through psychics, souls in Summerland can be contacted and summoned. This notion has led to a deluge of self-proclaimed mystics who claim that—for a fee—they serve as mediators between the living and the dead. In more recent times, the concept of Summerland has faded, as New Age practitioners have shifted emphasis to reincarnation and a continuous life cycle in the material world.

SWAHILI PARADISE   Swahilis believe in an AFRICAN PARADISE where human spirits are rewarded for their goodness. It is a glorious garden of lovely birds, plentiful fruit, and abundant game where all spirits exist in perfect harmony without even a hint of conflict. Swahili paradise was the sixth of the Almighty's creations and his most beautiful.

SWARGA   Swarga is the heaven of Hindu mythology located atop MOUNT MERU. The gods reside in Swarga, and "enlightened" human souls purged of all shortcomings are allowed respite in this enchanted realm. It is a fragrant garden of complete fulfillment.

Some legends name Indra, ranked second among Hindu gods, as Swarga-Pate, the "Lord of Paradise." Only Brahma, the "creator of all that is," holds a higher place in the pantheon and is thus "Supreme of heaven."

SWEDENBORG, EMANUEL
(1688–1772) Swedish philosopher Emanuel Swedenborg, the son of a wealthy Protestant bishop, reported having supernatural visions throughout his lifetime, beginning when he was a young child. Among these were journeys to the afterlife where he beheld ANGELS "while I was fully awake" in a "state of clear perception." After these celestial encounters, he began feverishly reading the Bible, trying to interpret these phenomenal experiences and make sense of the "divine messages" he believed he was being asked to deliver.

After much study and reflection, Swedenborg decided he had been "allowed to see what Heaven is like" in order to clear up misconceptions about

Philosopher Emanuel Swedenborg
ART TODAY

the afterlife. He began preaching that after death of the body, humans "become angels," growing spiritually and abandoning the "doubt and conflict" of humanity. This evolution continues throughout eternity. Swedenborg illuminated these theories about the afterlife in sixteen extensive tomes describing his visions and offering his imaginative conclusions.

According to his writings, heaven has four basic characteristics: (1) it is separated from earth by "only a thin veil"; (2) the afterlife is a continuation of earthly life with a desire for sensual fulfillment, (3) the saved are active both physically and mentally; and (4) marriage, communal love, and human relationships endure in the world to come. Swedenborg also rejects a THEOCENTRIC HEAVEN where the sole joy is contemplating the divine, stating instead that God is loved "through others" as well as directly.

The belief in REUNION of loved ones and peers is an important factor in Swe-

denborg's paradise. He contends that in the next world, humans continue to eat, drink, talk, and interact with friends in the same way they did while alive. Unfortunately, this also means taking "faults" to the afterlife, where they need to be overcome. Guiding angels help humans grow spiritually and correct these flaws, so they can ascend to "higher levels" of heaven. Eventually, virtuous human souls will be transformed into angels (an idea popularized in contemporary culture by movies such as IT'S A WONDERFUL LIFE and HIGHWAY TO HEAVEN).

Swedenborg believes that earth and heaven are separated by a gossamer thin veil, and so the pleasures of human life endure in the next world. In the "SPIRIT WORLD," a kind of gateway between life and eternity, are three distinct realms: a "natural," a "spiritual," and a "celestial" heaven. God does not judge souls and assign places; each spirit chooses the realm it wishes to inhabit.

Natural heaven is quite similar to earthly existence, only without the human pains and frailties that detract from enjoyment of life. Souls in this sector remain male or female and keep their former characteristics and personalities. Joys of natural heaven, too, parallel the pleasures of earth: delicious food, pleasant companionship, social interaction with loved ones.

The next level, spiritual heaven, offers a more cerebral paradise. Like the lower realm, here spirits can be male or female, but they inhabit an idealized society. The highest circle is celestial heaven. Here, the saved dwell with God in a restored Garden of Eden as purely spiritual beings. The naked souls are neither male nor female, having left all vestiges of their human existence behind. He explains that "the angels of the inmost heaven are naked, because they are in innocence," as Adam and Eve were before the fall in the Garden of Eden. They require no clothing, as they feel no shame over their human form. Swedenborg likens this realm to African society, which he calls "pure, primitive, natural and spontaneous" with all working toward collective goals, free of selfish motives.

In Swedenborg's model of that afterlife, there is no geographic distinction between heaven and hell. All agony and ecstasy lie in the individual's desires. Those who try to adapt to a place where they do not belong will feel spiritual pain and discomfort and will be compelled to leave. Pure souls will accept the aid offered them by angels and elevate themselves to angelic status. For the wicked, the fulfillment of what they crave ultimately brings torment, while the blessed are elated with their progress toward the divine. Those unwilling to improve themselves will find only paths to hell, defined as self-absorption, ignorance, and spiritual sloth.

Swedenborg soundly rejected the notion of a strictly contemplative heaven, calling the concept of a "perpetual Sabbath" tedious and unsustainable. His paradise is a place of constant movement and interaction. This continual flux keeps the HEREAFTER from becoming predictable. Eternal newness offers unending spiritual as well as psychological pleasure. To help preserve this dynamic

paradise, human angels also perform "jobs" or "tasks" designed to help them grow while contributing to the collective good.

Angelic activities include instructing less-developed spirits, guiding souls from the spirit world into higher realms, planning celestial festivities, and embroidering ceremonial tunics. Another important task is caring for children who die in infancy. Special angel nannies rear them to adulthood in the afterlife. And in some cases, angels could also be dispatched to earth to watch over the living or deliver divine messages. No duties are assigned; each angel is free to choose activities in accordance with its own interests.

The philosopher further contended that in heaven, the institution of marriage continues and is elevated to new heights. Souls could marry in "spirit weddings" (although not necessarily with their earthly spouses) complete with lavish receptions. Afterward, these "united spirits" could enjoy an enhanced version of sexual intercourse, which Swedenborg describes as the "ultimate delight." They would occupy houses, entertain friends, wear clothes, and enjoy "other things familiar to those which exist on earth, but, of course, infinitely more beautiful and perfect" in the world to come.

Swedenborg's theories are currently taught in the Church of the New Jerusalem. The philosopher also greatly influenced WILLIAM BLAKE, William Butler Yeats, and many modern poets.

SYMBOLS Certain symbols have been used to identify paradise, and many of these recur from culture to culture. Such icons as the LADDER, WEDDING FEAST, STAIRCASE, tropical garden, jeweled city, and PEACH have served as metaphors for blessed eternity and immortality. These symbols can be found in works of Zoroastrianism, the Bible, Koran, Jewish Torah, ancient myths, and modern POETRY.

Paradises of Asian origin routinely include tales of enchanted peach trees. By eating the fruit of this magic tree, humans become godlike and live forever. The symbol crossed over into European art as well and became identified with salvation. Paintings of the VIRGIN MARY and other SAINTS often include a peach or peach tree in the background.

Medieval Christian artists, obsessed with notions of hierarchy, depicted a mystic staircase of heaven. Holier souls (such as the Apostles, John the Baptist, and the ANGELS) were seated on the higher stairs, while less-worthy spirits were relegated to the lower ones. Many works of CHURCH ART AND ARCHITECTURE of this era show a very regimented paradise with distinct "stations" for the blessed according to their importance in Christian tradition. Other works show the stairway reaching from earth to paradise, often attended by guiding angels who assist departing human souls in their ascent.

During the Renaissance, CHRISTIAN PARADISE was depicted as a box with God at the top and a "garden of pleasure" at the bottom. The former levels of heaven were replaced by a courtyard where saved souls could mingle and interact. Virtually everyone inhabited the same plane regardless of piety or "merit." Residents of heaven were often naked, illustrating their purity and renunciation of material things.

In modern NEAR-DEATH EXPERIENCES, the passage to paradise is often represented as a "tunnel of light" that opens into eternity. In many accounts, it is lined with celestial spirits who encourage the departing soul to proceed. The term has since become synonymous with heaven.

TAJ MAHAL   The world-famous Taj Mahal in north India was constructed by seventeenth-century emperor Shah Jahan for his beloved wife, Mumtaz Mahal, who died soon after their wedding. Grief stricken at the loss of his lovely young bride, the shah ordered a MEMORIAL that would stand forever as a testament to her beauty and virtue. Hundreds of architects, artists, and scholars helped design and construct the Taj Mahal as an earthly representation of eternal paradise.

With its pearl columns set with precious gems, the Taj Mahal suggests a mystic place of joy and pleasure. The massive structure offers carved inscriptions about the afterlife from the KORAN (the holy book of Islam) describing the delights of DJANNA (Muslim paradise). There are also mentions of the coming LAST JUDGMENT, when all souls will be called before ALLAH to account for their lives. Islamic law forbids inclusion of il-

Sketch of the Taj Mahal. ART TODAY

lustrations or images in places of worship, so these texts, etched into black marble walls, serve as reminders of the glorious world to come.

Formal gardens around the Taj Mahal are likewise designed to represent the glorious afterlife. The flowering fields are elaborate, colorful, ever in bloom. Together, the monument and grounds symbolize the delightful court of Allah where blessed souls will live forever, Mumtaz Mahal foremost among them.

TALK SHOWS In recent years, radio and television talk shows have frequently taken up the subject of the afterlife. This trend coincides with the contemporary obsession with NEAR-DEATH EXPERIENCES, ESCHATOLOGY, and questions about human immortality. Topics typically include heaven, hell, the criteria for salvation, reincarnation, and the existence of God. Treatments of these issues range from serious debate by religious scholars to unbelievable claims by "psychics" who profess to have "visions" of the afterlife.

Talk show explorations of the supernatural also focus on the extraordinary experiences of ordinary citizens who believe they have been visited by ANGELS, SAINTS, or other religious figures. Guests often introduce themselves by stating that they are not churchgoers and never considered themselves particularly spiritual before the astounding event occurred. Some recall visitations by deceased loved ones; others describe mystic encounters with unfamiliar benevolent spirits. Many of these tales include illuminations about heaven and the afterlife.

The majority of these supernatural tales include common SYMBOLS of paradise, such as the LADDER or STAIRCASE, the "tunnel of light," and the enchanted garden. Contact with heavenly creatures conveys an overwhelming "sense of peace" or "indescribable happiness." And for most of the guests who have "touched" the mystic realm, the experience is life changing. Desire for heaven replaces all other pursuits and typically leaves the affected person "peaceful," "inspired," or "anxious to return again some day."

TAMOANCHAN Tamoanchan is the Aztec paradise reserved for women who die in childbirth. It is located in the west, beyond the sunset. It is one of the four paradises (each corresponding to a different direction) located below the POLE STAR, the pivot point of the Aztec universe. Spirits (called ciuateteo) in Tamoanchan spend eternity with the sun.

Restless ciuateteo can leave Tamoanchan to bring illness and disease to young children, so they must be placated with offerings of bread and milk.

Most, however, are content to dwell in paradise, consoled by the veneration and respect they receive from their kin.

"TEARS IN HEAVEN" After the tragic death of his four-year-old son Conor in 1991, songwriter Eric Clapton described his life as an abyss of sadness where "loss and emotional trauma" were "everyday feelings." Haunted by the memory of the beautiful child whose life ended prematurely when he fell from the window of his fifty-third-story apartment, Clapton sought therapy in his art. His pain served as the inspiration for a poignant speculation on the nature of the afterlife that has since become a modern classic. The lyrics of Clapton's masterpiece "Tears in Heaven" ask:

> *Would you know my name—If I*
> *saw you in heaven?*
> *Would it be the same?*

Clapton's lyrics are permeated with desolation yet rimmed with hope. For the artist also writes, "I know there'll be no more tears in heaven." He anticipates a paradise where loved ones enjoy a celestial REUNION and where sadness is obsolete. His song encompasses the strength of love—a bond that endures even after death—and the tenderness of heaven's mercy, reminiscent of the solace described in St. John's REVELATION: "And God shall wipe away all tears from their eyes; and there shall be no more death, neither sorrow, nor crying, neither shall there be any more pain: for the former things are passed away" (Rev. 21:4).

"Tears in Heaven" soared to the top of the sales and request charts in 1992 and swept the Grammy Awards, wining Clapton Best Song, Best Record, Best Album, and Best Pop Male Vocal Performance of the Year. Since that time, the melancholy ballad has become a fixture of adult contemporary music programs. In addition to its compelling artistic qualities, "Tears in Heaven" remains popular because it captures the imagination of a generation of Americans considered by many to be "spiritually homeless." The baby boomers, for the most part raised outside traditional religions, saw this as a New Age account of the HEREAFTER, free of the strings attached to CHRISTIAN PARADISE, DJANNA (Islamic heaven), and the strict criteria of other established faiths. Its touching lyrics and haunting melody stir a sense of sorrow tempered by the promise of joy, a gentle reassurance that pain is fleeting but happiness is eternal.

TENNIN The tennin are lovely maidens of paradise found in Buddhist lore, similar to the HOURI of Islamic belief. These supernatural creatures are also identified with ANGELS, since they too are represented as winged beings who "fly through the heavens" observing human affairs. In some tales, tennin visit the earth and interact with humans, usually helping them accomplish some significant task. Tennin appear in various Asian works of literature, including poems, plays, and songs about the afterlife.

THEOCENTRIC HEAVEN Some faiths teach that the ultimate joy of the afterlife is dwelling in the presence of the divine. This model of paradise is called "theocentric," meaning "focused on God." The notion rejects the belief that there will be any significant physical delights in the afterlife; everything else pales in comparison to the BEATIFIC VISION. True pleasure will exist solely in the spiritual fulfillment of union with the Almighty.

In CHRISTIAN PARADISE, the divine Father resides at the pinnacle of heaven. Scholars disagree on the specifics, but some claim that dwelling in the realm of God satisfies the soul's every need. Devout Muslims are rewarded by being allowed to gaze upon the face of ALLAH in the garden utopia of DJANNA. Other joys, such as a REUNION with loved ones and sensual pleasures, merely supplement this divine union.

Protestant founder Martin Luther embraced the concept of a theocentric heaven and soundly rejected the theory that in the afterlife the saved will be restored to their loved ones. According to his beliefs, there are no "human relationships" in heaven, since being in God's presence is the ultimate delight. No other pleasure is necessary. Based on Luther's theories, his pupil Philipp Melanchthon wrote a catechism depicting JESUS Christ as an explosion of light, surrounded by adoring ANGELS. After Luther's death, Melanchthon eulogized his mentor, telling followers that in eternity Luther sees his savior "face to face" in a realm of "unspeakable joy."

A century later, Puritan minister Richard Baxter wrote *Saints' Everlasting Rest* in 1649. The work claims that God—and God alone—is the reward of heaven. Like Luther, he rejects the belief that family and friends are reunited in paradise, going so far as to say there is "no human interaction" whatsoever in the world to come. The saved instead spend eternity in "perpetual singing of His high praises," oblivious to others around them. Baxter stresses the fact that spirits could meet and interact if they wanted to, but they simply do not because they are enveloped in the joy of the beatific vision. The author further advises that since the saved surround the throne of God with voices raised in song, singing HYMNS here on earth will give the living a glimpse of paradise.

In modern days, belief in a strictly theocentric heaven is on the wane. Most organized religions teach a paradise in which family and friends are joined in eternity for a grand celebration. Spiritualists and New Age practitioners have shifted emphasis to reincarnation and transmigration of souls, making the very idea of God and his divine court obsolete. The recent rash of reported NEAR-DEATH EXPERIENCES has also undercut the belief in a heaven of constant adoration, since most of these feature interaction with angels, blessed souls, and even deceased ANIMALS.

THESPESIUS *The Vision of Thespesius* is one of the few examples of VISION LITERATURE that predate the Middle Ages. It was written in the first century after the death of JESUS by Plutarch, a Greek author living in Rome. His *Thespesius* is a frightening work of fiction that reads like a factual account, causing many to speculate that the tale is based on actual experience. Stirred by its mystic imagery, many contemporary religious leaders used the story in sermons about the pleasures and punishments of the afterlife.

The story opens as Thespesius, who has fallen into a deep coma, is believed by all to be dead. While unconscious, he "wakes" on the other side of the grave and witnesses the judgment of departed human souls. As he stands in a vast field, Thespesius sees pure souls rise to heaven, luminous and beautiful as they ascend. Each blessed spirit becomes more brilliant and dazzling as it draws closer to paradise and eventually blends into the swirl of sacred worshipers around the throne of God. Tears come to his eyes as he watches this spectacle, and Thespesius has to look away.

Meanwhile, scarred and blotched spirits wither and are swept into a black abyss. Thespesius wanders among the damned and is horrified to find his own father in the depths of hell. The shamed man tells his son that he had been evil and violent in life, destroying others to advance his own petty schemes. Demons gather around Thespesius as the men speak, ready to devour this child of the "wicked seed." But Thespesius suddenly revives, escaping hell and its grotesque specter.

When he awakens, Thespesius tells the shocked mourners about his supernatural adventure. He admonishes all to repent of their sins, seek forgiveness, and devote themselves to virtue so that they, too, can join the celestial choir of heaven in the world to come.

THOTH Thoth is the keeper of afterlife records according to ancient Egyptian myth. He is the god of wisdom and magic who invented the alphabet and thus became the "scribe of the gods." Some legends name Thoth as author of the BOOK OF THE DEAD, a complex collection of instructions on reaching paradise. His symbol is the ibis (a sacred bird), and he is often depicted with the body of a man and an ibis's head.

According to ancient belief, when a soul dies, the jackal-headed ANUBIS conducts it to the Hall of OSIRIS, the lord of the dead. Here, Osiris weighs the spirit's heart (symbolizing the sum of its virtues and vices) against the "feather of truth" to determine the reward or punishment deserved. Thoth then records the verdict in the book of eternity. Worthy souls enjoy great pleasures in the next world, whereas wicked spirits face a variety of tortures in the gloomy underworld.

THREE LIVES OF THOMASINA, THE The tender 1964 drama *The Three Lives of Thomasina* explores the question of whether ANIMALS exist in paradise. Based on Paul Gallico's story, *Thomasina* sends a beloved ginger tabby to the great beyond when a skillful yet dispassionate veterinarian (played by Patrick McGoohan) is unable to save his young daughter's feline. Karen Dotrice (who later went on to star as Jane Banks in *Mary Poppins*) blames her father for "killing" the kitty and decides that he, too, is now "dead" to her.

Meanwhile, in cat heaven, the paunchy puss has her every whim fulfilled but longs to return to the little girl she left behind. Her wish is granted when a beautiful, mystic stranger played by Susan Hampshire performs a magic spell that restores the cat to life. Hampshire is also able to bring the widowed veterinarian and his little girl back together. *Thomasina*, which is told through the cat's perspective, ends as Hampshire and McGoohan are wed, providing a mom for Dotrice and a font of otherworldly powers that promise to help save other pets from departing to the HEREAFTER before their time.

TIAN   Tian (Thien) is the paradise preached by ancient Chinese philosophers, including CONFUCIUS. The earliest records of this heaven date back more than three thousand years; however, the specifics regarding Tian emerged between the eleventh and thirteenth centuries B.C. Tian means "sky," and the celestial realm is ruled by the god Tian-shen, a watchful deity who holds court in the celestial realm, keeping a record of every human action. Nobles, rulers, and the wealthy transcend human limitations and depart to Tian after death to spend eternity as part of Tian-shen's court. In some legends, humans who had lived exemplary lives could also be deified or could be recruited by Tian-shen to serve as his bureaucrats. Selected souls might be assigned such roles as overseer of crops and harvest, regulator of the

Ceremonial Chinese "heaven notes"

change of seasons, or supervisor of other earthly routines.

Tian is symbolized by the PI, a circle with a hole through the center. The pi is used in rituals involving the "Son of Heaven," a title bestowed on the emperor to reflect his divine origins. Through the pi, the reigning emperor could channel the favor of paradise and grant divine favors to the living.

An ancient funerary custom was to burn money during a loved one's burial ceremonies. These "heaven notes" were believed to accompany the deceased to the next world, where they will be needed to maintain a comfortable standard, purchase favors, and perhaps even bribe the overlords. Since more currency burned meant more joy in Tian, wealthy families could send their loved ones to a luxurious eternity, while the peasantry could hope for little more than an afterlife devoid of outright torture.

TIR NA N'OC   Tir Na n'Oc (Shimmering Land) is the enchanted island of Celtic belief. The isle lies on the other side of the ocean, five days' sail from Great Britain. In Tir Na n'Oc, souls enjoy eternal youth, fine feasts, and heavenly music. The blessed realm was eventually supplanted by the ISLE OF THE BLEST, a Briton mythic land that merged pagan notions with elements of CHRISTIAN PARADISE. According to legend, the Isle of the Blest was visited by SAINT BRENDAN during a supernatural voyage.

TI TSANG Ti Tsang is the Chinese Buddhist equivalent of the Japanese JIZO BOSATSU, the guide who leads souls to NIRVANA, the eternal paradise of enlightenment. In Chinese tradition, it is Ti Tsang who helps human souls shed the "self" and enter the "collective" cosmos where they will spend eternity in motionless union with the divine.

TLALOCAN Tlalocan is the paradise of Aztec myth reserved for people who die through the elements, such as drowning victims or those struck by lightning. It is located in the south, below the POLE STAR. Souls in Tlalocan dwell in perfect happiness in a garden paradise of fragrant flowers, gentle ANIMALS, and sweet rivers of purest water. Tlalocan is ruled by Tlaloc, god of thunder and lightning, who demands human sacrifices to appease him.

TREE OF IMMORTALITY The image of a heavenly tree with supernatural powers is part of a variety of beliefs. Spirits in the Buddhist heaven KHUN-LUN eat from a divine PEACH tree, as do souls in the EMPIRE OF JADE of Chinese

Taoist faith. This enchanted produce allows spirits to remain young and vibrant throughout the millennia and to continue to enjoy the splendors of the afterlife in good health.

According to the Christian Bible, Adam and Eve, the first man and woman, are expelled from the Garden of Eden for eating of the Tree of Knowledge, the only fruit forbidden to them. The devil tricks the humans by claiming that if they consume this food they will "live forever." Unwilling to cooperate with God's plan for their souls, Adam and Eve taste the fruit, only to be expelled from paradise. But even after this transgression, the Almighty promises to send a redeemer who will open the gates of heaven to them and to their children.

Islamic legend includes the SIDRET-EL-MOUNTEHA, a mystic tree that grows in the garden paradise of DJANNA. The magnificent plant has branches of gold and emeralds, and each leaf bears the name of a living person. During the month of Ramadan, Islam's holy season, leaves with the names of all those who will die in the upcoming year fall to the ground. Similarly, new leaves emerge, bearing the names of children to be born during the next twelve months. The tale of this enchanted tree spread through northern Africa and is known in this region as the CEDAR TREE OF THE END.

TRÈS RICHES HEURES DE DUC DE BERRY, LES *Les Très Riches Heures*, a BOOK OF HOURS composed for the Duke of Berry (brother of France's king) in the early 1400s, is the most luxurious and beautifully illustrated manuscript of its kind. Composed by the Limbourg brothers, the book offers dozens of miniatures of biblical events, including visits by courier ANGELS, the crucifixion of JESUS, the Christian Redeemer, and glorious portraits of saved souls savoring the glory of paradise.

Très Riches Heures also depicts the war in heaven described in St. John's REVELATION. The Limbourgs portray paradise as an exquisite realm of turquoise swirling with angels robed in brilliant sapphire. The archangel MICHAEL leads the celestial forces, a strong yet gentle warrior. The devil is likewise draped in royal blue garments, as are his rebels, differentiated from the loyal angels only by their horrifying facial expressions. Even the fallen spirits are beautiful, achingly beautiful, as they descend from the presence of God into the depths of hell.

Some drawings of the afterlife in this book of hours were inspired by contemporary examples of VISION LITERATURE. Such portraits were designed to offer a strong yet subtle warning to the infamous Duke of Berry (whose reputation for corruption was firmly established by 1413) about the fate of his immortal soul. He was encouraged to crave salvation and fear the underworld, in hopes that he might yet be "turned towards heaven."

TRIUMPH OF THE NAME OF JESUS *Triumph of the Name of* JESUS is an important work of Christian CHURCH ART AND ARCHITECTURE, as it blends several media in a unique portrait of paradise. Composed from 1672–1685 by painter Giovanni Battista Gaulli and sculptor Antonio Raggi, the work is part painting and part sculpture. The result is a striking depiction of the afterlife with a 3-D effect that mesmerized contemporary worshipers and instilled "holy fear" about the impending judgment.

Triumph of the Name of Jesus adorns the ceiling of II Gesù in Rome. The dazzling gold background is dotted with three-dimensional ANGELS that seem to swirl between heaven and earth. The top of the dome is painted to resemble a "window" looking into CHRISTIAN PARADISE. Angels and SAINTS, robed in luxurious garments, float on clouds and drift upward toward the pinnacle of heaven. The artist uses a radiant yellow spiral to draw the gaze upward, as if looking into the sun. This effect represents the EMPYREAN, an explosion of white and yellow so brilliant that viewers almost have to squint to behold its majesty.

Triumph of the Name of Jesus calls worshipers to cast their eyes to paradise and focus on the goal of salvation. In the face of such a majestic vision, the sacrifices and penances of earthly living pale in significance. Those beholding the grand accomplishment are encouraged to picture themselves among the blessed, vicariously joining the swirling ascent into the realm of God.

T-SHIRTS   T-shirts have become favorite "canvasses" for artists wishing to depict paradise in a decidedly informal setting. Examples range from humorous CARTOONS lampooning the great beyond to stylized reproductions of divine masterpieces. Some are preachy, others comical, and still others "inspirational." An all-cotton Proclamation of Christian concept bears the slogan "RAPTURE: Enjoy the ride," and shows a pious soul ascending to the skies. The heroes of heaven, such as ANGELS, JESUS, favorite SAINTS, and even God himself, have also been incorporated into these wearable emblems of eternity.

Not all heavenly Ts focus on religious notions. One pragmatic shirt suggests, "Heaven is living your hopes . . . Hell is living your fears." Another example, part of the recent explosion in ANGELWARE, is covered with multicolored angels. Its tag boasts, "You'll be embraced by celestial guardians, printed front AND back!" Sports humor is also a popular topic for wearable works of art. "If there's no Golf in Heaven," claims one shirt, "I'm not going!" The accompanying illustration shows a golf ball, complete with wings and HALO, bouncing through the clouds.

Images of heaven have also made their way onto MOVIE MERCHANDISING T-shirts. Scenes from such "otherworldly" films as *BILL & TED'S BOGUS JOURNEY*, *IT'S A WONDERFUL LIFE*, and *ALL DOGS GO TO HEAVEN* are available to consumers interested in advertising these cinematic paradises.

TUM The Muju of the Melanesian Islands believe in the paradise of Tum, a magnificent realm of sweet waters, succulent foods, and everlasting merriment. Souls travel to Tum on the back of a great serpent; however, only those with a mystic birthmark or tattoo are allowed entrance. The spirits in Tum recognize their own and forbid all others from joining their eternal celebration.

TUMBUKA Tumbuka is the Malawi place of the dead. In this paradise, souls experience eternal youth and all their earthly desires are met. Tumbuka is free of both physical and emotional pain, and spirits departing to this realm are assured of everlasting bliss.

TUNDAL The *Vision of Tundal* (Tyndal, Tundale), a classic of VISION LITERATURE, features a mystical journey through the afterlife in the company of ANGELS. The work describes the supernatural adventures of Tundal, a knight who has dedicated his life to sensual fulfillment rather than spiritual growth. According to the text, the dark nihilist "dies" and goes on a tour of heaven, PURGATORY, and hell before returning to life and renouncing his wicked ways.

The story opens as Tundal, overcome with fever, falls unconscious and is declared dead. Tundal's spirit leaves his body and travels to the "gates of eternity," where he meets with stern disapproval. In the distance, the knight can see heaven, a radiant orb beautiful to behold. ANGELS and SAINTS dance around the throne of God, singing HYMNS of praise. Tundal expects to ascend to the shining paradise; however, he is instead plunged into hell as punishment for his life of vice.

Demons seize his soul, chiding Tundal with shouts of "where are the good times now?" He is terrified at the prospect of being tortured by these vile beasts and struggles in vain to escape. As Tundal is about to despair, his guardian angel appears and commands the devils to release him. The stern angel then takes Tundal on a tour of hell, showing him numerous monsters, torture devices, and pits of agony.

The celestial guide tells Tundal that in the afterlife, only the purest souls can overcome the obstacles on the road to heaven. Tundal now notices that the path to paradise is beset with hazards and infested with hideous creatures determined to devour passing souls. As the two travel the road, Tundal is continually attacked by devils and tormented by vicious beasts. His angel must repeatedly rescue Tundal from these terrors. At one point, Tundal is devoured by a steel-beaked bird and defecated in the form of a serpent into a lake of ice where he is left, frozen, to suffer for eternity.

Seeing this, Tundal's angel takes pity on the man and restores him to human form. But the tortures continue, and Tundal is alternately melted in a fiery furnace, attacked by bloodthirsty mutants, and finally delivered to Lucifer, lord of the damned. After each encounter the angel must save Tundal and return him to his original state. Tundal begs his celestial guide for another chance at living piously, vowing that he has learned his lesson and is ready for a life of virtue.

The angel agrees and admonishes Tundal that the things he has seen are real and might still await him after death. Before restoring Tundal to life, the angel takes him to purgatory to show what spirits must endure in this transitional realm. Here, souls suffer only the human pains of hunger, thirst, sorrow, and longing for God. Tundal's guardian explains that these souls will eventually ascend to heaven once they have purified themselves and rid their spirits of every taint of sin.

Tundal awakens and resolves to reform his life. He dedicates the rest of his days to prayer, preaching, and performing acts of penance. And though he loathes having to relive his horrific vision, Tundal repeats his story again and again to serve as a warning to others.

The manuscript of the *Vision of Tundal* originates from the mid-eleventh century, and though the author's name remains unknown, historians can trace the text to a medieval Irish monk living in Germany. Copies of *Tundal* were illustrated by hand and translated into at least a dozen languages, then distributed throughout medieval Christendom. Several of these early ILLUMINATED MANUSCRIPTS are still in existence, many of which contain elaborate illustrations of the rewards of heaven and the torments of hell.

TURA Tura (Tengri, Tangara, Tengeri) is the paradise of Mongolian myth and also the name of God, the supreme being. Believers often separate Tura into two personages, one who controls the natural phenomena of harvest, weather, and seasonal cycles, while the other oversees human activity and controls each individual's destiny. Tura is thus routinely invoked in matters of fertility and prosperity as well as eternal salvation.

The kingdom of Tura is located "in the sky" and is therefore associated with the color blue. Souls in Tura enjoy a peaceful afterlife of human pleasures and spiritual fulfillment.

TWILIGHT ZONE Though Rod Serling's ground-breaking *Twilight Zone* series is better known for its spooky episodes about space aliens, deals with the devil, and surprise-ending mysteries, the show also devoted a number of episodes to the happier side of the afterlife. In these shows, Serling incorporates a variety of theories and SYMBOLS of paradise into his scripts. Taken as a whole, the "heaven programs" depict a realm of solace and fulfillment, where the dead truly do rest in peace.

Serling made his first foray into the realm of the blessed in October 1959 with his touching tale "One for the ANGELS." This tender episode stars Ed Wynn as a street corner pitchman who is not ready to depart to the HEREAFTER and asks his celestial escort for more time. Never having known financial success, Wynn is "beloved by children," which in the eyes of the Almighty makes him "a most important man." His one unfulfilled desire is to make "a pitch so big the sky would open up . . . a pitch for the angels!" When "Mr. Death" threatens to take a young girl in Wynn's place, he distracts the angel by pouring on his sales spiel. The ruse works, and the afterlife escort resorts to his original plan to deliver Wynn to his eternal reward. As the two depart, Wynn takes his case with him, noting, "You never know who might need something up there!"

Twilight Zone offers a very different vision of everlasting fulfillment in the 1960 "Elegy." The story involves the crew of a spaceship who make an emergency landing on a mysterious earthlike planet. At first the crew is excited to come upon a village, until they discover that everyone seems to be frozen in position, unable or unwilling to move a muscle. The men travel from house to house, finding the same suspended animation everywhere they go. Finally, they come upon a genteel old man (played by Cecil Kellaway) who is fully ambulatory. Kellaway explains that they have stumbled on a cemetery where wishes are fulfilled postmortem, and that he is its caretaker. He gives them refreshments, and they muse about their own "greatest wish." Each crewman has the same desire: to be back onboard their ship headed for home. So that is where Kellaway puts their corpses—having poisoned their food—to maintain peace in the silent graveyard.

Screenwriter George Clayton Johnson offers a much kindler, gentler vision of the world to come in the 1962 "Nothing in the Dark," which stars a young Robert Redford as a wounded policeman. Redford, shot by a fleeing criminal, begs an old woman (played by Gladys Cooper) to let him into her apartment to nurse his wound. At first Cooper refuses, certain that he is actually "Mr. Death" sent to claim her life. Moved by pity, she eventually takes in Redford and is relieved when he does not, as she feared, turn into a cruel monster. But when another man barges in and tells Cooper that her building is about to be destroyed, she realizes that he cannot see Redford. The young policeman *is*, in fact, Mr. Death, but he is not the harsh ravager she expected. Instead, he is revealed to be a gentle angel sent to escort the soul of a kindly old woman to paradise. Taking his hand, the two depart the shabby room into a brilliant, beautiful world of light.

"The Hunt" takes up the subject of whether there will be ANIMALS in heaven. Written by Earl Hamner Jr. (famous for his *Waltons* series), the episode features Arthur Hunnicut as a hunter who is killed while stalking a raccoon. He and his dog Rip then follow an unfamiliar path that leads to what Hunnicut takes to be the PEARLY GATES. But when the gatekeeper tells him that his dog is not allowed into heaven, he refuses to enter, opting instead to "keep walking." Farther down the road, Hunnicut and Rip come to the *real* gates of paradise, where an angel explains that the first gate actually led to hell. Rip was forbidden because he would have smelled the brimstone and alerted his master to the ruse. Hunnicut's loyalty to man's best friend pays off: He is welcomed into heaven, his faithful hound at his side.

"A Passage for Trumpet" includes an appearance by the angel GABRIEL, who is prophesied to sound his trumpet signaling the LAST JUDGMENT and end of the world. And in "The Bard," talentless screenwriter Julius Moomer (Jack Weston) uses black magic to call Shakespeare, Pocahontas, Abraham Lincoln, and George Washington back from the hereafter to help him write his history shows.

Overall, the heaven of Serling's series is a pleasant realm of happiness and fulfillment. *Twilight Zone* sends its blessed to a "better place" where wishes are granted and justice is served.

TWILIGHT ZONE MAGAZINE Inspired by the enduring cult following of Rod Serling's classic TWILIGHT ZONE television series, Montcalm Publishing launched *Twilight Zone Magazine* in 1981 to rave reviews. The monthly publication, under the directorship of Serling's widow, Carol, contained movie reviews, advertisements, and original fiction deal-ing with the unknown. During its nine-year run, *Twilight Zone Magazine* also ran numerous SHORT STORIES offering various interpretations of the blessed afterlife. These ranged from reverent forays into CHRISTIAN PARADISE to futuristic tales of interplanetary salvation.

The sentimental piece "Altemoor, Where the Dogs Dance" by Mort Castle imagines a paradise filled with the spirits of beloved ANIMALS. Castle's utopia lies just beyond the "rubber tree woods," on the banks of the "Happy-to-You River." In the story, an old man who has written seventeen books about the enchanted elsewhere of Altemoor is asked by his young grandson Mark what has become of Rusty, the boy's deceased pet dog. Grandpa responds that Rusty has journeyed to Altemoor to join the blessed beasts in dancing, singing, and games. This explanation consoles the sensitive boy, and his sadness over Rusty's death begins to subside.

Several months later, Mark awakens in the middle of the night and senses that his grandfather is dying. He quietly goes to the old man and takes his hand, then somberly reminds Grandpa how to find the mystical path to Altemoor. The old man thanks the boy, then departs for the place "where the dogs dance."

And though Mark will miss "so many things" about his grandpa, he knows that the man is truly happy, playing with Rusty in an endless summer field.

Jon Cohen's poignant "Preserves" tells the tale of an old woman who ventures down to her jam cellar to breathe her last. She opens a long-sealed jar, then expires with a smile on her face. A nurse finds the corpse, and no one can explain how or why they dying woman would choose to expire in the musty basement, an empty jam jar clasped in her hands.

Upon investigating these odd events, the woman's grandson discovers that his grandmother had a unique ability: She "preserved real days . . . the ones she wanted to keep forever." When Gramma knew that death was imminent, she escaped into one of these warm memories, then "took them with her" to the afterlife. "Preserves" includes elements of the REUNION theme of paradise, in which souls spend eternity with their loved ones, as well as the DREAM MODEL of heaven. This theory holds that people will pass the centuries reliving the actions of their lives, and that kind, loving people will enjoy splendid echoes in the world to come.

In a psychic foray into the unknown, "Crossing Over" by Jack McDevitt sends a telepathic woman into the void to "probe scientifically beyond the grave." Elizabeth, a young woman with the ability to "see" the thoughts and feelings of others, is hired to "join" consciences with a terminally ill man about to be taken off life support. She is devastated by the experience: While dying, the man flashes in and out of dozens of ugly images of his misspent life, haunted by visions of the wife he abused and the son he abandoned. Disillusioned, Elizabeth shares the story with her longtime friend Janice and Janice's devoted husband, Steve. They try to reassure her that perhaps his experience is not universal, but Elizabeth cannot be consoled.

That same night, the three are involved in an auto accident that leaves Janice dead and Steve dying. Elizabeth goes to his bedside, determined to "stay with him until the end." She melds her thoughts with his and is surprised to see a lush meadow brimming with fragrant flowers and singing birds that stretches into a brilliant light. Just before Steve "slips away," Elizabeth hears a distant voice that she recognizes as Janice's. "We are still one!" it says, as Steve joins his beloved in eternity. Elizabeth determines to celebrate the fact that she is "more than just a creature of a few summers" once her grief over losing Janice and Steve fades.

Reginald Brentor mixes biblical prophecies with alien encounters in his "Swing Low, Sweet Chariot," the tale of humanity's exit from earth. His work offers a new twist on the meaning of lyrics from a classic Christian HYMN:

Looked over Jordan, what did I see?
Comin' for to carry me home . . .
A band of ANGELS comin' after me
Comin' for to carry me home.

Brentor's revamped chariot is not the celestial carriage sent by God to ferry the

Hebrew prophet EZEKIEL but an intergalactic transport from outer space dispatched to collect earth's few survivors of a nuclear holocaust. The story's main character, Rev. Jonathan, believes that the event is "the fulfillment of the prophecy" of REVELATION, which describes the destruction of the world. He declares his flock to be the "chosen," deemed worthy of "a new heaven and a new earth" after a bloody LAST JUDGMENT in which most humans were annihilated. The spaceship's crew, he claims, are "messengers" sent from paradise, their luminous forms reflecting the GLORIFIED BODIES the saved will enjoy in the next world. Leaving the ghastly wasteland of wrecked earth, they depart for a "glorious, green, still-living world" promised to believers from old.

Other *Twilight Zone* short stories depict heaven as the place for fulfilling elusive dreams. In "The Bookshop," a browser discovers unknown titles by Shakespeare, Milton, Poe, and Dickens in a dreary little store. Thinking that this is either an elaborate hoax or "the greatest literary discovery of the century," he is about to ask the elderly clerk about the volumes when he comes upon his own unfinished novel. He had completed only three chapters, but this printed copy is complete and, leafing through he decides, masterful.

The old proprietor steps forward and gently explains that "only in this bookshop are stories high and sweet and true as their authors dreamed them." For this store exists in the afterlife, where death is "the final price of perfection." The young author is at first distraught at the thought of his demise, until the voices of generations of deceased authors call out to him "offering good fellowship" and an eternal forum for examining great literature.

"Five Minutes Early" by Robert Sheckley offers a soon-to-be-drowned sailor the chance to return to earth to come to terms with his impending death. When the "Recording Angel" discovers that the man has arrived before his time, the departed asks that his entry to the "Eternal City" be delayed so he can rejoin the living for a few more moments. Back on earth, the sailor spends the time storing up memories of simple pleasures, "like a man packing provisions for a long journey into a strange land." After purging himself of his mortal existence, he is ready for "what lay ahead."

In addition to speculating on the nature of heaven, *Twilight Zone* made forays into PURGATORY and LIMBO. Thomas Disch's "Carousel" sends a deceased traveler on an eternal journey from airport to airport, never reaching any ultimate destination. This afterlife fate is meted out to those who "didn't do anything bad enough" to be damned but failed to distinguish themselves as worthy of paradise. It is not a painful way to spend the aeons, just monotonous and devoid of joy.

Twilight Zone Magazine also ran numerous stories of ANGELS helping hapless humans and explored exotic paradises from ancient myths. Over the course of its run, the publication featured stories of King Arthur and AVALON, the Native American HAPPY HUNTING GROUNDS,

Nordic VALHALLA, and the Egyptian court of OSIRIS. Asian concepts of reincarnation and transmigration of souls were similarly probed in stylized fictional accounts.

In addition to mystic fiction, the monthly ran short articles probing "supernatural phenomena." One reported a "vision of JESUS Christ" in the rust pattern on an old oil tank in Ohio. According to the report, dozens of believers saw this as a sacred message from heaven. Pilgrims flocked to the site hoping for a glimpse of the Son of God in effigy and to assure their own place among the blessed.

Films focusing on the afterlife likewise received regular attention on *Twilight Zone*'s pages. Such cinematic treatments of ESCHATOLOGY as *BRAINSTORM* and *JACOB'S LADDER* appeared in each issue, complete with photos and behind-the-scenes interviews with the moviemakers. Rounding out the magazine dedicated to "the unknown" were advertisements for a variety of oddities, including solicitations for converts to mysticism, "cure yourself through psychic healing" kits, and trinkets of supernatural MOVIE MERCHANDISING.

TYMPANUM RELIEF The tympanum relief, a grand accomplishment in CHURCH ART AND ARCHITECTURE, was produced under the direction of French sculptor GISLEBERTUS for the Cathedral of St. Lazare in Autun. It took the artist and his creative team almost a decade to complete this interpretation of the LAST JUDGMENT (the event foretold in the Bible's REVELATION), occupying the

team from 1125 to 1136. The finished relief includes symbols of the afterlife from a range of sources, including religious doctrines, ancient myth, and Christian apocrypha.

The tympanum relief depicts both the joys of paradise and the tortures of the damned. Purified souls are shown entering heaven amid celebration and rejoicing, while doomed spirits are led off to eternal torment. A gallery of glorious ANGELS and SAINTS, enraptured with the ecstasy of paradise, look adoringly toward the throne of God. All citizens of paradise delight in the BEATIFIC VISION.

The tympanum relief is one of the first artistic compositions of the Middle Ages that can be positively linked to its creator. Earlier depictions of paradise and the Last Judgment are anonymous or otherwise unidentifiable by composer. Gislebertus, who signed his tympanum relief, had a flair for creating ruffled textures and often depicted humans as elongated and out of proportion. His unusual style and innovative technique are easily identifiable, enabling art historians to trace stylistic accomplishments copying his methods. Thus the tympanum relief had significant cultural as well as religious implications.

U

UNIVERSALISM Universalism is a philosophical belief held by people of various religions that virtually all human souls will be received into heaven. Hell in universalist belief is either temporary or nonexistent. Salvation is the only destiny of humanity, according to the teachings, since humans are created by a loving God who could not bear to see his creatures suffer in eternity. This theory is held by numerous followers of Judaism, Christianity, and Islam as well as by many who do not consider themselves members of any organized religion.

In addition to referring to a broad belief regarding human salvation, the term defines a separate sect of Christians, called Unitarians. The Unitarian Universalist Association, the modern American church of universalism, contends that God's greatest quality is his infinite capacity for mercy. Such a benevolent father would not allow any of his children to be tormented, and therefore all souls are destined for paradise. The church's doctrines further state that the sacrifice of JESUS, the Christian Redeemer, is sufficient to eradicate all evil from the created universe. Through the merits of Christ, good has conquered evil, and this victory will endure for all eternity.

URIEL   Uriel is one of the ANGELS charged with protecting paradise according to Judeo-Christian legend. His name means "flame of God," and he is believed to be the angel who stood guard at the entrance of the Garden of Eden after Adam and Eve were expelled, keeping them out with his fiery sword. According to some tales, Uriel is also the celestial messenger who was sent to warn Noah about the coming flood.

Milton's PARADISE LOST refers to the angel Uriel as the "sharpest sighted spirit in all Heaven." He is also featured in Dean Koontz's 1992 novel *Hideaway* as the protector who returns with the survivor of a NEAR-DEATH EXPERIENCE to fight off evil incarnate. Uriel is the angel of the month of September and is often invoked by people born during this month for special protection and favor.

V

VAIKUNTHA   Hindu mythology includes Vaikuntha, the "Paradise of Vishnu." It is an enchanted palace where souls who have lived according to "principles of Divine Essence" are rewarded with repose before rejoining the reincarnation cycle. After a brief respite in Vaikuntha, spirits are reborn in another life-form and continue the process of enlightenment with the ultimate goal of reaching MOKSHA, "oneness with all that is."

VALHALLA   Valhalla is the paradise of Germanic and Nordic myth. It is the "Hall of Slain Heroes," reserved for the souls of warriors who die in battle. Valhalla is surrounded by the river Thund, guarded by Valgrind, the "gates of death," and connected to earth by the BIFROST BRIDGE. Only stricken warriors could enter Valhalla; those who die by any other means depart to the dreary palace of Sleetcold ruled by the stern goddess Hel.

Legends tell that the VALKYRIES, daughters of the Norse god ODIN, search

Warrior souls in Valhalla

spirit stallions above the battlefields while deciding which warriors would die in combat. After rendering their judgments, the Valkyries take the heroic souls to Valhalla, where they will enjoy unending feasts and epic contests with their peers.

the battlefields for heroic warriors deserving of paradise. They then take the spirits from their slain bodies and escort them to Valhalla for eternal reward. The Valkyries ride magnificent horses whose hoofbeats sound like thunder as they race through the skies.

In Valhalla, souls of the dead enjoy fierce tournaments by day, then join for great feasting in a luxurious banquet hall every night. These courageous soldiers await the "Last Day" (a concept bearing similarities to the Christian apocalypse and LAST JUDGMENT), when the heroes of history will unite with the gods under Odin and fight an apocalyptic battle at Ragnarok. Until then, the spirits pass the ages in revelry.

Valhalla is mentioned in the epic "BALDER DEAD," in the PROSE EDDA, and in Wagner's opera *Der Ring des Nibelungen*.

VALKYRIES   Valkyries (meaning "choosers of the slain") are the daughters of the Norse god ODIN who select soldiers worthy of ascending to the paradise VALHALLA. The mystic maidens are beautiful and brave, riding majestic

VALLA, LORENZO (1405–1457) Lorenzo Valla, a fifteenth-century Italian humanist, offered a number of speculations on the afterlife that broke with contemporary doctrines. The most extensive is his 1431 *On Pleasure*, in which Valla blends notions of CHRISTIAN PARADISE with elements of CICERO, the ELYSIUM, the NEW JERUSALEM of the Book of REVELATION, and carnal delights. In his work, the main character, Antonio, dies and is escorted to heaven by ANGELS for a tour of the great beyond.

After drifting into the skies, Antonio passes through several "spheres of heaven," each more grand than the previous. When he arrives in paradise proper, he is greeted by a contingent of SAINTS including the VIRGIN MARY. Antonio also enjoys a REUNION with family and friends who enthusiastically invite him to sample the pleasures of the HEREAFTER. They then take him through opulent streets of gold and dazzling gems to the very throne of God. The newly arrived soul, overcome with joy, falls to his knees in worship and asks the Almighty to restore him to his beloved parents and brothers, long deceased, whom Antonio has waited for decades to see.

As a humanist, Valla depicted a paradise of delights for the body, soul, and intellect. In heaven, he anticipated being able to master all forms of language and art and to create great works of boundless expression. The GLORIFIED BODIES of the saved would be capable of flight, allowing human spirits to "play with our winged companions in the sky" and interact extensively with angels. Valla's paradise has souls passing the aeons talking with philosophers, soaring with angels, and unraveling the mysteries of the universe.

Valla fell from favor by proving that papal claims to disputed lands were based on forgeries. This act earned him the praise of fellow manuscript scholars and the scorn of church officials. Based at least partly on this incident, Valla's works came under mounting criticism. Within a hundred years of On Pleasure's publication, Valla's portrait of an afterlife rife with human pleasures was soundly rejected throughout Christendom. Both Roman Catholic and Protestant reformers declared that the ultimate joy of the next world is the BEATIFIC VISION, dwelling in the presence of God. His images of a dynamic paradise were replaced by a static heaven of silent, reverent divine adoration. This interpretation dominated notions of CHRISTIAN PARADISE for centuries and is still debated to day.

VICENTE, GIL (1470–1536) Gil Vicente, dubbed the "father of Portuguese drama," was among the first poets to write original religious plays in the native language of Portugal. Vicente's works bear strong resemblance to traditional MORALITY PLAYS, adding a touch of humanity and satire to the otherwise stern religious doctrines. His most fa-

mous work, a trilogy of dramas titled The Ships of Hell, Purgatory and Glory, has been called "the Portuguese DIVINE COMEDY." Like Dante's masterpiece, Vicente's Ships, written in 1517, describes the afterlife in lyric poetry. His heaven is a luminous realm of blessed souls, SAINTS, and ANGELS adoring the Almighty in his eternal courtyard.

VIRGIN MARY The Virgin Mary is the mother of JESUS, the Messiah of Christianity. She is hailed in the Bible as "full of grace" and is told "the Lord is with thee" from before Christ's miraculous conception. Scholars of the Roman Catholic church have given her the title Queen of Heaven and consider her to be a conduit of saving grace.

Other passages in the Bible reveal that Mary was visited by ANGELS, including the messenger GABRIEL. He appeared to the young girl to ask her if she would consent to becoming the mother of the Savior: "The angel Gabriel was sent from God unto a city of Galilee, named Nazareth, to a virgin espoused to a man whose name was Joseph, of the House of David, and the virgin's name was Mary. And the angel came unto her and said 'Hail, thou that art highly favored, the Lord is with thee, blest art thou among women' " (Luke 1:26–28).

The holy virgin also appears in St. John's Book of REVELATION, in which she is referred to as the "woman clothed with the sun."

Centuries of Christian scholars have likewise focused on Mary of Nazareth. Religious theorist Antonio Polti describes Mary as foremost among the

Vision of the Virgin Mary surrounded
by a choir of angels

blessed in his *On the Supreme Felicity of Heaven*, written in 1575. Polti's work, presented as a portrait of paradise, names an array of SAINTS and elaborates on the role of the virgin. The author places her at the center of creation, above even the angels, since her singular virtue made her worthy of bearing the Messiah. Polti calls Mary the "Queen of Angels" and "Empress of Heaven," titles that have been embraced by generations of Catholics.

As regent of paradise, Mary serves as an emissary between the living and the divine. Roman Catholics routinely pray to her, asking for aid in reaching paradise. The rosary, a sacred series of prayers, includes fifty recitations of a supplication to the holy woman called the Hail Mary. In part, the prayer asks: "Holy Mary, Mother of God, pray for us sinners, now and at hour of our death."

Two of the "mysteries" of the rosary (ideas to contemplate while praying) involve Mary's position as lady of paradise. The ASSUMPTION commemorates her delivery, body and soul, into heaven. (Pope Pius XII formally declared the doctrine of Mary's Assumption to be an official, infallible tenet of Catholic faith in 1950.) And the mystery of the CORONATION of the virgin reflects on the celestial celebration that took place when Jesus' mother was rewarded for her virtue with the crown of eternity.

She has also been called the Queen of PURGATORY, since her intercession is believed to be invaluable to souls languishing in this transitional realm. In a twentieth-century apparition to the child Lucia dos Santos, Mary gives the girl a vision of purgatory and hell, then dictates a prayer designed to help spirits find rest in the afterlife. This mystic event was later interpreted by surrealist Salvador Dali in his *Vision of Hell*.

Because of her awesome role in Christ's redemption of mankind, the Virgin Mary is depicted in examples of CHURCH ART AND ARCHITECTURE throughout the world. Her image is among the most popular subjects for statues, paintings, STAINED-GLASS WINDOWS, reliefs, and other artworks. Devotion to the holy mother as Queen of Paradise remains strong to this day.

VISION LITERATURE Vision literature is a vast, diverse body of works recounting the adventures of people who claim to have "witnessed" afterlife events firsthand. Most originate from medieval Europe, although records of these supernatural journeys are also found in African, Asian, and North, Central, and South American Indian cultures. There are even contemporary examples of vision literature written within the past decade. These various texts share one thing in common: They are presented as fact, not fiction, and are fiercely defended by their authors as legitimate reports of supernatural adventures.

The African legend of Kwasi Benefo describes a trip the mournful widower makes to ASAMANDO, the paradise of Ashanti belief. After Kwasi marries and then loses three subsequent wives whom he loved dearly, he decides to journey to the afterlife to join them on the other side of the grave. Kwasi contacts them in the land of the dead, and all three women assure him that his next marriage will not end in tragedy. Cheered by their words, Kwasi returns to his village, marries a young maiden, and enjoys many years with his new wife before departing to Asamando for good.

Vision literature unquestionably reached its high point during the Middle Ages when accounts of "visits" to the afterlife, often with intricate details of the rewards of heaven as well as the tortures of hell, were commonplace. Suddenly early versions of what we now call NEAR-DEATH EXPERIENCES were circulating throughout Christendom. Virtually all of these supernatural tales purported to be actual recollections of travels to the next world. And though details differed, alleged trips to CHRISTIAN PARADISE bore numerous similarities to one another and contained a number of shared elements.

Most feature sightings of biblical ANGELS such as MICHAEL, GABRIEL, and RAPHAEL. Another common component is a supernatural "guide" who leads and narrates the afterlife tour. DRITHELM is accompanied on his mystic journey by an angel, while an entire contingent of "heavenly hosts" escorts FURSEUS through the afterlife. Alberic of Settafrati is protected in eternity by none other than Christ's apostle and first pope of the Roman Catholic church, SAINT PETER, who is also legendary "keeper of the keys" to heaven. Other accounts include "benevolent spirits" and "steadfast shepherds" who usher human souls through the spiritual dimension.

Most medieval accounts also mention the SAINTS or MARTYRS, citing them as shining citizens of paradise. The VIRGIN MARY, mother of the Redeemer JESUS, likewise appears in numerous supernatural stories. She is always depicted as beautiful, gentle, and full of compassion. Some accounts further involve a REUNION of loved ones in paradise in which the "seer" is able to communicate with family and friends who have passed away. These touching episodes provide some of the most poignant moments in vision literature.

Another shared aspect of Christian vision literature is its emphasis on the need for "sinners, all of us" to live lives of virtue in order to see paradise in the next world. Examples of this include the accounts of TUNDAL, Furseus, BEDE, and Drithelm, all of which equate human behavior with afterlife fate. The majority of these visions were experienced by peasants; however, since commoners were illiterate, clerics were usually asked to transcribe the tales. The scribes no doubt stressed this "call to glory" and probably embellished the original accounts with religious edicts. Colorful illustrations were likewise often added to enhance the images, and these "fantastic witnesses" were then circulated throughout the Christian world. Tales of supernatural visions became so popular that worshipers attended Sunday services just to hear the latest surreal adventure.

The popularity of vision literature peaked toward the end of the Middle Ages, when it inevitably imploded. By the time the genre fizzled out in the fourteenth century, literally hundreds of people had claimed to have visited heaven, hell, and PURGATORY while "dead," only to be revived to tell their tales. The decline of vision literature's popularity can be attributed to several factors. First, the proliferation of these alleged journeys led to growing skepticism about their authenticity. Under the weight of so many conflicting and increasingly flamboyant accounts of heaven's pleasures and hell's pains, the fad eventually collapsed upon itself.

This was hastened by the growing scholarly debate over whether souls would be adjudicated immediately upon death, or would await the LAST JUDGMENT before entering heaven or hell. Many Christian philosophers taught that "visions" of spirits in the afterlife were impossible, since human souls would "sleep in Christ" until the end of the world. The final blow was the prominence of such fiction works as Dante's DIVINE COMEDY: THE PARADISO, which offer vivid, stylized descriptions of the HEREAFTER that rival the greatest tales of vision literature.

Despite the fact that vision literature as an industry died with the Middle Ages, it has by no means disappeared from the modern experience. The contemporary revival of "firsthand" accounts of the afterlife comes in the form of such books as *Embraced by the Light*, *Life After Life*, and scores of other near-death experience recollections. All of these feature stories about dying, visiting paradise, and returning to life that authors claim are true and unembellished. Most have come under fire for their questionable content, murky philosophy, and shaky credibility; however, they remain fixtures on recent bestseller lists.

VISION OF PAUL The *Vision of Paul*, an apocrypha written around A.D. 388, offers an early (although unsanctioned) rendering of CHRISTIAN PARADISE. The text describes the rewards that await the faithful in the afterlife and warns against the perils of falling into sin. Its text (attributed to St. Paul) details a mystic journey to heaven, where the author meets the VIRGIN MARY and talks with SAINTS, MARTYRS, and prophets of the Old Testament. The greatest joy of eternity is dwelling with God in perpetual adoration of the BEATIFIC VISION.

Though the *Vision of Paul* was supposedly discovered in St. Paul's former home in Tarsus, it has been ruled "unworthy of credence" by Christian authorities. Religious leaders found the treatise ludicrous; however, it became a cult classic among the common people. For decades after its discovery, priests and preachers drew on its images for use in their own descriptions of heaven.

Many ideas became institutionalized in concepts of Christian paradise and were incorporated into works of CHURCH ART AND ARCHITECTURE for centuries.

VISION OF PIERS PLOWMAN The fourteenth-century satirical poem *Vision of Piers Plowman* lampoons the traditional notions of CHRISTIAN PARADISE while decrying hypocrisy among the religious ranks. The *Vision of Piers Plowman* offers an account of what happens to the GOOD THIEF after JESUS allows him into heaven. Upon arriving in the HEREAFTER, the thief discovers that "justice" overrides "mercy," and his life of crime will not be overlooked in eternity. When, for example, he comes to the "banquet table" of the divine, the thief is forced to sit on the ground by himself, while the virtuous SAINTS and MARTYRS lounge comfortably at the feast looking down on the "petty criminal."

Heaven is also a cliquish realm where the pious congregate in close-knit groups, and the more "human" spirits are shunned. After wandering around paradise as a rogue and an outcast, the good thief realizes that joy is elusive for his kind, and salvation and redemption are not necessarily the same thing. *Vision of Piers Plowman* likewise mocks the notion of "levels" in heaven popularized by many works of Western literature, including Dante's DIVINE COMEDY: THE PARADISO. Such ridiculous assigned seating, according to the unknown author, would reduce paradise to a celestial piety competition where being "holier than thou" is more important than dwelling in the presence of God.

VOHU MANAH Vohu Manah (Good Thought) is one of the AMESHA SPENTAS, the six powerful ANGELS of Zoroastrian belief. Called "the firstborn of AHURA MAZDA" (the benevolent god of the ancient faith), Vohu Manah is responsible for recording the thoughts, feelings, and deeds of all humans to use in determining each soul's fate in the afterlife. He sits at the right hand of Ahura Mazda in ZOROASTRIAN HEAVEN and reads back the record at the time of a person's death. His account is reviewed by the lord of paradise and is used in making a final judgment about the spirit's destiny. Those who have lived virtuous lives will be allowed into paradise; but lazy, wicked, or indifferent souls will be cast into hell.

Vohu Manah is mentioned with the other "Beneficent Immortals" in the AVESTA, the sacred text of Zoroastrianism.

VOYAGE OF BRAN An ancient Celtic legend called the *Voyage of Bran* tells of a supernatural venture into the next world. The hero, Bran, is a blend of pagan legends and later Christian tales regarding a voyager with supernatural powers. In addition to offering tales of magic islands and mythic creatures, the story of Bran's adventures describes AVALON, the medieval Briton paradise.

According to the legend, Bran travels in an enchanted boat to the "OTHERWORLD," a place of timeless content, feasting, and heavenly music. This realm, likened to Avalon and CHRISTIAN PARADISE, is free of all human pain. Souls residing in the Otherworld remain eternally young. Bran enters this mystic place through a series of enchanted lakes and caverns. Some tales claim that he stayed in the paradise for several decades before returning home. Others say he could not depart from such a wonderful world and is there still, happily greeting blessed souls to the afterlife.

Bran is sometimes called "Bran the Blessed" and is credited with converting Britain to Christianity. Other versions of the *Voyage of Bran* have the legendary King Arthur calling on Bran for assistance in making his kingdom invincible and in overcoming attacks from outside forces.

WEDDING FEAST One of the most enduring images of heaven in Christian tradition is that of the wedding feast. This representation of paradise as a never-ending celebration where loved ones gather together to share their joy has long been used to illustrate the glories awaiting the faithful in the world to come. Unlike other analogies, the wedding feast combines notions of purity, tradition, and new beginnings, all of which are especially appropriate to the blessed afterlife.

JESUS, the Messiah of Christian faith, frequently invokes this symbol in his teachings about heaven. The wedding feast appears in several parables, such as that of the foolish virgins who fail to prepare for the celebration and are shut out of the festivities. The ten women were to carry lamps to light the way as the groom approaches; however, five of them did not bring enough oil and their torches burn out. While they are scrambling to find more fuel, the bridegroom arrives, "and they that were ready went in with him; and the doors were shut." When sometime later the five foolish virgins return, they find themselves locked out of the celebration, as the damned will be precluded from paradise.

In another lesson, Jesus warns that when the day of judgment comes, souls must be properly purified if they wish to enter the "kingdom of God." This parable also calls on the setting of a wedding feast in which a king sends his servants "into the highways" to invite everyone they encounter to attend. Nothing is asked of the guests except that they adorn themselves properly for the occasion. Harsh condemnation awaits those who fail to comply with this requirement: "And when the king came in to see the guests, he saw there a man which had not on a wedding garment: And he saith unto him, 'Friend, how camest thou in hither not having a wedding garment?' And he was speechless. Then said the king to the servants, 'Bind him hand and foot, and take him away, and cast him into outer darkness where there shall be weeping and gnashing of teeth. For many are called, but few are chosen' " (Matt. 22:11–14).

This parable likens those who waste their lives and neglect God to the fool who does not bother to dress properly for the wedding celebration. Too self-absorbed to consider what he should do, the man is caught unprepared for the festival. He therefore is not allowed to partake in the celebration, as sinners will be refused entrance into heaven.

The nuptial imagery is visited again in a passage from REVELATION in which God instructs the evangelist St. John: "Write 'Blessed are they which are called unto the marriage supper of the Lamb' " (Rev. 19:9).

The wedding feast served as an excellent metaphor for heaven during biblical times, since most people were illiterate and thus unable to study and comprehend the complexities of the holy texts. The peasantry could, however, relate to the concept of a marriage celebration since most had attended many during their lifetimes. Such festivities offered joy, color, and excitement in otherwise mundane lives. By comparing paradise to such parties, teachers gave the early Christians a distinct image that helped motivate converts and inspire the faithful.

During the ensuing centuries, the wedding feast metaphor was embraced by the SAINTS, many of whom denied themselves physical gratification in favor of spiritual growth. They looked forward to an unending festival in paradise that would more than make up for a lifetime of poverty, chastity, and obedience. The symbol had special meaning for nuns, often referred to as "brides of Christ," and some, such as CATHERINE OF SIENA, had mystic visions of this heavenly jubilee.

WHITE LIGHT The 1990 film *White Light* offers a NEAR-DEATH EXPERIENCE that suggests a mystic overlap between heaven and earth. The film portrays the "death" of a policeman (played by Martin Kove) who travels down the proverbial "tunnel of light" (in this case, a storm drainage pipe) only to be suddenly jolted back to the land of the living. After being revived, Kove is obsessed with visions of a beautiful woman whom he saw while "dead," unsure of who or what she is. He alternately considers that she might be one of the escorting ANGELS, a memory of some woman from his past, or perhaps just a hallucination brought on by powerful painkillers used in his treatment. Kove, ready to resign himself to the fact that this elusive beauty is simply an embodiment of his wish for true love, finally finds the girl of his ethereal dreams. She restores his faith in "something more" for his soul, in this world and the next.

WHITE MOUNTAINS The Mohave Indians of the Colorado River basin believe that departed spirits travel to the White Mountains, a paradise of abundant fruit and game. Stories passed down from generation to generation tell how the Mohave once lived in the mystic White Mountains before the cultural hero Matowelia led them to their present territory.

According to sacred belief, when a person dies, the family burns the body in a special ceremony invoking the aid of the tribe's ancestors. This act frees the soul and allows it to follow the ancient path to the White Mountains to dwell forever in peace. Spirits of those who do not receive the proper funerary rites will be reincarnated in the form of screech owls, who then haunt those responsible for their sad fate.

WIDE AWAKE   Writer-director M. Night Shyamalan's 1998 drama *Wide Awake* follows the desperate search of a young boy (played by Joseph Cross) for proof that heaven exists after his beloved grandfather (Robert Loggia) dies. Unconsoled by assurances from family members and teachers at his Catholic school that the man is "with God" and "in a better place," Cross fears that Loggia is simply "gone" forever. He desperately hopes that the promises of CHRISTIAN PARADISE are true and that they will one day enjoy a REUNION in paradise.

The film then embarks on a supernatural quest for validation. Cross begins by reading to his fifth-grade class, telling his schoolmates he and his grandfather "always watched out for each other." Now Cross feels lost and abandoned. He begins doubting the existence of the God he has been taught in his Catholic school, a benevolent father who loves his creatures. Loggia appears in flashback, tenderly trying to prepare Cross for the inevitable. But neither these touching words nor the insistence of his teachers helps settle his doubts. He begs for a "sign from heaven" that everything is all right.

Wide Awake also addresses such notions as the afterlife fate of unbaptized babies, (considered by some to ascend to LIMBO rather than heaven), the criteria for salvation, and the nature of paradise itself. Shyamalan also explores other beliefs, such as the edicts of the Islamic prophet MUHAMMAD, posing questions about how such divergent faiths can have similar goals. The film concludes with a poignant message uniting heavenly pleasures with earthly joys and affirming the beauty of God's design.

WILTON DIPTYCH   The *Wilton Diptych*, a panel painting from England's Gothic period (late fourteenth century), offers an example of the contemporary European tradition of blending politics and religion. Mingling religious imagery with patriotism, the unknown artist depicts heaven as a beautiful meadow dotted with fragrant flowers. Populating this CHRISTIAN PARADISE are such biblical heroes as the VIRGIN MARY, John the Baptist, and a legion of ANGELS. Among them kneel an array of SAINTS, including many deceased kings of England. All of the lovely blond angels wear symbols of the monarchy and are adorned with rose garlands symbolizing their allegiance to the British crown.

This merging of church and state was very common throughout Christendom for centuries. Paintings of paradise routinely included political figures, wealthy patrons, or other prominent citizens in the court of the Almighty. Most such compositions were commissioned by those wishing to see themselves or family members in blessed eternity. Living people included in such paintings were typically given a square HALO to indicate imminent salvation, whereas halos of the deceased were circular.

WODAN   Wodan (Voden, Votan, Woden, Wotan, Wuotan) is the Germanic equivalent of the Norse god ODIN. He is the supreme deity of the pantheon and ruler of paradise. Wednesday is Woden's day, and those who die on this day receive special favor in the afterlife. Brave and virtuous souls could be elevated to the "Palace of Wodan" after death, where they would be rewarded for their goodness.

Y

YAHOEL Yahoel (Jehoel) is one of the holy ANGELS who serve as consort to the Hebrew prophets. According tó ancient tradition, Yahoel dictated the Torah (the holy book of Judaism) to the patriarch Abraham and gave him advice and counsel on interpreting the sacred text. Later, Yahoel was sent to escort Abraham's soul to heaven at the time of his death. The celestial messenger then became Abraham's guide in the afterlife. In other legends, Yahoel is said to be the leader of the choir of paradise that sings eternal HYMNS at the throne of YAHWEH.

YAHWEH Yahweh is the God of Hebrew tradition and ruler of heaven described in ancient religious writings. He is named in many passages in the Old Testament, including in the prophecies of ELIJAH. The Almighty first reveals himself as Yahweh to Moses (although in many translations the name appears before Moses's time.) According to the sacred text: "God spake unto Moses, and said unto him, 'I am the Lord: and I appeared to Abraham, unto Isaac, and unto JACOB, by the name of God Almighty, but by my name Yahweh [Jehovah] was I not known to them' " (Ex. 6:2–3).

The name of Yahweh is sacred to Jews and Christians alike and appears in numerous HYMNS to the divine Father. The word *hallelujah*, used in sacred ceremonies to pay homage to the Almighty, literally means "shout praise to our god Yah." Yahweh is revered as the master of paradise whose mercy is essential to finding joy in the afterlife.

YAMBE-AKKA Yambe-akka (Jameakka, Jabmeanimo) is the goddess of death and the underworld of the Lapps of Scandinavia. A fearsome hag whose name means "old woman of the dead," Yambe-akka offers solace to the souls of children who die in infancy. Though most in her realm dwell in sorrow, the spirits of lost babes are soothed and comforted by Yambe-akka. Her sanctuary for these infants is similar to the Christian notion of LIMBO.

YAZATA The yazata are powerful ANGELS according to Zoroastrian belief. Their name means "adorable ones," and these celestial aids intercede between humans and the fair god AHURA MAZDA. They dwell eternally in ZOROASTRIAN HEAVEN but visit the earth to oversee the affairs of humanity and use their mystic abilities to help mortal beings. Yazata also guard the sun, moon, and stars are "too many to count in a thousand lifetimes."

One of the most influential yazata is Mithra (Mitra, Mithras), the "god of light." Mithra is the protector of truth and of agreements. People entering into contracts routinely ask Mithra to see to it that all parties live up to the terms. The brilliant angel could also be called on to punish those who cheat, lie, or defraud their fellow citizens. In other legends, Mithra is Ahura Mazda's second in command who leads the forces of good against the evil nemesis Ahriman. This role is similar to that of MICHAEL, the angel of Christian tradition who battles the devil according to the Bible's Book of REVELATION.

YOGA Hindus longing for a foretaste of eternal joy practice yoga, a series of disciplines designed to clear the mind and purify the soul. Since the Hindu paradise of MOKSHA is a state of being rather than a place, spirits in the temporal plane are able to transcend their physical state and find tranquillity. The yogis, teachers of this supernatural art, instruct the faithful in methods of dissolving passions, laying aside desire and merging with the "cosmic conscience." For millions of Hindus, exercising the principles of yoga offers a brief preview of afterlife bliss.

YOU NEVER CAN TELL The 1951 comedy You Never Can Tell takes an innovative look at the notion of ANIMALS in the afterlife. The film stars Dick Powell as a "humanimal," a deceased beast returned to earth in human form in order to resolve unfinished business. Powell plays a "reincarnated" German shepherd named King who leaves a huge inheritance to his present owner (played by Peggy Dow) at the time of his premature demise. Unhappy with his situation, the persistent pooch post-

pones paradise in favor of finding justice on this side of eternity.

After being poisoned by a greedy villain, the dog's spirit makes "the great ascension" to the "sanctuary of the golden oak," where he is judged by a majestic lion (the animal equivalent of SAINT PETER or the ancient OSIRIS). Being deemed "trusting, gentle, and loyal," King is allowed to enter the "happy fields" of paradise. But instead of taking up his new heavenly existence, the dog asks that he be allowed to return to the land of living in order to find his killer and clear the name of his beloved owner who is being blamed for the crime.

You Never Can Tell uses a variety of imaginative techniques to depict animal heaven. The entire afterlife sequence is shot in reverse, creating an otherworldly effect of unfamiliar light and shadow. Scenes of the blessed realm show a menagerie of chickens, elephants, dogs, cats, and other species mingling in harmony, no longer viewing themselves in terms of predators and prey. Disproportionate sizing completes the effect, as hens are now no different in size and stature from cows, conveying a sense of final equality in this animal eternity.

You Never Can Tell is in the vein of such classic afterlife-themed films as HERE COMES MR. JORDAN and its remake HEAVEN CAN WAIT, in which the deceased returns to life to right some wrong. The comedy's plot is reversed in the 1980 comedy OH, HEAVENLY DOG!, which stars Chevy Chase as the victim of violence who is reincarnated as Benji, a clever canine out for justice.

Z

ZOROASTRIAN HEAVEN The ancient prophet Zoroaster is believed to have lived about 700 B.C., around the same time as Buddha, CONFUCIUS, and the Hebrew prophet Jeremiah. Breaking with previous beliefs, Zoroaster rejected the contemporary concept of a pantheon of deities in favor of a dualistic system that envisions an ongoing battle between the forces of good and evil. According to Zoroaster, the benevolent god AHURA MAZDA strives to ease the plight of humans, even offering to them the hope of eternal paradise. Opposing him is the wicked Ahriman, a vile deity set upon corrupting human souls. Those who reject Ahriman's evil ways, obey the word of Ahura Mazda, and adhere to the teachings of Zoroaster can look forward to a blessed afterlife, sometimes referred to as the BEST EXISTENCE.

Zoroastrian belief teaches that when a person dies, the soul must cross the CHINVATO PERETAV, a perilous bridge that spans hell and leads to paradise. Some writings indicate that the prophet himself will appear to lead good souls across the narrow passage. Other tales claim that Ahura Mazda will send powerful ANGELS to help guide the deserving through the treacherous passageway. Once across, blessed souls will dwell eternally with Ahura Mazda and with his angels, the beautiful AMESHA SPENTAS and the luminous YAZATA. These and other teachings of Zoroaster are contained in the sacred text AVESTA, particularly in the GATHAS (songs), which includes HYMNS to Ahura Mazda, commentary on religious ideas, and descriptions of the faith taught by the ancient prophet.

The faith taught by Zoroaster was in many ways groundbreaking, abandoning earlier ideas that only the wealthy and powerful had any chance at immortality. In addition to proclaiming that virtually all people—from kings to slaves—could ascend to heaven, Zoroaster taught that body and soul would be reunited after death. This is necessary, because in eternity, rewards for the blessed are physical as well as spiritual. Zoroaster promised followers that in the world to come, the virtuous would inhabit perfect human forms with heightened senses, incorruptible, and impervious to disease or aging. (This Zoroastrian doctrine marks the first evidence of the concept of GLORIFIED BODIES in organized religion. Such a belief later became prominent in both Christianity and Islam.) Early followers of Zoroaster did not bury their dead but

Ancient prophet Zoroaster. ART TODAY

left corpses exposed to undergo the natural process of decay, confident that the creator would reassemble and glorify the pieces on the soul's adjucation.

The ancient prophet was also the first to promote the doctrine of a LAST JUDGMENT, when all human souls will be judged in eternity. Zoroaster prophesied that this would occur at some time in the future, when Ahura Mazda would defeat Ahriman and vanquish evil forever. Having destroyed "the lie" that corrupts material creation, the earth would then be restored to paradise, and the saved would reside in the new utopia for all eternity. Evil souls, having allied themselves with the forces of darkness, would be purged and eradicated from existence.

A wise and charismatic teacher, Zoroaster used his oratory skills to convert King Vishtaspa, who then declared Zoroastrianism the official religion of his kingdom. It remained the dominant faith for centuries, until it was suppressed around the year 333 B.C. when Alexander the Great conquered Persia and burned the capital city of Persepolis, destroying most of the written texts of Zoroastrianism. The young ruler then demanded that only Greek gods be worshiped in his territories. Despite this ban, Zoroastrianism flourished. It was the predominant faith of the Arab world until it was finally supplanted by Islam around the eighth century.

Even after the mass conversion to the teachings of Islamic faith, Zoroastrianism remained strong. Followers of Islam mingled many elements of the ancient faith with their new religion, keeping the old legends and tales but re-placing former heroes with the prophet MUHAMMAD. One notable holdover from Zoroaster's teachings is the Islamic article of faith mandating belief in the existence of angels. This is believed to be a homage to the Amesha Spentas (most notably Mithra, the "lord of light"), and the yazata, who were beloved and highly revered at the time of Islam's founding. Today, approximately 1 million people still practice Zoroastrianism and embrace the millennia-old ideas about a joyous world to come.

Acknowledgments

I extend my deepest gratitude and sincere appreciation to the following for invaluable contributions to this project:

Daniel Timothy Corcoran Jr.
Edgar Jerins
Gregg Pisani
Mary Ann Sullivan of the Blue Army of Our Lady of Fatima USA, Inc.
Maria Van Scott of *Miles Jesu/YOU! Magazine*, European edition
Harris McCarty Design Group of Manassas, Virginia
Michael Gariepy of *Art Today*
Dr. Bruce Joffe
Leon Fletcher
Staff and personnel of the Prince William County, Virginia, library system
Dolores and Cornelius Van Scott

Every attempt has been made to identify and credit sources used for this book. However, in the case of any verifiable errors, inaccuracies, or omissions, the author will gladly correct such in future editions. Please address any correspondence to the author in care of the publisher.

Bibliography

It is impossible to list every source consulted in the compilation of this book. The following works are offered as an annotated bibliography and are suggested for further reading on matters relating to the afterlife.

Andersen, Hans Christian. *Andersen's Fairy Tales.* New York: Grosset & Dunlap, 1945.

Apostolos, Diane. *Dictionary of Christian Art.* New York: Continuum, 1994.

Arberry, A. J., trans. *The Koran Interpreted.* New York: Simon & Schuster, 1996.

Baetzhold, Howard G., and Joseph B. McCullough, eds. *The Bible According to Mark Twain.* Athens, GA: University of Georgia Press, 1995.

Bensink, John R., ed. *Twilight Zone Magazine.* New York: Montcalm Publishing, 1981–89.

Bordman, Gerald. *American Musical Theatre.* 2d ed. New York: Oxford University Press, 1992.

———. *Oxford Companion to American Theatre.* New York: Oxford University Press, 1984.

Brown, Les. *Encyclopedia of Television.* 3rd ed. Detroit: Gale Research, 1992.

Budge, E. A. Wallis, trans. *The Egyptian Book of the Dead.* New York: Dover, 1967.

Camp, Joe. *Oh Heavenly Dog.* New York: Scholastic Book Services, 1980.

Campbell, Joseph. *Oriental Mythology.* New York: Arkana, 1991.

Carola, Leslie Conron, ed. *The Irish: A Treasury of Art and Literature.* Hong Kong: Hugh Lauter Levin, 1993.

Cavendish, Richard, ed. *Man, Myth and Magic: An Illustrated Encyclopedia of Mythology, Religion and the Unknown.* New York: Marshall Cavendish, 1995.

———. *Visions of Heaven and Hell.* New York: Harmony Books, 1977.

Cawley, John, and Jim Korkis. *The Encyclopedia of Cartoon Superstars.* Las Vegas: Pioneer Books, 1990.

Christie, Anthony. *Chinese Mythology.* London: Hamlyn Publishing Group, 1968.

Churchill, Robert. *The Cartoonist's Bible.* New York: St. Martin's Press, 1980.

Cotterell, Arthur. *The Macmillan Illustrated Encyclopedia of Myths & Legends.* New York: Macmillan, 1989.

Courlander, Harold. *A Treasury of African Folklore.* New York: Crown, 1975.

Daly, Kathleen. *Norse Mythology A–Z.* New York: Facts on File, 1991.

Davidson, Gustav. *A Dictionary of Angels.* New York: Free Press, 1971.

Delaney, John J. *A Woman Clothed with the Sun*. New York: Doubleday, 1961.

DK Direct Limited, ed. *Life Beyond Death*. New York: Reader's Digest, 1992.

Donaldson, E. Talbot, trans. *Piers Plowman*. Ed. Elizabeth D. Kirk and Judith J. Anderson. New York: Norton, 1990.

Ebert, Roger. *Roger Ebert's Movie Home Companion, 1993 Edition*. Kansas City: Andrews and McMeel, 1992.

Elkin, Stanley. *The Living End*. New York: Dutton, 1977.

Erdman, David V. *The Complete Poetry and Prose of William Blake*. New York: Doubleday, 1988.

Esposito, John. *Islam: The Straight Path*. New York: Oxford University Press, 1991.

Felleman, Hazel. *The Best Loved Poems of the American People*. New York: Doubleday, 1936.

Fitzgerald, Robert, trans. *The Aeneid*. New York: Random House, 1983.

Freke, Timothy. *Heaven: An Illustrated History of the Higher Realms*. Berkeley, CA: Conari Press, 1996.

Fremantle, Francesca, and Chogyam Trungpa. *Tibetan Book of the Dead*. Boston: Shambhala, 1987.

Gaskell, G. A. *Dictionary of All Scriptures & Myths*. New York: Gramercy Books, 1981.

Gaster, Theodor H. *The Dead Sea Scriptures*. New York: Doubleday, 1976.

Gilmore, John. *Probing Heaven: Key Questions on the Hereafter*. Grand Rapids, MI: Baker Book House, 1989.

Gleckner, Robert F. *The Poetical Works of Byron*. Boston: Houghton Mifflin, 1975.

Grimal, Pierre. *World Mythology*. New York: Excalibur Books, 1965.

Halliwell, Leslie. *Halliwell's Film Guide*. 7th ed. New York: Harper, 1989.

Hartt, Frederick. *Art: A History of Painting and Sculpture*. New York: Harry N. Abrams, 1993.

Hixon, Lex. *Heart of the Koran*. Wheaton, IL: Theosophical Publishing House, 1988.

Hunt, David. *Whatever Happened to Heaven?* Eugene, OR: Harvest House, 1998.

Ions, Veronica. *Indian Mythology*. New York: Peter Bedrick Books, 1967.

Janson, H. W. *The History of Art*. New York: Harry N. Abrams, 1995.

Knappert, Jan. *Kings, Gods, Spirits: African Myth*. New York: Peter Bedrick Books, 1986.

Kowalska, Sister M. Faustina. *Divine Mercy in My Soul*. Stockbridge, MA: Marian Press, 1987.

Kreeft, Peter. *Everything You Ever Wanted to Know About Heaven . . . But Never Dreamed of Asking!* San Francisco: Ignatius Press, 1990.

Larson, Gary. *Cows of Our Planet—A Far Side Collection*. Kansas City, MO: FarWorks, 1992.

Leonard, Sue, ed. *Life Beyond Death*. Pleasantville, NY: Reader's Digest, 1992.

Lewis, C. S. *The Great Divorce*. New York: Macmillan, 1946.

Lewis, James R. *Encyclopedia of Afterlife Beliefs and Phenomena*. Detroit: Visible Ink, 1995.

MacCana, Proinsias. *Celtic Mythology*. New York: Hamlyn Publishing, 1970.

Mack, Maynard, ed. *Norton Anthology of World Masterpieces.* 4th ed. New York: Norton, 1979.

Maltin, Leonard. *Leonard Maltin's Movie and Video Guide 1992.* New York: Penguin Books, 1991.

Mandelbaum, Ken. *Not Since Carrie: 40 Years of Broadway Musical Flops.* New York: St. Martin's Press, 1991.

Mayle, Peter. *Will I Go to Heaven?* New York: Corwin Books, 1976.

McDannell, Colleen, and Bernhard Lang. *Heaven: A History.* New Haven: Yale University Press, 1988.

Mercatante, Anthony S., ed. *The Facts on File Encyclopedia of World Mythology and Legend.* New York: Facts on File, 1988.

Moody, Raymond A., Jr. *Life After Life.* New York: Bantam Books, 1977.

New Catholic Encyclopedia. New York: McGraw-Hill, 1967.

Noffke, Suzanne, O. P., trans. *Catherine of Siena: The Dialogue.* New York: Paulist Press, 1980.

Ordway, Edith B. *The Opera Book.* New York: Sully and Kleinteich, 1915.

Pananen, Victor N. *William Blake.* Boston: Twayne, 1977.

Pinkwater, Daniel. The Afterlife Diet. New York: Random House 1995.

Prose, Francine. *Dybbuk: A Story Made in Heaven.* New York: Greenwillow Books, 1996.

Rhymer, Joseph. *The Illustrated Life of Jesus Christ.* London: Bloomsbury, 1994.

Rice, Anne. *Memnoch the Devil.* New York: Knopf, 1995.

Schouweiler, Tom. *Life After Death.* San Diego: Greenhaven Press, 1990.

Simon, Henry W. *100 Great Operas.* New York: Anchor Books, 1989.

Simpson, Jacqueline. *European Mythology.* New York: Peter Bedrick, 1987.

Skal, David J. *The Monster Show.* New York: Norton, 1993.

Smith, Dave. *The Official Encyclopedia of Disney A–Z.* New York: Hyperion, 1996.

Smith, Huston. *The Religions of Man.* New York: Mentor Books, 1958.

Sproul, R. C. *Surprised by Suffering.* Wheaton, IL: Tyndale House, 1979.

Sykes, Egerton. *Who's Who: Non-Classical Mythology.* New York: Oxford University Press, 1993.

Thurman, Robert A. F., trans. *The Tibetan Book of the Dead.* New York: Bantam Books, 1994.

Tine, Robert. *Bill & Ted's Bogus Journey.* New York: Berkley Books, 1991.

Turner, Jane, ed. *Dictionary of Art.* New York: Grove Dictionaries, 1996.

VideoHounds Complete Guide to Cult Flicks and Trash Picks. Detroit: Visible Ink Press, 1996.

Weintraub, Stanley, ed. *The Portable George Bernard Shaw.* New York: Penguin Books, 1977.

Wilde, Oscar. *The Fairy Tales of Oscar Wilde.* New York: Henry Holt, 1993.

Willis, Roy. *World Mythology.* New York: Henry Holt, 1993.

Zemach, Margot. *Jake and Honeybunch Go to Heaven.* New York: Farrar, Straus & Giroux, 1982.

Zicree, Marc Scott. *The Twilight Zone Companion.* New York: Bantam Books, 1982.